THOMAS MORE'S *UTOPIA*
IN EARLY MODERN EUROPE

Manchester University Press

Der Utopianer Alphabet.

a b c d e f g h i k l m n o p q r s t u x y

Vier Verß in Utopianischer sprach.

Vropos ha Boccas peula chama.

polta chamaan

Bargol he maglomi baccan

soma gymnosophaon

Agrama gymnosophon labarem

bacha bodamilomin

Voluala barchin heman la

lauoluola dramme pagloni.

Und ist die meynung diser obgeschribnen versen in Teütscher sprach souyl.

Utopus Hertzog hat mir gethon das/
Ein Insel gemacht/die ich nit was/
Und ich eyntzig vff erden fry
Hab on die kunst Philosophy
Alln tötlichen menschen zkennen geben
Zů füren ein Burgerlich leben/
Und was ich hab mitteyl ich gern
Will on Beschwärd gern Bessers lern.

A ij

Basel 1524: the Utopian alphabet. By permission of the British Library

THOMAS MORE'S *UTOPIA* IN EARLY MODERN EUROPE: PARATEXTS AND CONTEXTS

edited by
Terence Cave

For the project
*Dislocations: Practices of Cultural Transfer
in the Early Modern Period*
at the University of Oslo

Manchester University Press
Manchester and New York

distributed exclusively in the USA by Palgrave

Copyright © Manchester University Press 2008

While copyright in the volume as a whole is vested in Manchester University Press, copyright in individual chapters belongs to their respective authors, and no chapter may be reproduced wholly or in part without the express permission in writing of both author and publisher.

Published by Manchester University Press
Oxford Road, Manchester M13 9NR, UK
and Room 400, 175 Fifth Avenue, New York, NY 10010, USA
www.manchesteruniversitypress.co.uk

Distributed in the United States exclusively by
Palgrave Macmillan, 175 Fifth Avenue,
New York, NY 10010, USA

Distributed in Canada exclusively by
UBC Press, University of British Columbia, 2029 West Mall,
Vancouver, BC, Canada V6T 1Z2

British Library Cataloguing-in-Publication Data is available

Library of Congress Cataloging-in-Publication Data is available

ISBN 978 0 7190 8848 3 paperback

First published by Manchester University Press in hardback 2008

This paperback edition first published 2012

The publisher has no responsibility for the persistence or accuracy of URLs for any external or third-party internet websites referred to in this book, and does not guarantee that any content on such websites is, or will remain, accurate or appropriate.

This book has been published with the support of the Research Council of Norway

Printed by Lightning Source

CONTENTS

List of illustrations	*page* vii
Contributors	ix
Preface	xi
Acknowledgements	xvii

Part I Versions of *Utopia*: a European map

	Introduction	3
1	A Protean text: *Utopia* in Latin, 1516–1631	14
2	The German translations: humanist politics and literary journalism	32
3	The Italian *Utopia* of Lando, Doni and Sansovino: paradox and politics	47
4	The French versions of *Utopia*: Christian and cosmopolitan models	67
5	The English translation: thinking about the commonwealth	87
6	The Dutch translation: austerity and pragmatism	104
7	The Spanish translations: humanism and politics	110
	Afterword: transferring *Utopia*	128

Part II The paratexts

Principles and editorial conventions	145
The German paratexts	149
The Italian paratexts	171
The French paratexts	181
The English paratexts	205
The Dutch paratexts	219
The Spanish paratexts	233
A Latin paratext: Milan 1620	273
Tables of prefatory material in Latin editions	277
Bibliography	281
Index	295

LIST OF ILLUSTRATIONS

Frontispiece: Basel 1524: the Utopian alphabet. By permission of British Library
Leipzig 1612: Map of Utopia. By permission of British Library   1
Title-page, Amsterdam 1643. By permission of British Library   143
Title-page, Basel 1524 . By permission of British Library   149
Title-page, Venice 1548. By permission of British Library   171
Title-page, Paris 1550. By permission of British Library   181
Title-page, London 1551. By permission of British Library   205
Title-page, Antwerp 1553. By permission of British Library   219
Title-page, Córdoba 1637. By permission of the Biblioteca Nacional, Madrid   233
Title-page, Milan 1620. By permission of the Folger Shakespeare Library   273

CONTRIBUTORS

The following list represents the affiliation and status of the contributors in the later stages of preparation of the volume. The word 'researcher' has been used in a number of cases in order to avoid potentially misleading translations of local terms.

IFIKK: Department of Philosophy, Classics, History of Art and Ideas
ILOS: Department of Literature, Area Studies and European Languages

Warren Boutcher, reader in Renaissance studies, Queen Mary, University of London
Carlos F. Cabanillas Cárdenas, senior lecturer in Spanish, University of Tromsø, and doctoral researcher, Grupo de Investigación Siglo de Oro, University of Navarre
Terence Cave, emeritus professor of French literature, University of Oxford, and emeritus research fellow, St John's College, Oxford
Randi Lise Davenport, doctoral researcher in Spanish, ILOS, University of Oslo
Tyler Fisher, doctoral researcher in Spanish, Magdalen College, Oxford
Kristin Gjerpe, doctoral researcher in the history of ideas, IFIKK, University of Oslo
Lone Klem, emeritus professor of Italian, ILOS, University of Oslo
Gro Bjørnerud Mo, senior lecturer in French, ILOS, University of Oslo
Kathleen Mountjoy, doctoral researcher in Spanish, New College, Oxford
Vibeke Roggen, senior lecturer in Latin and neo-Latin studies, IFIKK, University of Oslo
Trond Kruke Salberg, professor of French literature, ILOS, University of Oslo
Kirsti Sellevold, postdoctoral researcher in French, ILOS, University of Oslo
Christina Sandhaug, doctoral researcher in English, ILOS, University of Oslo
Ronny Spaans, doctoral researcher in Dutch, ILOS, University of Oslo

PREFACE

A great deal is known about the initial fashioning of Thomas More's *Utopia* by a European network of humanists and printers and about its early reception. Particular attention has been given to its place in the Erasmian humanism of northern Europe and in the early modern history of ideas, and some local studies have been made of its emergence in the various national cultures of Europe.[1] What has been lacking up to now is a composite picture of how *Utopia* moved by means of translation from culture to culture and of the ways in which particular versions offered themselves to their readers; likewise, the prefatory and other texts that accompanied the translations have not been made available collectively. The primary aim of this volume is to make good those deficiencies. Part I consists of a series of chapters which provide a contextual and an interpretative framework for each national group of translations; in Part II, the substantive paratexts of all the extant translations of *Utopia* printed between 1524 and 1643 are reproduced both in the original language and in English translation.[2]

By the mid-seventeenth century, *Utopia* had been translated into six European vernaculars: German, Italian, French, English, Dutch and Spanish. Two

---

1 Essential information is provided in the two editions of *Utopia* currently regarded as authoritative: *The Complete Works of Thomas More*, vol. 4, ed. J. H. Hexter and Edward J. Surtz (New Haven and London: Yale University Press, 1965), and Thomas More, *Utopia*, ed. George M. Logan, Robert M. Adams and Clarence H. Miller (Cambridge: Cambridge University Press, 1995; paperback edition 2006). The second of these is, unless otherwise indicated, the edition of reference for this volume. The information it provides on the biography of More and the early printing history of *Utopia* is not repeated here unless it is directly relevant to a particular argument. For a study of utopian ideas in the early modern period, see J. C. Davis, *Utopia and the Ideal Society: A Study of English Utopian Writing 1516-1700* (Cambridge: Cambridge University Press, 1981); chapter 3 of this work, 'The re-emergence of utopia: the European experience 1521-1619' provides an overview which does not, however, give any account of the vernacular translations (for example, the English translation is not mentioned anywhere in the book). *La fortuna dell'Utopia di Thomas More nel dibattito politico europeo del '500* (Florence: Olschki, 1996) is a collection of papers on the fortunes of *Utopia* in various European countries; some of these are excellent, but no overall picture emerges.
2 We use the word 'paratext' to designate the materials that surround a given text, from its title-page onwards: the way it is packaged for its readers. Cf. Gérard Genette, *Seuils* (Paris: Editions du Seuil, 1987); Genette's exploration of the paratext in all its manifestations – particularly, perhaps the notion of a 'threshold' between different cultural moments – has been an important point of reference for us, but we limit the definition of the word to materials physically present in a given book. For the principles governing our selection and presentation of the *Utopia* paratexts, see below, Part II, 'Principles and editorial conventions'.

separate German translations and three different French translations appeared in print in this period; the first printed Spanish translation came late, but there is an early Spanish manuscript version. Several of the versions include only Book II of *Utopia* (or in one case a much abbreviated translation of Book I). The Dutch translation carries little evidence of its origins and destination, at least in its earlier printings; although its place in this book is thus relatively modest, it provides an important piece in the jigsaw puzzle we have sought to reassemble here.

The corpus on which this volume focuses is primarily a vernacular corpus, but *Utopia* was in its original form a Latin text and it continued to be published as such throughout the whole of this period. At various points, there are interesting connections or comparisons to be made between the Latin and the vernacular editions; furthermore, the complex and shifting group of paratexts that surround the first four Latin editions (1516-18) is clearly an important point of reference for the vernacular paratexts, even if relatively few of them featured in the translated editions of *Utopia*.[3] We have therefore included in the volume a chapter sketching the fortunes of the Latin paratexts and editions up to 1650, and a transcription of a single Latin paratext (a prefatory epistle from the 1620 edition) which has never, to our knowledge, been printed in modern times. Since all the other Latin prefatory epistles and poems are readily available in modern editions, we have excluded these texts, whether in the original Latin or translated into a vernacular language, from the Part II corpus. We have, however, included a table showing the way in which the Latin paratexts from 1516-18 appear, disappear and reappear in the Latin editions up to 1631, the last in our period; their presence and position in the vernacular versions is indicated for all the texts reproduced in Part II.

The Latin chapter is followed by six chapters devoted to the versions of *Utopia* in each of the six vernaculars, arranged in chronological order of the first translation to appear in that language; in Part II, the paratexts of each vernacular edition (together with the Latin prefatory epistle referred to above) are presented in the same order both in the original and in English translation.

This order was chosen rather than a strictly chronological one because it was necessary in some cases (Italian, English, Dutch) to follow the history of a given version through successive reprints or its displacement into a new textual configuration. In addition, we have in general given priority to the decisive first phase of vernacularisation in each culture, since the number of

---

[3] On the early Latin paratexts, see in particular Peter R. Allen, '*Utopia* and European humanism: the function of the prefatory letters and verses', *Studies in the Renaissance*, 10 (1963), 91-107.

new contexts multiplies as *Utopia* travels and to deal with them all in equal detail would have exceeded the scope of a volume of this kind. We have, however, aimed to provide a comprehensive map of the transfer of *Utopia* across the vernaculars in early modern Europe, with enough contextual and interpretative analysis to allow its plural trajectories to be grasped as a single complex phenomenon. Some of the pathways that More's work follows are highly individual, taking advantage of particular cultural or political conjunctions; others prove to be connected, sometimes obscurely or surprisingly. No study has yet attempted to trace out these various transformations and intersections in their concrete manifestation as moments in the history of a book, and it is hoped that this volume may provide a model for studies of clusters of paratexts that mediate the cross-cultural movement of other key works.

The methodology we have adopted is, like the object of study, plural. We draw primarily on the history of the book, charting the way that *Utopia* was relayed by printers, patrons and translators, by typefaces, formats and page layout, by prefaces, dedications and permissions. But the choice of these elements and the mode of analysis is flexible, serving at every point the priorities of a text in its particular history. The contributors to the volume are variously specialists in literature, the history of ideas, philology or textual scholarship. They use their different interpretative skills in order to uncover the implications of prefatory and other paratextual materials which are too often brushed aside as trivial or irrelevant if they do not engage directly with weighty matters of political thought.

It should be emphasised that we have used as our point of departure in each case the paratexts, those ephemeral materials that carry *Utopia* over the threshold into new cultural contexts and which therefore provide a rich repertory of signs indicating what was at stake in that act of *translatio*. We have not set out to examine the translations themselves as translations, although we have borne that question in mind and touched on it where it seemed directly relevant to the other questions we have pursued.

From the start, we have worked as a team, suggesting to each other new openings and new information, following up connections and contrasts, reading each other's drafts, correcting one another's errors. The introduction and the afterword seek to make that collective enterprise tangible, but it is in the detail of the work that its essential value lies. Inevitably, the character and style of the chapters vary considerably, partly because different materials required different kinds of approach, but also because we are a team of individuals. We believe that the enterprise has benefited as a result of that variety.

Since we are primarily concerned here with the presentation (the envelope or packaging) of *Utopia* rather than with the text itself, and since the

presentation changes with virtually every printing, we have frequently used the word 'edition' to refer to the successive appearances of the work. Thus straightforward reprints like Antwerp 1562 or Paris 1598 are counted as separate editions together with corrected editions such as London 1556 and of course new translations.

Since we refer in total to more than fifty different editions (in this sense) of *Utopia*, we have adopted the convention of referring to these wherever possible simply as 'Venice 1548', 'Basel 1563', 'Córdoba 1637', 'Cambridge 1995'. The advantage of this formula is that it preserves the two vital coordinates (place and date) for each edition. Unless otherwise indicated, full titles are provided in Part II for the vernacular editions and in the Bibliography for the Latin editions; the Bibliography also enables the abbreviated titles to be easily identified.

All quotations and translations from *Utopia* itself or from its early Latin paratexts are taken from Cambridge 1995 unless otherwise indicated. All other translations, whether in Part I or Part II, are by the author or authors of the chapter of Part I devoted to the language in question; exceptions are again indicated. For the principles and conventions used in transcribing and translating early modern materials throughout the volume, see Part II, 'Principles and editorial conventions'.

The translation of early modern words denoting political entities is notoriously difficult. In general, we have used 'republic' for early modern equivalents of the Latin *respublica*, even though its modern sense is different and could lead to misunderstanding. The early modern English word 'commonwealth' provides a direct translation, but it seemed less appropriate in the context of cultures other than English. 'Republic' also has the advantage that it echoes the title of Plato's founding work. All uses of 'republic' in this volume should therefore be understood according to the early modern sense (or senses) of the word unless otherwise indicated.

This project originated in a one-day workshop, held on 4 September 2004, which was designed as a pilot-study for the parent project 'Dislocations: practices of textual transfer [subsequently 'cultural transfer'] in the early modern period'. 'Dislocations' had been launched the year before by a group of colleagues and doctoral and postdoctoral researchers of the Faculty of the Humanities at the University of Oslo. Thomas More's *Utopia* was chosen as a classic instance of an important early modern text that was progressively transferred by means of re-edition and translation to different cultural contexts. The object of the 2004 workshop was partly methodological: the group had agreed to focus on the paratext as the site of transfer, and the para-

textual materials of the early modern editions and translations of *Utopia* were used as a first concrete example. Subsequently, the group decided to edit the collected paratexts, with translations and short introductory essays. The work for this project soon began to expand as members of the group discovered new translations and new editions or reprints of existing ones. A further one-day symposium, at which members of the team presented near-final drafts of their introductory chapters, was held in Vicenza on 4 May 2006 as part of a conference organised by the parent project.

The Utopia project team

ACKNOWLEDGEMENTS

The workshops, conferences and other research activities of the contributors have been funded by the Department of Literature, Area Studies and European Languages of the University of Oslo. The research team would like to express its appreciation of the Department's continued support.

We also wish to thank all those, too numerous to mention, whom we have consulted individually and collectively on questions arising from our work; the anonymous readers from whom Manchester University Press commissioned reports on our draft typescript, and whose constructive comments and suggestions were of great help in the final stages; and the staff of Manchester University Press itself for their interest in our project and for their friendly and efficient handling of the publication process.

Warmest thanks are due to Warren Boutcher for joining the team in the later stages of its work and for enriching it with his knowledge of the period, his methodological insights, his intellectual energy and his good humour.

Finally, the Editor would like to express his personal gratitude to Trond Kruke Salberg for his meticulous work on the index and to the whole team for their enthusiasm, professionalism and cooperation. Putting this book together was for him an unexpected but always fascinating excursion into areas of early modern culture that were largely unfamiliar to him.

PART I
VERSIONS OF *UTOPIA*:
A EUROPEAN MAP

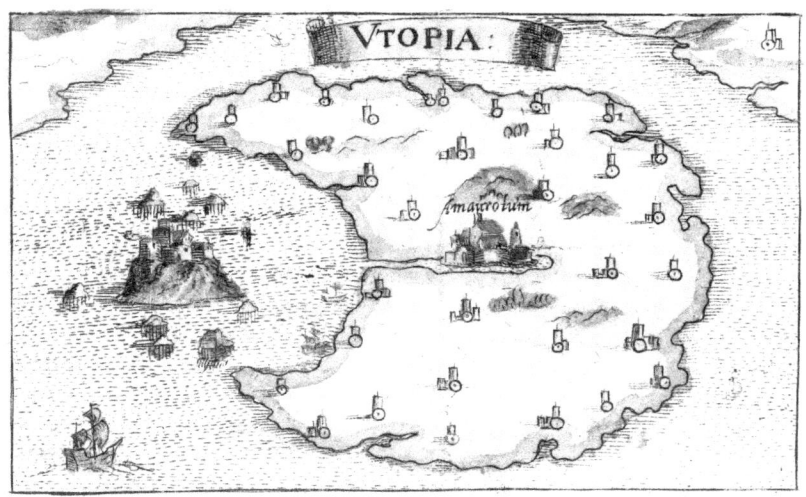

Leipzig 1612: map of Utopia. By permission of the British Library

INTRODUCTION

The first thing that emerges when one reviews the early modern transmission of *Utopia* in the European vernaculars is the variety of new contexts and guises in which it appeared. Between the anonymous sixteenth-century Dutch version, bare of all paratexts save the title, a permission and a privilege, and the sumptuous panoply of letters, prefaces, poems and authorisations in which Medinilla's Spanish translation is packaged, there is an enormous difference of cultural expectations, ideological implications and aesthetic preferences. More's work seems designed to travel: it adapts itself to the interests and tastes of its new readers to an extent that very few other works of the period can rival. The contextual studies in this volume give us a wide range of insights into this process and how it operated.

Let us first look at the simple distribution in time and space of the cluster of translations considered here. Only one was published in the aftermath of the early Latin editions: this was Claude Chansonnette's German rendering of Book II only, printed in Basel in 1524 and not reprinted in the early modern period. Basel was the city where the two 1518 editions of *Utopia* had appeared from Froben's printing house; these editions were to become the point of reference for most of the translations and Latin editions. It was also a humanist centre where More and Erasmus were held in high esteem and from where their views on religious questions as well as on education were widely disseminated. That a German translation should have been undertaken in that environment is not surprising, but neither is it self-evident; it immediately leads one to ask who read *Utopia* and for what purposes.

The only other translation undertaken in this first period was an anonymous Spanish version that was never printed as far as we know. It seems to have been executed – whether in Spain itself or in the Spanish-speaking southern Netherlands – in the early years of the reign of the Emperor Charles V, thus perhaps even before the German translation.

Almost a quarter of a century then elapsed before *Utopia* appeared again, whether in Latin or a vernacular language. During that critical time, the European Reformation begins to take shape; Henry VIII defies the Pope over his divorce from Catherine of Aragon and appoints himself head of the Church in England; Thomas More opposes him in vain, and is duly executed (1535). In 1548, the year after the death of Henry VIII, the Latin *Utopia* is printed in Louvain and an Italian translation appears in Venice. The two contexts

are sharply contrasted. The humanism of Louvain, with its 'College of the Three Languages', will from the mid-sixteenth century be promoted primarily by Jesuits for whom More is a Catholic martyr. Venice, by contrast, is a major trading centre, open to all kinds of interests, influences and styles of thought.

The paths followed by *Utopia* thus begin to proliferate, and the process continues apace. A French translation is printed in 1550, the following year sees the first edition of Ralph Robinson's English version, and in 1553 a Dutch translation is printed in Antwerp. The second edition of the English *Utopia* appears in 1556, a revised version of Le Blond's French translation follows in 1559, and the Dutch translation is reprinted in 1562. A parallel upsurge takes place in the Latin editions in approximately the same period: Louvain 1548 is followed by a cluster of others in the 1550s and 1560s.

How does one explain this mid-century burst of interest in *Utopia*? In the first place, one may conjecture that More's quarrel with Henry and his subsequent execution created a political and confessional turbulence that temporarily drew attention away from *Utopia*, or at least made it less easy for translators, printers and booksellers to identify a constituency of readers who would be interested in More's work as distinct from his public career. By the late 1540s, the dust is settling. In the humanist colleges of northern Europe and in other key humanist centres such as Lyon, the writings of More and Erasmus had always been regarded as an important model, and there is clear evidence linking those centres to some at least of the new translations: the Italian translator Ortensio Lando was in Lyon in the 1530s, as was Aneau, who revised Le Blond's version; Robinson was at the same moment (the moment of More's execution) beginning a course of humanist studies at an Oxford college founded by a friend of Erasmus and More.

More's Latin works are consolidated in the 1550s and 1560s by two contrasted publishing enterprises: the revival of *Utopia* and related humanist writings by the heirs of Froben at Basel, and the publication of the collected works in Catholic centres, especially Louvain, a project which is closely connected with the fashioning of a hagiographic biography of More as Catholic martyr. After the mid-1550s, by contrast, there are no genuinely new translations for some sixty years, and few reprints of existing ones. The one exception is what one may call the 'Sansovino cluster': Lando's Italian translation is included in Sansovino's often-reprinted survey of forms of government *Il governo* (1561), which carries *Utopia* with it when it makes the transfer into French a quarter of a century later.

As we move into the seventeenth century, the picture begins to change markedly. Gregorius Wintermonat translates *Utopia* in tandem with Joseph Hall's *Mundus alter et idem*, here called 'The Second Part of Utopia'. The

fact that the fourth edition of Robinson's English translation appears three years before the publication of Bacon's *New Atlantis* may be regarded as at least a significant accident. Other Utopian fictions have emerged since the mid-sixteenth century (Stiblin's *De Eudaemonensium republica*, Patrizi's *La città felice*, Doni's *Il mondo pazzo e savio*, Aneau's Orbe in *Alector*, and later Campanella's *Città del Sole*), and the name 'Utopia' becomes the principal identifying feature of the title of More's work in most of the Latin and the vernacular editions of the last decades of our period.[1]

The last four versions of *Utopia* in our corpus are sharply contrasted and demonstrate the almost bewilderingly different trajectories that *Utopia* followed on its way outward from the humanist circles of pre-Reformation Europe. Ralph Robinson's translation appears in a new guise, dedicated as an act of homage to More's great-grandson and biographer Cresacre More: the Catholic martyr has returned to England after nearly a century of exile. The Dutch translation is reprinted in Amsterdam, now with a Calvinist preface and accompanied by the paratextual letters of More, Erasmus and Budé. The paratexts of Medinilla's Spanish translation invest heavily in approbations and assurances of the orthodoxy of *Utopia* in order to satisfy the Catholic Inquisitor. Finally, Samuel Sorbière's French translation of 1643, closely connected through its printer with its Latin predecessor Amsterdam 1629, may have been designed to support the politics of the new Dutch Republic, while for its author it seems to have represented the first step in an intellectual career which was connected on the one hand with free-thinking circles in France and on the other with the political philosophy of Hobbes.

It is thus evident that More's work was available in a considerable number of different forms and contexts in western Europe, both in Latin and in the vernaculars, from the mid-sixteenth century onwards. Spain is a partial exception, since no printed version appeared there before Córdoba 1637; there seem to have been no editions of any kind in Portugal, Scandinavia or Eastern Europe.[2] This outline map could of course be refined by allowing for a reception beyond the scattering of printed editions and translations. Manuscripts

---

[1] The name of the island appears at the beginning of the title for the first time in Antwerp 1553. Basel 1563, like other collected editions, reduces the title essentially to 'Utopia', although the contraction is due in that case to the fact that *Utopia* there appears as one work among many. The paratextual letters of More himself, Erasmus and Budé indicate that their short-hand name for the work was 'Utopia' from the start, but it is important to distinguish this use from the way the title is presented to future readers in the printed editions.
[2] It is well-established that, already in this period, *Utopia* began to travel beyond Europe; the scope and purposes of our study made it impossible to give an account of that wider diffusion, but some reference will be made in chapter 7 to Utopian experiments in the New World.

such as the early Spanish translation may have circulated in elite circles of the Empire; early modern printed books circulated too, often beyond national borders, and could remain in use for decades: Quevedo is known to have possessed a copy of Louvain 1548. Periods of apparent silence may thus be misleading.

The map provided by the materials of this volume none the less supplies a wide range of valuable information. Much of this information comes packaged with the book as a cultural object: its printer and the history of his or her preferences, its format, its title-page, the authorisations or permissions it carries, its dedicatees, its prefatory materials, illustrations, marginal glosses and end-materials. There are also the choices made by editor, printer or translator with regard to the material included: many of the translations of *Utopia* omit Book I, or provide only an abridged version of it, thus removing most of the dialogue frame which provides a bridge between the fiction and the real world.

The primary method adopted by the contributors to this volume is to analyse these constantly shifting paratextual clusters both in their own right and as a means of access to the wider cultural context in which a particular translation was produced. In a case like the Italian translation, where the prefatory materials are very brief but the translator Lando and his sponsor Doni were themselves prolific men of letters, their other writings may also be considered as in some sense 'paratexts' to the *Utopia* translation, indicating (for example) generic and ideological preferences. Similarly, Aneau's writings on poetics and his novel *Alector* provide an immediate context for his reissue of the Le Blond version, while the intervention of a galaxy of politicians, theologians, administrators and writers in the paratextual apparatus of Medinilla's translation traces out the contours of a whole cultural and political microcosm.

The mobility of *Utopia*, its ability to adjust to different contexts, is especially visible in the tendency of its translated versions to change their paratextual materials at each appearance. The first Latin editions, printed between 1516 and 1518, are famous for the wealth of their prefatory letters and poems; the later editions for the most part reproduce a selection of these early paratexts without adding new ones. (We have included one late exception in this volume precisely because it is exceptional.) When *Utopia* is translated, however, most of these original paratexts are dropped and replaced by new vernacular paratexts referring to the context in which the translation was executed. Again there are exceptions: Chansonnette's preface borrows from Busleyden's letter to More; a French version of the whole of Budé's letter is included in Le Blond's translation, which also contains a series of woodcuts analogous to those of the early Latin editions; More's first letter to

Giles appears quite frequently as a preface to the work itself; sometimes the Utopian verses, and even the Utopian alphabet, are included. But because these are clearly selections, made for the particular purposes of that publication, they again carry important information about the way the text was meant to be read in its new context.

Utopia was thus from the outset a markedly cosmopolitan book. Its supposed conception in Antwerp is advertised in More's first letter to Giles, and its subsequent prefatory letters add to the network of overseas connections through which it was promoted. Budé sponsors it in Paris, Erasmus in Basel, Busleyden in the Low Countries. First printed in Louvain, it was not published in Latin in More's home country during our period: the Latin editions of the early modern period are scattered along a corridor that runs from the Low Countries in the north to Florence and Milan in the south, passing through Hanau, Wittenberg, Cologne, Frankfurt, and of course Basel. By the time the mid-sixteenth-century spate of translations was under way, however, the elite circle of humanists that had presided over the early Latin editions had become a thing of the past. More and Erasmus both died within the space of a year, and although they had disciples and admirers of various kinds, the cultural context was shifting irreversibly as schismatic religious reform began to put down roots and provoke major conflicts across Europe. The international crossovers of the later part of our period are less frequent and more opportunistic. The magpie translator Gabriel Chappuys, working at the Italianophile court of Catherine de Médicis and her sons, not only retranslated Lando's Italian version as revised by Sansovino, but also published a version of Doni's satire *I mondi*, with its Utopian episode *Il mondo pazzo e savio*. And as we have seen, Wintermonat coupled his *Utopia* translation with a version of Joseph Hall's *Mundus alter et idem*.

Despite these examples, the naturalisation of *Utopia* in particular European cultures and languages is in the main highly scattered, specific, even local: that is after all what one would expect of a work's vernacular transference. If one includes Latin editions in the map, clusters appear in the Low Countries in the 1550s and 1560s, then again between 1629 and 1643, but the ideological concerns that presided over each particular edition are far from unified. *Utopia* is a text that visibly keeps shifting with the context.

Rather than pursuing the local stories, however, the remainder of this introduction will sketch out the frames of reference within which the new versions of *Utopia* emerge, together with the ideological and generic issues to which they give substance. In keeping with the objectives of this volume, the starting-point will in all cases be the paratexts, the way *Utopia* surrounds itself with signs of intention directed towards its readers – not only the anonymous

individuals who buy and (perhaps) read the book, but also its dedicatees and patrons and censors.

The obvious place to begin is the way the figure of More himself is represented. The titles of *Utopia* in its various manifestations all carry the elements of a stereotype: More is 'famous', 'learned', 'eloquent', 'witty', and his rank and offices are usually cited, although one notes that the title of London 1551 reduces him to a simple 'citizen of London', perhaps because his disgrace was seen to deprive him of his rank and titles. Where the early Latin paratexts are preserved, these indications are enhanced by the voice of More himself and biographical details such as the circumstances of his visit to Antwerp. The woodcuts representing him in conversation with Giles and Hythloday are retained in Basel 1524, where the printer would have had access to Froben's blocks, and there is a series of such woodcuts in Paris 1550; much later, More's portrait is provided as a frontispiece in Leipzig 1612.

From the 1540s onwards, the figure of the humanist More, the friend of Erasmus and propagator of Erasmian humanism, is inevitably overshadowed by his dramatic fall and execution, which generate new stereotypes by making him either a traitor to his country or a martyr to his religion. The staunch defender of the Catholic faith, the martyr who persevered to the end, is particularly central to the Spanish paratexts. This is the idealised figure cultivated by the More family in exile and by their sponsors in Louvain and elsewhere; in this image-making process, the Jesuits played a leading role, combining an admiration for More's humanist learning with their mission of defending the Church as a transnational (literally 'catholic') institution. The first edition of the English *Utopia* presents the image of a man of great learning whose one grave error it is best to pass over; Sansovino turns this 'error' on its head by referring instead to the 'criminal desires' of Henry VIII. (In the Bodleian copy of Paris 1598, this passage is heavily scored out.) Doni's prefatory letter in Lando's translation says nothing at all about More, but is addressed to an exemplary *paterfamilias* whose qualities seem designed to recall that element of More's biography, graphically rendered by Holbein's famous painting and reflected, for example, in the late sixteenth-century English play *Sir Thomas More*. It is important to note, however, that the stereotypes relayed by the vernacular paratexts of *Utopia* only occasionally merge with the hagiographic biographies of More that gradually emerge during the later sixteenth century. The story of the More family in exile is largely distinct from the story of *Utopia* itself.

In the vernacular versions of *Utopia*, in other words, the name 'More' and the cluster of features attached to it have above all the function of signs advertising the character of the book. Next to these signs are the ones that indicate the class to which it is to be assigned, or the perspective in which it is to be read. The early Latin editions surround themselves with indicators of

this kind, from the title onwards. The doublet *salutaris* / *festivus*, for example, reissues the Horatian *topos* of the pleasing and the useful in the mode of Erasmian humanism, evoking the world of the *Praise of Folly*, the *Colloquies* and the *Adages*. Likewise, the paratexts designed to enhance the fiction – the map, the Utopian alphabet and verses, the prefatory letters that enter into the Utopian game – have the primary function of writing out the connotations of *festivus*, although we shall need to consider later precisely what the 'joyful' games are that can be played with *Utopia*.

As we have seen, however, the translations commonly strip away the early Latin paratexts and replace them with entirely different ones (or occasionally with none at all, other than the items on the title-page), a procedure that dramatically shifts the interpretative frame. The Dutch version, anonymous and unadorned as it is, retains throughout its reprints a title that emphasises the use of *Utopia* as a practical aid to government. The title of the founding Italian translation couples the 'useful' with the 'necessary'; it excludes any mention of the *festivus*, yet makes no reference to practicability. Instead, it stresses novelty, giving priority to the character of Utopia as a 'newly discovered' state. At the same time, astonishingly, it changes the name to 'Eutopia', which arguably brings the *festivus* back in again, although in a different perspective. It is also accompanied on the title-page by a complex image that seems to point to the allusive, playful nature of the text.

This contrast illustrates the very different trajectories that the reading of *Utopia* had already begun to follow in the mid-sixteenth century, and might also suggest a broad distinction between two opposed, or at least separate, destinations for the work. In some cases, it is presented in a way that aligns it with the tradition of treatises on the best (or ideal) form of the 'republic', from Plato to the fifteenth-century Francesco Patrizi of Siena.[3] Patrizi's work was translated in abridged form by Jean Le Blond, the author of the first French translation of *Utopia*; Lando's Italian version of Book II was included in Sansovino's popular survey of the forms of government of existing states, with a preface that explicitly links Utopia to Plato's Republic; and the Jesuit Gutiérrez's prefatory epistle to Medinilla's translation develops the 'Platonic' character of More's work at some length. The politics of dedication may well enhance these interpretative frames. The preface of Basel 1524, which also invokes the canon of political theorists (especially Aristotle), is addressed to the Mayor and city council of Basel; when Robinson chose William Cecil as the addressee of his translation, the young humanist-trained secretary to the King was on the threshold of his career as the leading statesman of his age;

---

3 This Francesco Patrizi is to be distinguished from his sixteenth-century namesake Francesco Patrizi da Cherso, author of *La Città felice* (1553), which also describes the optimal conditions for a city.

Chappuys's dedication of his (pirated) translation of Sansovino to Henri III shows that his choice of this work was grounded in the politics of the French wars of religion. Although most of the paratexts concede that Utopia is an ideal, an imaginary construction, there are cases – the title of the Dutch translation, and the whole tenor of Córdoba 1637, articulated as it is around the installation of Medinilla as regional governor – where they claim unequivocally that the book is a practical guide to governance.

Other versions emphasise the fictional strand that plays such a central role in the early Latin editions. Chansonnette's preface enters, if rather briefly, into the game of speaking as if Utopia were a real island, but it is Wintermonat's translation, nearly a hundred years later, that goes furthest in this direction, with its new map of Utopia, its resurrection of the Utopian alphabet (almost universally ignored in other translations) and its prefatory discussion of why, although Utopia has been discovered, so few people seem to have been there, not to mention its twinning with the elaborate fictions of Joseph Hall. Doni, the editor and publisher of Venice 1548, later wrote a satirical fantasy called *I mondi* which contains a Utopian world, while Aneau's extravagant novel *Alector* demonstrates its author's fascination with fictional scenarios.

This apparent separation fails, however, to do justice to the complex strands of *Utopia*'s reception. With one or two possible exceptions like the Dutch translation, all of the cases I have mentioned are in fact mixed. *Utopia* is not a treatise like Patrizi's, and Le Blond, who translated them both, is well aware of the fact: taking up key aspects of Budé's letter, he explores the complex question of how More's work is to be read. Conversely, Sansovino (followed by Chappuys) says that he has placed *Utopia* at the end of his survey of existing states so that the reader will be led to reconsider them in the perspective of More's imagined ideal. *Utopia* is above all an instrument for thinking with.

The early French paratexts are instructive here. By translating Budé's letter and echoing it in his own paratexts, Le Blond relays to a new audience Budé's notion of *Utopia* as an *exemplary* text. It is clear that neither Budé nor his translator envisages a direct, practical application of the Utopian political system. Budé's story of how he received and read More's work while he was preoccupied with the management of his personal estates allows him to inflect its purport towards the fundamentally non-materialist values of Christianity, and thence a radical rethinking of one's mode of life. Aneau subsequently revises this reading, replacing the evangelical frame of reference with a markedly classical one: *Utopia* becomes an exemplar of both Ciceronian eloquence and Stoic virtue. Yet here again, the 'model' is one that cannot be achieved, only aspired to: Utopia does not exist, it is a fiction. Aneau saw such fictions in Platonist terms as 'fables', myths that cloak profound truths in pleasing imaginary forms, a hermeneutic tradition that Budé himself had drawn on

copiously and which had been familiar to More also. Gutiérrez, as late as 1637, is still working essentially within this framework, and although the other paratexts of Medinilla's translation focus primarily on practical governance, they do so in the language of a high Baroque rhetoric which arguably constructs the parallel between Utopia and Córdoba as a poetic image, a myth.

Whatever the readings that may emerge in particular cases, our paratexts revert insistently to the conception of *Utopia* as a heuristic text, a fable that speaks obliquely and disconcertingly about matters of grave import. This conception is present in the opening anecdote of Robinson's 1551 preface, with its Lucianic emblem of the observer on the side-lines who apparently indulges in the 'useless' or irrelevant activity of rolling his tub (writing ironic fictions) as a substitute for 'real' involvement in everyday affairs. The anecdote would have been immediately recognised by More and Erasmus, whose translations of Lucian accompanied the 1519 Florence edition of *Utopia*, and it was disseminated in France via the Prologue to Rabelais's Third Book, which also begins with an episode of Utopian colonisation. The title-page of Lando's version, with its complex interplay between title and emblematic image, enters into the same game, which was entirely familiar to Doni, Lando and their circle. Indeed, the fact that it was Lando who translated *Utopia* in 1548 tells us a great deal about the generic and intellectual category to which the work was seen to belong, since Lando was famous above all for his revival of the Ciceronian paradox, which must be understood here in its classical sense, namely a proposition counter to, or on the margins of, common opinion. *Utopia* is a paradox in precisely this sense, since it constructs an 'ideal state' based on the absence of that which was generally believed to be essential to all human society, namely personal property and monetary exchange. This aspect of *Utopia* comes to the fore on the final page, where 'More' as narrative persona appears to reject the notion that an ideal polity can be constructed without wealth. Much discussion has focused on this page, but the decisive factor in any interpretation must surely be the phrase 'such is the common opinion' ('ut publica est opinio'), hidden discreetly in a parenthesis. By attributing to common opinion (*doxa*) the notion that wealth and distinction of rank are essential in any society, More in fact expressly distances himself from that opinion, and consequently gives licence to the 'paradox' on which Utopia is founded.

Thus the translations of *Utopia*, considered collectively, do not merely make a valued text available to a much wider audience. They also identify it as a special kind of text, requiring skilled reading practices, and they transfer the practices as well, rephrasing them in the different idioms of reading that their audience will recognise. In fact, one could go further and suggest that, while there were certainly readers who would recognise those practices and

know how to handle them, the paratexts of the vernacular Utopias are also concerned to pass on such skills to a new generation of readers. In that sense, the cultural transference of More's work was a doubly heuristic exercise: it mediated a text which was a special kind of instrument for thought, and it enacted the reading scenarios in which that instrument could be explored and used.

The versatility of *Utopia*, its ability to adapt itself to different contexts, is also illustrated by the history of the various kinds of censorship to which it laid itself open. The first thing to note here is that there is no sign that what for us is the most radical aspect of Utopian society, the absence of private property, gave rise to censure or censorship. In England, More's fall and execution clearly presented a potential obstacle to publication of his works during the reigns of Edward VI and Elizabeth I. However, as Robinson's first preface shows, this could be negotiated by acknowledging it and then setting it aside. The successive orthodox Catholic editions, from the mid-1560s onwards, 'correct' or 'expurgate' the text: they remove an offensive marginal gloss implying that there are too many priests in 'our' world, a part of the dialogue with the Cardinal in Book I, and two passages in Budé's prefatory epistle, one praising Erasmus, the other implying a negative view of canon law. Of the translations, only the Spanish is accompanied by a set of official authorisations, stating explicitly that it is in no further need of expurgation. In addition, the issue of the toleration of plural belief in the chapter 'On the religions of the Utopians' is raised and negotiated by means of a markedly casuistic argument in Medinilla's preface to his translation, while Quevedo's prefatory epistle also defends More's religious orthodoxy against his detractors, although in more general terms.

It is important to stress that all these corrections and apologetic arguments were manifestly designed to 'save' More's work, to enable it to be published, and that none of them affects the fundamental model I have sketched out above. Most of them are responses to issues that shift with the hardening of confessional dividing lines as the rapid rise of heterodox movements of reform resulted in a fragmentation of the Church that was to prove irreversible: for example, Budé's carefully non-schismatic reformism looked very different as seen from the theological and political viewpoint of the 1560s. At the same time, variations of local cultural context can have the effect of 'detoxifying' apparently suspect authors: even in ultra-orthodox Spain, Quevedo mentions Erasmus and Budé's prefatory letters (not in fact included in the Spanish translation) as evidence of More's scholarly credentials.

What emerges from all this is perhaps above all the ability of *Utopia* not

only to survive cultural transfer, but also to flourish on it. From the start, it was supplied with safety devices, in the way it was written but especially in the way it was presented, and it proved capable of generating new ones for itself as it followed its unforeseeable trajectory through the minefields of early modern institutions and ideologies. It is a text that lends itself to translation, transference, transplantation; it is *resilient*, in the etymological sense of the word, constantly rewinding its spring, renewing its forces. When Montaigne chose the motto 'Vires acquirit eundo' ('It gathers strength as it goes on') for the title-page of his *Essais* in the 1588 edition, he was referring to the tendency of his writings not only literally to expand, but also to acquire more confidence in their purpose. *Utopia* doesn't, of course, expand textually, and its purpose may be reinterpreted as it passes from one cultural moment to another. Yet the motto is appropriate in another sense. Thomas More could have had no notion that, as we now perceive it, he lived at the threshold of the 'early modern' period.[4] He worked with inherited materials and traditions, but was able to inflect them, thanks to the Erasmian milieu to which he belonged, in a way that created an opening for new possibilities of thought. More perhaps than any other paradox of the period, the Utopian paradox demands of its readers the ability to think otherwise, to avoid blind confrontation between existing political and social forces and find an alternative way forward. No other Renaissance Latin work had anything like the staying-power of *Utopia* – not even Erasmus' most successful writings, which are now known only to specialists. Machiavelli's *The Prince*, itself a paradox, had an enormous impact because of its stark political message, but is written in assertive rather than imaginative mode. Few other texts of that period – Montaigne's *Essais* is arguably its only close rival – embodied in such a high degree the possibility of the 'early modern', the invention not so much of new contents as of new instruments of thought.

Terence Cave

---

4 Together with other humanists, he was no doubt conscious of participating in a wide-ranging renewal of culture, a 'new age' profoundly different both from Antiquity and the 'Middle Age'. But he could have had no conception of what we call 'modern', which in turn defines our notion of the 'early modern'.

1 A PROTEAN TEXT: *UTOPIA* IN LATIN, 1516–1631

Long after *Utopia* had become available in Western European vernaculars, the book continued to be published in the original language. Of the printed editions that appeared before 1650, twenty-five are translations, whereas there are twenty editions in Latin.[1] Little attention has been paid to the majority of these, since the main interest of modern editors and other scholars has been the cluster of early editions directly connected with the circle of humanists to which More belonged. However, in the present volume the object of study is the movement of the text through the early modern period as a whole; in that context, *all* the editions are of interest.

Although all the early Latin editions have been examined for the present study, some of them in more than one copy, it has not been possible to make complete collations. Textual variants have been studied primarily on the basis of those reported in Cambridge 1995. A tabular survey of the paratexts in the examined editions is presented at the end of this book; the editions themselves are listed chronologically in the Bibliography, section 1. The perspectives provided in this chapter arise directly from that evidence, which the reader is invited to consult as necessary.[2] A section is also devoted to Milan 1620, which is the only one among the Latin editions after 1518 that presents a new dedicatory epistle; the epistle itself is reproduced in Part II.

A survey of the editions

The first edition of *Utopia* (Louvain 1516) presents itself on the title-page as a 'golden book' on the best form of a state and on a new island. In this epoch of discoveries, readers were not likely to observe immediately that Utopia was not newly discovered but newly invented, and that this was not another travel

---

1 Walter Berschin's survey of Latin editions in his article on Utopian literature seems to be complete; see 'Neulateinische Utopien im alten Reich (1555-1741)', in W. Berschin, *Mittellateinische Studien* (Heidelberg: Matte, 2005), pp. 377-87 (379).
2 Information provided in the introduction and editorial materials in Cambridge 1995 will in general not be repeated here, although certain basic points concerning the early editions and their paratexts will necessarily be recapitulated. On the early paratexts, see in particular Peter R. Allen, '*Utopia* and European humanism: the function of the prefatory letters and verses', *Studies in the Renaissance*, 10 (1963), 91-107. For a graphic evocation of the Erasmus-More circle at the time *Utopia* was going to press, see Lisa Jardine, *Erasmus, Man of Letters: The Construction of Charisma in Print* (Princeton, NJ: Princeton University Press, 1993), pp. 27-41 and 175-80.

book but a literary invention. (They were meant to realise that later.) The paratextual material on the following pages would confirm the illusion: a map of Utopia and the alphabet of its language. After that, they would find poems and letters written by scholars and poets, from Europe as well as from Utopia, a common feature of these texts being the movement from reality to fiction and back. From the correspondence of Erasmus and More and their circle in 1516, it is evident that these well-known humanists greatly enjoyed preparing the book for the press.

Utopia's first printer was Dirk Martens, a pioneer of printing in the Low Countries, whose services Erasmus had been using for many years. Peter Giles (Petrus Aegidius), whose central role as *Utopia*'s first editor is made clear on the title-page, was a corrector for Martens, in addition to his work as a city clerk in Antwerp.[3] In March 1517 Erasmus asked More for a corrected copy of the printed book; the plan was to have a second edition printed in either Paris or Basel.[4] More preferred Paris, and *Utopia* was sent to Gilles de Gourmont, a leading French printer and another of Erasmus' contacts. The young humanist and corrector Thomas Lupset was to be responsible for preparing this edition. According to the title-page, it has been purged of innumerable errors, and it is true that some better readings have been introduced. But apparently, something went wrong during the production, and Erasmus was not at all satisfied.[5]

More and Erasmus next turned to the scholar-printer Johannes Froben, whose press in Basel was a major centre of humanist activity. Froben produced two editions, in March and November 1518;[6] unlike the 1516 and 1517 editions, where *Utopia* appeared alone, they both include the collected epigrams of More and Erasmus. Froben's books had a reputation for beauty, not least because of the woodcuts, and in the case of *Utopia*, too, one sees that priority was given to the visual presentation. Not only were the Utopian alphabet and poem included again, having been omitted in the Paris octavo, but a new map of the island was also made, together with a woodcut depicting the colloquy of Book I. There are many parallels between the two Basel editions; among the differences is a new title-page for the November printing, signed by Hans Holbein, and some considered changes in the text demonstrate that editorial work was done during the months that had passed.

The last edition printed in More's lifetime, Florence 1519, differs from its

---

3 This Peter Giles or Aegidius from Antwerp should not be confused with a contemporary scholar (1488-1555) by the same name from Albi in Southern France who, among other things, translated Aelian's *Historia animalium* from Greek into French.
4 Cambridge 1995, p. 271.
5 New Haven 1965, p. clxxxv, with references to epistles.
6 The two Basel editions will henceforth be referred to as Basel 1518M and Basel 1518N respectively.

predecessors in that it seems to have no direct connection with the circle of Erasmus and More. It was printed by Filippo Giunta's heirs, who also produced works in Italian by early modern writers (Petrarch, Boccaccio) alongside classical texts in Greek and Latin and other humanist works, including *The Praise of Folly* (1518). Giunta printed *Utopia* at the end of a volume devoted to Erasmus' and More's translations of works by Lucian; it almost looks like an afterthought. The volume reveals little about its origin: it names no editor and carries no new preface or introduction. The first text after the title-page is a letter that Erasmus had written some thirteen years earlier, dedicating his first piece of translation of Lucian to Richard Foxe, Bishop of Winchester and a patron of learning.[7] None of the *Utopia* paratexts added after 1516 is included in the volume, but textual variations reveal that the exemplar of the 1519 edition was Basel 1518M.[8]

After the first five editions, published within the space of three years, no other Latin edition appeared for almost thirty years. But in 1548 *Utopia* appeared once more in Louvain, printed by Servaes van Sassen and financed by Arnold Birckmann's widow, and it looks as if the link from the first editions to what we may call the second generation of *Utopia* editions goes through the Birckmann family of booksellers and printers in Cologne.[9] Arnold's brother Franz, who had died nearly twenty years earlier, had been active as a disseminator of books, and was, it seems, a well-known figure at the great Frankfurt book fairs; *Utopia* may well have been among the books that he sold for Froben, with whom he had close connections.[10] A second link goes through Franz's brother-in-law, Johannes Grapheus: *his* brother was Cornelius, the author of a paratextual poem in *Utopia*. The Birckmann family is also the link that connects Louvain 1548 with Cologne 1555, which was printed by Birckmann's heirs. The Louvain edition follows Froben's very closely as far as the paratexts are concerned: it even presents them in the same order. Only the map and the Utopian alphabet have been left out. Cologne 1555 presents exactly the same group of paratexts as its predecessor – four poems and five letters – but in a different order. And in these first posthumous editions, More is still presented as vice-sheriff of London, the title he held in 1518.

The next edition of *Utopia* was printed in 1563 in Basel by Froben's

---

7 The first edition of the Lucian translations was *Luciani opuscula ... ab Erasmo Roterodamo et Thoma Moro ... in Latinorum linguam traducta* (Paris: Josse Bade, 1506). On Foxe, see below, pp. 88, 90.
8 Cambridge 1995, p. 270.
9 Louvain 1548 copies readings from Basel 1518N, against the first three editions, e.g. 'meus vero sermo' against 'mea vero oratio' (Cambridge 1995, p. 96, line 16) and 'parvulus' against 'puerulus' (Cambridge 1995, p. 152, line 19).
10 See *Allgemeine Deutsche Biographie*, vol. 2 (Leipzig: Duncker & Humblot, 1875), art. 'Birkmann', pp. 663-4.

grandson, Nicolaus Episcopius. Nicolaus the elder had married Froben's daughter Justina and started a printing house together with his brother-in-law Hieronymus Froben.[11] He had had close connections with Erasmus, who lived in Basel in his later years and who held a high opinion of the young man. Nicolaus the younger established his own printing house in 1553. The volume containing *Utopia* is the first collective edition of More's Latin works, published under the title of *Lucubrationes*; *Utopia* is placed at the beginning of the volume.

Basel 1563 may have served as a spur for editors and printers in Louvain, where More's collected Latin works appeared only two years later in a rival edition, this time ostentatiously Catholic, and with More's position correctly described as 'former chancellor of England'. Four editions were published in the course of 1565 and 1566. The privilege carried by these editions states that no printer other than Bogard and Zangre was allowed to print More's works or to sell them during the next six years. It is dated 14 October 1565 and was signed in Brussels by a certain de Facuwez, acting as representative for the royal authorities;[12] the same official had signed the privilege in Louvain 1548. Apparently, the two printers produced *Utopia* as a joint venture. What appear as different editions were in fact printed from the same forms. Only the title-pages differ, each printer referring to his own sign.[13] The editors of this group made a serious attempt to make the collection of More's Latin works as complete as possible: they even translated his incomplete English play *Richard III* into Latin. As far as *Utopia* and its paratexts are concerned, they used at least two former editions: three marginal notes that were added in Basel 1518N are included here, and also the letter and poem by Paludanus, omitted by other editions from 1518 onwards. The *Utopia* paratexts are located directly after two brief epitaphs for More, without a new title-page or even a subtitle.

Wittenberg 1591 is clearly based on Louvain 1516. The title is the same, word for word, and the contents are identical and in the same order, except that the map, the Utopian alphabet and the Utopian poem are missing. It appears that the printer or bookseller had acquired the *editio princeps* seventy-five years after it came out.

On the threshold of the seventeenth century, there appeared a new edition, printed by Saur in Frankfurt am Main. The editor, Eberhard von Weihe,

---

11 *Allgemeine Deutsche Biographie*, vol. 6 (1877), art. 'Episcopius, Nicolaus', p. 155.
12 The king in question was Philip II of Spain; in the very same month a group of noblemen took an initiative that led to the Dutch War of liberation.
13 Zangre adds, after his name on the title-page, 'sub Fonte' ('at the sign of the fountain'), with the picture of a fountain; Bogard adds 'sub Bibliis Aureis' ('at the sign of the golden Bibles'), with the picture of a book, among other things.

followed the readings of Basel 1518N against the first three editions,[14] and as in the 'Birckmann' cluster of editions, More is given the title he held at the time he wrote *Utopia*. This 1601 edition was financed by Peter Kopff, as was its successor, printed by Henne in Hanau in 1613. Although the two editions were not printed from the same form, Hanau 1613 follows its predecessor closely from page to page. However, it makes no mention of von Weihe, and omits a puzzling phrase from the title-page (see below, p. 28). Hanau 1619 belongs to the same group of editions; with the exception of the marginal notes,[15] it contains the same paratexts, and even in the same order. But the editor, Caspar Dornau, has used More's text as an element in his own project, to make a collection of playful texts from Antiquity to his own age.[16] The result is some 1150 pages in folio, entitled *Amphitheatrum sapientiae Socraticae joco-seriae* ('An amphitheatre of Socrates' joking-serious wisdom'). The amphitheatre makes it possible for the reader to study the objects from many angles, and Dornau's theatre presents a systematically organised collection of mocking poems, parodies, dissertations and the like. Under 'passer' one finds Catullus' poems, of course, and then a number of imitations. Tiny animals are praised in a humorous way, and the subject of 'nature' is also extended to bodily functions. Among the dissertations there are three or four written by Dornau himself, and also one by Eberhart von Weihe, the editor of Frankfurt 1601. There are extracts from Alciati's *Emblemata* and Erasmus' *Praise of Folly*, there is a text by Stefano Guazzo, the 'Encomium adulationis' ('Praise of flattery'), and even Melanchthon has not been left out. Among the Greek texts in the volume is the Homeric mini-epic 'The Frog-Mouse War'.

The first Hanau edition of *Utopia* was printed by an insignificant printer, but this one bears Wechel's name on the frontispiece, the name of one of the printing dynasties. 'Typis Wechelianis' was a mark of quality, since Wechel's set of Greek types had been used. But who printed the book? The title page reveals that the costs were paid by Daniel and David Aubri and Clemens Schleich - relatives and successors of Andreas Wechel, who ran a printing house together from 1617 on.[17] As Hanau was a Calvinist centre, the Wechels

---

14 Where textual variants are concerned, Frankfurt 1601 depends upon the tradition from Basel 1518N. For example, the 1601 edition shares the reading 'intersunt' with Basel 1518N; Louvain 1516 and Paris 1517 have 'inter se sunt' and Basel 1518M has 'inter sunt' (Cambridge 1995, p. 112, line 4). And whereas Basel 1518M has 'obiecisse', Frankfurt 1601 shares the reading 'obiecisset' with the other three early editions (Cambridge 1995, p. 218, line 25).
15 It seems as though the marginal notes were forgotten in Hanau 1619; they first appear in the middle of the chapter 'Slaves' ('De servis') in Book II.
16 For a study of Dornau, see Robert Seidel, *Späthumanismus in Schlesien: Caspar Dornau (1577-1631). Leben und Werk* (Tübingen: Max Niemeyer Verlag, 1994). The *Amphitheatrum* is discussed in chapter 11, pp. 338-64.
17 R. J. W. Evans, *The Wechel Presses: Humanism and Calvinism in Central Europe 1527-1627* (Oxford: The Past and Present Society, 1975), p. 5.

were a Calvinist family; Andreas was among the Huguenots who had to flee from the massacre on St. Bartholomew's Day, Paris 1572.[18]

A century after Florence 1519, a Latin *Utopia* was printed in Milan. In an introductory epistle, the printer and editor Bidelli dedicates the book to the president of the Milanese senate. From the text on the respective title-pages, it seems clear that the exemplar was one of the editions financed by Kopff. The book includes *Utopia* only, and it has no illustrations except for the printer's device. Many of Bidelli's editions are beautiful; his edition of *Utopia*, however, was apparently made as a pocket-book, as cheaply as possible.

The last Latin editions in our period form a strange threesome. The title-pages carry the names of three different printers and two cities: Cornelius ab Egmond, Cologne 1629; Willem Blaeuw, Amsterdam 1629; and Jan Jansson, Amsterdam 1631. Nevertheless, the books are strikingly similar: the collections of paratexts are the same, there are no marginal notes, and the format is 32°.[19] A closer comparison reveals that the same copper plate – a picture of three women - has been used for both 1629 editions. It is generally accepted that 'Cornelius ab Egmond' is a fictitious name, adopted by Blaeuw to promote his books in Catholic areas.[20] Thus Blaeuw printed two versions of the same book. Of the two 1629 editions, the one from Cologne says on the title-page that it is corrected in accordance with the index of expurgated books by the Archbishop of Toledo, and it does in fact have 266 pages as against 268 in its Amsterdam twin. Blaeuw must have had more than one earlier edition at his disposal, since he appears to be the first to print both Erasmus' letter to Froben and Paludanus' letter and poem in the same edition. Jansson's edition copies the one that has Blaeuw's name on it page by page and line by line, with few exceptions. These two Amsterdam printers are often mentioned as rivals; in the case of *Utopia*, it seems that Janssonius produced what we would now call a pirated edition.

The paratexts

The collection of paratexts surrounding the earlier Latin editions of *Utopia* is impressive both for their number and for the celebrity of certain of their authors. Contributions by two of the leading humanists of the day were added after the first edition: a letter by Budé in the second edition and one by

---

18 Evans, *The Wechel Presses*, p. 3.
19 See the Tables, below, pp. 278–80. The first Latin edition of *Utopia* that appeared in England (Oxford: W. Hall, 1663) is almost identical with this cluster of editions.
20 For example, it is taken for granted in Edouard Rahir (ed.), *Catalogue d'une collection unique de volumes imprimés par les Elzevier et divers typographes hollandais du XVII siècle* (Nieuwkoop: B. de Graaf, 1965 (1896)), p. 484. Sorbière's French translation (Amsterdam 1643) was printed by Willem Blaeuw's son Jan or Jean; see below, pp. 82, 84, 86.

Erasmus in the third. Their most striking feature, however, is their mobility: paratexts come and go from one edition to the next. Whatever the reasons for these changes, and they are sometimes difficult to assess, they certainly have to do with the local perspectives of those who assembled the editions, whether editors or printers. Let us look, then, at some key elements in this shifting package of promotional texts.

We may begin with the title. Although More and Erasmus in their 1516 correspondence refer to the text by the name of the island, it was a long time before the word 'Utopia' became generally accepted as the title of the book.[21] In the first edition, what we may call the title is presented as follows: 'A truly golden little book, no less beneficial than entertaining, on the best form of a state and on the new island of Utopia'. In the second edition, the text on the title-page is addressed to the reader, and the title as such is the grammatical object of the verb *habes* ('you have'): 'To the reader. You have a truly golden little work by Thomas More, no less useful than elegant, on the best form of a state and on the new island of Utopia.' What was in 1516 a *libellus* that was *salutaris* and *festivus* is now an *opusculum* that is *utile* and *elegans*. Froben preferred the version from 1516, but with the elements in the opposite order: 'On the best form of a state and on the new island of Utopia, a truly golden little book, no less beneficial than entertaining'. Florence 1519 followed Froben, and so did Louvain 1548 and Cologne 1555. The picture changes in the 1563 edition of More's works, partly because *Utopia* is here only one work among many: it is presented on the title-page of the volume as a whole as *Utopiae libri II*. The Louvain collected works followed suit. When *Utopia* was again published separately, 'Utopia' was no longer the title. In Frankfurt 1601, the title has reverted to a variant of Froben's: 'On the best form of a state and on the new island of Utopia, two books: a truly golden piece of writing, no less beneficial than entertaining'. This edition also introduces the new practice of giving the author's name *before* the title of his work. Milan 1620 copies the title from one or other of the editions financed by Krafft, but leaves out the second part ('a truly golden ...'). It is only in the Amsterdam-'Cologne' group of editions that the title is reduced to the single word 'Utopia'. A parallel shift, as subsequent chapters will show, also occurs in several of the vernacular editions of the seventeenth century.

The two main paratextual genres deployed in the first four editions of *Utopia* are the poem and the epistle, but we should also count the marginal notes, together with the map and the Utopian alphabet. The paratextual

---

21 Nor was Utopia at the outset the name of the island: in their correspondence of September and October 1516, More and Erasmus had used the Latin equivalent 'Nusquama'. See *Opus epistolarum Des. Erasmi Roterodami*, ed. P. S. Allen, vol. 2, 1514-17 (Oxford: Clarendon Press, 1910), epistles 461, 467, 474, 477, 481.

material as a whole seems designed to foster the illusion of Utopia as a new or new-found island, but this is especially true of the map and the alphabet, placed as they are in a key position on the pages following the title-page. In the haste of preparing More's manuscript for the press for the first time, a map of the island of Utopia was apparently given priority: as late as 12 November 1516, it was no more than a sketch, made by 'some excellent artist' ('quidam egregius pictor').[22] The master of the 1518 map has been identified as Ambrosius Holbein, and in comparisons between the maps, it has become customary to assert the superior quality of his. However, one should also notice that whereas the first map follows More's text in representing the island with a bay, the later map has turned the bay into land so that the island has become roughly circular. Apparently, the later artist used the 1516 map as a model instead of reading the text and misunderstood the representation of the bay. Bishop has put forward the interesting hypothesis that the shape of the island has been deliberately made to look like a skull, as a *memento mori*,[23] apparently one of the many puns on More's name that contemporaries liked to make (Erasmus' *Encomium Moriae* being the most famous example). As for the Utopian language, it is the result of skilful effort, according to Hexter, with a vocabulary that is constructed in a logical way, for example *la* (not) and *uoluala* (willingly) combine to form *lauoluala* (unwillingly).[24] But arguably, the alphabet itself is less sophisticated; it consists of only a few basic forms, like the circle and the square, and the shapes of the letters are based upon the order of the Latin alphabet.[25]

Those responsible for preparing the early editions appeared to think that it was more important to promote the idea of Utopia than to surround the work with encomiastic poems to the author, as was the general practice: *Utopia*'s paratextual poems concern themselves primarily with the island's history, philosophy and way of living, although More is praised as 'London's pride' in the verses of Noviomagus and Grapheus. More's first letter to Peter Giles and Book I of the work itself (which is also a kind of paratext in its own right) confirm Utopia as a contemporary discovery and make Hythloday one among a group of participants in a dialogue. Just as Hythloday is seen in conversation with More and Giles in Book I, the Utopian poet Anemolius, like the anonymous author of the opening Utopian quatrain, is treated on a par with his real European counterparts. This tendency is even stronger in

---

22 *Opus epistolarum Des. Erasmi Roterodami*, ed. Allen, epistle 487.
23 Malcolm Bishop, 'Ambrosius Holbein's memento mori map for Sir Thomas More's *Utopia*. The meanings of a masterpiece of early sixteenth-century graphic art', *British Dental Journal*, vol. 199 (2005), 107-12. For example, part of the ship at the front of the picture may be seen as teeth (perhaps this is why the article was printed in a periodical for dentists).
24 New Haven 1965, pp. 277-8.
25 Compare, for example, a–f (circles) with r–y (squares); see above, frontispiece.

later editions, where all the poems are placed together in a single group and the Utopian quatrain is given in Latin only.

This merging of the fictional scenario and the historical world of More's humanist network is of course essential to the way the work as a whole commutes between the 'ideal' world of Utopia and the lived reality of the early sixteenth century. The prose paratexts make various kinds of choice between these polarities, but most allude to the fictional game in one way or another, and most also reflect on the value of Utopia as a construction analogous to Plato's Republic. The short epistle from Erasmus to Froben in the Basel editions does neither; instead, it emphasises More's rootedness in English affairs and in his own household, an image connected by analogy with the idea of good governance. In these various ways, the paratexts prepare for and enhance the engagement with 'domestic' English politics in Book I, which many of the vernacular versions will partially or entirely omit.

Marginal annotations are a standard feature of early modern books and they commonly combine a purely indicatory function, like section titles and running heads, with value-judgements and occasional witticisms. *Utopia*'s marginal notes are no exception, but as they are imitated in some of the vernacular versions and are also, as we shall see, in certain cases the object of censorship, they deserve attention. It is not entirely clear who supplied them. In his letter to Busleyden, Giles says that he has added the Utopian quatrain and 'some marginal notes'.[26] Although he is here adopting the fictional frame of reference (he claims that Hythloday had showed him the poem), this passage is usually taken to mean that he himself supplied these elements of the publication.[27] On the other hand, the title-page of Paris 1517 seems to imply that it was Erasmus who had written the notes, as Prévost asserts in his modern French translation: 'En plus de la correction d'innombrables fautes en maints endroits, on y trouve des annotations d'Érasme et une lettre de Budé.'[28] However, the phrase 'Erasmi annotationes' appears in a list of improvements or elements added to the present edition, and the marginal notes were not new. It is possible that the intended meaning is that the purging of errors was carried out in accordance with Erasmus' annotations on Louvain 1516,[29]

---

26 Cambridge 1995, pp. 26-7.
27 Cf. More's way of describing his composition of *Utopia* in his preface addressed to Giles: 'All I had to do was repeat what you and I together heard Raphael relate' (Cambridge 1995, p. 31).
28 André Prévost, *L'Utopie de Thomas More* (Paris: Mame, 1978), p. 226, with a facsimile of the 1517 title-page on p. 227; translated into English, Prévost's version reads: 'Besides the correction of innumerable errors in many places, it contains annotations by Erasmus and a letter by Budé.' The Latin text is 'Cui quidem ab innumeris mendis undequaque purgatio *praeter* [my italics; the word is expressed by an abbreviature] Erasmi annotationes ac Budaei epistulam.'
29 In this case, 'epistulam' is a misprint for 'epistula', and the abbreviature should be interpreted

which corresponds better to what we know about the circumstances of the 1517 edition. Opinions remain divided,[30] but whatever the truth of the matter, the connection of Erasmus' name with the marginal annotations may have drawn the attention of later Church censors to two satirical notes in the later part of the work.

The process of taking out paratextual material started with the second edition. The elements not included are the map and the Utopian alphabet and poem; priority was given to producing a cheaper book in the format of a handbook, which excluded the use of the original woodcuts, even if one assumes that they were available to Gilles de Gourmont. As one would expect, Froben had new woodcuts of high quality made for his editions, but most of the later printers left these elements out, no doubt mainly, again, for practical and economic reasons.

The most authoritative among the early editions were those with Froben's device on them; these editions seem to have been the most widely distributed and read, and Froben's choice of paratexts had considerable influence on later editions. For example, Froben chose not to reprint More's second letter to Giles, and it was never reprinted in early modern editions. He also omitted the two contributions by Paludanus, which were reprinted only rarely. Of the three letters to Peter Giles, the first editor of *Utopia*, Froben prints only the one (More's) that has the function of a preface; on the other hand, he emphasises his own key position through the added letter to himself, written by Erasmus and placed immediately after the title-page. It seems that it was Erasmus who had authorised the editor of the Froben editions, Beatus Rhenanus, to omit Paludanus' letter and poem; this may be either because Desmarez (Paludanus) was simply not famous enough, or because both texts make slighting remarks about the Dutch people, which were not likely to please Erasmus. Similarly, one of the marginal notes to Book II was omitted for what look like nationalistic motives: people from Basel would not care to read, as a commentary to a description of the barbarous neighbours of the Utopians, 'A people not so unlike the Swiss'.[31] Such were the local factors that helped to shape the presentation of *Utopia* as it passed from place to place and printer to printer.

Florence 1519 did not use paratexts to enhance the game, the illusion that

---

as 'propter', not 'praeter', and translated as 'in accordance with', not 'besides'. Cf. Adriano Cappelli, *Lexicon abbreviaturarum: Wörterbuch lateinischer und italienischer Abkürzungen* (Leipzig: J. J. Weber, 1928), pp. 293-4.
30 'Perhaps both contributed glosses; or perhaps the 1517 edition is wrong' (Cambridge 1995, p. 27, n. 23). John Freeman finds that the marginal notes were supplied by Erasmus ('Discourse in More's Utopia: Alibi/pretext/postscript', *English Literary History*, 59 (1992), 289–311 (301)).
31 See Cambridge 1995, p. 208, n. 47.

Utopia was a real place; not even Anemolius' poem was included. Instead, the edition focuses on Utopia as a political work, not least through a title-page where the word *tyrannicida* occurs four times (in connection with tracts by Lucian). One wonders why this edition has left out the epistle by Budé,[32] a contributor whose name is prominent on the title-page of other editions. The Budé letter was among the elements of Utopia that were expurgated later on, but it would be wrong to project the opinion of later censors back on to this early edition. A more plausible reason for the omission is Budé's nationality, since this was a period of military threats from France against Italian territories: only three years before, France had reoccupied Milan.

One understands why editors did not want to include More's second letter, which spoils the ongoing joke of Utopia as a real place; besides, since it was not included in Froben's editions, some of the later editors would not have known it at all. Erasmus' letter to Froben, like the Budé letter, was dropped in Florence 1519; it is also absent from the Louvain collected works. Of the letters and poems from 1516, only five are included in all the Latin editions: Giles's letter to Busleyden, Busleyden's epistle to More, the poems by Noviomagus (Geldenhouwer) and Grapheus (de Schrijver), and More's important first letter to Giles. But even so, the status of these paratexts may vary with their location in the volume and with their title. For example, More's letter to Giles is entitled 'Preface to the work on the best condition of a state' in 1516; in the following editions the title is 'Thomas More sends his greetings to Peter Giles', as if this were an ordinary letter. And whereas the 1518 editions have the word 'preface' in the running title, Paris 1517 leaves out that important word; so do some later editions, such as Louvain 1565/1566.

Some editions omit all marginal notes, but most adopt those of the early editions, sometimes adding or omitting one or two. Basel 1563 goes further: here, the editor has given himself the liberty to rephrase existing notes and invent new ones at will.

The early editions thus belong by and large to the ambiance of the international humanist network of which Erasmus was the acknowledged leader; *Utopia* is represented as a brilliant new variation on the device of *serio ludere* which had been made famous by the *Praise of Folly*. Even Florence 1519, which is in many ways independent of the first four editions, prints the text alongside the Lucian translations. Yet this uniformity is at least partly deceptive: the lines of force shift from edition to edition, with different local contexts and concerns coming to the fore. *Utopia*, from the outset, is already a mobile text, lending itself to transfer and transplantation.

---

[32] The edition does not include any paratexts added after 1516, although its exemplar was the edition from Basel 1518M (Cambridge 1995, p. 270).

Utopia, religion and censorship

The religious dimension of *Utopia* is not especially prominent, despite the chapter on Utopian religions, which seems to evoke the pre-Reformation tolerance prevalent in Erasmus' circle at the time it was written. In a similar spirit, Budé's letter brings out the strain of Christian anti-materialism which is implied by the abolition of personal property in Utopia. It is true that there are some satirical remarks about priests and friars, particularly in the 'conversation with the Cardinal' in Book I, but More's work was not provocative in the sense that the *Praise of Folly* undoubtedly was.

The image of the humanist, moderate More was at least partially overtaken by events in the later part of his career; his confrontation with Henry VIII in the 1530s and subsequent execution, together with his persecution of Lutherans, was to turn him in due course into a Catholic martyr for some and a traitor for others. Yet this polarisation did not have an immediate effect, as is shown by the connections between the editions printed in Louvain and Basel in the mid-sixteenth century: the transfer of *Utopia* between these locations seems to have been unmarked by religious conflict until after 1560. Although the city of Cologne permitted no Reformists of any colour to reside there and bore the motto 'Holy Cologne, faithful daughter of the Holy Roman Church' ('Sancta Colonia sanctae Romanae Ecclesiae fidelis filia'), Cologne 1555, like Louvain 1548, makes no mention of the author's role as a martyr. And in Basel 1563, the author is presented, not with his official titles, but as 'England's distinguished jewel' ('Angliae ornamenti eximii'); this may be seen, perhaps, as an attempt to avoid conflict and to deflect attention from the status and position that More occupied during his later years, in order to focus on his writings.

Two factors brought about a change in this situation. One was the dramatically shifting politics of the English schism. The sudden upsurge of Catholic loyalty under Queen Mary of England and its subsequent suppression led in the following years to the construction by pious Catholics in exile and their sympathisers of monuments to More's memory in the form of biographies and complete works.[33] In such a context, it is perhaps not surprising that the Louvain *Opera omnia* appear as ostentatiously Catholic: More's *virtus* is emphasised on the title-page, and the image of the author as a martyr is underlined through the decision to locate his epitaph as the first among his works, thus focusing the reader's attention on his death. This edition also includes polemical works such as More's response to Martin Luther, which

---

33 See Hugh Trevor-Roper, 'The image of Thomas More in England 1535-1635', in *La fortuna dell'Utopia di Thomas More nel dibattito politico europeo del '500* (Florence: Olschki, 1996), pp. 5-23 (pp. 7-9).

carries a number of acrimonious marginal notes.[34]

The other factor was no doubt the Catholic reaction to the steady rise of schismatic tendencies in Europe, in other words the phenomenon known in general as the Counter-Reformation, which can be dated from the hardening of confessional divides in the 1560s following the publication of the decrees of the Council of Trent. In Louvain 1548, as we have seen, there is no sign of active censorship. Cologne 1555 again contains no statement on the admissibility or otherwise of the contents of the book, but it is hardly accidental that it omits a marginal note in Book II exclaiming that the priests of Utopia are much holier than our own; as we shall see, this is a sign of things to come. Ten years later, the two Louvain editions contain a paragraph stating that More's Latin works might be presented to the reading public, and that they might also bring 'piety and a not irreligious pleasure' if they were 'thus corrected'. Budé's letter was left untouched, but a whole page of Hythloday's 'conversation with the Cardinal' is deleted.[35] This was the work of Johannes Hentenius, professor of theology at Louvain and himself a Dominican friar; he was also a Biblical scholar and editor of considerable experience and repute. Later in Book I, Hentenius shows his genius where censorship is concerned. To Hythloday's claim that preachers are clever men who adjust Christ's doctrines to people's morals – since the opposite is unrealistic – Hentenius has added the little word 'nonnulli': *some* preachers do this.[36]

The fact that the Catholic world recognised Thomas More as an exemplar of Christian faith did not prevent Cardinal Gaspar de Quiroga, Archbishop of Toledo, from putting *Utopia* on the Index of prohibited books (1583). In the case of Utopia, certain passages would have to be omitted before publication because the general public might misunderstand them.[37] The passages he deleted in *Utopia* are a negative remark in Budé's letter on the proliferation of canon law, which pre-Reformers of the early sixteenth century regarded as a purely human and pernicious accretion to the divine laws that have scriptural authority; two unflattering jokes about priests and friars in the 'conversation with the Cardinal'; and the marginal note

---

34 E.g. 'Luther's boasting' ('Iactantia Lutheri') and 'You didn't get this doctrine from heaven, did you, Luther?' ('Num hanc doctrinam coelo habes Luthere?') (Louvain 1565, fols 59 (error for 60) r and 62 v).
35 Cambridge 1995, from p. 78, line 4 to p. 80, line 13.
36 The passage is not annotated in Cambridge 1995, p. 98, line 16.
37 The expurgation is carried through in Gaspar de Quiroga, *Index librorum expurgatorum* (Madrid: Alfonso Gómez, 1584), fol. 193. Cf. Francisco López Estrada, 'La primera versión española de la *Utopía* de Moro, por Jerónimo Antonio de Medinilla (Córdoba, 1637)', in M. P. Hornik (ed.), *Collected Studies in Honour of Américo Castro's Eightieth Year* (Oxford: Lincombe Lodge Research Library, 1965), pp. 291-309 (p. 291 n.).

which had been omitted in Cologne 1555.[38] A similar note praising the small number of priests in Utopia,[39] omitted from Milan 1620, is not on Quiroga's list. But one cannot draw the conclusion that he allowed this note; apparently he never saw it. The edition he used was Basel 1563,[40] where the note is absent (on the notes in Basel 1563, see above, p. 24).

This evidence is corroborated by occasional signs of censorship exercised by early book-owners. In the copy of the 1555 edition in the Vatican library, ten pages have been cut out; it is hardly coincidental that these contain the letters by Budé and Erasmus. And in the copy of Louvain (Zangre) 1566 in the library of Bergamo, an early hand has added on the title-page: 'With expurgation of two passages in Guillaume Budé's letter to the Englishman Thomas Lupset'.[41] The expurgation itself was also made by hand, and the first of the censored passages is the one that was expurgated in Quiroga's Index. This deletion is somewhat half-hearted, but the second passage cannot be read at all: it praises Erasmus as 'a most distinguished man who has contributed so much to every sort of literary study, whether sacred or profane'.[42] There is a mark on the verso of the title-page, showing that the book was formerly held by the library of the Capucin order at Bergamo, and it seems likely that the annotation was made while in the possession of the order. In this connection, it should be noticed that in the Portuguese Index of 1561, which bears Cardinal Iffante's name, Erasmus was among the (many) authors whose works were generally forbidden.[43]

Milan 1620 presents an example of a censored Catholic edition from the early seventeenth century. On the title-page, the reader is informed that the edition was 'emended at the command of the superiors'. The superiors were a group of three obscure figures, representing the Milanese Holy Office, clergy and senate. Among other things, three marginal notes have been deleted, the two previously mentioned and 'The Utopians' confession'.

The last example of such an edition in our period is Cologne 1629, which asserts on the title-page that it was 'corrected in accordance with the Cardinal and Archbishop of Toledo's Index of expurgated books'. However, this edition suppresses more than Quiroga did. For example, where he deletes one sentence from the 'conversation with the Cardinal', Cologne 1629 removes a whole page of the same discussion, as did the Louvain complete works expurgated

---

38 In Cambridge 1995: p. 12, lines 17-20, p. 76, line 32, p. 78, lines 9-11; cf. also p. 232.
39 Cambridge 1995, p. 232, lines 14-15.
40 López Estrada, 'La primera versión española', p. 290 n.
41 'Cum expurgatione duorum locorum in epistula Guilielmi Budaei Thomae Lupseto Anglo.'
42 'clarissimi viri ac de literis sacris, profanis, omneque genus meritissimi' (Cambridge 1995, pp. 16-17).
43 Francisco Bethencourt, *História das Inquisições: Portugal, Espanha e Itália* (n.p.: Temas e Debates, 1996), p. 175.

by Hentenius. But 'Cologne' 1629 is not an exact copy of Louvain 1565/1566; for example, Hentenius' added 'nonnulli' is not found there.

We may close this treatment of *Utopia* and religion with the edition from Frankfurt am Main 1601. Its editor, Eberhard von Weihe, had been professor of canonic law in Protestant Wittenberg and rector of the university there until he was expelled from the city in 1591 for his Calvinist sympathies. In Frankfurt he became counsellor to the young Count of Hessen-Kassel, Moritz the Learned ('der Gelehrte'), who came from a Lutheran family. However, some five years after *Utopia* was published, Moritz turned to Calvinism; one may guess that he was influenced by his counsellor. According to the text on the title-page, this *Utopia* was edited 'in order to please the politicians'; furthermore, the book was 'now at last snatched away from the graves of books' ('nunc tandem bibliotaphis subreptum'). The expression *bibliotaphos* was often used to describe the situation when manuscripts were in private hands and remained unpublished.[44] But the situation for *Utopia* was different, and we can only guess that von Weihe was referring in a hostile way to the city that had expelled him: in that case, the grave of books is Wittenberg, where *Utopia* was printed in the very year von Weihe was exiled.

Milan 1620 and its dedicatory epistle

After 1518, the only new paratexts with which the Latin *Utopia* surrounds itself are variant titles, permissions, signs of censorship and the like. The one exception is Milan 1620, which contains a fresh dedicatory letter, reproduced below in Part II. Through this letter and other paratextual material, the edition gives a glimpse of the situation in Milan. Although the city was under Spanish rule, its religious leaders had refused to submit to the Spanish Inquisition. This policy of independence had been initiated in the late sixteenth century by Archbishop Carlo Borromeo, who was canonised only twelve years after his death.[45] Federico Borromeo, a cousin of the saint, was archbishop at the time when *Utopia* was published in Milan, and adopted the same clerical policy as his predecessor.[46] As a result, the publication of books depended on the censorship of a group of local officials. Borromeo is not mentioned by name

---

44 E. J. Kenney, *The Classical Text* (Berkeley, Los Angeles, London: University of California Press, 1974), p. 16.
45 Marc Venard (ed.), *Il tempo delle confessioni (1530-1620/30)*, in *Storia del Cristianesimo: Religione-Politica-Cultura*, vol. 8 (Rome: Borla/Città Nuova, 1992), pp. 520-1.
46 Among Federico's own merits is the founding of the famous Ambrosian library, to which he also donated his collection of books; see 'Borromeo, Federico cardinale', *Enciclopedia Italiana di scienze, lettere ed arti*, vol. 7 (Rome: Istituto della enciclopedia italiana, 1949), pp. 512-13. It is not unlikely that the founder of the library was also the first owner of its copy of the 1620 *Utopia*.

in the book, but one of the three men who examined *Utopia* before it was printed was a provost acting 'on behalf of the archbishop'.

The world of politics further infiltrates this edition via its addressee, the president of the Milanese senate, Giulio Arese, who was born into a Milanese family of senators and lawyers. During his time as a student of law in Pavia, he had made friends with whom he shared scholarly interests; this can be seen from poems and books they dedicated to him later. When in 1604 the so-called 'Academia degli Inquieti' was founded for the promotion of the sciences, Arese was present, perhaps as one of the founders.[47] The dedicatory letter refers to Arese's position in the privy council, of which he was a member from 1613, a high political post. But it is above all Arese's role as president of the senate that is emphasised in the edition, a post to which he had been elected only the preceding year.

The editor of the book and the author of the dedicatory letter was the printer Giovan Battista Bidelli.[48] Bidelli started out as a bookseller, and from about 1612 he owned a printing house. His output as a printer was voluminous and wide-ranging, focusing in particular on books by contemporary authors in various genres. Among his editions are a few in Spanish, including the comedies of Lope de Vega (1619), another sign of the cultural connections between Milan and Spain in this period; he also published the first edition of Paolo Giovio's Latin lives of the dukes of Milan.[49]

The dedicatory letter is brief but rather rhetorical in style, deploying for example the topos that *Utopia* is small in size but great in wisdom. A flattering comparison between More and Arese is also implied, a recurrent strategy in this kind of paratext. Unlike the authors of letters in the early editions, Bidelli makes no attempt to enter into the Utopia game; instead, he presents the book explicitly as one where serious matters are treated in a playful way;[50] according to Bidelli, this will be of value to Arese in his work for the privy council. Bidelli claims that he is Arese's greatest admirer, and the tone of the letter reveals that it was written to a man whose position in society was considerably higher than his own. But he is not afraid repeatedly to stress his aim of obtaining protection for the book. One of Bidelli's arguments is the well-worn 'do ut des': I am giving you a book, so you must in turn protect the book.

---

47 See *Storia di Milano*, vol. 10 (Milan: Fondazione Treccani degli Alfieri, 1957), p. 464.
48 On the lives of Arese and Bidelli, see *Dizionario biografico degli Italiani*, vol. 4 (Rome: Istituto della enciclopedia italiana, 1962), p. 83 (Arese), and vol. 10 (Rome: Istituto della enciclopedia italiana, 1968), p. 358 (Bidelli). However, *Utopia* is mentioned neither among the books dedicated to Arese nor among those printed by Bidelli.
49 *Storia di Milano*, vol. 11 (Milan: Fondazione Treccani degli Alfieri, 1958), p. 437.
50 See Part II, pp. 274–5: 'the truths he expressed in a playful spirit' and 'advice and precepts that he – seriously, through humour – gave...'.

Conclusion

Bidelli's brief paratext shows once again how *Utopia* was supplied with local credentials as it traversed Europe. On the other hand, the very fact that it is an exception also reminds us that the Latin *Utopia* was, relatively speaking, more conservative and stable than the vernacular versions, preserving fragments of the original paratextual apparatus well into the seventeenth century. As we have seen, however, prefatory epistles and poems only provide part of the story: titles, authorisations, marginal notes and the like may be equally eloquent in their own way. Like Proteus, *Utopia* changed its shape, depending on the aim of the edition: to emphasise More's martyrdom, to encourage local politicians, to see to it that such an interesting and entertaining text was made available to the reading public, or just to make money. Such differences are of course often underpinned by broader contextual factors: changes in society and religion, or the establishing of 'Utopia' as a concept in the history of ideas.

Among the first four editions, the two printed by Froben were by far the most influential. One reason for this was, surely, Erasmus' authority, embodied in his letter which prefaces these editions, together with the fact that he was not pleased with either of the first two editions. It also seems that one of Froben's contacts, Birckmann, played an important part at a crucial point in the transmission of the text. More generally, the humanist milieu of Basel clearly helped to make *Utopia* accessible to subsequent generations of readers: it was there that the first vernacular edition was published, and it was there, too, that the first collection of Latin works by Thomas More was printed in 1563.

But how easily available was *Utopia* in the period up to 1650? Hentenius and Blaeuw each used more than one edition as exemplars, but other editors and printers were apparently barely able to lay their hands on *one* copy of *Utopia*. That seems to be what is implied by the curious phrase on the title-page of Franfurt am Main 1601, that *Utopia* has 'now at last [been] snatched away from the graveyard of books'. Bidelli's opening phrase in his dedicatory epistle points in the same direction: 'This little book, truly small in size but great in wisdom, came into my hands, noble President, to my great advantage.' Overall, the number of Latin editions is quite high, but there is a clear tendency for them to appear in groups: two were financed or printed (or both) by Birckmann, four were produced as a common project by two Louvain printers, two were financed by Kopff, and the 1613 Hanau edition was followed by another Hanau edition. Finally, there is the group of editions from Amsterdam. Of the fifteen editions printed between More's death and 1650, only three, as it seems, are independent of these groups: Basel

1563, Wittenberg 1591 and Milan 1620. The fact that different investors and printers continued to repeat the act of publication over the years implies that the Latin *Utopia* found plenty of readers and buyers, but looked at in this way, the number of publishing milieux from which it emerged between 1548 and 1650 is reduced to seven.

The long-standing success of *Utopia* was initially launched by Erasmus' efforts to establish it as an important book. Erasmus had the contacts of all kinds that were needed for this first impetus: fellow scholars to praise the book in prose and verse, printers, correctors, and wealthy and powerful patrons to read and promote the book. What happened in the hundred years that followed the death of Erasmus and More is a rich and manifold story, even if one restricts oneself to the Latin transmission. Its broadest outline may be seen in the development from the first presentation of Utopia as a new island – inviting the reader to play the Utopian game – up to the point where the concept of Utopia has become so well established that the name of the island alone was sufficient as the book's title. *Utopia* had founded a new genre.

Vibeke Roggen

2 THE GERMAN TRANSLATIONS: HUMANIST POLITICS AND LITERARY JOURNALISM[1]

Utopia was translated into German twice during the period that is covered by this volume; as we shall see, these translations are as different from each other as two translations of the same text may well be. The first was made by Claude Chansonnette (Claudius Cantiuncula) in 1524, the second by Gregor(ius) Wintermonat in 1612. Chansonnette's translation was reprinted photographically in 1980.[2]

The title-page of the 1524 translation is reproduced below.[3] The last page has a woodcut depicting More, Peter Giles and Hythloday[4] and underneath the following text: 'Printed at Basel by Johann Bebel in the year 1524, on the 16th day of the month of June' ('Gedruckt zů Basel durch Joannem Bebelium. Im M D. XXiiii. jar. am sechtzehenden tag des Brachmons'). The dedicatory preface has been transcribed once before in modern times and the first part of it freely rendered into Modern New High German.[5]

The title-page of the 1612 translation, also printed below,[6] informs us that the publisher is Henning Grosse. On the last page, after a line filled with a typographical ornament, we find the following text: 'Leipzig, printed by Michael Lantzenberger,[7] in the year 1612' ('Leipzig / Gedruckt bey Michael Lantzenderger / *Anno MDCXII*'). As far as I have been able to discover, this book has not been reprinted.[8]

Basel 1524: contents

Chansonnette, as the title-page makes clear and as he himself points out in his preface, only translates Book II of More's work. He also leaves out all the paratextual material found in the Latin editions except the map of Utopia, the alphabet of the Utopians ('Der Utopianer Alphabet'), the 'Four lines in

---

1 I wish to state at the outset that I could not have done this work in an adequate manner without the invaluable help of Professor Heinz-Peter Prell of the University of Oslo.
2 All my work is based on this reprint, which is listed below in the Bibliography.
3 Part II, pp. 149–50.
4 This picture also appears on fol. A vi v.
5 Guido Kisch, *Gestalten und Probleme aus Humanismus und Jurisprudenz: Neue Studien und Texte* (Berlin: Walter de Gruyter & Co., 1969), pp. 323–8 and 247–9.
6 Part II, p. 162.
7 The text says 'Lantzenderger', clearly a misprint.
8 All my work on this translation is based on a copy of the 1612 edition in the British Library.

the Utopian language' ('Vier Verß in Utopianischer sprach') and the short text that follows the words 'End of Book Two' in More's work. The alphabet of the Utopians is presented, with a roman transcription, and the four lines are rendered in the Utopian alphabet as well as in transcription. Chansonnette also provides a translation into German of the little poem.[9]

The text that follows the end of Book II in the original is translated by Chansonnette with two small but not insignificant changes to which we shall return shortly. In his version, it reads as follows:

> The end of the speech that Raphael Hythloday made about the laws and customs of as the island of Utopia (as yet known to very few people), first written in Latin by the well-born and highly learned Sir Thomas More, Knight and Chancellor of the Most Glorious and Most Mighty King of England.[10]

Apart from these materials, the book contains only one paratext: a preface, or more properly a long dedication (eight pages). This preface will be our main concern in what follows.

Basel 1524: the shorter paratexts

If one compares Chansonnette's title-page with the Latin title of the work,[11] one notices that the 'Citizen and Undersheriff of the Famous City of London'[12] has become 'knight and treasurer of the most glorious and most mighty king of England': More had been knighted and made Under-treasurer in 1521.

Chansonnette's printer, Johann Bebel, exercised his profession in Basel from 1523. He is known to have printed about 100 works, among them a Hebrew Bible, a German translation of the works of Aristotle and editions of a great number of classical authors, among them Galen and Proclus.[13]

As for the map of Utopia and the picture of the three friends, they are

---

9 See Part II, pp. 150–2.
10 'End der red so Raphael Hythlodeus von den gesätzen und gewonheiten der Innsel Utopia (so noch gar wenig lüten bekant) gehebt hat / durch den wolgebornen und hochgelerten herrn Thomam Morum Fryherr / und des durchlüchtigisten / großmechtigisten Künigs zů Engelland Schatzmeister erstlich zů latin beschriben.'
11 The comparison must be made with the Basel 1518 editions. Since Chansonnette's translation, too, was printed in Basel, it would *a priori* be natural to suppose that Chansonnette would use one of these (rather than Louvain 1516 or Paris 1517). But the fact is proved by the error 'zwentzigtusent schrytt' (fol. Bii r) as in the two 1518 editions: '20,000' is an error for '12,000', which is what the two first editions have; see Cambridge 1995, p. 112, n. 4.
12 'inclutae civitatis Londinensis civis et Vicecomitis'.
13 See the *Historisch-biographisches Lexicon der Schweiz* (Neuenburg: Viktor Attinger, 1921–34), vol. 2, p. 64 and Walther Killy (ed.), *Deutsche biographische Enzyklopädie* (Munich, New Providence, London and Paris: K.G. Saur Verlag, 1995–2003), vol. 1, p. 364. On Bebel, see also Rudolf Wackernagel, *Geschichte der Stadt Basel* (Basel: Helbing und Lichtenhahn, 1907–24), vol. 3, p. 443.

taken from the editions of 1518; no doubt Bebel had borrowed (or bought) the plates from his colleague Johann Froben. The Utopian alphabet with the corresponding letters of the Latin alphabet printed in roman lettering also corresponds exactly to what one finds in the 1518 editions. The same is the case for the text and transcription of the Utopian poem. The German translation of the Latin translation of the poem is remarkably accurate, and it is certainly pleasing enough in an appropriately ingenuous way. The final paratext, the one that comes after the end of Book II, echoes the title-page in giving More his new titles; it also omits the information that Hythloday's discourse was *pomeridianus*, that it took place after lunch: for the lunch takes place in the untranslated Book I.

Basel 1524: the translator and his preface

Claude Chansonnette or Claudius Cantiuncula (1490–1549) was one of the leading jurists of the Renaissance: he is recognised as such both by his most important contemporaries and by modern scholars. From 1518, he was employed at the University of Basel and joined the famous circle of humanist scholars there.[14] He was also legal adviser (*syndicus* or *advocatus*) to the Basel Town Council. By 1524, however, he had decided to leave: reformist ideas were gaining ground in the city, and he himself was a man of orthodox beliefs with no taste for religious controversy. But before leaving he published his translation of the second book of *Utopia*, presenting it as a farewell gift to the Town Council.[15]

The essential argument of Chansonnette's dedication to the town councillors seems to be the following: 'I wish to give you a farewell present. The reason a translation of the second book of More's work can function as a present to you, is that you, as rulers of the excellent polity of Basel, will naturally like to read about that other excellent polity, Utopia.' The superiority of the Utopians,

---

14 The most important of them, of course, was Erasmus of Rotterdam. One may note that both More and Chansonnette were praised by Erasmus in his *Dialogus Ciceronianus*, ed. Pierre Mesnard, *Opera omnia* (Amsterdam: North-Holland Publishing Company, 1969–), Part I, vol. 2, pp. 674–5 and 677–8; trans. Betty I. Knott, *Collected Works of Erasmus* (Toronto, Buffalo and London: University of Toronto Press, 1974–), vol. 28, pp. 421–2 and 423. On the 'Basler Humanismus', see Wackernagel, *Geschichte*, vol. 3, pp. 421–38, René Teuteberg, *Basler Geschichte* (Basel: Christoph Merian Verlag, 1986), pp. 178–201, Hans R. Guggisberg, *Basel in the Sixteenth Century: Aspects of the City Republic before, during and after the Reformation* (St. Louis (Missouri): Center for Reformation Research, 1982), pp. 10–17, and for the later period, Amy Nelson Burnett, *Teaching the Reformation: Ministers and Their Message in Basel 1529–1629* (Oxford: Oxford University Press, 2006).

15 On Chansonnette's life and career see Guido Kisch, *Claudius Cantiuncula: Ein Basler Jurist und Humanist des 16. Jahrhunderts* (Basel: Helbing und Lichtenhahn, 1970). On Chansonnette in Basel, see also Wackernagel, *Geschichte*, vol. 3, p. 429.

Chansonnette goes on to say, that which separates them from other famous nations, is that they uphold three essential virtues: common ownership, equality and civic peace. Now Basel was certainly not a communist egalitarian society. But the economic life of the time (with its guilds, corporations, monopolies and the like) was basically regulated, that is to say political, 'common'.[16] And it must be noted that Chansonnette's conception of egalitarianism is a very relative one: it is wrong, he says, to receive in the same way 'the good and the bad, the well-born and the base, the wise and the foolish'.[17] The distinction between 'well-born' and 'base' assumes a traditional equivalence between social status and moral value. And as for Utopia, it is after all a strictly regulated, hierarchical society, with its condemned criminals, its slaves, its political and religious leaders and so on. So perhaps Chansonnette could have made his case: looking at Basel with an idealising intention and looking at Utopia with an analysing intention one might conclude that the two societies conform, as far as the two first virtues are concerned. But what about the 'peaceful unity among the citizens living together', the 'fridsamme einhelligkeit burgerlicher bywonung'? This third virtue is given particular weight by what follows in the text: the destructiveness of the three vices the Utopians succeed in avoiding ('strife, greed for money and ambitiousness')[18] is illustrated by the fall of Rome. I think Hoyer is right in supposing that one must see here 'a warning in the face of the confessional strife among the citizens and in the Council'.[19] It is in fact quite likely, as we shall see, that this warning has a specific political meaning.

This interpretation of the preface is admittedly somewhat conjectural.[20] But it is perhaps supported by a curious reason Chansonnette gives for not translating Book I: he says that it deals with matters 'that only concern the English

16 This regulated character of the economy was in fact becoming more pronounced in Basel during the first part of the sixteenth century. Thus in 1526 a new *Gewerbordnung* made it illegal to import and sell such goods as were produced by the Basel guilds (see Wackernagel, *Geschichte*, vol. 3, p. 388 and Paul Burckhardt, *Geschichte der Stadt Basel* (Basel: Helbing und Lichtenhahn, 1942), p. 3 and *passim*). Politically, as we shall see shortly, this corresponds to the demise of the old merchant patricians and the establishment of a regime built on the artisan guilds; see Hans Füglister's *Handwerksregiment: Untersuchungen und Materialien zur sozialen und politischen Struktur der Stadt Basel in der ersten Hälfte des 16. Jahrhunderts* (Basel and Frankfurt am Main: Helbing und Lichtenhahn, 1981), pp. 282 ff and *passim*. See also Guggisberg's *Basel in the Sixteenth Century*.
17 'die gůten unnd bösen / die wol herkommen und schnöden / die vernünfftigen und thoren' (Part II, pp. 156–7).
18 'zwytracht / gytz des gelts / und eergyrigkeit' (Part II, *ibid.*).
19 'eine Mahnung angesichts der konfessionellen Zwistigkeiten in der Bürgschaft und im Rat' (Siegfried Hoyer, 'Utopia deutsch. Zu den Gleichheitsvorstellungen im Basler Humanistenkreis', *Jahrbuch für Geschichte des Feudalismus*, 5 (1981), 237–54 (240)).
20 One may note, however, that a similar interpretation of *Utopia* itself is given by Busleyden in his letter to More. Busleyden mentions the downfall of Sparta, Athens and Rome, and then goes on to say that More's purpose must have been to prevent the great modern polities from suffering the same fate (Cambridge 1995, pp. 252–3).

and that are of no use for the understanding of the conditions of Utopia'.[21] But is it not clear that More meant to contrast *Europe*, or rather *Christendom* with Utopia, and that England was only the example closest to hand? I believe Chansonnette left out Book I for a more fundamental reason. The whole logical structure of his argumentation is different from that of More. First look at the sorry state of Christendom, More says (Book I), and then see how much better many things are arranged in Utopia (Book II). But we have one essential thing the Utopians lack: Christianity. However, now that the Utopians have come into contact with Christians, it seems certain that they will adopt the true faith. It is to be hoped that we will also adopt some of the practices of the Utopians. Chansonnette's argument takes a quite different direction: Basel is a marvellous city, he says at the beginning of his preface, and Utopia is also a marvellous society. They have much in common. But now it seems that we are losing one of the things we have in common with the Utopians. That must be avoided. For Chansonnette, then, the negative contrast to Utopia is situated in the future, it is a *threat*. He has no need for Book I.

This function of the preface as a warning may arguably be linked to Chansonnette's highly motivated choice of dedicatee. It is of course not surprising that a text dedicated to a town council should more particularly be dedicated to the mayor. But Basel regularly had two mayors: from 1516 onward, it had been the custom to elect one man from among the merchant-patricians (the 'Hohe Stube' or 'High Hall') and another from one of the artisan guilds. In 1524, Heinrich Meltinger was the mayor from the Hohe Stube and Adelberg Meyer the mayor from the guilds.[22] Only Meyer is mentioned in the dedication. This is no doubt significant.[23] For by 1524 the traditional conflict between merchant-patricians and artisans had been compounded by the religious controversy of the time; in fact there were three groups among the councillors: the patrician *Altgläubigen* ('Old Believers'), the radical reformers, and a middle group that wanted above all to maintain the peace and the authority of the Council, and who therefore advocated a certain degree of religious tolerance. Adelberg Meyer was the leader of this middle party.[24] One may conjecture that the political point of Chansonnette's undertaking was to mobilise the prestige of Basel's humanist circle in support of Meyer's

---

21 'so die Engellender gar nach allein betreffend / und zům verstand des Utopianischen wesens von unnöten' (Part II, pp. 158–9).
22 See Füglister, *Handwerksregiment*, p. 162.
23 Documents were (almost) always directed simply to the 'Mayors and Council of the City of Basel' ('bürgermeister und ratt der statt Basel'); see Emil Dürr and Paul Roth (eds), *Aktensammlung zur Geschichte der Basler Reformation in den Jahren 1519 bis Anfang 1534* (Basel: Verlag der historischen und antiquarischen Gesellschaft, Staatsarchiv, 1921–1950), vol. I, p. 81 and *passim*.
24 See Wackernagel, *Geschichte*, vol. 3, pp. 464–5, and Burckhardt, *Geschichte*, pp. 15 ff. On Meyer see also Wackernagel, *Geschichte*, vol. 3, p. 418.

group:[25] hence the emphasis on the 'peaceful unity among the citizens living together'. The choice of More's *Utopia* as the vehicle for this strategy is easily explained: strong political authority, civil peace and relative religious tolerance are among the chief characteristics of the imagined society.[26]

This preference for balance and moderation in external matters must, I think, be regarded as the context for another of Chansonnette's pronouncements: 'A good theologian', he says, likes to hear 'only about the pure holy scripture.'[27] This sounds like Erasmus's call – advertised in his 1516 edition of the New Testament and further promoted, for example, in the *Ratio verae theologiae* of 1518 – for a theology and a religious practice based directly on Scripture; given Chansonnette's distaste for extreme reform, it can hardly be read as an early version of the more radical principle of *sola scriptura* propounded by Luther and others. More specifically, the translator is no doubt referring here to the Basel *Predigtmandat* ('preaching ordinance')[28] of May/June 1523: preachers of all categories are told to follow 'only the holy gospel'[29] and it is ordered that 'every preacher should apply himself to discover and to propagate exclusively the pure truth of holy scripture.'[30] Chansonnette uses the same key words: *allein, luter*.[31]

We need now to address a quite different aspect of the preface, namely the

---

25 It may be possible to indicate another such attempt: at one point the Council actually asked Erasmus's advice on certain religious matters. Erasmus was not thrilled; Wackernagel (*Geschichte*, vol. 3, p. 465) thinks he feared that the Lutherans were setting him a trap. So he was exceedingly cautious when giving his answer. At the same time, however, he went out of his way to emphasise on the one hand the need to respect authority and tradition and on the other hand the need for tolerance, moderation and forbearance. This is how the text ends: 'I think you should continue to act prudently and moderately, as you have done in the past, until experience teaches us whether what is happening now is of God or not. In the meantime everything which encourages sedition must be assiduously rooted out' (trans. A. Dalzell, *Collected Works* (Toronto, Buffalo and London: University of Toronto Press, 1974–), vol. 11, p. 16) ('prudenti moderatione vobis utendum censeo, quemadmodum hactenus fecistis, donec res ipsa doceat utrum hoc quod nunc agitur, a Deo sit an aliunde. Interim omnia seditionum seminaria diligenter sunt excludenda' (*Opus epistolarum*, eds P. S. Allen *et al.* (Oxford: Clarendon Press, 1906–58), vol. 6, p. 11). It was, perhaps, exactly the answer Meyer was hoping for. Wackernagel asserts that Erasmus gave his answer in the autumn of 1524, but Allen dates Erasmus's letter 'c. January 1535' (*ibid.*, p. 6) and the translator concurs (*Collected Works*, vol. 11, p. 11).
26 On the affinity between the literary and ideological aspects of humanism and the 'moderate politics of the northern European humanists', see below, pp. 99–100, 103.
27 'ein rechter Theologus allein von der lutern heiligen geschrifft' (Part II, pp. 154–5).
28 See Wackernagel, *Geschichte*, vol. 3, p. 358 and pp. 463–4, Burckhardt, *Geschichte*, p. 9 and Teuteberg, *Geschichte*, pp. 211–12.
29 'allein das heilig evangelium'; I quote from Dürr and Roth (eds), *Aktensammlung*, vol. 1, p. 67.
30 'ein jeder predicant die blosse lutere warheit der heiligen geschrifft zů entdecken und zů verkünden sich übe' (*ibid.*, vol. 1, p. 68).
31 Modern German *lauter*; the corresponding verb is *läutern*, to rinse, cleanse, purify. The two words thus convey between them a strong sense of exclusivity.

curious passage listing a whole series of constitutions that are inferior to that of Utopia. The first two are 'Socrates' first polity, which he devised, but which nobody adopted' and 'the second polity of the same, which the Magnesians adopted for a time'.[32] This refers respectively to the *Republic* and to the *Laws*. But even if we admit that the 'Athenian' of the *Laws* is Socrates, the constitution elaborated for (New) Magnesia[33] is clearly presented as a *project* (702b-d). Where is it said that it was actually accepted and 'adopted for a time'? And later on we are told that the first polity of Socrates would imply a 'simple undifferentiated common ownership of all things, with no exceptions, so that everyone would be allowed to do what he liked'.[34] Is that supposed to be the society imagined in the *Republic*? Also very problematical is the next item on the list: 'Phaleas' polity in the city of Carthage' ('die policy Phalee in der Statt Carthago'). Phaleas of Chalcedon's ideas are known to us only as far as they are criticised by Aristotle in his *Politics* (1266a-7b). And nothing that is known about Carthage, as far as I can see, indicates a close connection with these ideas. Perhaps the link with Carthage is due simply to the fact that Aristotle discusses the constitution of this state in the same work (1272b-3b). Next comes the polity of Hippodamus 'among the Milesians' ('by den Milesiern'). The case is very similar to the last one: Aristotle criticises Hippodamus' theories (*Politics*, 1267b-8b), and Hippodamus was a citizen of Miletus, but there is no tradition of the Milesians (or anybody else) having tried to *apply* these theories. Even if the three following names (Minos, Lycurgus and Solon)[35] are used in a more conventional way, it is clear that Chansonnette, in this passage at least, is not so much using historical arguments as entering into a literary game, quite in the spirit of the Latin paratexts.

Another good example of this is the way he uses an idea taken from Giles's letter to Busleyden. Giles argues for the real existence of Utopia by pointing out the possibility that the ancients may never have found the island or that 'the name that the ancients gave it was later changed'.[36] Chansonnette simply mentions the first, reasonable, explanation in passing; on the other hand he sets out to prove the plausibility of the second by a long and rather superfluous array of (perfectly authentic) examples.[37]

---

32 'die erste policy Socratis / die er angesehen aber nyemand angenommen hatt / die andere policy desselbigen / so by den Magnesiern ein zyt gewert' (Part II, pp. 154-5).
33 i.e. the planned town which, as the 'Athenian' suggests in the *Laws*, may take its name from Magnesia (see *Laws* 969a).
34 'schlechte unverscheydne gemeinschafft aller dingen / gar nüt ußgenommen / dadurch eim yeden was im gelieben ouch erloubt würde' (Part II, pp. 156-7).
35 It can hardly be an accident that all the six constitution-makers mentioned in Chansonnette's preface also appear in the *Politics* (Solon: 1256b, 1266b, 1273b-4a, 1281b, 1296a; Lycurgus: 1270a, 1273b-4a; Minos: 1271b, 1329b).
36 'nomen quo veteres sint usi postea sit commutatum' (Cambridge 1995, pp. 28-9).
37 Part II, pp. 158-61.

This brings us to Chansonnette's tendency to compensate for the translation's omissions by using elements of what was omitted. This goes for the description of the narrative setting for Hythloday's story,[38] the reference to Plato,[39] the evaluation of More's style[40] and the idea that the Utopians have *three* essential virtues.[41]

But the most important of the borrowings from the omitted Latin paratexts concerns the comparison between the Utopian constitution and those of the great nations of the past, the virtues upheld and the vices avoided by the Utopians, the downfall of the old great nations because they did not follow these principles, and the risk present nations run for the same reason. The development of this theme may be taken from Busleyden's letter to More.[42] Chansonnette's argumentation is however more analytical and more rigorously structured, his historical references are more specific, and he gives his reasoning as a whole a particular slant, which, if my interpretation is correct, is due to the fact that it is meant to be applied to the actual situation in Basel in 1524.

Leipzig 1612: contents

Wintermonat translates both books of *Utopia*, but he leaves out most of Book I,[43] replacing it with the following lines:

> For he [Hythloday] had lived more than five years in this same [island of Utopia], nor would he, as he says, ever have left it, if it had not been in order to discover this new world to us Europeans.[44]

Like Chansonnette, Wintermonat also reproduces the 'Four lines in the Utopian language' ('Vier Verß in Utopianischer Sprach'), but only in the transcription in roman lettering. The text is printed in italics, as is the Latin translation that follows, which is preceded by the words 'Translated into Latin word for word, these lines sound like this' ('Diese Verß lauten von wort zu wort in Lateinischer Sprach also'); after the Latin version comes the German translation.[45] A map of Utopia is also included.

---

38 See Part II, pp. 158–9, where elements from Book I are used.
39 See above, p. 38; cf. Giles's letter to Busleyden (Cambridge 1995, pp. 24–5).
40 Compare Part II, pp. 158–9, with Budé's letter to Lupset (Cambridge 1995, pp. 16–17) and More's letter to Giles (pp. 30–3).
41 See above, p. 35; cf. Budé's letter to Lupset (Cambridge 1995, pp. 12–13).
42 See Cambridge 1995, pp. 252–5.
43 Corresponding to Cambridge 1995, pp. 47–106.
44 'Dann er uber die fünff Jahr in derselben [Insul *Utopia*] gewohnet / were auch / wie er saget / nicht mehr heraus kommen / da es nicht deßwegen geschehen / damit er dieselbige newe Welt uns Europeern entdeckete' (Leipzig 1612, p. 10).
45 See Part II, p. 166.

To the short text at the end of Book II following the formula 'secundi libri finis' in More's work corresponds in Wintermonat's version the following text, which is printed above the line of typographical ornament: 'The end of the description of the marvellous, until now little-known island of Utopia. Glory to God alone' ('Ende der Beschreibung der wunderbarlichen / noch bißher wenig bekanten Insul *Utopia*. *Soli* DE[O] *gloria*'). All other paratexts of the Latin original are omitted by Wintermonat, but he adds some of his own. To the title-page and the short text on the last page must be added above all the preface, which will be our main concern in what follows, but there is also a new division of the text into chapters, a table of contents, a portrait of More, a number of marginal notes, and a running title on most pages. Underneath the portrait we find the text 'Thomas More, once the most dignified Chancellor of All England' ('Thomas Morus quondam totius Angliae cancellarius digniss[imus]), followed by the signature 'Jan Fab: Jün:', to which we shall return shortly. As for the marginal notes, they are not a translation of those found in the early Latin editions and commonly attributed to Peter Giles or Erasmus or both, nor do they contain anything remarkable on matters such as religion.[46]

Leipzig 1612: the shorter paratexts

The title-page is close to that of the 1518 editions, but More has now become 'High Chancellor of the kingdom of England' ('des Königreichs Engelland Obristen Cantzler'). More became Lord Chancellor in 1529.

The one intriguing element of the title-page is the fact that the translator's name is given in Utopian letters. Why this should be so is something of a mystery, since the translation does not include the Utopian alphabet. But if one uses the key given in other translations and editions, one may conclude that Wintermonat calls himself SMDYGMXIRNHDRH MXISOFM (in two lines). We may be dealing with some kind of code, acronym or (more or less) private joke.[47] But I think we would do better to consider this *emphatic* anonymity, so to speak, as emblematic. As opposed to many other versions of *Utopia*, this book does not present itself as a message sent from one person

---

46 See above, pp. 22–3.
47 It is interesting to note, however, that the name of the translator is also written in Utopian letters on the title-page of Gregorius Wintermonat's rendering of Joseph Hall's *Mundus alter et idem*. The translation is said to be 'Durch GREGORIUMHVEMV ME?VIVM' (I have here represented by '?' a symbol that is new to the Utopian alphabet). The beginning at least makes sense and the rest might be a garbled version of a latinisation of the name 'Wintermonat'. The *Mundus alter et idem* is also said to be 'UTOPIAE PARS II', it was published in 1613 and the British Library copy is bound with the translation of *Utopia*. But since that book is not called 'UTOPIAE PARS I', the decision to translate Hall was probably made after the printing of the first translation.

to another person or group of persons. The translator does not give his name, and he addresses his preface to an equally anonymous 'good reader'. This work does not seem to be meant to have a function in a specific situation in a particular place. I do not believe that it would be helpful to ask what was happening at Leipzig or in Saxony in 1612 that might provide a context for this translation. Leipzig was the centre of German book production and the site of a famous book fair. The translation is aimed at the German-reading public *in general* and is not meant to induce anyone to take any kind of *action*: the contrast with Basel 1524 and many of the other editions of *Utopia* is striking. In this sense, Wintermonat is not so very 'early' modern'. He seems to present *Utopia* mainly as a culturally prestigious curio from the past: it is interesting, but not really relevant to any particular contemporary matter.

One may see an interesting parallel here to the way Wintermonat presents 'news', for example the discovery of the North-East Passage mentioned in the preface.[48] It is true that this discovery has a function in the mock-serious discussion about the reality of Utopia. But I also have the impression that this, in fact, is 'news'. As Neil Postman has shown, the use of this word may imply 'that the value of information need not be tied to any function it might serve in social and political decision-making and action, but may attach merely to its novelty, interest, and curiosity.'[49] Wintermonat has no thought of any political purpose he might serve. In the preface of his *Calendarium historicum*, he presents an apology for what may be called historical journalism: 'For histories of our time are no less useful than very old ones.'[50] Wintermonat may be thinking of the classical notion of *exemplum*.[51] And yet his work is typical of the phenomenon that Postman treats under the title 'Now ... this':[52] each item of news presented is simply juxtaposed to the next; it is part neither of an analysis (which might have a conclusion) nor of a history (which might have a moral). This is not *exemplum*, but something entirely different.[53] A

---

48 Part II, pp. 164–5.
49 Neil Postman, *Amusing Ourselves to Death: Public Discourse in the Age of Show Business* (New York: Viking, 1985), p. 65.
50 'als haben die jetzigen Historien ... nicht weniger ihren Nutzen als gar die uralten.' This preface is reprinted in part in Edgar Blühm and Rolf Engelsing (eds), *Die Zeitung: Deutsche Urteile und Dokumente von den Anfängen bis zur Gegenwart* (Bremen: Carl Schünemann Verlag, 1967), pp. 18–22; for the passage quoted, see p. 21.
51 What I have in mind is the ancient rather than the medieval notion of *exemplum*. See Claude Bremond, Jacques Le Goff and Jean-Claude Schmitt, *L'«exemplum»* (Turnhout: Brepols, 1996), especially pp. 13–14 and 45. This volume also provides a large number of useful references.
52 Postman, *Amusing Ourselves*, ch. 7. What Postman denounces is of course not 'news' in the sense of 'new information', but 'fragmented, irrelevant information'.
53 Wintermonat, quoting the Latin proverb 'happy the man whom other people's dangers make cautious' (p. 22), seems to suggest that *each single* story may have its moral. In fact he is not only a practitioner but even an apologist of the 'Now ... this'. After 300 years of 'news', he does not sound entirely convincing.

fact recorded by Livy is at the same time a part of a meaningful history and an element in a certain ideology; it was *highly* relevant to Roman 'political decision-making and action'. Have the classical historians lost this relevance today? The question is no doubt debatable. But my point is that Wintermonat does not use his preface to claim any such relevance for *Utopia*. He insists on how *prestigious* the work is. It is one of those books one 'ought to have read'.

Henning Grosse was one of the most important men in the publishing business of late sixteenth- and early seventeenth-century Germany. He published the first general catalogue for the Leipzig Book Fair in 1594 and from then on saw to it that this catalogue appeared regularly. It is in great measure due to his efforts that Leipzig came to take the place of Frankfurt as the centre of the German book trade. He is known to have published almost a thousand works in the field of theology alone.[54] The colophon informs us that the printer was Michael Lantzenberger, who is known above all for printing works on theological and ecclesiastical matters.[55]

The division of the texts into chapters is based on the original in the sense that Book I becomes Chapter I and that each of the five chapter-titles in Book II are retained as such in the translation.[56] But some of the original chapter-titles really only account for the beginning of the section of the text that follows. So Wintermonat introduces new chapter-titles of his own, giving his translation a total of sixteen chapters. The effect seems to me reasonable enough.

One may regret the fact that Wintermonat left out the Utopian alphabet (particularly since he uses it on the title-page). As for the German translation of the poem, it seems to me just as adequate in its own way as the one provided by Chansonnette.

The portrait of More is clearly an engraving based on the oil painting by Hans Holbein the Younger,[57] whose name appears in abbreviated form in the inscription under the picture.[58]

The map is much simpler than those of the 1516 and 1518 editions. It may not give a good idea of Utopia's geography, but the island is roughly

---

54 See the *Allgemeine deutsche Biographie* (Leipzig: Duncker and Humblot, 1875–1912), vol. 9, pp. 748–9 and the *Deutsche biographische Enzyklopädie*, vol. 4, p. 194.
55 See the *Allgemeine deutsche Biographie*, vol. 17, pp. 701–2.
56 I assume that Wintermonat used Basel 1518 (March). This assumption is justified by the fact that the translator mentions it at the start of his preface and by his use of several of the paratexts it includes. On may also note the error '20. Welsche Meilweges' (p. 16); see above, p. 33, n. 11.
57 The two portcullises hanging from More's Lancastrian Collar of Esses have, however, been omitted. Possibly the artist was not aware of the function of the portcullis as a royal heraldic badge in England.
58 Jan = Hans, Fab. = *faber* (artist), Jün. = (der) Jüngere (the younger).

crescent-shaped and the mistake in the second map (that of the 1518 editions) is avoided.[59]

The text that follows the end of the last chapter is much shorter than the corresponding one in the Latin original. Given the essentially redundant character of texts of this type, that is hardly remarkable. As for the phrase *Soli Deo gloria*, it may have been chosen by Wintermonat as a counterweight to the plurality of religions described in the final chapter: Wintermonat's phrase is emphatically singular. But it is equally likely that it may have been due to the initiative of either the editor or the printer. Such mottoes were commonly used in the colophon, and Grosse and Lantzenberger were both, as we have seen, in the business of producing religious books.

Leipzig 1612: the translator and his preface

Very little is known about Gregor Wintermonat. An examination of the catalogues of a few major libraries reveals him as the editor of the *Calendarium historicum decennale oder Zehnjährige Historische Relation* (Leipzig, 1609) and of a long series of continuations to this work (perhaps as many as thirty): here we find him again to be unambiguously interested in recent events, a form of 'news'. He also wrote a *Historia ecclesiastica Romana* or *Newe Bäpst Chronica* (Leipzig, 1614) and, as we have seen, he translated Joseph Hall's *Mundus alter et idem*. Zedler's *Universal-Lexicon* calls Wintermonat 'an unknown historian from the first half of the seventeenth century'.[60] This is correct. Even the *Allgemeine deutsche Biographie* does not mention him.

The main feature of his preface is its insistence on the importance and status of *Utopia*. Not only is More's standing evoked,[61] we also find references to the authority and prestige of Erasmus, Budé, Geldenhouwer, Giles, Busleyden, and De Schrijver. Of course some of these men are not so very famous, but the real point is undoubtedly that they all contributed to the paratexts of the March 1518 edition. The last person named, Jean Bodin, falls into a different category. Given his critical attitude towards More's ideas, it is perhaps somewhat surprising that he should be mentioned at all. But the very fact that Bodin refers to *Utopia* and clearly considers it an important work is sufficient for Wintermonat's purpose here: all news is good news.[62] The

---

59 For a reproduction of the 1612 map, see above, p. 1.
60 'ein unbekannter Historicus aus der ersten Helffte des 17 Jahrhunderts', Jacob August Frankkenstein *et al.* (eds), *Großes vollständiges Universal-Lexicon aller Wissenschaften und Künste* (Halle and Leipzig: Johann Heinrich Zedler, 1732–54), vol. 57, col. 991.
61 That is to say his standing as 'royal councillor and Chancellor of England' ('Königlicher Rath und Cantzler in Engelland') (Part II, pp. 162–3). His role as a Catholic martyr is irrelevant in a Saxony that was as yet staunchly Protestant.
62 See R. J. Schoeck, 'Bodin's opposition to the mixed state and to Thomas More', in Horst

reference to Chansonnette's translation has a similar function: if the great jurist thought it worthwhile to translate the book, it must be important. The reference also shows that the 1524 translation was still remembered and – presumably – available nearly a century after it was printed, even though it had never been reissued.

The last part of the preface makes a new contribution to the mock-serious discussion of the reality of Utopia. We have already heard that it is difficult for strange ships to land on the island and that the ancient cosmographers may have known it under another name or that it may have been unknown to them. Now we are told that if anybody *did* get to Utopia from Europe, they would not be eager to return.

The translations

In his activity as a translator, Chansonnette seems above all to be motivated by a desire to render the Latin text exactly: his rendering in fact sometimes follows the original more closely than does the English translation in Cambridge 1995. In the part of the text I have examined, I have found only one important omission. Characteristically, it is the sentence 'The oldest of every household, *as I said*, is the ruler':[63] what has already been said can safely be left out.

Wintermonat, on the other hand, treats the original with much greater liberty. He leaves out parts of the text he considers immaterial, for example most of the praise allotted to Henry VIII and to Cuthbert Tunstall.[64] And there are numerous other small abridgements and modifications. Thus when More says that he may return to some of the things Hythloday said on another occasion, 'especially those that it would be useful not to be ignorant of', Wintermonat reduces the relative clause to the simple adjective 'gedenckwürdig'.[65]

Denzer (ed.), *Jean Bodin* (Munich: C. H. Beck, 1973), pp. 399–412. The preface of *Les Six Livres de la république* in the edition published in 1579 contains the following sentence: 'However, neither would we like to present an ideal impracticable polity, such as was imagined by Plato and by Thomas More, Chancellor of England; we shall content ourselves with following the laws of politics as closely as possible' ('Toutefois, nous ne voulons pas aussi figurer une République en Idée sans effet, telle que Platon et Thomas le More, chancelier d'Angleterre, ont imaginé: mais nous nous contenterons de suivre les règles Politiques au plus près qu'il sera possible' (quoted by Schoeck, 'Bodin's opposition', p. 400). The sentence is to be found neither in the 1576 edition nor the 1583 edition. There are two other explicit references to More in the *Six Livres*: vol. 4, p. 169 and vol. 6, p. 286 (not p. 288 as the 'Table' mistakenly says); I follow the edition published by Fayard in 1986.

63 'Antiquissimus (*ut dixi*) praeest familiae' (Cambridge 1995, pp. 136–7; my italics); cf. Basel 1524, fol. D iii v.
64 Cambridge 1995, pp. 40–1; Leipzig 1612, pp. 1–2.
65 'praesertim quicquid ex usu fuerit non ignorari' (Cambridge 1995, pp. 48–9); Leipzig 1612, p. 10; 'gedenckwürdig' means literally 'worthy of thought'.

On the other hand he thinks it worthwhile to remind the reader that Ulysses is 'weiterfahren'[66] and that Plato is a 'hochgelärter Philosophus'.[67] The general impression is that of an effort to adapt the text for a somewhat wider audience than that for which the original was intended. This agrees well with what I have already said about the presumed aims of the translation.

Chansonnette, as we have seen, translates only Book II. It is not surprising that Wintermonat too removes most of the first book: its political dialogue belongs to a genre very different from the narrative of Book II. It is interesting to note, however, that what he offers corresponds almost exactly to what modern scholars think of as the 'first version' of *Utopia*: it is assumed that this consisted only of what is now Book II and the beginning of Book I.[68] As for the short text that replaces most of Book I (see above p. 39), I believe that it is logically linked to what is said on the last page of the passage left out. Here we are told how the Utopians profited from the arrival of a single European ship about 1,200 years before Raphael Hythloday's visit to their island. But Hythloday does not believe Europeans would have been able to profit from a similar visit from Utopia. Indeed, if any such visit has taken place it has been forgotten, as future Europeans may very well come to forget Hythloday's sojourn in the island.[69] According to the translation, however, Hythloday has returned with the express intention of discovering Utopia to the Europeans. Does that not in itself imply a grain of optimism?

In Chansonnette's career the translation of *Utopia* must no doubt be considered something of a footnote; his reputation is founded on the fact that he is *Cantiuncula*, one of the most important jurists of the Renaissance. Gregor Wintermonat, on the other hand, is simply an 'unknown historian'; all we know about him is that he was one of those who – as an English novelist puts it – 'labour on in the valley of the shadow of books'.[70] It is to be hoped that his association with More's *Utopia* will gain him a little immortality. One has the feeling that the thought would have pleased him.

As for Chansonnette, I have suggested that part of his purpose was to warn against the consequences of civil strife and more specifically to support the 'middle party' in the Town Council of Basel. That may have been in vain.[71]

---

66 Cambridge 1995, pp. 42–3; Leipzig 1612, p. 5; 'weiterfahren' means 'widely experienced' or more specifically and originally 'widely travelled and therefore experienced'; the allusion is no doubt to the first lines of the *Odyssey*.
67 Cambridge 1995, pp. 44–5; Leipzig 1612, p. 5; 'hochgelärt' means 'very learned'.
68 See Cambridge 1995, pp. xx–xxiii.
69 Cambridge 1995, pp. 106–7.
70 George Gissing, *New Grub Street*, ch. 24.
71 The Basel revolution of 1528–29 meant the victory of the radical reformist party; Mayor Meltinger had to flee (see Burckhardt, *Geschichte*, pp. 16 ff; Teuteberg, *Geschichte*, p. 214). But the Reformation and Peasants' War were much less bloody in Basel than elsewhere, and

But when he left, the Council in its turn gave him a farewell present: a silver gilt cup.[72] Not all intellectual efforts are that well rewarded.

Trond Kruke Salberg

Meyer's group may have contributed to this. The Basel Council even acted as a mediator abroad; see Burckhardt, *Geschichte*, pp. 11–12.
72 See Kisch, *Claudius Cantiuncula*, p. 33, n. 23.

3 THE ITALIAN *UTOPIA* OF LANDO, DONI AND SANSOVINO: PARADOX AND POLITICS

The female figure depicted on the title-page of the first Italian vernacular edition of Thomas More's *Utopia* is seated cross-legged on a tree trunk from which sprouts a fresh branch of olive, her dress torn at the bottom. Her slightly twisted posture elegantly repeats the swirling movement of her mantle as it is blown back by the wind. She is holding a mask up in front of her face, but we cannot know if she is about to lift the mask to reveal or cover herself. In any case she is turned away from the viewer so that we only see her young profile.

With its precisely drawn flowing lines, the stylistic quality of the image is high. The artist, unknown, shows confidence in the new early sixteenth-century manner of depicting the human body – slender, serpentine, michelangiolesque. The single iconographic elements are recognisable and not too hard to interpret, but their combination is unusual and intriguing. Both the trunk and the torn dress may indicate old age and death, whereas the fresh olive demonstrates that out of the old something new and fruitful might emerge. Read as a political treatise, the text behind the image is clearly in line with such a meaning, embodying a desire for a new way of ordering society, yet one in accordance with early Christian communalism. Also the mask, indicative of play, simulation and theatre, seems a fitting enough emblem for a book whose literary form was based on an amusing intermingling of fiction and reality.[1] But some readers might have recognised the picture from the frontispiece of certain other books and hence connected it to the Florentine editor and writer Anton Francesco Doni. They might even have recalled a motto that – as we shall see – sometimes accompanied it; if so, the image would have evoked for them a different set of associations.[2]

When the small octavo appeared in Venice in 1548, it constituted the first European vernacular translation of More's *Utopia* complete with Books I and II.[3] Title, dedicatory letter and headings were printed in roman, the table of contents and the main bulk of the text in space-saving italics, with

---

[1] For the trunk with the olive, see for example Jennifer Montague, *An Index of Emblems of the Italian Academies* (London: Warburg Institute, 1988), p. 73. For the masked woman as symbol of simulation and theatre, see below, p. 53, n. 23.
[2] Modern bibliographers and historians of book illustrations have, however, not made this connection between the *Utopia* frontispiece and the other versions of the same picture.
[3] This remained the only Italian translation until the nineteenth century.

simple woodcut headpieces and initials. The title-page bears the place and year of print, and the name of the English author, but not that of the printer or translator, who therefore remain as enigmatic as the woman behind her mask. Apart from the fine frontispiece image, the paratextual apparatus is modest in both scope and size, restricted to six pages of prefatory material: a scant three-page dedicatory preface to M. Gieronimo Fava signed Doni, and a table of contents over the next two and a half pages. The translation itself, which occupies sixty folios, is stripped of all the original appended material – letters, verses, Utopian alphabet and map – except More's first letter to Peter Giles. The name of the translator, Ortensio Lando, is not mentioned at all; only the preface to the 1561 reissue of Book II in a larger compilatory work in comparative politics, *Il governo* by Francesco Sansovino, reveals his name, an identification usually not called in question.[4] Nor can one find the name or mark of the printing-house, believed to be that of Aurelio Pincio where Doni – who appears to be the editor – had several books printed in the course of the following years.

The function of the many prefatory letters and verses written for the first four Latin editions of More's *Utopia* is commonly said to have been to identify the text as a humanist document, its context defined by the careers of the men behind this paratextual material.[5] When *Utopia* was transferred to vernacular Italy three decades later, however, it met with other men and other careers.[6] The discarding of most of the Latin paratexts also meant that much of *Utopia*'s original context disappeared. What had been 'a corporate product of Erasmus' humanist circle'[7] now became the product of rather different circles. The recontextualisation that is the theme of this introduction was the work not of great humanist scholars but of lesser known polygraphers – all-purpose editors, *literati*, minor writers – who rushed to liberal cosmopolitan Venice, the printing capital of Europe, during the middle decades of the sixteenth century. The major figures in the Italian vernacular appropriation of More's *Utopia* were Lando, who translated it, and Doni who published it, both of them friends of the infamous Pietro Aretino; later, the historiographer Sansovino (son of the celebrated architect) recycled Book II of the Lando-Doni *Utopia* and made it more widely known. All three of them were involved in

---

4 But see Christian Rivoletti, who raises a slight doubt over the attribution of the translation to Lando in his *Le metamorfosi dell'Utopia: Anton Francesco Doni e l'immaginario utopico di metà Cinquecento* (Lucca: M. Pacini Fazzi, 2003), p. 37n.
5 See e.g. Peter R. Allen, '*Utopia* and European humanism: the function of the prefatory letters and verses', in *Studies in the Renaissance*, 10 (1963), 91–107.
6 For the general reception of More in Italy, see the fundamental work done by Luigi Firpo, especially 'Thomas More e la sua fortuna in Italia', in Firpo (ed.), *Studi sull'Utopia* (Florence: Olschki, 1977), pp. 31–58.
7 Cambridge 1995, p. 276.

THE ITALIAN *UTOPIA* OF LANDO, DONI AND SANSOVINO   49

literary activities of diverse kinds and had their writing printed in Venice, to which they came from Milan, Florence or Rome, and where they stayed for extensive periods of their lives.[8] In 1548 and 1561 respectively, they prepared More's text for a new and larger reading public, one no longer restricted to the circle of learned Latin-speaking humanists.

Their interest in Utopia, however, went much further than editing, translating and publishing More's work. The impact of *Utopia* on other literary products from their pens (and presses) was significant and cannot be overlooked if one wants to understand the way Utopia was being situated in the Italian landscape. Removing most of the work's original paratexts, which had done so much to foreground its ludic aspects in the early Latin editions, did not necessarily mean suppressing its learned literary game and inserting it exclusively into the tradition of political philosophy, as claimed by some critics (although Sansovino, as we shall see, moves in this direction).[9] On the contrary, Lando and Doni show such involvement with the Utopian fiction that in a certain sense we could speak of whole books of theirs as paratextual in relation to More's *Utopia*. In addition, Lando's parasitic relationship to Utopia – the idea of the island as well as the actual book – throughout much of his writing life almost makes the man himself a 'paratext'.[10] This, then, will be my perspective here: to consider what roles Lando, Doni and Sansovino played in transferring More's *Utopia* to the Italian scene, and how those roles were further acted out in other writings of theirs.

Dell'isola Eutopia: title and preface

How was the book – without its original wrapping – presented to the new audience of Italian readers? Visually, the most striking feature of the title-page is the picture. But the title itself also attracts attention, departing as it does from the Latin originals in significant ways.[11] Where the original Latin titles spoke of the 'new island of Utopia', the Italian title makes a surprising change: the isle is named 'Eutopia', a choice not explained in the preface. To exclude the marginal possibility that 'Eutopia' could be a dictation or printing error,

---

8 For a description of this environment, see Paul F. Grendler, *Critics of the Italian World 1530–1560: Anton Francesco Doni, Nicolò Franco and Ortensio Lando* (Madison: University of Wisconsin Press, 1969).
9 Rivoletti writes that the main function of the original literary 'frame' was to set in motion an exchange between a fictional world and a real one, a game in which, he claims, the vernacular translations no longer participated (*Le metamorfosi*, pp. 52–7).
10 The translation of *Utopia* was but the corollary of Lando's intellectual experience, writes Silvana Seidel Menchi ('Ortensio Lando cittadino di Utopia: un esercizio di lettura', in *La fortuna dell'Utopia di Thomas More nel dibattito politico europeo del '500* (Florence: Olschki, 1996), pp. 95–120 (97)).
11 See Part II, pp. 171–3.

we only need to look at the table of contents, where we find the same version of the name repeated twice; indeed, 'Utopia' is never mentioned there.[12] Nor does Doni use it in his short preface.[13] He talks of having in his possession a booklet on the 'best form of a republic', but omits altogether the name of the republic, and the name of the book, with the result that the Italian reader did not meet the word 'Utopia' before starting to read the translation of More's letter to Giles.

In other words, 'Utopia' became 'Eutopia' in the new paratextual material. Why? The pun on the Greek words for 'no-place' (*outopia*) and 'good place' (*eutopia*) was made explicit in the early Latin editions only in the poem of the fictive Anemolius.[14] This poem was left out in the Italian version, as in most vernacular editions of the time. What was lost with this omission was thus strikingly reintroduced, changing the whole title of the book as if in response to the imperative of Anemolius's last line: '"The Good Place" [*Eutopia*] they should call me, with good cause.' Whether Doni, by noting this alteration, wanted to suggest to his readers that the society described by More is not only desirable but also possible to put into practice, remains an open question.[15]

The other significant deviation is the break with the Horatian notion of combining the instructive with the entertaining – the *salutaris* and the *festivus*, as the pair runs in some of the Latin titles. The Italian title uses instead the words *utile* and *necessario*, thus acting as if only the seriousness of the political tract is the issue here. In the preface, however, Doni corrects the imbalance when he tells Gieronimo Fava that he will derive from the book 'the highest pleasure and no little satisfaction'. He dutifully adds that there is a lot to be learnt from the book as well: 'you will learn of very beautiful things.'

The preface is unclear – deliberately so, one might think – about how and where the book came into Doni's hands, and it says nothing of the translator, nor of the translation itself. At one point, Doni refers to himself in the third person in order to make a pun on his surname, the plural for *dono* (gift). This play on words introduces a tone of slight mockery in the otherwise conventional dedication, so that we cannot entirely trust the flattering comparison

---

12 See fol. A iiii r: 'Tavola del libro secondo. Descrittione dell'Isola d'Eutopia ... Qual era il nome antico dell'Isola Eutopia ... '. Firpo, on the other hand, suggests that it is a translation error ('Thomas More e la sua fortuna in Italia', p. 48).
13 See Part II, pp. 172–5 (this reference covers the whole of the following discussion).
14 Cambridge 1995, pp. 18–19.
15 Elena Moro ('Dall'utopia all'eutopia: dal disegno ideale della città alla sua concretizzazione', in Nadia Minerva (ed.), *Per una definizione dell'utopia. Metodologie e discipline a confronto* (Ravenna: Longo, 1992), pp. 449–55) associates 'eutopia', the beautiful place, with Filarete's attempts to design an ideal (i.e. beautiful, well-ordered, harmonious and symmetrical) urban plan, like Sforzinda, described in his *Trattato di architettura* (1465). In the 1580s, at least one such ideal town was built, Sabbioneta in the province of Mantua.

he suggests between the perfect society described in the book and the praiseworthy state of affairs in Fava's household: 'I immediately decided to send it [the book] to you, so that you could compare it to the Republic of your home.'[16] The parallel between the government of the family and the state is of course a commonplace which goes back to Aristotle and Xenophon, and which in Renaissance Italy received ample theoretical treatment, from Alberti to Speroni, Della Casa and Torquato Tasso. In relation to More, famous for his family life and good domestic government, it had indeed become a mini-topos in its own right. To the extent that Doni's preface is a portrait of the dedicatee's father as an exemplar of good government, it is a conscious rewriting of this story in terms of Doni's own circle of protectors.

With its elaborate frontispiece image and freely composed title, the editor has certainly left his mark on the Italian *Utopia*. What mark had *Utopia* left on him, prompting him to have it printed? To answer this question, one will need to look beyond the polite dedicatory preface.

Anton Francesco Doni (1513–1574)

It is possible that Doni's interest in More's *Utopia* began many years before he prepared the Italian translation of the text for printing and sale in 1548. Florence, where Doni grew up and began his literary career, had been the first town on the Italian peninsula to welcome More's little text into print. The fifth and last edition of *Utopia* in Latin to appear in More's lifetime was printed here by the Giunta family in 1519 as an appendix to a selection of Lucian's works translated from the Greek by More and Erasmus in collaboration, the *Luciani opuscula*.[17] The Giunta press, furthermore, had published Erasmus' *Praise of Folly* the previous year, and they were also the first to issue (clandestinely) the Bible in Italian. This means that they had become a driving force in promoting Erasmianism as well as the reformist attitude of so-called 'evangelism', with which both Doni and Lando have been associated and which is likely to have influenced their interest in More's *Utopia*. The Bible translator Antonio Brucioli, another Florentine, might moreover have been one of the first readers of Florence 1519: his dialogue *Della repubblica* (1526) has been shown to contain traces of More's work.[18] Doni, too, as a young man, might well have obtained a copy of the *Luciani opuscula*: if so, his perception of *Utopia* would have been conditioned by a textual environment (paratexts in a broad sense) that anticipated the Lucianic, satirical mode he himself will adopt in his own writings.

---

16 Gieronimo Fava was a noble from Ferrara in whose villa Doni had probably been a guest on one or more occasions, and this was no doubt his way of expressing his appreciation.
17 See above, p. 16.
18 See Rivoletti, *Le metamorfosi*, p. 59.

Those writings were to be prolific, but not uncommonly so for men of his standing who attempted to make a living from their pen independently of demanding patrons, and succeeded. The titles bearing Doni's name – as author, translator, printer or editor – total more than forty in his lifetime, and seven of them have as their frontispiece a variant of the woman with the mask.[19] This picture, then, was not devised for *Utopia* in particular. It had been used before and was to be used again, always on books edited by Doni.

What emerges, in fact, is that Doni used it on books that may be regarded as his most personal and philosophical works. To include *Utopia* among these is a strong statement in itself: the frontispiece image becomes a visible sign of Doni's personal appropriation of More's work. The first book to emerge from Doni's own press in Florence, a collection of his own letters (1546), already carries the image. Before leaving his home town definitively, Doni used it again in three more publications (including a second volume of his letters), now accompanied by a motto: 'What hurts me most, I hide and keep silent about' ('Quel che piú mi molesta / ascondo et taccio'). In Venice, where he continued his printing activity, using the press of Pincio and Marcolini, it shows up again in *Utopia* and then in the frontispiece of three more titles – a translation of Seneca's letters and two books on ancient moral philosophy – with a Latin variant of the previous motto.[20] Presumably these woodcuts were Doni's property and had been brought to Venice by him, or were cut again on the basis of the same drawings, which originated in the rich artistic environment in Florence which Doni is known to have frequented.[21] According to Gertrude Bing the signification of the motto in conjunction with the picture is that the virtuous man must conceal behind a mask the wounds he receives from fortune's arrows; she argues that this was Doni's public statement of a philosophical attitude.[22] However, Bing also makes it clear that the picture

---

19 Whereas the entry on the Italian *Utopia* in *EDIT 16* of the *Istituto Centrale per il Catalogo Unico* (*ICCU*) provides no link to translator, editor, printer or title-page illustration, the entries on the other books Doni had printed do provide such a link (http://edit16.iccu.sbn.it, page consulted 16.04.06). For Doni's bibliography, I have also consulted the 'Appendix' in Grendler, *Critics of the Italian world*, pp. 240–9.

20 Doni also has another variant woodcut, showing a woman burning a mask, which he used twice in 1546 in Florence, then again in Venice on a reissue of Seneca's letters and of the third book of ancient moral philosophy, with another Italian variant of the motto.

21 See e.g. M. Plaisance, 'L'Académie Florentine de 1541 à 1583: permanence et changement', in D. S. Chambers and F. Quiviger (eds), *Italian Academies of the Sixteenth Century* (London: The Warburg Institute, 1995), pp. 127–35. To track down a particular artist's name behind the picture seems, however, difficult. The Medici court painters Agnolo Bronzino and Francesco Salviati have both been suggested, but the attribution must probably be left open. I am grateful to Dr Sharon Gregory for kindly providing me with information on this question.

22 'The mask is Doni's means of hiding the wounds inflicted by the slings and arrows of outrageous fortune. It enables him to play his role, to transform himself into the character which fate expects him to bear, but the stage on which he perform is only the phantasmagoria of the actual world ... The mask enables a man to put a distance between himself and the

could be used independently of the motto, and that 'there may be instances where literary and pictorial evidence may develop on different lines'.[23] By dropping the motto in the *Utopia* print, Doni in fact leaves the reading of the picture open to an interpretation in line with the work to which it is attached. The 'masked woman', then, was not his printer's device as such;[24] it was rather a kind of personal device in that it was used on certain books presumably in order to give a visible indication of their close relationship to Doni himself. Situated, like all frontispiece pictures, in the borderland between the reader and the text, it helped to condition the reader's perception of that text; whatever its iconographic meaning, it tells a publishing story of the editor and of how he wanted to put his own personal stamp on the books in this group. In other words, *Utopia* – in spite of being a work by someone else – must have been seen to belong to such a category of personal writings.

There are other indications, too, that Doni strongly identified himself with the Utopian case. Doni's most popular literary work was *I Mondi*, a Lucianic description of seven different 'worlds', printed four years after the Italian *Utopia*. In twelve pages of chapter six we find Doni's own version of Utopia, in which an entirely new 'wise-mad' world is described in a dream.[25] Where Doni in his dedicatory preface to Fava had rendered More's work apparently harmless by drawing it into an atmosphere of family life, a very different direction is taken here, one which might give us a better clue to the real interest Doni took in *Utopia*. The interlocutors of the mock-philosophical dialogues of *I mondi* belong to Doni's (perhaps fictional) academy of travellers or strangers, the 'Academia peregrina'. The two we meet in chapter six are the Wise Man ('Savio') and the Madman ('Pazzo'), and Savio narrates a dream beginning with two strangers one day coming to visit them to take them to a new and different world. 'It seemed like a dream,' says Savio; 'I told myself that it couldn't be real.'[26] Savio continues his story while drawing a circle on the ground, demonstrating the perfect circular shape of the city they

---

world of vanities, as an actor views the part which he plays' (Gertrude Bing, 'Nugae circa Veritatem: notes on Anton Francesco Doni', *Journal of the Warburg Institute*, 1 (1937–38), 304–12 (310)). Bing discusses the motto (and variants like 'Quod molestius / patior taceo') in relation to the woodcuts, but the *Utopia* frontispiece was apparently not known to her.

23 Bing, 'Nugae circa Veritatem', 306, note 4. One such instance is provided by the reappearance of the woman with a mask in Cesare Ripa's *Iconologia* under the headings 'Imitatione' and 'Simulatione'. Here, the mask represents the imitation of human action on the stage.

24 As Firpo, the only *Utopia* scholar to mention the image, believed: he calls the picture 'Doni's usual vignette' ('Thomas More e la sua fortuna', p. 48n). Doni's mark as a printer was another smaller emblem showing a lion holding a flower, symbol of the city of Florence. See Alessandro Cecchi, 'In margina a una recente monografia sul Salviati', *Antichità viva*, 33 (1994), 12–22 (17).

25 See 'Mondo savio e pazzo' in A. F. Doni, *I Mondi e gli Inferni*, ed. P. Pellizzari (Turin: Einaudi, 1994), pp. 158–87.

26 'Ben mi pareva sogno, ben diceva io: la non è cosa che possa essere' (*ibid.*, p. 162).

were taken to.[27] Savio's description clearly imitates the communal principle of More's island society: everything is held in common. Whether it can be called wise or mad depends, it is said here, on how it is judged.

The ontological status of Doni's wise-mad world is therefore not so easy to grasp. When a shift of scene in the next dialogue takes us to heaven, the line between dream and reality becomes as blurred as that between the fool and the wise man, a mad world and a sane world. We learn that the two men who in the dream led Savio and Pazzo to the other and better world were Jupiter and Momus descended to earth in the guise of travellers. Jupiter suggests – by citing illustrious leaders in ancient history – that the purpose of the dream was political: to provide guidelines and a goal for political reform. And Savio – perhaps a mouthpiece for Doni himself – has been chosen to realise the dream on earth. Through fictional literature, then?

If in Doni's dialogues the political purpose recedes into the background, this does not imply, therefore, that politics is replaced by playful wit purely for the sake of laughter. 'It is sufficient that this is dream, wisdom, popular opinion, madness,'[28] Savio is made to say at one point, echoing the *Praise of Folly* (which Doni, as we have seen, could have read in the 1518 Giunta edition). What it is not, however, is false. The complex exchange of wisdom and foolishness in the dialogue between Savio and Pazzo creates a space for thought where the question of truth versus falsity is suspended. This intellectual stance may perhaps in certain respects be associated with sixteenth-century scepticism, but more specifically it shows an attitude where something seemingly impossible, or contrary to common sense, is, for all its implausibility, presented as if it is possible.

And is it not the possibility, rather than the impossibility, of the imagined Utopian world that constitutes its strongest appeal, and must have done so to many sixteenth-century readers? In this it emerges as paradoxical, and even more so when the fictional or dream world is narrated in the first person singular, which ensures that the link to the everyday world is not broken. Does paradox, then, disappear when the paratexts shrink, as Françoise Lavocat interestingly suggests?[29] In the case of Doni this was clearly not so. Rather the taste for paradox conditioned the project as such. Five years prior to Doni's printing of the Italian *Utopia*, a book had been issued by a Lyon printing house that made Doni want to get to know its anonymous author: *Paradossi*

---

27 The French translation of 1578 by Gabriel Chappuys (see below, pp. 81) has a picture of Doni's star city, reprinted as fig. 8 in Grendler, *Critics of the Italian World*, p. 178.
28 'basta che questo è sogno, questa è saviezza, questa è opinione degli uomini, questa è pazzia' (*I Mondi*, pp. 167–8).
29 F. Lavocat, 'Fictions et paradoxes: les nouveaux mondes possibles à la Renaissance', in *Vox Poetica* 20/02/2006, www.vox-poetica.org/t/lavocatart.html (page consulted 12.03.06), p. 15.

cioè sententie fuori del comun parere ('Paradoxes, that is to say propositions outside the realm of common opinion'). 'I so much liked this work,' he writes to a friend. 'If only I could get to know that brilliant mind and become his friend!'[30] And so he did.

Ortensio Lando (1512–ca. 1555)

'These doctrines are surprising, and they run counter to universal opinion', is Cicero's definition of the genre in the preface to his little book of six Stoic paradoxes, which became a model for Renaissance humanists.[31] It was first printed in Venice in 1488, then reprinted again and again, for example by the Giunta press in Florence in 1513, and it was soon made available in vernacular translations.[32] The Italian *Paradossi* of 1543 was with its thirty paradoxes the first extensive and original imitation and emulation of Cicero's work to appear in the vernacular. As Corsaro argues, it is a much more serious text than the printer's letter to the reader would suggest in calling it a 'capricious freak' ('capricciosa bizzaria'). The erudite play on words for which More and other humanists were renowned here gives way to a genuine evangelical spirit where the radical 'foolishness of Christ' outdoes any moderate Ciceronian Stoicism; the author of the *Paradossi* appears in the end as a veritable anti-Ciceronian (in the philosophical, not stylistic, sense).

It could not have been too difficult for Doni to pin down the name of the author of this influential text: the book ends with a little Latin enigma, 'SUISNETROH TABEDUL', which, read backwards, means that Ortensio was playing or having fun. And at the end of the volume there follows a letter to the readers saying that 'the author of the present volume was MOLM with

---

30 'Quest'opera ... m'ha gustato tanto ... S'io conoscessi quel chiarissimo intelletto, io piglierei tanta letitia d'esserli amico'; quoted by A. Corsaro in his introduction to *Paradossi* (reprint of the 1543 Lyon edition; Rome: Edizioni di storia e letteratura, 2000), p. 11. The fifth paradox, 'It is better to be mad than wise' ('Meglio è d'esser pazzo che savio'; *ibid.*, fol. D i v), may have been the most immediate source for Doni's dialogue between Savio and Pazzo in *I Mondi*.
31 'admirabilia contraque opinionem omnium' (*Paradoxa Stoicorum*, 4; translation from Loeb Classical Library, Cicero IV, p. 257). This definition renders the etymological sense of the Greek word; the title of the book printed in Lyon is a free rendering of Cicero's phrase. In Greek patristic literature, this word is used to characterise what is hard to believe, the greatest theological paradox being the Incarnation itself, where God became man – a contradiction in terms. It is no doubt from such self-contradictory conceptions that the more common modern use of the word arose. On Ciceronian paradox in the Renaissance, see Agnieszka Steczowicz, *The Defence of Contraries: Paradox and the Late Renaissance Disciplines*, unpublished D.Phil. thesis, University of Oxford, 2006.
32 The French and English editions are briefly mentioned by Elizabeth McCutcheon, 'More's Utopia and Cicero's *Paradoxa Stoicorum*', *Moreana*, 86 (1985), 3–22 (8). For the Italian translation (1528), I have consulted *EDIT16*.

the nickname 'Tranquillus':[33] in other words, Messère Ortensio Lando Milanese.

Unlike Doni, Lando did not publish his letters and remains an obscure figure, even if close to thirty texts exist from his hand – original works, paraphrases and translations, many published anonymously, some of the titles of which endorse the picture of him as a rather bizarre person with a taste for deceit and play.[34] He had been an Augustinian monk and a priest with unorthodox views, before earning his living from a sharp pen. After humanistic and medical studies in monasteries in Milan, Naples and Bologna he went for some time into exile, accused of heresy. Known to have led an irregular and erratic life – his travels took him to France, Switzerland, Germany and the whole of Italy – he was labelled *vir inconstantissimus*, a very restless man, by the famous Lyon printer Sébastien Gryphe. But when received in the Accademia degli Elevati in Ferrara in 1540, he was given the name 'Tranquillus': an ironic antiphrasis, or possibly an indication of inner peace of soul in contrast with his constant wandering.[35]

It is, however, another pseudonym that interests us here, because it reveals Ortensio Lando's longstanding relationship to the Morian Utopia. This is the one he gave himself in a sketch for the third paradox ('Better to be ignorant than learned') in a manuscript 'dialogue against the men of letters' dating from 1541.[36] The manuscript is anonymous, being signed simply 'Filalete, citizen of Utopia' ('Filalete' is a Greek coinage meaning 'lover of truth'). This signature can be traced back to the crucial year of 1535, the year of More's execution, when Lando, then 23 years old, stayed at the Buonvisi family's Villa di Forci on the outskirts of Lucca, one of the Italian city-states that most actively fostered evangelical reform. If Lando had not encountered *Utopia* before – in Lyon, in Paris?[37] – it certainly came into his hands now, thanks to this wealthy and cultured Lucca family: Vicenzo Buonvisi, whom Lando had befriended in Lyon, was the brother of Thomas More's personal friend, the London-based merchant Antonio Buonvisi, to whom one of More's last

33 'L'autore della presente opera, il qual fu MOLM detto per sopra nome il Tranq.' (fol. O 8 r).
34 Among these is a book called *Pazzia* ('Madness'), which the title-page declares to be printed in India, but which was printed in Venice in 1550, and a book containing funeral orations on the death of various animals (Venice, 1548).
35 That would be in accord with his *Trattato della vera tranquillità dell'animo* (Venice, 1544), sometimes attributed to Isabella Sforza, the author of the preface.
36 Soon to be paraphrased in French, anonymously, as *Paradoxe contre les lettres* (Lyon, 1545). Significantly, it is this third paradox that contains a mention of Thomas More, on the death of the learned: 'a Tomaso Moro s'è visto mozzar il capo' ('Thomas More was seen to have his head cut off'; *Paradossi*, fol. C 3 v)
37 Or in his early Italian years, when he could have read Florence 1519; his reading of Erasmus (whose translations of Lucian were published in this volume together with More's) was extensive.

letters from prison is addressed.[38] The conversations that grew out of this stay are recorded in the form of the learned Latin dialogue *Forcianae questiones*, which is the first of several works signed by the anonymous author and citizen of Utopia and which marks the beginning of Lando's lifelong relationship with the Utopian idea. Here Lando presented himself as 'Filalethe, citizen of Polytopia'.[39] So if *Utopia* was a non-place and its Italian translator in the paratexts of Venice 1548 a non-person, in other cases Lando appeared in a Utopian disguise, a curious and very literary self-fashioning quite unlike the political self-fashioning and self-cancellation Stephen Greenblatt notoriously attributes to More.[40]

Lyon became decisive for Lando's involvement with More's *Utopia* in more than one respect. It was here, as we have seen, that he befriended Vicenzo Buonvisi and so came into contact with More's personal friends; it was here, too, that nine years later he had his *Paradossi* printed, the book that subsequently put him in contact with Doni. And Lyon could also have been the city where he made the decision both to write in the vernacular and to become a translator, inspired perhaps by his friend Etienne Dolet and his brief treatise on translation.[41]

A year or two after the *Paradossi* was issued, Lando and Doni, who in several ways had led parallel lives, had the chance to meet, in Piacenza or in Venice.[42] This might indeed have been the moment when they started to plan the translation of the paradox writ large that is *Utopia,* or alternatively, the moment when Lando presented Doni with a complete translation of a work that they had each, independently, long been familiar with.

The attraction of *Utopia* for a wanderer like Lando would not only have been its paradoxical nature, but also its simulation of an explorer's tale. In the very year of the publication of the Italian *Utopia*, Lando's own travel account of a voyage through the Italian peninsula was issued in Venice.[43] The printer is not mentioned, nor the name of the real author, but by now Mr. Anonymous

---

38 *The Correspondence of Sir Thomas More*, ed. Elizabeth Francis Rogers (Princeton, NJ: Princeton University Press, 1947), letter no. 217; see Firpo, 'Thomas More e la sua fortuna in Italia', pp. 31–2.
39 Further variants appear in works published in 1540, 1548, 1550 and 1555. For a list of Lando's 'Utopian texts', see Seidel Menchi, 'Ortensio Lando cittadino di Utopia', pp. 98–9.
40 See S. Greenblatt, *Renaissance Self-Fashioning: From More to Shakespeare* (Chicago: The University of Chicago Press, 1980), pp. 11–73.
41 *La maniere de bien traduire d'une langue en aultre* (Lyon, 1540).
42 In 1544, Doni reports that he is preparing for the press an unnamed dialogue of a 'M. Hortensio', who could be Ortensio Lando; see Grendler, *Critics of the Italian world*, pp. 31–2.
43 Lando, *Commentario delle più notabili e mostruose cose d'Italia e altri luoghi. Catalogo de gli inventori delle cose che si mangiano e beveno*, eds Guido and Paolo Salvatori (Bologna: Edizioni Pendragon, 1994).

from Utopia could not have been too difficult to identify.[44] Here the Utopian fiction allows Lando to approach his own country from the outside, reversing so to speak the direction of the voyage:

> since I had read in the old stories so many wonderful things about the Italians ... the wish to see Italy for myself started to burn in my breast, an extreme desire, not only to see it, but to live there as long as I lived ... in our country, which is called the Kingdom of the Lost, there arrived by chance, blown off course by the winds, a ship from the isle of Utopia ... Amongst the many men on board, there was a Florentine named Tetigio ... I asked him to come with me and be my guide on my Italian journey.[45]

Behind this Florentine we can easily detect Amerigo Vespucci, but perhaps it would not be too far-fetched also to see another Florentine, Lando's friend Doni.[46] The perspective is in any case totally altered: instead of heading out from Italy across the ocean to unknown continents, these travellers turn to Italy itself, almost as if to give birth to the enduring notion of the 'Italian journey', a genre that began to establish itself in the course of the sixteenth century. Here, too, however, the perspective is altered in favour of what we may call a Utopian outlook: the travelogue becomes a catalogue of vices compared to what Italy ideally could – or could not – have been. Lando shows himself to be not only an acute observer of popular customs and culinary specialities but also a critic of contemporary Italian society, the hypocrisy of the rich, the lifelessness of erudition and the absurdity of theological disputes, a stance typical of the outsider or exile. For, as Hugo Tucker has shown, exile could be used in a positive way to create a new fictional identity.[47]

This was of course also a time when accounts of discoveries in the New World were proliferating and Venice naturally became a centre of printed

---

44 In a recommendation of the *Commentario* placed after the text, as in the *Paradossi*, the initials of the real author (MOL) appear, and the last page of the *Catalogo* has another Latin 'enigma' similar to the one in the *Paradossi* (see above, pp. 55–6).

45 'avendo letto nelle antiche storie tante meravigliose cose dalli Italiani ... nacquemi nel petto un ardentissimo disio e vennemi un'estrema voglia, non sol da vederla, ma di abitarla mentre vivessi ... nel paese nostro, che si chiama il regno de' Sperduti, capitasse, spinta da contrari venti, una nave dall'isole di Utopia ... sopra della quale, fra molti, vi era un fiorentino chiamato Tetigio... Io chiesi se voleva rimanersi meco ed essermi guida nel viaggio d'Italia' (*Commentario*, p. 3).

46 There is yet another fiction here: on the title-page, Lando presents the work as a translation from Aramaic. The I-persona from the Kingdom of the Lost Ones has written his account in Aramaic, whereas the anonymous 'Utopian' author – that is, Lando himself – is only the translator.

47 G. H. Tucker, *Homo Viator: Itineraries of Exile, Displacement and Writing in Renaissance Europe* (Geneva: Droz, 2003). Tucker devotes a chapter to Lando ('Dialogue, irony and paradox in the comings and goings of the "Poly(u)topian" Ortensio Landi'; pp. 270–80), mainly on his satirical dialogues *Cicero relegatus* and *Cicero revocatus* (1534) and the notion of exile.

information about the New World and the East; the fame of Venice in the 1540s as a polyglot city was closely linked to its busy port and the tales of the many seafarers, explorers and merchants who passed through it.[48] Publishing More's *Utopia* in the vernacular fitted in well with this kind of activity.

But for Lando as for Doni, the real value of travelling to Utopia in writing was the position of exile offered through its fiction, and thus a space for thinking alternatively about the world.

Francesco Sansovino (1521–1586)

In 1561, Book II of the Italian *Utopia* was included at the end of Sansovino's compilatory work on different governments, *Il governo*, first printed in Venice that year and reissued in 1566, 1567, 1578, 1583 and 1607; it was also translated into French.[49] The prolific polygrapher Francesco Sansovino, a translator of Greek and Latin, was thus responsible for making *Utopia* available to a much wider reading public in Italy and France.

He was also responsible for making Ortensio Lando known as the translator of *Utopia*: 'the Republic of Utopia was ... translated from More's Latin by Hortensio Lando', he writes in the general preface.[50] This disclosure of the identity of the hitherto anonymous translator of *Utopia* may be seen as a consequence of Sansovino's enthusiasm for the vernacular, as witness his many works on questions of language; for him, the aspiration towards the best possible government (the overall theme of *Il governo*) seems to have included a national language politics.[51] He is also likely to have known Doni personally, and perhaps Doni finally found that the time had come to credit the name of his friend, now dead. In all later editions of *Il governo*, however, it was removed: one may conjecture that the increasingly sharp confessional divide made it unsuitable to name an author of heterodox beliefs. Only once, then, was Ortensio Lando openly credited as the translator of More's Latin.[52]

---

48 See Peter Burke, 'Early modern Venice as a center of information and communication', in J. Martin and D. Romano (eds), *Venice Reconsidered. The History and Civilization of an Italian City-State 1297–1797* (Baltimore & London: Johns Hopkins University Press, 2000), pp. 389–419.
49 See below, pp. 78–82.
50 'la Rep. d'Utopia fu ... tradotta dalla Latina del Moro da Hortensio Lando' (Venice 1561, fol. *3 v).
51 See for example Sansovino, *Ortografia delle voci della lingua nostra, o vero dittionario volgare et latino: nel quale s'impara a scriver correttamente ogni parola cosi in prosa come in verso, per fuggir le rime false e gli altri errori che si possono commettere favellando e scrivendo* (Venice: F. Sansovino, 1568).
52 Sansovino himself was therefore often taken to be the translator, as witness the Portuguese Inquisitor who in 1624 attributed to him the translation of the prohibited *Utopia*; see José V. de Pina Martins, 'L'*Utopie* de Thomas More au Portugal', *Moreana*, 69 (1981), 137–56 (144–5).

Sansovino is, however, not entirely happy with the translation and explains that he had to improve it in some measure. Lando, he goes on to say, was

> truly a man well-versed in letters, but not very precise in matters regarding the vernacular language, for it seemed to him, although he was writing in his own tongue, that he was not only a Tuscan but a serious prose writer, and in this, too, it was appropriate that I should make a bit of an effort.[53]

Exactly what kind of efforts Sansovino made to improve Lando's prose is not clear; a comparative study of the two versions has, to my knowledge, not been carried out. But Sansovino's derogatory remarks on Lando's linguistic capacity imply a problem with his regional dialect. The written vernacular had come to mean Tuscan on the model of Dante, Boccaccio and Petrarch, whereas Lando obviously wrote with a touch of his native spoken Milanese. In the dedicatory preface to the *Paradossi*, Lando himself makes it clear that the anti-Tuscan and non-conformist choice is a deliberate one, although it needs to be explained and defended: 'I haven't even cared, my lord, for writing Tuscan-wise, as is nowadays the rule; rather I have written them [the paradoxes] in the form I usually speak with my closest friends.'[54]

Modern critics agree in that they also spot the Lombardan vein, but they are less judgemental about it. Scrivano speaks of Lando's translation as being in 'an Italian that is loose, flowing, and characterised by regionalisms', while Firpo remarks that 'in Lando's prose we can recognise, even if marked by not excessively strident Lombardisms, a pleasing liveliness and a powerful effect of concentration.'[55] Only Seidel Menchi – whose discussion is regrettably lacking in concrete examples – is more severe in her critique, although her concern is not with dialect. But she, too, ends on a positive note.[56]

Whatever the qualities of Lando's prose, it must have rendered the vivid naturalness of More's text effectively enough to make a man concerned with

---

53 'huomo nel vero di molte lettere, ma delle cose della lingua volgare poco accurato, percioche a lui pareva, scrivendo secondo la sua lingua, d'esser non solamente Thoscano, ma un solenne prosatore, e ancho in quella mi è convenuto affaticarmi un pezzo' (Venice 1561, fol. *3 v).
54 'Non mi sono neanche, Signor mio, curato di scrivere toscanamente, come oggidì s'usa di fare, ma gli ho scritti nella forma che solito sono di parlare con e miei più familiari amici' (*Paradossi*, Dedicatoria I, fol. A 3 v).
55 R. Scrivano, 'Ortensio Lando traduttore di Thomas More', in *Studi sulla cultura lombarda: in memoria di Mario Apollonio*, vol. 1 (Milan: Pubblicazioni della Università Cattolica del Sacro Cuore, 1972), p. 100; Firpo, 'Thomas More e la sua fortuna', p. 50.
56 'The translation is not in the least concerned with being faithful; nor is it obsessed with completeness, and it is far removed from any kind of pedantry. The translator did not have the mental habits of the scholar: the textual divergences of the translation from the Latin original are numerous, ample and substantial ... These deviations do not reduce the impact of the text; in fact, they increase it, precisely as a result of the translation's concentration and simplification' (Seidel Menchi, 'Ortensio Lando cittadino di Utopia', p. 97n, my translation).

serious political history interested in it. In his collection of political topographies, Sansovino describes – mostly by quoting and paraphrasing other (acknowledged) authors – a whole range of real countries and cities, paying special attention to their forms of government and administration; the only exception is of course Utopia itself, placed at the end. By 1583, the year of the last edition to appear in Sansovino's lifetime, the number of countries or treatises included in the anthology had risen from seventeen to twenty-two, but Utopia was still the last, now even appearing on the title-page of the whole work together with the other names of the states.[57] Sansovino explains why it is placed at the end: 'I have striven to tell the truth [in all the books up to the last] as far as I was able. The final Republic, that of Utopia, is all fiction, but beautiful in its effect, and therefore I decided to place it at the end.'[58]

The explanation belongs to one of two paratextual items of relevance. The first is the passage dealing with *Utopia* in this general preface. The other is a brief note prefacing the book of *Utopia* itself.[59] Both prefaces were, to the best of my knowledge, reproduced in all subsequent reissues of *Il governo*, with some slight alterations.[60] What emerges from these two prefaces, together with the whole context of *Il governo*, is a version of *Utopia* that differs significantly from the one promoted by Lando and Doni.

First of all, the work is given a special aura by the brief hagiographic note on its author in the *Utopia* preface: Sansovino calls More 'a man of most saintly life' and refers to the consequences of his courageous opposition to Henry VIII.[61] Sansovino's *Utopia* thus takes definitive leave of the evangelical milieu that had fostered Lando's translation and adopts instead the Counter-Reformation agenda (More as saint and martyr) which became a familiar element of the Latin complete works of the same decade.[62]

Another major deviation regards the question of literariness, fiction, truth. Sansovino clearly distances himself from the literary game that More and his humanist friends invited the reader to participate in when they deliberately blurred the lines between real-life persons and fictional characters, actual politics and an imaginary island. The first step in that direction is a feature that Sansovino shares with many other editors and translators of *Utopia*: he only includes Book II. The second and more unusual step is his explicit

---

57 See below, Bibliography.
58 'io mi sono ingegnato di dir la verità piu che mi è stato possibile. L'ultima Republica d'Utopia è tutta finta, ma bella in effetto, e però la ho voluta metter nell'ultimo luogo' (Venice 1561, fol. *3 v).
59 See Part II, pp. 176–9.
60 One alteration in the general preface has already been noted: Ortensio Lando's name is left out.
61 Sansovino's account implies that *Utopia* was actually written as a consequence of his disapproval of Henry VIII's regime.
62 See above, pp. 25–6.

attempt to make clear from the outset that the last book treats of a state that is not real: compared to the previous books of *Il governo* where he has, he says, striven to tell the truth, it is 'all fiction' (*tutta finta*). This remark – which by informed readers of the period would have been read as a deliberate reversal of Machiavelli's celebrated strictures on 'imagined' republics[63] – is repeated in the prefatory note to *Utopia* itself when he writes of it as a *piacevolissima fittione*, something that pretends to be true but is not, however pleasing.[64] In the 1583 edition, the last to be revised by him personally, he even adds a sentence to further this point: *Utopia* invites an 'imaginary reading'. In other words, Sansovino is at pains to draw a distinct line between the previous books which treats of *cose vere* (true things), and *Utopia* which is entirely fictitious and imaginary.

Yet the inclusion of Utopia in a volume consisting of treatises on real and historical states makes it partake in a context that is broader than the tradition of imaginary or ideal states (like Plato's republic, which he also mentions in the prefatory note). Of this effect Sansovino seems to be fully aware. First of all, he chooses for the last book of *Il governo* the title *On the government of the Republic of Utopia*, so that it actually fits in with the previous titles: it doesn't, so to speak, break the line. Finding itself placed at the end of a whole series of descriptions of real-world governments, *Utopia* is thus entirely recontextualised. Secondly he stresses in both prefaces that, although *Utopia* does not tell the truth, it may – with its elaborate description of 'a republic governed by the best laws and brought to a state of absolute peace' – teach people how to live more happily and quit the corrupt habits that More was weary of. It is to this useful end that Sansovino lets the book of Utopia have the famous last word: it shows the ultimate meaning and direction of all the previous discussions on various ways of governing states. Only with such high ideals in view may reform of governments or the founding of new and good republics be obtained.

It may not be competely coincidental that the passage on *Utopia* in the general preface contains a brief reference to Contarini's Republic, that is Venice.[65] Sansovino also wrote about Venice: in the same year as *Il governo*

---

63 See *Il Principe*, Book 15: 'but as it was my intention to write something that might be of use to anyone who understands it, it seemed to me more appropriate to go straight to the practical truth of the matter rather than to an imaginary conception of it. And many have imagined republics and principalities which have never been seen or known to exist in reality' ('ma, sendo l'intento mio, scrivere cosa utile a chi la intende, mi è parso piú conveniente andare drieto alla verità effettuale della cosa che alla immaginazione di essa. E molti si sono immaginati republiche e principati, che non si sono mai visti né conosciuti essere in vero'; Niccolò Machiavelli, *Il Principe*, ed. Mario Martelli and Nicoletta Marcelli (Rome: Salerno Editrice, 2006), pp. 215–16.
64 See Part II, pp. 178–9.
65 This is the widely read book in political thought, *De magistratibus et Republica Venetorum*

was printed, his city-guide *Venetia città nobilissima et singolare* appeared for the first time. It became even more popular than *Il governo*, and was to be reissued again and again in steadily expanded and altered editions into the next century. Perhaps, for Sansovino, the beauty and power of Venice – a city built on water – had come close to the unreal and ideal state of *Utopia*.

After 1600: Zuccolo and Campanella

A similar patriotic attitude recurs after the turn of the century in another of the ever-proliferating authors of Utopias in Italian.[66] Ludovico Zuccolo, a political thinker concerned with the *raison d'état* and with Italy's progression toward modern statehood, tells of a beautiful province in Asia, 'in the nearest vicinity of the Isle of Utopia', called Evandria.[67] In this dialogue, dating from 1621, Evandria emerges with many traits reminiscent of Italy itself, or the idealised version of it that Zuccolo wished to see (and partly saw in the Venetian Republic).[68] But in several places it also imitates More's *Utopia*, which Zuccolo could have read in one of the Sansovino editions, or perhaps the new Latin edition printed in Milan in 1620 – so much so that the author after a few years may have felt the need to distance himself from it. For in yet another dialogue, *L'aromatorio, ovvero Della repubblica d'Utopia* (1625), More's book is the subject of ridicule and harsh criticism from a pragmatic point of view; in particular, the speakers attack the dissolution of private property that is essential to More's programme.[69]

(Paris, 1543) by Cardinal Gasparo Contarini, which reinforced the so-called myth of Venice as the perfect state; in Venice 1583, the Italian translation of this text (or parts of it) appears at fols 85r–91r. Interestingly, More has been suggested as an inspiration: 'One intriguing suggestion is that the book may have originated in a dinner-table conversation between Contarini and Thomas More in Bruges in 1521. More's *Utopia* had appeared five years earlier, and Contarini could easily have read it. Yet Contarini makes no mention of the book and remarks merely that More was a "very learned gentleman"' (Elisabeth G. Gleason, *Gasparo Contarini: Venice, Rome, and Reform* (Berkeley: University of California Press 1993), p. 111).

66 To the titles treated here should be added Francesco Patrizi da Cherso's *La città felice* (1553), Matteo Buonamici's *L'isola di Narsida* (1572), Ludovico Agostini's *La repubblica immaginaria* (1585), Fabio Albergati's *La repubblica regia* (1627), Giovanni Bonifacio's *La repubblica delle api* (1627), Vincenzo Sgualdi's *La Repubblica di Lesbo ovvero della ragione di stato in un dominio aristocratico* (1640), and Tomaso Tomasi's *La Spinalba* (1647).
67 Ludovico Zuccolo, *La Repubblica d'Evandria e altri dialoghi italiani*, pref. R. de Mattei (Roma: Colombo Editore, 1944).
68 The very name has a nationalistic air. In Greek, 'Euandros' means 'good man'; in Virgil's *Aeneid* VIII.313, Evandros is an involuntary exile from Greek Arcadia who settled in Latium, where Rome was later built. Possibly Zuccolo took the name from *Punica* VII.18, which refers to 'the Evandrian kingdoms' ('regna Evandria'), i.e. the Roman Empire, founded by Evandrus.
69 This work was printed together with *Belluzzi ovvero La Città felice* (Venice, 1625), which had San Marino as its model.

But this was not the only stance taken in Italy on Utopian matters a century after the book's first appearance on the market. At about the same time, Tommaso Campanella's *La Città del Sole* was printed, a radically proto-communist text. In contrast with Doni, Lando, Sansovino and Zuccolo, Campanella is one of the few authors of Utopias who acted on his ideas. As a Calabrian of poor origin, he became in 1597 the leader of a Calabrian conspiracy against the Spanish rule in southern Italy with the aim to establish a society based on the community of goods (and wives), clearly inspired by More's Utopia. Captured and condemned to death, he only saved his life by feigning insanity. He wrote *La Città del Sole* in 1602 while incarcerated for life in Naples. That it was not printed until 1623, and then in a Latin translation in Frankfurt, may say something about the stricter political and religious climate of this period as compared to that in the mid-sixteenth century, but its origin and survival may tell us even more about the enduring force of the Utopian vision.

Conclusion

The appropriation of *Utopia* by Lando, Doni and Sansovino, men closely linked to book production while independent of court milieux and of particular institutions of learning, illustrates the active work done by readers and writers in the wake of More's death. It shows how new meaning was produced not only through the insertion of More's *Utopia* into the context of early modern printing culture in Venice, but more particularly through the insertion of More's ideas into the creative minds of the work's translator, editors and imitators.

As a hybrid between a political treatise and an imaginary travel description, More's *Utopia* belongs, in a wide sense, to the sixteenth-century genre of the 'philosophical fiction'. Of this hybrid in general it has been said that its emblem 'might perhaps be something like ... the cosmographies that complete their image of the "real world" with merely possible islands.'[70] In the case of *Utopia*, that sounds more like a precise description of the project as such. In its combination of strangeness and familiarity, drawing on elements from different levels of reality, this genre poses particular problems for the modern interpreter who seeks to grasp the responses that such a text elicited from its readers five hundred years ago. But the problem was already there at the time, as a problem of reading. To study the immediate reception of More's *Utopia* through the vernacular translations and the texts and the people that surrounded these translations is to let this problem come to the fore.

---

70 Terence Cave, 'Epilogue', in Neil Kenny (ed.), *Philosophical Fictions and the French Renaissance* (London: Warburg Institute, 1991), pp. 127–32 (p. 127).

Yet perhaps we should not call it a problem. In the case of the Italian translator, editors and imitators, the reading of More's little text must have aroused an enthusiasm that spurred them on to integrate his work into their own in order to continue its provocatively mixed discourse. Lando's travelogue, Doni's burlesque allegory, Sansovino's study in comparative politics, like Zuccolo's pragmatic *Repubblica d'Evandria* and Campanella's revolutionary *Città del Sole*, were direct responses to a text that appealed to them in many ways, a text they italianised and transformed with their own literary imagination. Although none of them displays any theoretical interest in the hybrid genre of the book, each has obviously been most receptive of precisely this aspect. While apparently taking the political tale at face value, they voluntarily let themselves be absorbed by the fiction.

We have also seen that they acted this fiction out in different ways. Whereas Lando and Doni pushed *Utopia* further into an entirely fictional world, Sansovino and, much later, Zuccolo attempted to integrate *Utopia* into their own political and patriotic projects. Campanella's visionary mode, born of real poverty, marks, on the other hand, a very different turn in the history of Utopian literary practice. And whereas Lando is the stranger coming from outside and looking critically at Italy from a Utopian point of view (a forerunner of the modern anthropologist's), Doni cannot decide if the perfect world envisioned in a dream is wise or insane; both of them create suspension through paradox. For Sansovino, only Book II of *Utopia* is of interest; he rids himself of the literary frame as well as of the original Northern European context. More's *Utopia* is thus placed alongside accounts of governments in real countries. Indeed, Sansovino seems to have ended up projecting Utopia onto his beloved Venice. Some decades later, in a different political climate, this patriotic line is developed into nationalism: Zuccolo's literary invention, the peninsula *Evandria*, is his sober vision of what a unified Italian state could be. Arguing fervently against More's 'communism', Zuccolo maintains – in striking contrast with his contemporary Campanella – a pragmatic view of human nature and society.

Ultimately, it seems to me that the question is not so much whether the various Utopian texts were political, but rather how, by what means, and why. *Utopia* was from the outset a political text, but its early modern reception indicates that it was so in very different ways and that these differences are partly traceable in the contrasting conceptions of the nature of such political prose. If fictional, how fictional? How close to the real world, or how far from it, or contrary to it? And by what means should a political message be argued? By way of logical discourse, or analogy, or rather reversed analogy, the image of something opposite or alternative – paradoxical in the classical sense, that is? If the alternative was to be truly compelling, it had to be conceived of as

'possible' at one level or another, in spite of its 'Utopianism' (as we would call it). This it achieved in that all its individual elements were familiar or natural: they had a referent in the real world (which in the sixteenth century included the classical literary heritage from Antiquity). The imagined world will appear natural, or very possible, on an empirical level (hardly any supernatural events take place there), so that only human nature makes it unreal and unrealisable.

Is human nature, then, the target? We cannot infer from Doni's and Lando's readings and rewritings of *Utopia* that their aim was radically to change human nature, although Lando's reformist inclination may point in the direction of an evangelical change of heart. What we do see is an adherence to More's text as a model, both stylistically and otherwise, for paradoxical literature – that is to say, a form of writing that constantly questions established truths and accepted realities by turning them upside down.

Kristin Gjerpe

4 THE FRENCH VERSIONS OF *UTOPIA*: CHRISTIAN AND COSMOPOLITAN MODELS

If one wants to uncover the cultural contexts into which translations of *Utopia* were introduced in France in the sixteenth and seventeenth centuries, a good place to begin is the trace of More's work in the form of allusions, imitations or borrowings. Of these, Rabelais's comic fictions provide some of the clearest and most inventive examples. The first-published book (*Pantagruel*, 1532) alludes to Utopia as Pantagruel's soon-to-be-inherited kingdom, contains a sample of spoken Utopian, and plots in the imaginary island as a projected stopping-point on his and his friends' itinerary; *Gargantua* (1534) contains a scene of imaginary world conquest which is indebted to a passage in Book 1 of *Utopia* and ends with the Abbey of Thélème, a Utopian château offering a kind of training-ground for well-born men and women before they enter 'real' society; and the *Tiers livre* (1546) begins with the wholly beneficial colonisation of the conquered land of Dipsodie by the Utopians.[1]

Other early references to More and *Utopia* include the pamphlet *Misocacus civis utopiensis Philaletis ex sorore nepotis Dialogi tres* (probably from 1526), supposedly printed in the Utopian city of Amaurot, and Geoffroy Tory's *Champ fleury* (1529), which reproduces the Utopian alphabet along with a reference to its author and the book from which it is taken.[2] Such allusions provide evidence that *Utopia* was already part of a common fund of textual knowledge in France during More's lifetime, even if this knowledge was sometimes superficial.

Large-scale imitations come somewhat later. The description of the city Orbe in Barthélemy Aneau's novel *Alector* (1560), while clearly related to More's work, as we shall see, derives its architectural characteristics from other contemporary Utopian works.[3] Half a century later, there appeared another imitation of *Utopia*, the *Histoire du Grand et Admirable Royaume*

---

1 See François Rabelais, *Œuvres complètes*, ed. Mireille Huchon and François Moureau ([Paris]: Gallimard, 1994).
2 A full account of these is provided by Jean Céard, 'La fortune de l'*Utopie* de Thomas More en France au XVIe siècle', in *La fortuna dell'Utopia di Thomas More nel dibattito politico europeo del '500* (Florence: Olschki, 1996), pp. 43–75, and V.-L. Saulnier, 'Mythologies pantagruéliques. L'*Utopie* en France: Morus et Rabelais', in R. Klein (ed.), *Les Utopies à la Renaissance* (Brussels: Presses Universitaires, 1963), pp. 137–63.
3 See Barthélemy Aneau, *Alector ou le coq. Histoire fabuleuse*, ed. Marie Madeleine Fontaine, 2 vols (Geneva: Droz, 1996); vol. 1, p. xiii; vol. 2, pp. 757 ff.

d'Antangil (1616), by the still unidentified 'I. D. M. G. T'.[4] Both Aneau and this anonymous seventeenth-century imitator provide examples of the way in which More's book gave rise to a genre of literary utopias that was to become established in France from the mid-seventeenth century.[5]

Among all the pathways available for exploring the cultural context of the reception of *Utopia* in France, however, the cluster of its early French translations proves perhaps the most promising. The first thing that one notes is that the number of translations is relatively large (two new translations, two retranslations and one revised version up to 1643). Translators acquired a strong position in France in the course of the sixteenth century,[6] and often occupied high-ranking, or at least highly visible, social positions, close to the King or within the clergy, as is the case of Gabriel Chappuys and Jacques Amyot.[7] For them, translation took its place alongside a number of other intellectual activities, and the works they translated often reflect their own scholarly, literary or political interests. This is true of all the translators of *Utopia* considered here. Their paratexts are less numerous than those of the early Latin editions, but they have a strategic value in advertising the text and in some cases also propose highly independent interpretations of Utopian society. The translators, in other words, aimed at controlling the reader's interpretation, or at least orienting it in particular directions; they thus provide us with an indispensable barometer for measuring the way More's work is successively reinserted into different cultural contexts.

The translation of Jean Le Blond (1502-1553)

The young Jean Le Blond may have had ambitions of becoming a poet – in 1536, he published a volume of poetry and an epithalamium to James V of Scotland and Madeleine of France – but his main impact in the realm of letters is as a translator. He produced versions of the ten books of Valerius Maximus and three neo-Latin works, all of which have political content of one kind or another: More's *Utopia*, a chronicle of the reign of François I by Johann Caron (1553), and the *Livre de police humaine* (1544), which Le Blond based on a shortened version (by Gilles d'Aurigny) of the popular treatise by Francesco Patrizi of Siena. The preface to the 1549 edition of the Patrizi

---

4 See Céard, 'La fortune de l'*Utopie*', p. 61 ff.
5 See Saulnier, 'Mythologies pantagruéliques', p. 139.
6 According to R. Zuber (*Les 'Belles Infidèles' et la formation du goût classique* (Paris: Armand Colin, 1968), ch. 1), translation was considered a genre in its own right during the sixteenth century in France.
7 Chappuys became Henri III's historiographer in 1583 and royal interpreter of foreign tongues to Henri IV in 1596; Amyot was Bishop of Auxerre and Grand Aumônier of France.

translation takes the form of a defence of the French language, claiming not only that it is superior by right of primogeniture, but also that it acquired its excellence well ahead of the languages of Antiquity.[8] Le Blond's hyperbolic defence is one of a number of such promotional texts published during the first half of the sixteenth century; it antedates Joachim Du Bellay's famous *Deffence et Illustration de la langue françoyse* by at most a few months.[9] It only appears in this third edition of the *Livre de police humaine*, but Le Blond puts forward another and more subtle view of the excellence of the French language in one of his prefaces to the translation of *Utopia*.

Le Blond's choice of texts to translate and the content of his prefaces thus show that he considers language, *a fortiori* the promotion of the French language, to be deeply connected with politics. Let us now turn, then, to the paratexts surrounding the translation of *Utopia*, beginning with the title.[10] When one compares it with that of the first Latin editions, it emerges that Le Blond may have used Paris 1517 as his source text. The title ends with a reference to Guillaume Budé's letter, which seems to echo the title of Paris 1517 ('Budaei epistolam'), and part of it consists of a borrowing from the letter itself: the phrase 'the model of a happy life' ('l'exemplaire de vie heureuse') is a quite precise rephrasing of 'beatae vitae exemplar.'[11] In addition, Céard has argued that the notion of a mirror in the title may echo the letter of Jean Desmarez (Paludanus) which was included in the first two editions of *Utopia*.[12] Finally, the hypothesis that Le Blond used an edition prior to 1518 is corroborated by the 'twenty-mile test'.[13]

This is not the whole story, however. Le Blond's translation is presented in an elegantly decorated edition, containing twelve woodcuts in total; all except three head the chapters of the second book.[14] The illustration that introduces the short description of the book preceding Book I represents the dialogue between Raphael Hythloday, Thomas More, Peter Giles and More's servant Clement, and is particularly interesting in that the same scene also features in the two Basel 1518 editions.[15] As these are the only two Latin editions that

---

8 *Le Livre de police humaine, contenant briefve description de plusieurs choses dignes de memoire ...*, trans. Jean Le Blond (Paris: Charles l'Angelier, 1549). This fifteenth-century Francesco Patrizi should not be confused with his sixteenth-century namesake, the author of *La Città felice* (1553). On Le Blond's preface, see Robert E. Hallowell, 'Jean Le Blond's defense of the French language (1549)', *Romanic Review*, 51 (1960), 86–92.
9 The *achevé d'imprimer* is dated 20 February 1548 (i.e. 1549, new style).
10 See Part II, pp. 181–7.
11 Cambridge 1995, p. 16.
12 Céard, 'La fortune de l'*Utopie*', pp. 47–8. Desmarez, who taught in Louvain from 1483 to 1525, contributed both a letter and a poem to these editions.
13 See above, p. 33, n. 11.
14 For a description of the woodcuts, see Part II, p. 184, n. 1. Some are repeated, perhaps to reduce the cost to the printer; there are seven different variants.
15 See above, p. 15.

include the woodcut, it appears that Le Blond or his printer must have seen at least one of them.[16]

Returning to the title, one notes finally that there is a marked shift of focus in relation to the early Latin titles, which advertise the book's political import by putting the form of government first. The order of Le Blond's title, by contrast, evokes its character as a fictional topography: this edition thus contributes to the progressive shift towards the emergence of 'Utopia' as the distinctive name of the work.

The other paratextual items include (in order) a privilege, a complete translation of Guillaume Budé's letter, a short poem and, following the two books of *Utopia*, two notes of a prefatory character and a table of contents. The first of the two notes is addressed by the 'author to the reader'. Here Le Blond speaks as a professional translator, defending his use of paraphrase 'in order to render the author's intentions more intelligible' and arguing in favour of neologism, a practice currently being promoted by the younger generation of French poets generally referred to as the Pléiade. Relative freedom in relation to the source text is common enough in the early modern period,[17] but the specific emphasis on paraphrase here may be significant, since this was the mode adopted by Erasmus and others to make biblical texts (in particular) more perspicuous and accessible.[18]

We now come to the important group of paratexts which promote the connection of Le Blond's translation with Budé, and in particular with the prefatory letter that he wrote for Paris 1517. As we have seen, the connection is already announced by the title and immediately confirmed (after the privilege) by the letter itself, which is absent from all other French editions of *Utopia* in our period. We shall return to this key document in a moment, but we need to point out first that Budé is present in both the poem and the second note to the reader. The poem – which in other respects is a remake of the prefatory Latin poems in praise of Utopia – is built, in fact, upon several borrowings from Budé's letter. In proposing to replace the notion of the 'Elysian Fields' with 'Utopian Fields', described as a 'paradise' governed by 'saintly customs', it

---

16 Céard ('La fortune de l'*Utopie*', p. 49, n. 20) pins it down to the second Basel edition: Le Blond follows that edition's erroneous rendering of a phrasing in Budé's letter. One may note, with Céard, that in Le Blond's translation the figures are clad in toga-like garments, which gives them a more classical appearance (in the Basel woodcuts, they are dressed in contemporary style).

17 Michel Jeanneret (introduction to Paris 1970, p. xv), and Brenda Hosington ('Early French translations of Thomas More's *Utopia*: 1550–1730', *Journal of Neo-Latin Studies*, 33 (1984), 116–34 (118)) both point out that Le Blond's version remains relatively faithful to the original: the use of paraphrase should be distinguished from the kind of freedom in which the translator departs from the sense of the source text or adds material it does not contain.

18 Paraphrase was of course already a feature of ancient rhetorical theory, recommended notably by Quintilian (*Institutio oratoria* VIII.iii.89).

accentuates the immateriality of the island, located outside of time and space, as conveyed by the notion 'Elysian Fields' used by Budé himself.[19]

In the second note to the reader, the status that Le Blond gives to Budé's letter is quite explicit.[20] Rather than presenting his own judgement of the content of the book, which was a standard feature of translators' prefaces of that time,[21] he refers instead to Budé's, assigning to it an authority at least equal to More's own. He also concludes his brief note, at the very end of the book, with a routine but none the less pointed reference to the utility of the work to the 'republic'.[22]

Budé's letter thus becomes the dominant paratext of this edition. All of the early Latin paratexts, when transferred to a new vernacular edition, carry a memory, but in this case the memory is particularly powerful and targeted. In the first place, the letter records in its opening lines the first arrival of *Utopia* in France: Budé eloquently thanks Thomas Lupset for the copy that he has given him. The scene of presenting a gift, a gesture originally designed to promote the book in France, is thus replayed in an entirely new context some thirty years later.[23]

Secondly, the letter preserves not merely a eulogy but also a highly original interpretation of More's work. Here again the memory takes the form of a scene in which Budé records the effect the reading of *Utopia* had upon him. Since for the past two years he has devoted most of his time to looking after his country house, he has brought the book with him to the country. The carrying around of the book in his hand,[24] implying constant reading, has however *almost* made him neglect his domestic duties.[25] In the light of what he has learnt about the customs of Utopia, the seemingly innocent bustling about with practical affairs appears in a negative light as a 'business of constantly accumulating more and more'. The reading of Utopia has in other words had a sort of defamiliarising effect, by which Budé sees his own apparently routine activities in a new light.

This experience of defamiliarisation leads him on to a reflection on the laws governing the society to which he belongs. Famous for his own commentaries on the Roman legal corpus, he shows not only civil and canon law but also natural law to be based not on true equity but on insatiable greed, the

---

19 See Cambridge, 1995, p. 15. For the poem, see Part II, pp. 182–3.
20 See Part II, p. 186–7.
21 B. Hosington, 'Early French Translations', p. 123.
22 It is curious that Le Blond announces the letter as following immediately after the note, whereas it in fact precedes the text of *Utopia* itself; no doubt the decision to change the order was made at the last moment, possibly by the printer.
23 Cambridge 1995, pp. 6–9; Paris 1550, fol. ii v.
24 This idea of the book as a manual (*enchiridion*), something to carry about and learn by heart, is also present in the title of Paris 1517.
25 Cambridge 1995, pp. 8–9 (line 14, 'paene'); Paris 1550, fol. iii r ('quasi j'ay interrompu …').

very antithesis of the 'rule of mutual charity and communal property' that Jesus Christ practised among his disciples. In the second part of the letter this 'rule' of Christ turns out to be uniquely in harmony with the customs of Utopia, supported as they are by three principles: 'equality of good and evil things among the citizens', 'dedication to peace and tranquillity' and 'utter contempt for gold and silver'. This merging of Christian and Utopian values is what enables Budé to put forward Utopia in the last part of the letter as a 'model of the happy life and rule for living well'.

Budé's interpretation echoes Erasmus' emphasis, in his preface to the 1516 New Testament and elsewhere, on the supremacy of the divine law of charity as opposed to the proliferation of human laws, and one might conclude that the opening anecdote is designed to suggest that Utopian society should be a model for action rather than simply a theoretical idea. Furthermore, such a conclusion might seem to be supported by the fact that Budé proposes a fixed location for Utopia, something which the other early paratexts had notably failed to do. However, the location of Utopia somewhere in the region of the Elysian Fields rapidly makes it clear that, far from providing it with a concrete point of reference, Budé wants to assign it to a mythical realm; as we have seen, it is precisely from this mythical dimension of Utopia that Le Blond constructs his poem. It is clear that Budé is eager to furnish himself with an entrance ticket to More's skilful combination of the serious and the playful, and he shows himself to be a confident player of the fictional game. Turning Hythloday into the founder of Utopia, and changing the name of Amaurot to Hagnopolis, he has no hesitation in modifying certain details of the story. As Marie-Madeleine de La Garanderie has argued,[26] the name Hagnopolis confers on Amaurot the status of both an unknown and a holy place; it thus confirms the earlier merging of Christian and Utopian customs and establishes the capital of Utopia as a pure, sanctified city.

This interplay between the ethical ideal and its points of contact with the 'real world' is carried through into the conclusion of Budé's letter, where More's narrative is called 'a seedbed ... of elegant and useful concepts' from which our own age and ages to come 'will be able to borrow practices to be introduced into their own several nations and adapted for use there'.[27] But the ambivalence was there from the outset: Budé knows exactly how to play More's game even while shifting its emphasis. For, as we have seen, the effect of the defamiliarising experience that Budé describes is qualified by the little word 'almost': the practical outcome, the application of the lesson, is as it were

---

26 'Guillaume Budé lecteur de l'*Utopie*', in *Miscellanea Moreana: Essays for Germain Marc'hadour* (Medieval & Renaissance Texts & Studies, Binghamton, New York: 1989), pp. 333–4.
27 Cambridge, 1995, pp. 18–19; Paris 1550, fol. [viii] r.

deferred. The defamiliarising experience of reading *Utopia* thereby acquires a primarily heuristic value, and the anecdote becomes the key to a profoundly serious rereading of More's book.

By appropriating this letter, Le Blond may have wanted, among other things, to promote its evangelical message at the very moment when the non-schismatic French pre-reformers known as 'evangelicals' were on the point of extinction. Their leader and protector at court, Marguerite de Navarre, sister to François I, had died in 1549, and the confessional polarisation brought about by Luther, Calvin and their followers was now moving unstoppably towards schism.

However that may be, one may say that the paratexts of Le Blond's translation advertise a specifically *French* reception of *Utopia* that began as early as 1517, when Budé was given a copy of the book together with an invitation to write a prefatory letter for it. In this French reception story, Budé's Christian moral perspective is an important strand, especially perhaps because he discloses the heuristic value of the book, which depends precisely on its playful aspects. To this must be added the Utopian echoes we looked at earlier, the importance of translation in France in this period, and also the close connection between language and politics. By packaging *Utopia* with the first translation of Budé's letter into the French vernacular, Le Blond was thus making a positive intervention into a whole series of intersecting cultural fields.

Le Blond's translation revisited: Barthélemy Aneau (1505?-1561)

One may wonder why Barthélemy Aneau, who was Rector of the Collège de la Trinité in Lyon as well as a well-known writer and translator, appropriated and reissued Le Blond's translation of *Utopia* only nine years later. He is, however, known to have revised and written prefaces to a considerable number of translations,[28] and it is not unlikely that he was asked to perform the task by the printer Jean Saugrain in Lyon, with whom he had already cooperated before. Perhaps Saugrain saw the potential for market success in publishing another French version of *Utopia*, noticing that Le Blond's translation had attracted an increasing interest in the book.

The title announces that the work has been translated 'nouvellement', a word which could be taken to mean either 'newly' or 'recently'.[29] Since Le Blond's name and almost all his paratexts were removed, one might easily suppose that Aneau was trying to present the translation as his own: Lyon 1559 was in fact considered a translation in its own right as late as the eighteenth

---

28 See Brigitte Biot, 'Barthélemy Aneau, lecteur de l'*Utopie*', in *Moreana*, 121 (1995), 11–28.
29 See M. Jeanneret's introduction to Paris 1970, p. xviii, n. 28.

century.[30] However, Aneau's name does not appear either: the only thing that makes the attribution possible is that the prefatory note is signed 'M. B. A.' It is true that signing by initials is not uncommon in the period, and it is a device that Aneau uses in many of his other works. However, Aneau seems not to have been unduly worried about letting his version appear as a remake of Le Blond's: he left in place his predecessor's motto and, more significantly, his poem. Anyone who knew Paris 1550 would in other words quite easily have recognised this version to be a revision of it; in fact, Brenda Hosington's detailed comparison of selected passages shows that Aneau made relatively few changes to Le Blond's text.

It cannot have been a matter of mere coincidence that Aneau undertook the revision of *Utopia*; judging from his other works, he took a particular interest in More and admired him and his writings.[31] One may also assume that the intellectual milieu of Lyon was an important factor in drawing Aneau's attention to More's *Utopia*. Between 1520 and 1565, Lyon became one of the major commercial and cultural centres of France, known for its many printers, humanists and poets (both neo-Latin and vernacular). It provided an attractive stopping-place on the itinerary of humanist travellers, like Ortensio Lando, the translator of the Italian *Utopia*, who spent several periods in Lyon in the 1530s and 40s.[32] They would have encountered there the particular strand of Ciceronianism that developed in Lyon in this period, which concentrated on the historical figure of Cicero, as conveyed in particular by his correspondence, creating the image of a man invested with Stoic qualities and exposed to the risks of political commitment.[33] Both Lando and Aneau published or translated works on Cicero: Lando's double dialogue *Cicero relegatus* and *Cicero revocatus* was published in Lyon in 1534, and Aneau translated one of Cicero's speeches (1542).[34]

Aneau provides a new explanatory note ('advertissement'), which replaces all of Le Blond's paratexts except his poem and motto.[35] One might think, then, that Budé has completely disappeared from the scene in the new

30 See Paris 1970, p. 119.
31 In his enigmatic play *Lyon marchant*, Aneau evokes More's tragic fate, and in his poem *Juris Prudentia*, More appears as the culminating figure in a series of divinely inspired legislators and as an imitator of Plato and Cicero; see Biot, 'Barthélemy Aneau, lecteur de l'*Utopie*', 14.
32 For Lando, see above, pp. 55–9.
33 See Marie Madeleine Fontaine, 'Quelques traits du cicéronianisme lyonnais: Claude Guilliaud, Florent Wilson, Barthélemy Aneau et Simon de Vallambert', in *Scritture dell'impegno dal rinascimento all'età barocca* (Fasano: Schena, 1994), pp. 35–72.
34 See *ibid.*, also above, pp. 55, 58 n. 47.
35 In addition to the explanatory note, there is also a sort of glossary of the words invented by More, placed at the end of the book. I have been unable to consult a copy that contains this glossary, which is absent from those held by the British Library and the Bibliothèque Nationale de France. It is mentioned, however, by Jeanneret (Paris 1970, pp. xviii–xix), Céard ('La fortune de l'*Utopie*', pp. 51–2) and Biot ('Barthélemy Aneau, lecteur de l'*Utopie*', 21).

edition, but his shadowy figure is still detectable in the background. We have for instance seen that Le Blond's poem builds on textual borrowings from Budé's letter, and in the second part of his note, Aneau alludes to Budé's interpretation of More's work several times. More important still is an implicit reference in the first part of the note, since it shows how the humanist milieu of Lyon has inflected the reading of *Utopia*. In Aneau's perspective, Utopian society is no longer an image of the charity of Christ, but of the perfection of the Stoic sage and the Ciceronian orator.[36] A parallel reading of Budé's letter and Aneau's note shows that the underlying Christian values on which Budé founded Utopian society are here replaced by Stoic ones.

The adjectives used in this passage ('*perfect* sage', '*perfect* orator' and '*most excellent* form of government') reveal another side of More's 'ingenious invention and eloquence' to which Aneau will return with an almost obsessive insistence, namely its imaginary character. Throughout the explanatory note Aneau establishes a close link between the notion of perfection, the idea of a place that does not exist, and Utopia, and in fact uses Budé to authorise the connection between the last two: 'and Master Budé in his magnificent prefatory epistle to the work named it Udepotia, that is, which never existed'.[37] If we go back to Budé's reference to Udepotia, however, we see that this is more a remark in passing ('The island of Utopia, however, which I hear is also called Udepotia ...') than a confirmation of Utopia's status as a place that does not exist. In promoting one of the alternative names of Utopia, Aneau thus insists much more strongly than his predecessors on Utopia's imaginary status. The first conclusion one might draw from this, then, is that, for him, *Utopia* must have been much less a practical model than it was for Budé. Although he preserves the notion of a model ('the model of this Utopian polity'), and although the word 'perhaps' ('and perhaps never will') keeps open a small possibility for it to materialise, the overall impression is that More's *Utopia* represents for Aneau an ideal that real states cannot achieve. This move away from the conception of Utopia as a practical model is particularly clear in the last line of the explanatory note, where perfection is joined to timelessness, making Utopia an archetypal model which can only be imitated by approximation: 'the perfect archetype of a true government, which all others ought to conform themselves to, or at least approach as closely as possible'.[38]

Biot has argued that Aneau, in insisting so strongly on Utopia as a perfect, unobtainable ideal, missed the deeper implication of More's book that Budé

---

36 See Part II, pp. 190–1.
37 *Ibid.*
38 As Céard has shown ('La fortune de l'*Utopie*', p. 53), Aneau describes Plato's *Republic* in more or less the same terms in his *Juris Prudentia* (1554); he thus establishes a clearer parallel between *Utopia* and the classical tradition of ideal states than More himself did.

brought out so nicely by means of his personal anecdote, namely its cathartic effect, its ability to bring about a conversion from the craving for worldly goods.[39] This may well be the case, since neither More nor Budé describes Utopia as a perfect state. Another reading becomes possible, however, if one focuses on Aneau's understanding of the nature of this kind of fiction. In the opening lines of the explanatory note, Aneau draws an analogy between More's 'fictional narration' and the 'mythological fable' of the ancient poets, the function of which is to 'conceal the true philosophy'. Just as those poets used allegorical fictions to represent the truth, More has used the cover of 'a fictional narration of the new Isle of Utopia ... to represent a moral republic and a most perfect form of government'.[40] The deeper moral implications of *Utopia* are thus not conveyed directly, but by means of something akin to allegory. In constructing this analogy, Aneau draws on neo-Platonist elements in order to describe More's book, combining these with the Ciceronian-Stoic strand to which we have already referred.

That *Utopia* in Aneau's view is a 'fable' (a myth) is also corroborated by the adjustment of the title to stress utility. The title is in fact the one element of Le Blond's translation that Aneau modified completely.[41] The focus on 'style' in Le Blond's title is replaced by 'profit', which is presumably the truth hidden in the fable. That this shift of focus from style to utility does not exclude the entertaining aspects of the book becomes evident later in the explanatory note, where the allegorical dimension of More's fiction is further nuanced (as it is in the neo-Platonist theory of allegory) by the theme of pleasure.[42] Profit and pleasure are thus the two faces of the same coin in *Utopia*'s progressive revealing of the truth.

The close connection between fiction and fable is also reflected in the subtitle – 'histoire fabuleuse' – of Aneau's highly inventive chivalric romance *Alector*, published in 1560, shortly after the revision of *Utopia*. There is in fact more than one connection between *Utopia* and *Alector*. Aneau worked on *Alector* while revising Le Blond's translation, and the term 'chorographical fiction' ('fiction chorographique'), which designates the topographical description of a city or a particular place,[43] and which Aneau coins to describe More's

---

39 Biot, 'Barthélemy Aneau, lecteur de l'*Utopie*', 22–3.
40 One may note that Aneau uses here the word 'adombrer', which he also uses to describe the allegorical nature of ancient poetry in the preface ('preparation de voie à la lecture et intelligence des Poëtes fabuleux') to his partial translation of Ovid's *Metamorphoses*, *Trois premiers livres de la Metamorphose d'Ovide, Traduictz en vers François. Le premier et second, par Cl. Marot. Le tiers par B. Aneau* (Lyon: Guillaume Rouille, 1556), fol. a 4 v.
41 See Part II, pp. 188–9.
42 *Ibid.*, pp. 188–93.
43 See Fontaine's note in Aneau, *Alector*, vol. 2, pp. 757–8.

project, also appears in the heading of the twenty-fourth chapter (out of twenty-six) of *Alector*: 'Chorographie de la ville d'Orbe'. This chapter thus displays a highly interesting description of another chorographical fiction, the city of Orbe, which – somewhat belatedly – has come to be regarded as 'the first Utopian city of French literature.[44] As already mentioned, Aneau not only uses elements from More's *Utopia* to describe Orbe but also draws on the tradition of the description of ideal states. As its name indicates, for instance, Orbe is circular in form (by contrast with Amaurot, which has no particular form): this was a common feature of utopias from Plato's description of his ideal city in *Laws* VI to the early modern period.[45] Furthermore, both cities are surrounded by rivers, Anyder and Cloterre respectively, but whereas the function of Anyder is only mentioned in passing, Cloterre supplies a cleaning system for the city's streets, houses and inhabitants. This description is inspired by Vitruvius and Alberti, and Aneau in fact centres his description of Orbe on its architectural aspects, that is to say on an extremely detailed survey of the architecture of four huge buildings situated on a vast square in the middle of the city. Orbe thus conforms much more literally to the term 'chorographical fiction' than does Amaurot.

Aneau's detailed description of the architectural structures of Orbe has been said to represent not only a Utopian city, but also an idealised version of Aneau's own city Lyon,[46] which reveals some interesting similarities between the way More and Aneau respectively construct their fictions. Aneau was at the time involved in several of Lyon's spectacular Entries, of the King and other notables such as archbishops, and was even responsible for one of them.[47] On these occasions the city was decked out in such a way as to virtually become an idealised version of itself, and it is not unlikely that Aneau transferred the experience he acquired of mixing reality and fiction by organising these events to his description of Orbe. In that sense, his detailed 'chorography' of Orbe is a perfect imitation of More's fictional model, in particular its blend of reality and fiction.[48]

44 Biot, 'Barthélemy Aneau, lecteur de l'*Utopie*', 28. The recent upsurge in reseach on Aneau studies dates from Biot's 1992 thesis, published as *Barthélemy Aneau, régent de la Renaissance lyonnaise* (Paris: Champion, 1995), and Fontaine's critical edition of *Alector* (1996).
45 For a detailed account of these predecessors, see Fontaine's note in Aneau, *Alector*, vol. 2, pp. 760–2.
46 See B. Biot, 'Barthélemy Aneau, lecteur de l'*Utopie*', 26–7.
47 The Entry of Archbishop Jacques de Saint-André in 1550. Aneau is also reputed to have participated, as assistant to the poet Maurice Scève, in the Entry of Henry II and his wife Catherine in 1548; see Richard Cooper (ed.), *Maurice Scève: The Entry of Henri II into Lyon. September 1548* (Tempe, Arizona: Medieval & Renaissance Texts & Studies, 1997); also Peter Sharratt, 'The Imaginary City of Bernard Salomon', in Philip Ford and Gillian Jondorf (eds), *Intellectual life in Renaissance Lyon* (Cambridge: Cambridge French Colloquia, 1993), pp. 33–49.
48 One recalls, for example, the parallel between Amaurot and London in the marginal notes of Book II (Cambridge 1995, pp. 116–17).

When it comes to More's 'fictional narration', however, Aneau's imitation of More's Utopian society reveals, again, more differences than similarities. There is here no social hierachy, and interestingly no system of pedagogy; the inhabitants occupy no profession and their only activities take the form of entertainment. Money too, is an important aspect of the life of the city. Finally, Orbe is infested by evil and terror: a huge snake living in one of the main buildings is only kept in check if it is fed one man every third day in expiation of the inhabitants' lack of moral behaviour. This dystopian aspect of Orbe is part of the overall structure of the novel, an indispensable element for the resolution of the plot, namely the liberation of the city by the young hero Alector in the last chapter, and may for this reason be said mainly to serve the demands of a romance fiction. It remains the case that, in the twenty-fourth chapter, romance fiction is replaced by a chorographical fiction which, in joining the topographical description of a particular place to the notion of fiction, elegantly creates an impression of narrative probability ('verisimilitude historiale'). Used to characterise both More's Utopia and his own Orbe, this notion suggests that Aneau not only grasped the novelty and strangeness of More's mixture of fiction and reality – as indeed is demonstrated in the explanatory note ('he sought to represent it ... by means of a new and strange story')[49] – but produced his own highly independent imitation of it.

Gabriel Chappuys (c. 1546–1611): real and imaginary governments

The notion of a chorographical fiction may also prove useful in considering the status accorded to Utopia by the third disseminator of More's text in France in our period. As we have seen, Gabriel Chappuys was closely connected to the centre of power in France in the last decades of the century, and in 1585 he published a work dedicated to Henri III, entitled *L'Estat, description et gouvernement des royaumes et republiques du monde, tant anciennes que modernes*, the twenty-four chapters of which describe different forms of government in Europe, the Middle East and North Africa. In the general preface, Chappuys places his work within the compilatory genre, saying it is based not just on his own research but also on extracts from different contemporary sources. The description of these states, kingdoms and republics is furthermore neither fictitious nor imaginary ('n'est fainte ny imaginaire'),[50] except for the twenty-fourth and last chapter, which he claims to have translated from Thomas More's Latin work. This third French translation of *Utopia*, then, no longer appears as an autonomous text, but is part of a larger work on existing states.

Chappuys translates only Book II, however, of which he also omits the

---

49 Part II, pp. 190–1.
50 Paris 1585, fol. a iii r.

epilogue. As Nathalie Hester has shown,[51] the work of which it forms part does not quite conform to his own description; rather than a compilation, drawn from Chappuys's own research and from contemporary sources, it appears in fact to be largely a disguised translation of the Italian Francesco Sansovino's work *Il governo*.[52] Published several times between 1561 and 1607, Sansovino's work expands over the years from eighteen books to twenty-two, but *Utopia* always keeps its place at the very end of the work, that is to say in a position likely to catch the eye of the reader. *Utopia* occupies this same focalised position in both editions of Chappuys's version (Paris 1585 and 1598). However, in a third French edition (1611), translated not by Chappuys but by 'F. N. D.' (the initials have not to my knowledge been identified), *Utopia* is relegated to a non-focalised position as the twenty-second of a modified set of twenty-four chapters. It remains the case that the dissemination of Sansovino's work in Italy and France must have been a major vehicle for making *Utopia* known to a larger public at the turning point of the century.

According to Hester's study of the relation between Sansovino's and Chappuys's work, nine of Chappuys's chapters are more or less direct, literal translations of *Il governo*, another nine chapters are a combination of extracts from Sansovino and other sources, four have identical titles but with a different content, whereas two chapters are entirely absent from Sansovino's work. This is in sharp contrast to what Chappuys says himself in his general preface. If he is prepared to admit having been inspired by certain authors, he says, this is only to forestall the criticism of those critics who judge his work to be a 'translation, hotch-potch or rhapsody', rather than something akin to an 'invention'.[53] But even if one might concede that Chappuys perhaps made an indirect concession to Sansovino in saying that certain of his sources are Italian ('je me suis aydé de plusieurs Autheurs de renom, et sçavoir François, Latins, et Italiens'), it is hard to avoid the conclusion that, in disclosing his minor sources and hardly mentioning his major source,[54] he commits in this work a form of literary piracy.[55]

As we have seen, Chappuys claims to have translated More's text from the Latin. But since he, like Sansovino, leaves out not only the first book but also

---

51 'Stolen texts? Gabriel Chappuys' *L'estat, description et gouvernement des royaumes et républiques du monde*', in P. Cherchi (ed.), *Sondaggi sulla riscrittura del cinquecento* (Ravenna: Longo, 1998), pp. 133–48.
52 On which, see above, pp. 59–63.
53 'Ce que je dy, pour clorre la bouche à une infinité de Contrerooleurs, qui appelleront plustost cecy traduction, ramas ou rapsodie, qu'invention ou autrement' (Paris 1585, fol. a iii v).
54 According to Hester ('Stolen texts?', p. 141), Chappuys mentions Sansovino only three times.
55 But see also Kirsti Sellevold, 'Some "hardis repreneurs" in sixteenth-century France: Du Bellay, Aneau, Chappuys', in Hall Bjørnstad (ed.), *Borrowed Feathers: Plagiarism and the Limits of Imitation in Early Modern Europe* (Oslo: Unipub, 2008), pp. 53–65.

the epilogue of the second, it is more likely that his source text in this case too was the Italian translation, which, as Sansovino states in his preface, was a modified version of Lando's.[56] One of the strategies that Chappuys uses to disguise his dependence on Sansovino is to change the order of Sansovino's short biographical note on More that prefaces the chapter consisting of the second book of *Utopia*. Whereas Sansovino introduces the reader to More first as a martyr and only secondly as the author of *Utopia*, Chappuys reverses this order, adopting the sequence in which the two events happened, as if the writing of *Utopia* had some influence on the later tragic fate of its author.[57]

It will be evident that, whatever the order of the biographical note, Chappuys preserves its apologetic function: as in the Italian version, More is advertised as a paragon of the saintly life and as the martyred victim of a wicked king. This emphasis is corroborated by a passage in Chappuys's general dedication of the volume to Henri III where the translator exhorts the King to protect the true faith as his predecessors have done and uproot any new heresies that may have been introduced; Henri's own devotional behaviour is also praised.[58] In that light, the biographical preface may be read as a disguised warning, since it shows another King Henry in a highly unflattering light: despite his reputation for extravagant demonstrations of piety, Henri III was, in 1585, far from being a militant Counter-Reformation monarch, and his legitimate heir was the Protestant Henri of Navarre. Chappuys is using More as a front for a position of no compromise, a position identifiable with the extremist 'Ligue' party in the closing years of Henri III's reign.[59]

We need now to consider the question of what happens to the status of *Utopia* when inserted into a work on existing states. Céard is surprised to find *Utopia* in Chappuys's work, especially as he claims to be a historian, not a legislator, but this set aside, Chappuys's stripped version of *Utopia* may, in Céard's view, be considered as a sort of theoretical programme for practical governance.[60] As we have seen, however, it is not Chappuys but Sansovino who had the idea of inserting *Utopia* into a work on real states. That does not of course exclude the possibility that Chappuys concurred with some enthusiasm in Sansovino's project. But what was that project? Was it simply to propose a series of exercises in political practice? In his dedicatory epistle to Henri III, Chappuys says that his somewhat ridiculous attempt to describe kingdoms the King knows so well (France and Poland) might be repaired by

---

56 See above, pp. 59–60.
57 Compare Part II, pp. 176–9 with pp. 194–7.
58 Paris 1585, fols [a v] v–[a vi] r.
59 Like certain other vernacular versions of *Utopia*, this one reduces the plurality of religions described in the last chapter of the work to one.
60 Céard, 'La fortune de l'*Utopie*', pp. 54–5. Neither Hosington nor Céard seems to be aware of the fact that Chappuys's work translates large parts of Sansovino's.

the pleasure of 'the reading of something that will perhaps seem new to him in the description of the other empires and states that follows his own'.[61] The customs of Fez and Tunisia might well seem as new, remote and foreign as those of Utopia. In other words, the imaginary state, juxtaposed with other 'existing' ones, becomes modified in the light of the others and vice versa: this is explicitly signalled in the short prefatory note to *Utopia*.[62] In that sense, the volume presents a series of new and unfamiliar forms of government that opens up multiple possibilities and that challenges, as indeed Thomas More did,[63] the borderline between fiction and reality. Aneau's description of *Utopia* and his own Orbe, as chorographic fictions, may thus serve as emblematic for the status that *Utopia* acquires when it becomes part of Sansovino's work and its French offshoots.

There is other evidence that Chappuys was genuinely interested in *Utopia* and the generic problems it posed. A few years earlier, in 1578, Chappuys had translated a work similar to that of Sansovino, except that this was not about states of this world but celestial worlds, namely Doni's *I mondi celesti*. This makes the connection to *Utopia* explicit, since Doni edited, printed and wrote the preface to its Italian translation, and *I mondi* contains its own Utopia, *Il mondo savio e pazzo*.[64] Through Chappuys's translation of *I mondi*, Doni comes back into the picture, revealing that Chappuys was not just fascinated by the political aspects of *Utopia* but also by its imaginary and hence fictional content. As he says in the preface to his translation: 'new regions, new worlds are described [here] by means of new abstractions and pleasing fantasies.'[65] Through his description of Doni's coupling of politics and fiction, so germane to More's project, we see the ramifications of cross-cultural contextual references that go well beyond the borders of countries.

61 'la lecture de quelque chose, qui luy semblera paravanture nouvelle, en la description des autres Empires et Estats, qui suivent les siens' (Paris 1585, fol. aii r).
62 See Part II, pp. 178–9 and 194–7; Chappuys translates the relevant sentence from Sansovino's preface quite literally. One might note that, in a text first published three years after the appearance of Chappuys's compilation, Montaigne – like Machiavelli before him (see above, p. 62) – speaks contemptuously of imaginary republics: 'And certainly all those contrived, fictional descriptions of polities prove to be ridiculous and ill-suited to be put into practice' ('Et certes toutes ces descriptions de police, feintes par art, se trouvent ridicules et ineptes à mettre en practique'; Michel de Montaigne, *Les Essais*, ed. P. Villey and V.-L. Saulnier (Paris: PUF, 1965), p. 957).
63 In for instance More's letter to Giles: 'Truth in fact is the only thing at which I should aim and do aim in writing this book' (Cambridge, 1995, p. 31).
64 See above, pp. 53–4. This Utopia takes the form of a dream which, to Savio (who dreams it and then describes it to Pazzo), seems true; cf. the claims made for the truth of the Utopia story by More and others in the Latin paratexts.
65 'nouvelles regions, nouveaux mondes ... sont descrits par nouvelles abstractions et plaisantes fantasies' (*Les Mondes, celestes, terrestres et infernaux. Le Monde petit, Grand, Imaginé, Meslé, Risible, des Sages et Fols, et le Tresgrand ... Tirez des œuvres de Doni Florentin*, trans. Gabriel Chappuys (Lyon: Barthelemy Honorati, 1578), fol. *3 r–v).

We need finally to take a closer look at Paris 1611. Although it is of course a variant of the Sansovino-Chappuys story, it belongs to a different political moment, the year after the assassination of the relatively moderate Henri IV. Without conducting a detailed comparison between Chappuys's and F. N. D.'s translation, it is impossible to state with certainty whether the latter was aware of his predecessor's version, but it is clearly a new translation. For example, unlike Chappuys, F. N. D. follows the order of the original preface to the book containing *Utopia*. Furthermore, Sansovino is mentioned on the title-page as the author of the work, while there are no references whatsoever to Chappuys; his long general preface is replaced by a dedicatory epistle to François de Montagu, a nobleman in the most intimate circle of the King. Paris 1611 does, it is true, contain the same number of chapters as Chappuys's version, but the two states in Chappuys that are not in Sansovino – Scotland and the 'republic of the Hebrews' respectively – are replaced in 1611 by Egypt and Ethiopia (a letter from the Emperor of Ethiopia to the Pope is annexed after this chapter, which is the last in the volume). The Utopia chapter precedes those two chapters. It seems most likely that F. N. D. used one of Sansovino's early editions, as he does not include an addition to be found in the biographical preface in Venice 1583. Understandably, F. N. D. omits Sansovino's justification for making *Utopia* the last chapter of his book, a passage which is of course retained by Chappuys.[66]

Paris 1611 is interesting in our perspective above all because it makes *Utopia* available to readers on the threshold of the reign of Louis XIII. This is a period when the centralisation of France and the rise of the doctrine of absolutism leave less space for speculation about modes of government. Those circumstances may not explain why *Utopia* no longer appears in a focalised position in this edition, but they may well constitute one of the reasons why the next French translation of *Utopia* was published in Amsterdam and no new edition or translation was to appear in France until 1713.

The translation of Samuel Sorbière (1615–1670)

Amsterdam 1643 was printed by Jean Blaeu, whose father had published its Latin predecessor Amsterdam 1629, and the two books are remarkably similar in appearance: both are pocket-size books with simple titles focusing on the name *Utopia*. The title-page of the vernacular edition, however, makes more effort to attract the reader. The title itself appears on a curtain attached to a frame at the top and reaching halfway down the pag (see below, p. 143). Underneath, as in a scene from a play, three figures sit at a table in a

---

[66] We may also note that F. N. D.'s general preface emphasises above all the value of history and that he removes the references to fiction in the preface to *Utopia* itself.

garden; on the table, there is a map, half unrolled, and a pair of compasses. The figure facing out of the picture is not difficult to identify as Hythloday, telling his story to More and Giles. The scene is clearly a remake in seventeenth-century terms of the woodcut image that appeared in the early Latin editions. The map that had also appeared in those editions is now available only to the figures in the picture, but it and the compasses suggest that they are not merely learned humanists: they take the arts of travel and exploration seriously, as readers from the trading and sea-faring culture of the United Provinces might expect.

Like his Utopian predecessors, the translator Samuel Sorbière earned his living from various intellectual activities – as, among other things, a teacher, doctor, historiographer and author of a sceptical treatise – but in contrast to them, he spent most of his adult life struggling to secure himself financially.[67] These problems could have been avoided if he had accepted the parish offered to him in 1639 by his uncle, Samuel Petit, Principal of the Collège de Nîmes and a well-known Protestant priest. Instead he made his way to Paris. There he became acquainted with the *libertin* circle and befriended, among others, Grotius and Gassendi. His readings in philosophy, theology and science appear to have led him to question the religion into which he had been born: accused by the Protestant Church of making heretical statements, he lost the preceptorship which he had occupied at the time and in 1642 decided to move to the Hague in the northern Netherlands.[68] It was there that he translated *Utopia*, having meanwhile secured himself a new position as tutor to the children of Frederik Magnus, Count ('Rhinegrave') of Salm.

The translation contains one item from the original paratexts, More's first letter to Giles, although Sorbière certainly knew others, since he mentions 'the homage paid to [*Utopia*] by Erasmus, Budé and all men of learning': the prefatory epistles of More, Erasmus and Budé appear in that order at the beginning of Amsterdam 1629, which could well have been the edition on which Sorbière based his translation. He supplies one new paratext of his own that provides useful evidence of the context within which he conceived his version of *Utopia*. This is a preface dedicated to his new patron Count Frederik, who, as we see from the heading, was not only a serving officer of high rank but also governor of Sluis. Some five years later, Magnus was to be appointed governor of Maastricht, a position he held until his death in 1673. Through his grandmother and aunt, he was closely connected to the house of Orange, in whose service he spent his entire career, and in 1635 he had married

---

67 For details of Sorbière's life and career, see René Pintard, *Le Libertinage érudit dans la première moitié du XVIIe siècle*, 2 vols (Paris: Boivin, 1943), pp. 334–46, 383, 418–20, 425–7, 552–8.
68 See Pintard, *Le Libertinage érudit*, pp. 338–9.

Marguerite Tissart, a niece of Cardinal Richelieu.[69]

Not only was Frederik Magnus connected to leading French families, he also moved in a French-speaking milieu: French was the primary language of the ruling house of Orange and was also widely used in élite diplomatic, political and cultural circles.[70] This explains why Sorbière was able to publish a French translation of *Utopia* in Amsterdam and dedicate it to a leading political and military figure in the newly emerging United Provinces. As chapters 1 and 6 in this volume show,[71] there was considerable interest in *Utopia* in the United Provinces, marked by a cluster of editions in Latin and in Dutch translation; Sorbière's French rendering – published as we have seen by the son of the printer of Amsterdam 1629 – provides unambiguous evidence that this interest penetrated to the highest ruling classes.[72]

Frederik Magnus may clearly be regarded as one of the group of politically prominent men, immersed in the day-to-day business of administration, to whom translations of *Utopia* were dedicated – the Mayor of Basel (Basel 1524), William Cecil (London 1551), Henri III of France (Paris 1585), or for that matter Medinilla, whose version (Córdoba 1637) was designed to publicise and exemplify his own political achievements as governor. Seen from this angle, Sorbière's preface seems thus to be in line with those of earlier translators who offered their translations as in some sense a manual for practical government. But as we have seen, even in the versions of Sansovino and Chappuys, who bring Utopia close to the real world by integrating it in a compilation on existing states, the equivocation between the real and the imaginary does not disappear entirely. Like Aneau, for instance, Sorbière attributes to Utopia the status of a fable.[73] But whereas Aneau inscribes the fable explicitly into the classical tradition, making its pleasing and entertaining aspects a (secondary) means of delivering the 'useful', that is to say moral truth, it has a more independent status in Sorbière's account. The focus is markedly on its entertaining aspects in that More seems, says Sorbière, by so ingeniously blending the useful and the agreeable, to have written his book 'solely to entertain those who read [it]'. If the readers happen to acquire a purified judgement, imbued with good sense along with it, this is an unexpected advantage of which they are completely unaware. As is clear from his reference to 'those pens that we see

---

69 See *Nieuw nederlandsch biografisch woordenboek* (Leiden: A. W. Sijthoff, 1911–27), vol. 2, col. 1258.
70 See Maria A. Schenkeveld, *Dutch Literature in the Age of Rembrandt: Themes and Ideas* (Amsterdam/Philadelphia: John Benjamins Publishing Company, 1991), p. 139.
71 See above, p. 19 and below, pp. 108–9.
72 Another constituency of French-speaking readers who might well have added to Jean Blaeu's sales figures for this book were Huguenot exiles from France; Sorbière himself came from a similar background.
73 See Part II, pp. 198–201.

nowadays so well-sharpened in the use of our language' (my italics), Sorbière is here drawing on the French literary culture of the mid-seventeenth century, where any overt display of learning or didacticism is scorned and the most serious reflections must be disguised in an engaging, unpretentious form and in the language of polite society. Presented thus, Sorbière's preface has a character very different from that of the seventeenth-century editions of the Dutch translation, which, in keeping with its strikingly Calvinist tone, contains only a brief mention of the fable and its qualities, insisting much less on its agreeable than on its useful aspects.[74]

The phrasing of this part of the preface also seems at times to echo that of the preface to *Utopia* in Sansovino's *Il Governo*, which Sorbière might well have been familiar with in one of its French versions, given his interest in forms of government. For example, when he says that 'Plato ... did not treat this subject with such clarity' ('avec tant de netteté'), he seems almost to be translating Sansovino's 'it appears to be much more thoroughly worked out [*risoluta*] than Plato's'.[75]

Since Sorbière proposes no independent interpretation of *Utopia*, one might assume that the translation was executed primarily in order to assure the continued protection (financial and otherwise) of Frederik Magnus: according to the preface, Magnus had already been providing work for Sorbière for some time. In this he may have been successful, since he married and stayed in Holland until 1650. However, the translation also marks the beginning of an intellectual career devoted to politics, and more precisely to the study of the political ideas of Thomas Hobbes: Sorbière's reputation today is in fact rather that of the main disseminator of Hobbes's ideas in France than of a thinker in his own right.[76] He agreed to edit Hobbes's *De cive*, publishing it in the Dutch Republic in 1647 and 1648, together with a translation of the same work in 1649, and he also translated the *De corpore politico* in 1652. This translation helped his own political ideas to mature and in 1653 he published his *Discours sceptiques*, which combines sceptical and Machiavellian ideas.

This account, however, leaves out several important pieces of the picture. When Sorbière became acquainted with Hobbes's political doctrine in Paris in 1642, the year before his translation of *Utopia* was published, his first response was not assent but refutation.[77] This is entirely compatible with his interest in *Utopia*, which of course represents a kind of political imagination

---

74 See below, p. 107.
75 See Part II, pp. 178–9, 198–9; compare also Sorbière's 'the pleasures that the imagination receives from the beauty of fictions' with similar phrases in the later part of Sansovino's preface (including the addition of 1583).
76 Sorbière's treatise *Discours sceptiques* has, however, recently appeared in a new edition by Sophie Gouverneur (Paris: Champion, 2002).
77 See Pintard, *Le Libertinage érudit*, pp. 552–3.

very different from that associated with Hobbes. It seems that the translation represents an early stage in Sorbière's political thought, before he became converted to the Hobbesian perspective.

We may now return to the immediate context of the translation. It seems probable that two principal factors came together here, Sorbière's emerging interest in political philosophy and his choice of a dedicatee and patron who occupied a prominent position as a highly-placed governor connected to the house of Orange. In addition, the Blaeu family of printers must have played a role in encouraging, or at least willingly accepting, the publication of a French translation of a work which had already attracted considerable attention in the United Provinces. Such a convergence of determining factors is unlikely to be accidental. As the chapter in this volume on the Dutch translation argues, the evidence suggests that More's work was used as a point of reference for a newly formed state that was still seeking an identity, politically and culturally. It is important to emphasise here the relative unimportance of religious disputes in this context. More and his work could, as the history of its transmission shows, be recognised as a model by both Catholics and Protestants, and in the culture of the United Provinces, where different religious factions lived in relative harmony, *Utopia* had the considerable advantage of offering a political model that was not dependent on a specific Christian theology.

A salient feature of Sorbière's preface is consistent with this reading. In order to glorify Magnus, Sorbière relates not only the count's recent deeds: he also anticipates a glorious *future* for him and his two sons. As we have seen, Magnus would indeed continue to play an important role in the development of the Dutch state. In this light, Sorbière's translation may indeed be seen as a successor to the cluster of re-editions of the Latin text and of the Dutch translation some ten years earlier, proposing a model for the formation of one of the most important and powerful polities of the early modern period.

The distance between Le Blond's version and Sorbière's is considerable. Whereas Le Blond had used Budé's letter to recall the early transfer of *Utopia* into a French context, Sorbière's translation marks a shift into an alternative, cosmopolitan Francophone world that will reach its peak in the eighteenth century. The French adaptations of Sansovino already anticipate that wider vision, both in their content and in their mode of textual transfer. What looks at first like a marginal, offshore translation of More's work may thus be read as a further realisation, in a new historical and cultural context, of the profoundly cosmopolitan character it had displayed from the outset.

Kirsti Sellevold

5 THE ENGLISH TRANSLATION: THINKING ABOUT THE COMMONWEALTH

Thomas More's *Utopia* makes a modest entrance in 1551 into the world of English letters. It is a small, inexpensively produced book in black-letter type, without illustrations or elaborate paratextual materials, and the translator is an obscure, poorly paid clerk with no other visible pretensions as a writer. Yet Ralph Robinson's version was to hold its place as a landmark in the English reception of More's work. It was reissued four times in the period covered by this volume; no rival translation was produced until Gilbert Burnet's version appeared in 1684; and, despite some unflattering comments on its qualities as a translation, it has remained in circulation in the last hundred years or so, thanks to editions from Joseph Lupton's bilingual version of 1895 to the Everyman and World's Classics editions currently in print.[1]

Robinson translates both books of *Utopia*, preceded by More's letter to Peter Giles in all printings except 1639. The 1556, 1597 and 1624 editions add translations of a handful of other Latin paratexts. No map of Utopia is provided, and the Utopian alphabet, although promised by the printer in a note at the end of the 1556 edition, never materialises.

In the earlier printings, the title broadly follows the order of the original in giving priority to the political theme. In 1624 and 1639, however, the book announces itself as *Sir Thomas More's Utopia* and *The Common Wealth of Utopia* respectively, with '... *the best state of a Publike Weale*' relegated to secondary status. Following a trend which is also apparent in the Latin editions and some of the other vernacular versions, the name 'Utopia' is asserting its priority in England: More's fictional conceit is thus establishing itself as one of a class, if not yet as a genre.

Robinson adds only one new prefatory text in the first edition, a dedicatory epistle to William Cecil, who was at that time, as the header tells us, one of the principal secretaries to the young King Edward VI. This letter is replaced in the 1556 edition, the only other published during Robinson's lifetime, by a preface from 'the translator to the gentle reader' explaining at greater length the circumstances of his decision to translate the work and subsequently have it printed. The title now advertises his status as 'sometime fellowe of Corpus Christi College in Oxford' and makes the claim, commonplace in reprints,

---

[1] See Oxford 1895, London 1992 (based on the 1551 printing of Robinson's translation) and Oxford 1999 (based on the 1556 printing of Robinson's translation).

that the work has been 'newlie perused and corrected'. The 1597 printing, while preserving the 1556 set of translated materials, omits the translator's preface; it has no new paratexts and thus provides little evidence of the context or motivation of the reprint. In the 1624 and 1639 editions, the printer Bernard Alsop adds a brief but hyperbolically encomiastic dedicatory epistle to Cresacre More, the great-grandson of Thomas More, who had between 1615 and 1620 written what Trevor-Roper calls 'the last of the tributary biographies issued from the devoted family circle'.[2]

What can this fragmentary record of the emergence and insistent return of Robinson's translation tell us about the transmission and reception of *Utopia* in early modern England? The first thing one notices is that a single translation establishes itself for nearly a century, and that it seems to have been well enough known after Robinson's death for other printers to take it up again and reprint it despite considerable lapses of time. This is the more striking in that its apparent success has nothing to do with the fame of the writer, who as far as we know published no other work and who lived out his life far from the public eye. The other self-evident feature of the print history is that Robinson's translation travels, apparently without difficulty, between quite different political and cultural moments, but that it is differently packaged each time it appears. Let us now return to the two editions printed during Robinson's lifetime and examine the story he tells us about how and why he undertook the translation.

The translator and his friends

Like many other clever boys of slender means, Ralph Robinson had acquired a solid education at grammar school and then proceeded in 1536, just before his sixteenth birthday, to Corpus Christi College, Oxford, where he took his bachelor's degree in October 1540.[3] Corpus was then a new college, founded in 1516 by Richard Foxe to provide an education along humanist lines. This provides us with a first link to the *Utopia* translation: Foxe was a close friend of Erasmus and More, and – as we shall see shortly – a dedicatory letter to him from Erasmus features prominently in the paratextual materials of Florence 1519. It seems certain that the works of Erasmus and More were studied at Corpus as models of humanist Latin composition, although one should bear

---

2 Hugh Trevor-Roper, 'The image of Thomas More in England 1535–1635', in *La fortuna dell'Utopia di Thomas More nel dibattito politico europeo del '500* (Florence: Olschki, 1996), pp. 5–23 (p. 15).
3 For these and other details of his biography, I have consulted John Bennell, 'Robinson, Ralph (1520–1577)', in *Oxford Dictionary of National Biography*, Oxford University Press, www.oxforddnb.com/view/article/23863 (accessed 27.08.05). See also Oxford 1895, pp. lxxi-vi.

in mind that More's fall and execution had taken place in the years immediately preceding Robinson's arrival there, so that a first potential clash arises here between the model humanist and his exemplary disgrace.

Robinson must have displayed a more than average academic talent, since he was elected to a probationary fellowship in 1542. Two years later, however, he left Oxford for London, where he became an apprentice goldsmith, then a member of the Goldsmiths' Company in 1546. By the time his translation of *Utopia* was first published, he was about thirty years old and was working as a clerk of the Company in the Tower mint, an insecure and ill-remunerated job. The 1551 and 1556 prefaces show that he belonged to a circle of literate friends who, like himself, were members of guilds and thus full citizens, as the 1551 title emphasises. Robinson refers to one of these, a haberdasher called George Tadlowe, as the prime mover in the project of translating *Utopia*. Although Tadlowe was, in Robinson's words, 'wittie, and also skilful', he lacked his friend's humanist education and had little or no Latin.[4] It was apparently for that reason that, together with other unnamed friends, Tadlowe encouraged the former Fellow of Corpus Christi to translate More's work for him and then subsequently to have it printed.

Robinson's story of how he came to translate *Utopia* is not likely to have been simply invented. In the first place, he chooses to name Tadlowe not only in the preface but also on the title-page of the first edition: ambitious authors might thank their friends, but the names they advertise in the title are usually well-known or impressive ones that will bring them credit and credibility. Similarly, since the circle of friends he refers to is far from being an illustrious group of scholars or noble figures, one must assume that there were such friends, and furthermore that they must have discussed *Utopia* among themselves before the project of translation was conceived. One may conjecture that Robinson was the most scholarly member of the group, and that he described More's work so enthusiastically to Tadlowe and the others that they wanted to read it for themselves.

The first conclusion we can draw from this paratextual evidence, then, is that, in London in the reign of Edward VI, *Utopia* was being actively read and discussed by people of modest means and education who then had the idea of disseminating it more widely for people like themselves whose Latin was not up to the task of reading the original.[5]

Now, when Robinson says that he only wrote the work for a private circle

---

4 See Part II, pp. 208, 210.
5 Although no Latin edition was printed in England until 1666, copies of the early editions, and perhaps also the 1548 Louvain edition, were no doubt held in private and academic libraries. We do not know which edition Robinson used for his translation, but the 1516 and 1517 editions are ruled out by the 'twenty-mile' test (see above, p. 33, n. 11).

of friends, that it was done rapidly, that it makes no pretensions to polish or eloquence, and that he never intended to publish it, he is using a commonplace not unlike those that Erasmus deploys in the *Praise of Folly*; indeed, More himself uses a similar tactic in his prefatory letter to Peter Giles.[6] Such protestations often accompany texts that in some way challenge prevailing opinion, and the fact that Robinson is only the translator here, not the author, makes little difference, especially as the controversial character of the original work had by this time been far outstripped by its author's final challenge to royal orthodoxy.

That Robinson meant to insert himself into the lineage of Erasmus and More – even if his claims to humility are a good deal more plausible than theirs – is corroborated by his opening move in the 1551 preface. He cites an anecdote from Lucian which is in fact a variant of the topos of the modest author. Lucian was of course one of the favourite authors of Erasmus and More and a model for their use of entertaining fictions as a vehicle for controversial themes. As another contributor to this volume reminds us,[7] they had collaborated in translating a selection of Lucian's works into Latin, first printed in 1506, with a preface by Erasmus addressed to Richard Foxe, none other than the future founder of Corpus Christi. In the 1519 Florence edition, *Utopia* is reprinted after the Lucian translations; the letter to Foxe is reproduced here too, and its place at the beginning of the volume gives it the status of an additional paratext to *Utopia* itself. This configuration of texts and humanist interests provides a crucial piece of evidence in the pre-history of Robinson's translation.

Neither Erasmus nor More chose to translate Lucian's *How to Write History*, from which this anecdote is derived, but both were undoubtedly familiar with it. The story itself runs as follows: seeing that his fellow-countrymen the Corinthians are busy preparing for battle as the armies of Philip of Macedonia approach, Diogenes takes the barrel he lives in and begins to toss it energetically around. When asked why he is doing this, he says that, seeing everyone else so busy on matters of national importance and having nothing to contribute, he is trying at least to imitate their activity. Lucian uses this as a mock apology for not writing a history of his own,[8] and the device is borrowed by a number of early sixteenth-century humanists, particularly in France.[9] The most flamboyant instance is indisputably the prologue to Rabelais's *Third Book*, first printed in 1546, and it is not impossible that Robinson

---

6 Cambridge 1995, pp. 31–3.
7 See above, p. 16.
8 Lucian, *How to Write History*, 3–4.
9 Guillaume Budé provides a version in the dedicatory epistle of his *Annotationes in Pandectas* (1508).

had read Rabelais's comic fictions: Rabelais situates some of the narrative action in Utopia, and certain key episodes are clearly indebted to More's example. Whether Robinson borrowed the Lucian anecdote from Rabelais or from a common source, the parallel is equally illuminating. The translator is fully cognisant of the humanist mode of *serio ludere* in which he is writing. Furthermore, it is not only a mode of writing he gestures towards, but also a mode of action: the action of someone who stands in the margin, seeing that the public world is so preoccupied with the immediate business of state that it fails to tackle the really important issues.[10] No issue was more important during the minority of Edward VI than bringing into being the best possible commonwealth. Robinson, Tadlowe and their friends were obviously not in a position to do anything concrete about this: all they could do was roll the fictional barrel they had inherited from More. But Robinson knew one person who might make a difference, and indeed did in the end make a difference beyond any expectations that anyone could have had at the time. This was William Cecil, the dedicatee of the 1551 edition, and we need now to turn our attention to this important figure, and to another conjectural story of how the English translation of *Utopia* came into being.

The translator and his patron

The object of a grammar school and university education, for someone of Robinson's social standing, was not to turn him into a scholar but to equip him to make his way in the world: others of similar background – like Thomas Cromwell, Henry VIII's right-hand man at the time of the Anglican schism – had in their lifetime risen to positions of extraordinary power. Robinson was clearly not an achiever on that scale. All he could do was use his acquired skills and his schoolday contacts to keep himself and his family afloat. In 1551, his job at the mint was apparently not secure, and he needed support from high places. At the grammar schools of Grantham and Stamford, he had become acquainted with William Cecil, the son of a flourishing and well-connected landowner who had acquired the lordship of Burghley through marriage and was to build on the foundations laid by Cromwell.[11] Cecil had in the two

---

10 David Weil Baker points out that Robinson changes the balance of the topos in that the 'busyness' observed by the narrator includes the writings of learned men whose new 'inventions and devices' for the furtherance of the commwealth's affairs are viewed in a positive light (*Divulging Utopia: Radical Humanism in Sixteenth-Century England* (Amherst: University of Massachusetts Press, 1999), pp. 117 ff.); by reducing the satirical point of the anecdote, however, this shift if anything strengthens the political implications of the topos as used by Robinson.

11 See Michael A. R. Graves, *Burghley: William Cecil, Lord Burghley* (London and New York: Longman, 1998), p. 214: 'Burghley must take full credit for his prominent role in the preservation of the national state and church created by Thomas Cromwell.' On Burghley's

previous years risen rapidly and was now one of the secretaries of Seymour, the protector of the young Edward VI. Robinson refers to him as his 'Master', and Lupton (followed by King) asserts that he was a clerk in Cecil's service, although the reference may simply indicate that, since he worked in the royal mint, Robinson was also a servant of the royal secretary.[12]

At all events, in May 1551, Robinson wrote to Cecil asking for his help: his family was poor, he had to support his two brothers, and he was in debt. The dedication of his translation to Cecil was undoubtedly part of the same strategy of using this valuable contact to secure his position. The concluding passage of the prefatory letter makes it clear that, although the two men had not met for some time (perhaps not since their school years), Cecil had helped Robinson materially, both 'in the time of our olde acquayntance, and also now lately again'. Robinson would hardly have said this if his earlier letter asking for help had gone unanswered, despite the fact that no record of a reply has survived.

The critical point in this minor drama, however, is not Robinson's financial fortunes but the transaction itself: the connection between this particular gift and this recipient. One does not offer an already famous book about the government of the commonwealth to a highly-placed official without some sense of what one is doing, especially when the author's name is anathema to the regime. Why *Utopia* rather than, say, Cicero's *De officiis*, which is said to have been one of Cecil's favourite books?[13] The choice must have been quite deliberate, and it is reasonable to infer not only that Robinson himself and his friends admired *Utopia*, but also that he believed that Cecil admired it too. It is known that, at least from his Cambridge years, Cecil had taken a particular interest in classical writings on citizenship and governance:[14] he seems consciously to have prepared himself for a career in which he was in fact to help shape the key institutions of the emerging English state, and although most of this career was still in the future when Robinson offered Cecil his English *Utopia*, one may assume that he was aware of Cecil's interests.

There is further evidence to support these conjectures. Cecil was already, at the age of thirty, using his patronage to support writers.[15] He was also closely acquainted with Sir Thomas Chaloner, whose English translation of

---

education and career, see also Wallace T. MacCaffrey, 'Cecil, William, first Baron Burghley (1520/21–1598)', *Oxford Dictionary of National Biography*, Oxford University Press, www.oxforddnb.com/view/article/4983 (accessed 06.11.05).

12 See Oxford 1895, p. lxxii; John N. King, *English Reformation Literature: The Tudor Origins of the Protestant Tradition* (Princeton, NJ: Princeton University Press, 1982), p. 111.
13 See Graves, *Burghley*, p. 210.
14 See MacCaffrey, 'Cecil', section entitled 'Education and early life'. Like Robinson, Cecil also attended a humanist college, St John's College, Cambridge.
15 On Cecil's patronage, see King, *English Reformation Literature*, pp. 108–11.

The Praise of Folly had appeared in 1549,[16] and it seems entirely natural that Cecil should give protection to the translator of *Utopia*, since the two works were widely perceived to belong to the same category. But in this case protection was perhaps precisely what was needed, in addition to modest financial support. More's fatal attempts to resist schism were still fresh in everyone's memory in 1551, and Robinson is careful to cover himself against potential condemnation even while praising More's 'excellent qualities' and appealing to his international reputation:

> it is much to be lamented of al, and not only of us English men, that a man of so incomparable witte, of so profounde knowledge, of so absolute learning, and of so fine eloquence was yet neverthelesse so much blinded, rather with obstinacie, then with ignoraunce that he could not or rather would not see the shining light of godes holy truthe in certein principal pointes of Christian religion: but did rather cheuse to persever, and continue in his wilfull and stubbourne obstinacie even to the very death.[17]

Robinson appears also to want to transfer to Tadlowe 'the daunger, whyche upon this bolde, and rashe enterpryse shall ensue'.[18] It seems unlikely that he is merely speaking here of his own rashness in presuming to translate this eloquent work, rather than of the more serious danger of censure, since the point is made with considerable emphasis and reinforced by an appeal to Cecil in the following sentences to afford him his protection. Cecil had in fact been appointed a member of Seymour's censorship committee in 1549, and continued to have a powerful influence on patronage and censorship even after Dudley ousted Seymour in that same year.[19] The blazoning of Cecil's name on the title-page therefore implied that Robinson could rely on the intervention of the King's secretary should difficulties of that kind arise.

Let us now consider what the relation might be between the stories I have sketched out. Neither of them is likely to be 'merely' rhetoric: clearly Robinson read *Utopia* with Tadlowe and others, and equally clearly, his old school-friend played a role in mediating this translation, whether Cecil was actually the prime mover behind the scenes or, on the contrary, only grudgingly allowed Robinson to use his name. In fact, the stories are not incompatible. The very gesture of *translation* is significant here. It was not for Cecil himself that an English version was needed: he would undoubtedly already have read *Utopia* in Latin. The point of translating it was to make it better known and more

---

16 *The praise of Folie. Moriae Encomium a boke made in latine by that great clerke Erasmus Roterodame. Englisshed by Sir Thomas Chaloner knight* (London: Thomas Berthelet, 1549). See Baker, *Divulging Utopia*, p. 108. Cecil was chief mourner at Chaloner's funeral in 1565.
17 Part II, p. 207.
18 Part II, p. 208.
19 See King, *English Reformation Literature*, pp. 76, 85–6, 109–10.

widely read, and Robinson must have thought that Cecil would approve of that aim too. What is critical is that an important book by a condemned author surfaces here at a particular site: not in a university, or in a great house where a patron employed budding writers, but at the point of intersection between an everyday world of literate but not Latinate culture and the very centre of government. Such an event is unlikely to occur accidentally.

A new edition for a new regime

The virtual narrative continues with the removal of the dedicatory letter in the 1556 edition. This has been interpreted as one element in Robinson's creation of a new image for himself as he gained confidence in his own status as a writer: he now refers in the title to his Oxford fellowship, as if to give the translation greater authority; he adds translations of several of the original paratexts, together with marginal notes; the new preface is addressed to the 'gentle reader', which suggests that the print is aiming at a somewhat higher social stratum; Tadlowe, by contrast, is no longer mentioned by name (having in fact died in the previous year) and Robinson refers to the 'meanness of his learning'.[20]

Whatever weight one may give to these changes, the overriding factor determining the context in which the translation was reissued is the abrupt change of regime and of public culture that had occurred with the accession of the ultra-Catholic Queen Mary in 1553. In her reign, there was no need to apologise for Thomas More or his writings: on the contrary, it was the Marian regime that initiated the construction of More as a martyr.[21] There are accordingly no apologies in the 1556 preface. Likewise, Cecil had withdrawn from public office skilfully and diplomatically enough to avoid drawing down upon himself the wrath of the establishment for his support of the Henrican schism, and he may well have preferred not to have his name cited in a connection which would have reminded readers of his former position.

At the same time, the printer Abraham Vele must have sold enough copies of the first edition to make it worth investing in Robinson's translation again: the English *Utopia* is beginning to make its way in the world independently of great names. Let us now look, then, at the kinds of book that Vele was producing between the late 1540s and around 1560. He apparently specialised in books for the popular market. They are crudely printed in black-letter, enlivened with woodcuts, and show no signs of aspiration to humanist elegance in

---

20 See Baker, *Divulging Utopia*, p. 108; this interpretation is developed in more detail in an unpublished paper by Per Sivefors, '"Yet their characters we have not": the Utopian alphabet and the production of textual control', pp. 19–22. I am grateful to Mr Sivefors for allowing me to refer to it here.
21 See Anne Dillon, *The Construction of Martyrdom in the English Catholic Community, 1535–1603* (Aldershot and Burlington, VT: Ashgate, 2002), pp. 37 ff.

appearance or content. Some are unambiguously Protestant moral tracts, like *The Christen state of Matrymonie*, translated from Bullinger by Miles Coverdale. Others are manuals for everyday life, such as a version of the *Regimen sanitatis Salerni*, or *The boke of hawkynge huntynge and fysshynge with all the propertyes and medecynes that are necessarye to be kepte*. Vele's interest in translated works appears again in *Xenophon's treatise of housholde*.[22] Another group again consists of stories in the late medieval tradition where intermittent sentential moralising and the interlacing of Biblical stories with secular ones licenses some sexually explicit narratives. Not surprisingly, there are no unambiguously Protestant texts after 1553: Vele seems to have adapted his production to suit the ruling culture, and was probably glad to be able to reprint Robinson's translation at a moment when there would be no problems over More's reputation.

This evidence is consistent with Robinson's modest aspirations, and it also supplies a micro-context for the everyday culture in which he participated. Of those on Vele's list, Xenophon's *Oeconomicus* is no doubt the closest to *Utopia*, in that it belongs to the same broad tradition of works on management, whether of a family, an estate, or a whole realm. It is the sort of book that a moderately well-to-do person might regard as seriously useful reading, given its combination of venerable antiquity and practical advice. At all events, *Utopia* re-emerges here at a considerable distance from the circle of Erasmian intimates in which it was originally conceived, and also from the Latin editions which are beginning to multiply at about this time. If Robinson's aspirations were somewhat more scholarly in the 1556 edition, the shift is only a modest one when viewed in this context: he did not, for example, seek to have his translation published by a more genteel or scholarly printer.

The addition of further paratexts from the early Latin editions provides another kind of evidence of what Robinson was aiming for in this second printing.[23] The decision to include the four-line poem in Utopian, together with a note from the printer promising the Utopian alphabet in due course, marks a willingness to enter into the more playful aspects of More's text, especially as the verse translation of the economical Latin version both expands the text considerably and makes it less transparent, as if Robinson wanted to 'foreignise' it.[24] His rendering of the Anemolius poem likewise indulges in

---

22 This translation was printed (by the royal printer, Thomas de Berthelet) as early as 1532.
23 For these paratexts in Robinson's translation, see Oxford 1991, pp. 124–8.
24 This is echoed in the final printer's note on the Utopian alphabet, where the 'strangeness' of the alphabet is said to surpass that of 'the Indian, the Persian, the Syrian, the Arabicke, the Egyptian, the Macedonian, the Sclavonian, the ciprian, the Scythian, etc.' One should also note that these paratexts are placed at the end of the book rather than at the beginning, as in the early Latin editions, so that the fictional game is less prominent. On these questions, see Sivefors, 'Yet their characters we have not', pp. 20–2.

some word-play on Plato's name for which there is no parallel in the original; on the other hand, it also provides an explanation of the name 'Eutopia'. As for the poems by Noviomagus and Grapheus, they provide Robinson with a voice to praise More, 'London's immortal glory', in terms that would hardly have been conceivable in 1551.

The choice of the letter from Giles to Busleyden is no doubt also not a random one. In the first place, it has the function of introducing the Utopian poem, which itself is linked generically to the two encomiastic poems, so that these paratexts form a coherent group in this vernacular edition as they do in many of the Latin editions. The letter is also connected with the Utopian poem in that it enters into the fictional game, telling the anecdote of the whispering servant and the unfortunate cough that prevent Giles from hearing where Utopia is located. Like the poems of Noviomagus and Grapheus, too, it praises More with unqualified licence: the letter begins with a eulogy of the ecphrastic power of More's writing as surpassing even the eloquent narrative of Hythloday himself, and includes an admiring aside on More's judgement ('prudence') in analysing the implications of Utopia for the success or failure of a commonwealth.

Perhaps the most significant passage for Robinson's purpose, however, was the concluding lines of the letter, since these are addressed specifically to Busleyden, the patron whose support was essential to the early promotion of More's work. Giles tells Busleyden that *Utopia* was

> most worthy to go abrod into the handes of men, yea, and under the title of youre name to be publyshed to the worlde: either because the singular endowmentes and qualities of master More be to no man better knowen then to you, or els bicause no man is more fitte and meete, then you with good counselles to further, and avaunce the commen wealth.[25]

As rendered into Robinson's English, these lines might perfectly well have been addressed to William Cecil, who, like Busleyden, had also been counsellor to a monarch. Was this the discreet acknowledgement of a patronage which could not be openly declared in these difficult times, but which Robinson continued to value? Cecil was certainly an experienced enough reader to take the point.

One final detail may bear some relation to the ideology of Queen Mary's reign. In this printing, as the title page tells us, Robinson has added 'divers notes in the margent'. As in the early French editions, some of these are translated from the Latin text, others are modified or invented by Robinson himself, which shows that he must have reflected on the meaning and function of the glosses. In the chapter 'Of the religions in Utopia', the Latin editions carried

25 London 1556, fol. [S vi] r.

two glosses pointing satirically at the excessive number of priests in 'our' world and at their lack of true piety. Robinson replaces these with a single phrase, 'The majestie and preeminence of priestes'. As chapter 1 of the present volume shows (see above, pp. 26–7), the two Latin glosses exercised the Catholic censors in the 1560s, since by this time the confessional polarisation had made it virtually impossible to hold the moderate, non-schismatic reformist position that Erasmus and More had shared at the time *Utopia* was written. Robinson, it seems, was already sensitive to this point, and – whatever his personal beliefs – thought it prudent to remove this inflammatory material.[26]

Utopian allusions in the Elizabethan era

Robinson and his printer may well have expected good sales for the 1556 printing and for another to follow in due course. The next year saw the publication of More's complete English works, with a dedication by William Rastell to Queen Mary celebrating her suppression of heresy; a biography of More was already under way, and an edition of the Latin works could also have appeared in England within the next few years.[27] However, Mary's death put an end to the budding cult of More as an English martyr, and John Foxe was soon to demonise him as a persecutor of Protestant martyrs. *Utopia* was not to be printed again until the closing years of Elizabeth's reign, more than twenty years after Robinson's death in 1576. Meanwhile, in 1572, Robinson had written another letter requesting support from Burghley, who was now, having been ennobled by the Queen, at the height of his career, with wide-ranging powers and interests in Elizabeth's administration. This renewed contact with his patron provides no firm evidence of Burghley's continued interest in the *Utopia* translation, but it is none the less a detail which helps one to construct a broader picture.

In the absence of a printing of *Utopia*, we may look briefly here at two well-known references which show that More's work was an established landmark in Elizabethan literary culture. The first is the allusion by Sir Philip Sidney, in *A Defence of Poetry*, to *Utopia* as an example of a 'feigned image of poetry' which tells the truth better than 'the regular instruction of philosophy'. In order to help his readers to understand Aristotle's argument for the superiority of plausible fictions over historical discourse, Sidney cites an instance which is not only modern but also politically charged: More's work is the highest and the most relevant form of 'poetry', despite its faults:

26 See also Sivefors, 'Yet their characters we have not', p. 19, note 24.
27 See Trevor-Roper, 'The image of Thomas More', pp. 7–8; Dillon, *The Construction of Martyrdom*, pp. 37–9, 41–5.

because where Sir Thomas More erred, it was the fault of the man and not of the poet, for that way of patterning a commonwealth was most absolute, though he perchance hath not so absolutely performed it.[28]

Sidney is writing for an elite circle of readers in the 1580s, but those readers at least must have been familiar with More's work, otherwise the example would have been without effect. Whether they read it in Latin or in Robinson's English must remain uncertain, but it seems likely that some at least would have been glad enough of the translation. Equally important is the sophistication of the argument. Elizabethan readers were evidently entirely capable of grasping the essential point that the power of *Utopia* to deliver its high political message is inseparable from its character as a fiction (although it might well be separable from the character of the person who wrote it).

The other reference comes from Thomas Nashe's *The Unfortunate Traveller*, first printed in 1594. Nashe's picaresque satire recognises the precise generic location of More's work by pairing it with Erasmus' *Praise of Folly* as mirror-images of one another: whereas Erasmus satirises the 'indiscretion of princes in preferring of parasites and fools', More 'travelled in a clean contrary province' and laid down 'a perfect plot of a commonwealth or government.'[29]

If *Utopia* was as well known as this, it seems strange that it is not alluded to in Anthony Munday's play about More, probably written in the early 1590s and revised a few years later, but apparently never performed.[30] The very existence of the play demonstrates at least that such a portrayal was beginning to be politically viable in the later part of Elizabeth's reign as memories of the political dramas of the 1530s gradually faded: the question of the royal marriage can now be simply airbrushed out, and what More obstinately refuses to sign, in the last act, is left entirely vague.

However, it is possible to read a kind of Utopian subtext in More's speech to the rebellious townspeople, commonly said to have been added in Shakespeare's hand.[31] More here invites his audience to put themselves in the position of the foreigners they are attacking: how would they feel if they were

---

28 Sir Philip Sidney, *Miscellaneous Prose*, eds Katherine Duncan-Jones and Jan van Dorsten (Oxford: Clarendon Press, 1973), pp. 86–7. The reference to More's 'fault' is ambiguous: the later part of the sentence implies that it was *Utopia* itself that was defective (although 'perchance' leaves that opinion open to doubt), whereas the 'fault of the man' sounds more like a reference to More's refusal to support Henry in the marriage crisis.
29 Thomas Nashe, *The Unfortunate Traveller and Other Works*, ed. J. B. Steane (London: Penguin, repr. in Penguin Classics, 1985), pp. 290–1.
30 For a detailed reconstruction of the composition of the play, see *Sir Thomas More: A Play by Anthony Munday and Others*, ed. Vittorio Gabrieli and Giorgio Melchiori (Manchester and New York: Manchester University Press, 1990), Introduction.
31 For a different contextual reading, see Warren Boutcher, '"A French Dexteritie, & an Italian Confidence": new documents on John Florio, learned strangers and Protestant humanist study of modern languages in Renaissance England from c.1547 to c.1625', *Reformation*, 2 (1997), 39–109 (39–40).

themselves in exile in a foreign country? This is exactly the kind of imaginative reversal (or paradox, in the strict sense of the word) on which the fiction of Utopia is based, and both appeal to a geographical and not only cultural distancing of perspective.

This textual conjunction, whether it is accidental or not, points to the outlines of a hypothesis that would fit all of these fragmentary glimpses of a sixteenth-century English *Utopia*. Before More's image was torn apart by the religious politics of the Reformation, he was, like Erasmus, a moderate humanist seeking new and imaginative solutions to old problems.[32] That message became in the course of the sixteenth century the hallmark of the city of Basel, where editions of the Latin *Utopia* and the 1524 German translation were printed. It was no doubt passed on to young students at Corpus Christi College, Oxford and St John's College, Cambridge, and thus to Robinson and Cecil. It was certainly taken up in France also by non-schismatic reformers like Budé and Rabelais and still pursued, despite the outbreak of the wars of religion in the 1560s, by major statesmen, local *magistrats*, diplomats and men of letters (Montaigne was all of these), and even by members of the ruling house of Valois, in other words by the eclectic group that came to be known as the *politiques*. Drawing its members from both Protestant and Catholic confessions, this party sought to avoid extremism and achieve national peace through reconciliation. One of the moves that was considered in order to achieve this aim was to arrange a marriage between a Valois prince and Elizabeth of England. This of course never came about, but Burghley was a prime mover in the negotiations.[33] We can be quite sure, then, that he knew about the *politiques* and what they stood for: the idea that the welfare of the nation – the 'common weal' – must have priority over religious principle, sincerely though that principle be held on either side. Burghley was certainly a good Protestant, even a hard-line Calvinist, anxious to the point of paranoia about Popish plots to supplant Elizabeth with a Catholic monarch; his insistence on the execution of Mary Stuart, despite the reluctance of the Queen, is the most famous example. But it would be wrong to see him as a fanatic. The evidence of his career, taken as a whole, points the other way. As Patrick Collinson has argued, he disliked extremist positions on both sides of the confessional divide: he was a mediator, a man for all seasons.[34] If a position

---

32 On the 'radical humanism' of the sixteenth century, see David Norbrook, *Poetry and Politics in the English Renaissance* (rev. edn) (Oxford: Oxford University Press, 2002), especially chapter 1, 'The *Utopia* and radical humanism'.
33 See Graves, *Burghley*, p. 51.
34 Patrick Collinson, 'Sir Nicholas Bacon and the Elizabethan *via media*', in *Godly People: Essays on English Protestantism and Puritanism* (London: Hambledon Press, 1983), pp. 135–53 (p. 137). See also Dillon (*The Construction of Martyrdom*, pp. 15–16, 80, 148–9) on Burghley's distinction in his tract *The Execution of Justice* (1583) between treason and

like that of the *politiques* was held by anyone in England (and the circumstances were of course very different), Burghley, with his devotion to the ideal of the commonwealth, fits the profile. As a humanist administrator, he must have seen More's imaginary state not as an ideal to be put into immediate practice, but as a place of radical reflection on the principles and presuppositions of good governance: a work of negotiation that belonged to the prehistory of the *politiques*.

A Stuart revival

The English *Utopia* was printed once more in the sixteenth century, just one year before its erstwhile patron's death in 1598, by Thomas Creede, who two years later brought out Shakespeare's *Romeo and Juliet*. This printing has no contemporary prefaces and no printer's note, but otherwise it reproduces the contents of the 1556 edition. It shows once again that More's work was not itself regarded as suspect and that a printer thought it would sell to a new generation of readers.

The two seventeenth-century editions belong, in many respects, to another world. The House of Tudor has come to an end; the House of Stuart has always had French and Catholic connections, now prominently represented by Henrietta Maria, and the regime, by the 1620s, is much less concerned with 'Popish plots': the threat to the Crown will come from the other end of the confessional spectrum. The More family, which had lain low, whether in England or in exile abroad, is one of a growing number of English Catholic families who are no longer exposed to direct persecution.

In this more favourable environment, the various biographical materials which had been circulating privately since the mid-sixteenth century[35] were at last beginnning to appear in print in English:[36] they were still published abroad, but with English dedicatees. One of these was composed by Cresacre More, More's great-grandson, between 1615 and 1620 and printed some time after 1630 (no date of publication is indicated).[37] It was dedicated to the Queen, that is to say Henrietta Maria, and is extravagantly hagiographic: More has become a legend, a saint in the making.

---

religious dissent; he also distinguishes between the proselytism of Catholic priests, which he believes should be prosecuted, and the discreet religious practices of lay persons 'of good possessions, and lands' who do not challenge the authority of the state. This double distinction allows for a certain freedom of conscience, although Burghley's Catholic adversaries inevitably heaped scorn on his supposed tolerance.

35 See Trevor-Roper, 'The image of Thomas More', pp. 7–9.
36 Thomas Stapleton's Latin biography had been printed in Douai in 1588 (see Trevor-Roper, pp. 11–12)
37 Trevor-Roper, pp. 15 and 17.

Bernard Alsop, the printer of both the 1624 and the 1639 editions of the English *Utopia*, had been Thomas Creede's apprentice and took over his business when he retired (or died) in 1616. His approach to More's work, however, is much less anonymous. The changed political context enabled him to adopt a self-consciously encomiastic tone in his short dedicatory epistles to Cresacre More: he makes no apologies for publishing 'this glorious Common wealth'. In these paratexts, then, the family story at last comes together, albeit briefly, with the acclaimed text that Robinson had translated. The printer's aim was not so much, one suspects, to provoke political reflection as to participate in the newly fashionable celebration of More. The politics of Utopia was of course never markedly Catholic, and the printer makes scant mention of the place or of its value as a model of government, none at all of its character as a paradox (although the 1624 printing still preserves the group of early Latin paratexts that had been appended in 1556 and 1597). At most, by indulging in some word-play in the 1639 dedication, Alsop gestures towards the by now canonic 'wit' of the book and its author.

This moment of triumph, however, soon becomes history: England will within a few years be ruled by a Puritan regime. The irony is that Cromwell's Commonwealth, with its marked austerity and its show of egalitarianism, was arguably a good deal closer to the governance of Utopia than was the Stuart monarchy that preceded and followed it.

The fact that Robinson's translation comes back again and again, like the Vicar of Bray, from one reign to the next, for close on a hundred years, makes it reasonable to infer that it is the character of *Utopia* rather than the religion of its author that must have been the determining factor in the translation and its dissemination. *Utopia* makes its way in England, through thick and thin, as a paradigm of detached political reflection unprejudiced by religious commitment.

Questions of translation

The value of Robinson's translation as a means of access to his interpretation of *Utopia* is relatively limited, since there are few occasions when his deviations from the original give any clear indication of a particular preference. We have already seen that one of the marginal notes in the 1556 edition removes a satirical allusion in the Latin glosses, and Robinson omits the sentence 'There is no need for farm labour, in which they have been trained, where there is no land left to be planted'[38] in the passage in Book I describing the unemployment that results from the enclosures. It is conceivable that Robinson

---

38 'Nam rusticae rei cui assueverunt nihil est quod agatur ubi nihil seritur' (Cambridge 1995, pp. 62–5). A more literal translation of the last phrase would be 'where nothing is planted'.

thought the point was politically sensitive in some way, but it seems more likely that this was simply an accidental omission.

Considered as a literary work in its own right, Robinson's *Utopia* is a remarkable achievement. It is hard to imagine that it would have been reprinted without rivals for a hundred years had its readers not found it idiomatic, inventive and entertaining. It has been suggested that the qualities of its prose – a highly literate version of the current spoken vernacular – are at least in part indebted to the English Prayer Book, an early version of which was printed in 1549, two years before Robinson's *Utopia*.[39] However, no single precedent can account adequately for this kind of phenomenon. A full-scale study in the context of other vernacular and Latin writings of the mid-century seems to be called for; in the absence of such a study, it is only possible to point to a few salient features.

Robinson adopts the mode of translation generally favoured in the sixteenth century, the one that Florio will famously use half a century later in his version of Montaigne's *Essais*. He does not feel bound to remain faithful to the original at every point, allowing himself at times to expand phrases and even whole sentences in order to create an arresting effect.[40] Here is a particularly colourful example, with added or expanded phrases in italics:

> For not only gently mens servauntes, but also handy craft men: yea and almoste the *ploughemen of the countrey*, with all other sortes of people, use muche *straunge and prowde newe fanglenes* in their apparell, and to muche *prodigal riotte and sumptuous fare* at their table. Nowe *bawdes, qweynes, hoores, harlottes, strumpettes*, brothelhouses, stewes, and yet an other stewes, wine tavernes, ale houses, *and tipling houses*, with so many *noughty lewde and unlawfull* games, as dice, cardes, tables, tennyes, bolles, coytes, do not al thys sende the haunters of them streyght a stealynge when theyr money is gone.[41]

From this and other instances, it looks as if Robinson was thoroughly familiar with the Erasmian technique of *copia*, which was widely taught in the 1530s, when Robinson was learning to write Latin. That he is able successfully to

---

39 See Oxford 1895, p. lxxiii.
40 Most commentators, ignoring the predominance of this mode of translation in the sixteenth century, are patronising in their assessment of Robinson's skills as a translator. See Oxford 1895, p. lxxiii; Reed Edwin Peggrum, 'The first French and English translations of Sir Thomas More's *Utopia*' (*Modern Language Review*, 35 (1940), 330–40); James Binder, 'More's *Utopia* in English: a note on translation' (*Modern Language Notes*, 62 (1947), 370–6); Knud Sørensen, 'Notes on the first English translation of More's *Utopia*', in Graham D. Caie and Holger Nørgaard (eds), *A Literary Miscellany Presented to Eric Jacobsen* (Copenhagen: University of Copenhagen, 1988), pp. 326–37. These value-loaded judgements have unfortunately led some distinguished scholars to belittle Robinson's grasp of the import and complexity of the work he was translating; see for example Norbrook, *Poetry and Politics*, p. 26.
41 London 1551, fol. D i r. See Cambridge 1995, pp. 64–6, for the Latin text.

transfer the method to English prose is an indication of the rapid vernacularisation of humanist culture in sixteenth-century England.

Passages like this also suggest that Robinson must have enjoyed reading Erasmus' and More's Latin translations of Lucian, Erasmus' *Praise of Folly* and *Colloquia*, and no doubt other witty and imaginative texts. But the contemporary writer who immediately comes to mind here, particularly because of Robinson's use of the Lucian anecdote at the beginning of his preface, is Rabelais. Robinson is of course less exuberant than his French counterpart (even a free translation imposes limits), but the love of colourful vocabulary and of cumulative effect is common to them both. The parallel is suggestive of the direction taken by the vernacular styles of northern Europe in the mid-sixteenth century in the wake of the more playful of the Latin works of Erasmus and More. In England, one thinks of Skelton's satirical poems, or of William Baldwin's satire *A Marvelous Hystory Intitulede, Beware the Cat*, composed in 1553 although not printed until 1570, which projects a fictional world of talking cats on to the topography of contemporary London;[42] or again Thomas Nashe's avowedly Rabelaisian *The Unfortunate Traveller*.

This is of course not only a question of style. The moderate politics of the northern European humanists is deeply linked to the style in which they present their often provocative ideological moves: allusive, satirical, paradoxical (again in the earlier sense of the word), at times jokingly prolix, their manner of writing is designed to carry a policy, or more fundamentally a way of thinking. Dialogue and plurality are of the essence here: it is not an accident that the first book of *Utopia* is a dialogue, or that engravings in several of the early modern editions shows More conversing with Giles and Hythloday. Rabelais produces a virtuoso variant of both the manner and the message; later in the century, Montaigne invents a special kind of polyphonic syntax that enacts the speaker's habit of looking at everything from more than one angle. The ultimate example of this northern European manner is of course Shakespeare, who gives a voice to everyone. He never directly evokes Utopia, but he does ask the question, over and over again, of the right way to run a commonwealth, be it the England of the Wars of the Roses, Coriolanus' Rome or the imaginary micro-state of Prospero's isle. Robinson's translation is perhaps best read as one moment in the pre-history of that extraordinary cultural move towards a pluralisation of the body politic and its voices.

Terence Cave

---

42 William Baldwin, *Beware the Cat: The First English Novel*, ed. William A. Ringler, Jr. and Michael Flachmann (San Marino, CA: Huntingdon Library, 1988); see King, *English Reformation Literature*, pp. 387–406.

6 THE DUTCH TRANSLATION: AUSTERITY AND PRAGMATISM

From the outset, *Utopia* was deeply connected with the Low Countries and its culture.[1] As More says in his prefatory first letter to Peter Giles, it was in 1515 in Bruges, while conducting trade negotiations on behalf of Henry VIII, that he began work on *Utopia*, finishing it, in its first version at least, during the summer of that year in Bruges and Antwerp. It was first printed in Louvain – at that time at the forefront of humanist innovation, with a 'College of the Three Languages' about to be established in 1517 – and its entry into the world was surrounded by Dutch scholars and patrons: Giles, its first editor, Martens, its first printer, Busleyden, its rich patron, and of course Erasmus. The fiction of Hythloday's appearance on the scene and his subsequent dialogue with More and Giles is equally set in Antwerp: indeed, one could argue that the whole strategy of Book I and the paratexts in creating a plausible frame of reference for the Utopia narrative of Book II consciously exploits the pragmatic, down-to-earth culture of the Low Countries as a this-world counterpart to the strange 'new world' described by Hythloday. Like Venice, Antwerp was a major trading centre, a place where travellers from all parts of the known and unknown globe might meet, and this is the place where the Utopian fiction becomes anchored to the everyday world.

As chapter 1 of this volume has recalled, the first posthumous Latin edition of *Utopia* (1548) appeared in the scholarly environment of Louvain, but it was in Antwerp that a Dutch translation first appeared in 1553. It seems that it had been completed some years earlier, since the privilege is dated 29 October 1550. It is a plainly-printed little book containing only *Utopia*, Books I and II. The Latin paratexts have disappeared, and no new prefatory materials have been added except the privilege and a statement at the end of the

---

1 We use this loose term to designate the geographical area corresponding approximately to modern Belgium and the Netherlands. When speaking of the northern provinces after their secession, we use the name 'United Provinces', even if the provinces were a loose federation rather than a single political entity, as 'united' might suggest. On the problems of nomenclature, see Simon Schama, *The Embarrassment of Riches: An Interpretation of Dutch Culture in the Golden Age* (London: Collins, 1987), pp. 54–5. On the transfer of More's work into the culture of the Low Countries, see Vincent Buyens, 'Over edele tegenvoeters en welvarende Hollanders: ideal en droom in de zeventiende-eeuwse literatuur', in A. Decelle and A. Faems (eds), *Aan de voet van de regenboog: De utopie in de Nederlandse literatuur* (Leuven: Peeters, forthcoming).

book that it has been approved by a learned theologian under the authority of the Emperor.[2]

The title, however, shows a striking departure from those of the Latin editions.[3] The standard reference to the 'best state of a republic' has disappeared, and the name of the country is now given priority, without reference to its fictional status as a new-found island. The name 'Utopia' is followed by the author's own name and erstwhile position as Chancellor of England and the fact that he is no longer alive is made explicit. The phrase 'golden little book' has gone; 'beneficial and entertaining' have been rendered by the plainer 'profitable and pleasing'. However, the most significant change is the gloss that follows this Horatian commonplace: the book is especially profitable and pleasing to read 'for those who in the present day have to rule a town and district, a purpose which it is above all suited to serve'. The phrasing is quite unambiguous: *Utopia* is a practical book, containing useful advice for administrators. Unfortunately, in the absence of the name of a translator or dedicatee, or of any official body such as a town council or guild, it is hard to interpret. All we can say is that More's playful work, once the focus of a high-spirited humanist dialogue, is now presented to the sort of readers who feature in the large assemblages of officials one sees in certain early modern civic paintings. The playfulness has not entirely disappeared; few readers of the mid-sixteenth century would have been likely to think that Utopia was anything but a fiction, and Book I preserves a memory of humanists in conversation. But neither the translator nor the printer has thought it necessary to add paratexts from the early editions such as the map and Utopian alphabet, still less to enter into the game themselves. Whether the book actually assisted any of the first readers of this translation in their civic duties must remain an open question, but if so, it must have been by fostering reflection on the principles of government, not by providing directly applicable guidelines.

The book appears to have sold well enough for the same printer, Hans de Laet (Johannes Latius), to reissue it in 1562. De Laet, who was active between the mid-1540s and his death in 1566, was an important and prolific printer who collaborated with Plantin from 1555; a wide range of works came from his presses. It is perhaps a sign of the times that the second printing of the Dutch translation appeared just before the Latin *Utopia* began to be reissued in the collected works of Basel and Louvain. Perhaps De Laet knew of the efforts being made in Louvain to assemble a monument to More and decided that he could exploit the wave of interest in the English martyr. In the last three years of his life, that is to say at exactly the same time as the Louvain editions, he also printed a number of Catholic works written in English.

2 See Part II, pp. 220–1.
3 *Ibid.*

In the mid-sixteenth century, the Low Countries formed an important part of the imperial domains, subject to the rule of Charles V until his abdication in 1556, and thereafter of his son Philip II. Charles had been born in Ghent and spoke Dutch, probably as his mother-tongue, whereas Philip had grown up in Spain. However, the new Emperor had lived in the region intermittently since 1548; after his marriage to Queen Mary of England in 1554, he continued to reside in Brussels in order to conduct the war against France in alliance with England. More importantly for our purposes, he imposed a religious policy in the Netherlands which was much more militantly orthodox than it had been under Charles V: until 1556, the different reformist sects had lived in relative peace with moderate Catholics. Like his English queen, however, Philip was zealously anti-Protestant, bringing the Jesuits to the region to help root out heresy; the Spanish Inquisition was also implemented there. Even after the death of Mary and Philip's return to Spain the following year (1559), the same policy continued, despite fierce resistance from the reformers and moderates. The eventual outcome was the secession of the northern provinces, to which many committed Protestants from the south – especially Calvinists – subsequently fled.[4] Antwerp remained in Spanish hands, but at the expense of losing its status as a major trading centre; Amsterdam was in due course to take over that role.[5]

This is the context for the re-emergence of the Dutch *Utopia* in the earlier seventeenth century. No less than sixty-seven years after the second edition, the translation was published again, this time in Hoorn – not far from Amsterdam – by the printers and booksellers Martin Gerbrantsz and Isaäc Willemsz: like Robinson's English version, this anonymous Dutch translation, despite its modest appearance, is a survivor. In fact, a cluster of new editions was issued between 1629 and 1634. The first is dated 1629 on the title-page and 1630 in the colophon. The last, dated 1634, has a title modified to include a reference to the translations of early Latin paratexts which are a feature of all of these editions. The University Library of Utrecht has a copy dated 1630 in which the earlier date has disappeared and where the title has already been modified in this way. It appears that Gerbrantsz and Willemsz cooperated to produce this new version of the sixteenth-century translation and issued it in slightly different formats. However, in all essential respects, these three versions are identical, and we have – albeit somewhat arbitrarily – counted them as two editions (Hoorn 1629 and Hoorn 1634) for the sake of this account.

---

4 For a detailed general history of the Dutch Republic, see Jonathan I. Israel, *The Dutch Republic: Its Rise, Greatness, and Fall. 1477–1806* (Oxford: Clarendon Press, 1995).
5 See Maria A. Schenkeveld, *Dutch Literature in the Age of Rembrandt* (Amsterdam and Philadelphia: John Benjamins Publishing Company, 1991), p. 3.

The decision to add the letters of More, Erasmus, Budé, Busleyden and Giles, together with the poems of 'Anemolius', Noviomagus and Grapheus, shows that the early Latin paratexts had not been forgotten, thanks no doubt to their recurrence in the Latin editions, and could now be used once more for a new promotion of More's text. Whoever translated them must of course have had access to a Latin copy; the short text that introduces the paratexts is for the most part a translation of the original title, and a much more literal one than the version provided by the sixteenth-century translator.[6]

In the new northern 'Republic', or 'United Provinces', it was safe to publish texts by those, like Erasmus and Budé, now perceived to be forerunners of the Reform: safe, but not unproblematic. The official religious culture at this time was Calvinist; other Protestant groups were allowed freedom of worship, and even the substantial Catholic minority were tolerated provided they resorted to *schuilkerken* ('hidden churches'). But only members of the Calvinist Church could apply for important public offices, and a degree of literary censorship was imposed, not least on classical and humanistic writings.[7] That perspective is abundantly apparent in the short preface 'To the Christian reader who is eager for knowledge'.[8] Its rhetoric is unequivocally Calvinist, with its tone of sober admonition, its series of Old Testament references, its Biblical phrasing and its concluding call to prayer.[9] It identifies the well-being of the state with absolute subjection to the service of God and promises apocalyptic destruction for errant nations, whether those of the Old Testament or contemporary ones like the southern provinces. If any country wishes to improve its political establishment, it should follow the advice of Jethro and other Old Testament authorities. It is only after this message, hammered in over more than half of the preface, that the reader is told that the 'elegant portrayal of the polity that the learned Thomas More ... has sketched out in his Utopia' may in addition not be unprofitable and may even be enjoyable. The cautions and double negatives continue throughout, however. The anonymous author

---

6 See Part II, pp. 228–9. The Dutch phrase 'Een recht gouden Schrift, ende niet min heylsaem als geneughlijck' exactly renders the 'libellus vere aureus nec minus salutaris quam festivus' of the Latin editions. There are signs, too, that the author of the preface did not rely exclusively on the sixteenth-century version he was introducing. When characterising More's work, he uses the expressions 'niet ondienstelijck' and 'met geneuchte' ('not unprofitably' and 'with enjoyment') instead of the adjectives 'profijtelijck' and 'vermakelijck' that are found in the 1553 and 1562 editions of the translation; he also refers to More's 'cierlijcke afbeeldinghe' ('elegant image') of a polity, a phrase which recalls the early humanist paratexts and (no doubt accidentally) the title of Paris 1517.
7 On these questions, see Schenkeveld, *Dutch Literature*, pp. 39–40; on the 'great toleration debate', which 'was at its most intense and decisive phase in the late 1620s', see Israel, *The Dutch Republic*, pp. 499–505.
8 See Part II, pp. 224–7.
9 This rhetoric is common to Calvinist culture throughout Europe; on its specific value to Dutch Calvinists, see Schama, *The Embarrassment of Riches*, pp. 94 ff.

of the preface evokes and endorses More's own reservations in the concluding passage of the work concerning some of the aspects of Utopian government (here naming only their military and religious practices), and later inserts the qualification that the reader should seek to put More's suggestions into practice 'where they are not contrary to God's word'.

The preface thus systematically removes from the Utopian model any possibility of equivocation. In this respect, it echoes what the translator had already done in that concluding passage, where More's remark that many of the laws and customs described by Hythloday were 'really absurd' becomes 'there was much that I would have rebuked or condemned',[10] and the crucial phrase 'in the popular view' ('ut publica est opinio') is simply not translated.[11] What all this amounts to is a kind of virtual censorship. The Catholic authorisation that accompanied the sixteenth-century editions has of course been removed, but it has been replaced by one which is more severe in its effects than the adjustments and exclusions imposed by the Catholic censors in other editions. No actual suppressions are required, but the reader has been supplied with a rule that rigorously restrains the intellectual and ethical openness that characterises More's work.

It is possible, of course, that the preface is there precisely to pre-empt potential objections and suspicions from religious authorities. Perhaps it was the price that needed to be paid, given the Calvinist hegemony, for such a work to be made available. In favour of such a view, one could cite the evidence already presented elsewhere in this volume that there was a demand for *Utopia* in this period and milieu. The new editions of the Dutch translation coincide in date with the small-format Latin editions, now called simply *Utopia*, that appeared in Amsterdam in 1629 and again in 1631. Did Willems and Gerbrandtsz exploit the revival of More's work for readers literate in Latin by reissuing the old vernacular version? Did the markets overlap? Was there a reason why More's work was suddenly relevant again?

The most obvious answer is that this was a period when the question of Dutch national identity became critical. When the northern provinces broke away from the Empire and declared themselves to be a free republic, the status and grounding of such a republic came in question. What was to be the relationship between the orthodox Calvinist Princes of Orange on the one hand and, on the other, the Parliament and civil authorities, who were for the most part rich bourgeois merchants of liberal views? One major argument put forward in favour of the legitimacy of the new state was historical. The Batavians, a people who lived in the region in Roman times, become the

---

10 'soo had ick veel dat ick ... soude berispt ende bestraft hebben' (Hoorn 1629, p. 200; compare Cambridge 1995, p. 246–7).
11 See above, p. 11.

model for a national identity grounded in antiquity and continuity: painters such as Otto van Veen and (later) Rembrandt provide striking illustrations of this theme.[12] In that context, More's *Utopia* takes on an unexpected relevance: Utopia is represented as an ancient republic, and is at the same time a new ideal state, tolerant yet tightly controlled, ethically austere yet prosperous and indeed comfortable for its hard-working citizens.[13]

Such local considerations must undoubtedly have played a role in the revival of More's work in the northern provinces. In the wider context that this volume provides, however, it is clear that a similar revival was taking place elsewhere in Europe at this time, as Cologne 1629, London 1624 and 1639, and Córdoba 1637 testify. And not many years later, the son of the printer of Amsterdam 1629 will publish a new *French* translation, apparently conceived in a quite different spirit. The one thing that these strands of a publishing history make abundantly clear is that, throughout our period, the Low Countries remain a key focus for the transfer of *Utopia*.

Ronny Spaans and Terence Cave

---

12 See Schama, *The Embarrassment of Riches*, pp. 76–7.
13 See *ibid.*, p. 68, on the convergence of Roman and Old Testament models; pp. 78–82, on the social and ethical characteristics projected on to the Batavians. The parallel with Utopia is striking. The potential contribution that More's *Utopia* may have been thought to make to discussion of the founding of a new Dutch republic is also attested by the fact that a copy of the 1630 edition is bound together with Johan de Brune the Elder's *De Grondsteenen van een vaste Regieringe, gheleyt end wthestelt tot bericht end nuttigheyt van alle goede Vader-landers* (Middelburgh: Hans vander Hellen for Ian Pieterssen vande Venne, 1621). De Brune was a well-known author and statesman and a Calvinist moralist; his treatise asserts that 'the service of God and righteousness is the only foundation and mode of operation of a stable and spiritually beneficial polity', a view identical with that of the anonymous preface to the Dutch *Utopia*: it is indeed not inconceivable that De Brune wrote the preface himself. Although De Brune's writings are characterised by a thorough knowledge of classical and modern literature, Calvinism remained the defining feature of his work.

7 THE SPANISH TRANSLATIONS: HUMANISM AND POLITICS

There are two chronological contexts for the early modern cultural transfer of Thomas More's *Utopia* to Spain. The first, contemporary with More himself, is the culture of the early sixteenth century, a prosperous period for Spanish humanism; the second is the Spanish political scene in the seventeenth century, when the decline of the Spanish empire spawned a vast number of political tracts and treatises offering solutions to the crisis. However, the first Spanish translation of *Utopia* was never printed, and it was not until 1637, 121 years after the first Latin edition, that More's work was published in Spanish, translated by Jerónimo Antonio de Medinilla y Porres and printed in Córdoba. We shall deal briefly with the manuscript before focusing on Córdoba 1637, where the contextual and paratextual evidence is much richer.

The Gondomar manuscript

The anonymous sixteenth-century translation of *Utopia* is to be found in the Biblioteca Real de Palacio in Madrid.[1] The manuscript came to the Library of the Royal Palace through the splendid collection of Diego Sarmiento de Acuña, Count of Gondomar (1567–1626). The volume consists of forty-seven folios, and two different handwritings can be identified. The second hand makes corrections on the first as well as some annotations in the margin on the lacunae of the first copyist.[2] This scrupulousness may indicate that the text was made for the manuscript collection of a noble or that it was the clean copy made for printing.

The external evidence shows that this is a sixteenth-century text, but there are also internal indications that help to date the manuscript. When referring to 'Charles, the most serene Prince of Castile', the phrase 'now Emperor' is added;[3] furthermore, there is no mention of More's death. Practically all

1 Shelfmark: II/1087. Manuel Serrano y Sanz, 'Libros manuscritos o de mano', *Revista de Archivos, Bibliotecas y Museos*, 8 (1903), 65–8, 225–8, 295–300, made the manuscript known, but this information was forgotten until Francisco López Estrada recovered it for his works on *Utopia* in Spain. For a description of the manuscript, see López Estrada, 'Une traduction précoce de *L'Utopie* de Thomas More', *Moreana*, 111–12 (1992), 15–18.
2 The two different hands also include differences in the translation. For example, in the headings to each part, the translation of More's title, 'Vicecomitem', has been rendered as 'Viceconde' in Book I (fol. 3 v) and as 'Gobernador' in Book II (fol. 16 v).
3 Gondomar MS, fol. 17 r; cf. Cambridge 1995, p. 41. Charles I of Spain (reigned 1516–56) became the Emperor Charles V in 1519. We refer to him throughout as Charles V.

Spanish texts posterior to his execution refer to him as 'martyr' and this would surely have been the case for the manuscript also. This does not allow us to determine the exact date of the translation, but it was probably made after 1519 and before 1535.

The reign of Charles V saw an important upsurge of humanist scholarship and thought in Spain.[4] It should suffice to mention the editing of the so-called *Biblia políglota complutense*, a task initiated in 1502 and led by Cardinal Francisco Jiménez de Cisneros at the University of Alcalá. It was actually printed in 1514, but not issued until 1517, the year after Erasmus' *New Testament*. Erasmus had a great defender in Alfonso de Valdés, secretary to Charles V, and his works were widely read in Spain. It is in this period of relative religious tolerance and humanist activity that the first translation of More's *Utopia* must have circulated in manuscript, perhaps among the intellectuals of the court.[5] However, by the 1550s the situation had changed considerably; Catholic orthodoxy was reaffirmed by the Council of Trent (1545–1563), the Inquisition was reinforced, and Spanish humanists would have found it difficult to take a work like *Utopia* to the printing press.

Latin copies were also taken to America in the sixteenth century: Vasco de Quiroga, bishop and judge in Michoacán (Mexico), wrote a report to Charles V in 1535 proposing the organisation of an ideal polity in the manner of *Utopia*.[6] According to this *Información en derecho*, he also made a partial translation of More's work which was to accompany the report, but unfortunately this appendix has not survived, or at least it has not resurfaced since the sixteenth century.[7]

The original used for the Gondomar translation must be an edition no earlier than Basel 1518. The text includes the letter from Giles to Busleyden and More's first letter to Giles, and at the end of Book II, Busleyden's letter to More. It omits the letters from Erasmus to Froben and from Budé to Lupset, together with all other early paratextual materials such as the map of Utopia and the Utopian alphabet and verses. The title is translated at the beginning

---

4 See e.g. Marcel Bataillon, *Erasmo y España*, trans. A. Alatorre (Mexico: Fondo de Cultura Económica, 1966; original version 1937), chapters 5–8.
5 The early Latin editions were read in Spain by a scholarly public; see López Estrada, *Tomás Moro y España: sus relaciones hasta el siglo XVIII* (Madrid: Editorial de la Universidad Complutense, 1980), pp. 53–4, and 'La fortuna de Tomás Moro y su *Utopia* en la España del Siglo de Oro', in *La fortuna dell'Utopia di Thomas More nel dibattito politico europeo del '500* (Florence: Olschki, 1996), pp. 75–91.
6 See Fernando Gómez, *Good Places and Non-Places in Colonial Mexico: The Figure of Vasco de Quiroga (1470–1565)* (Lanham, New York, Oxford: University Press of America, 2001), pp. 154–8.
7 See Vasco de Quiroga, *La Utopía en América*, ed. Paz Serrano Gassent (Madrid: Dastin, 2002), pp. 233–4. Silvio Zavala was the first to provide this information in 'Vasco de Quiroga, traducteur de l'*Utopia*', *Moreana*, 69 (1981), 115–17; he believes the translation to have been of Book I only, but this is not explicitly stated by Quiroga.

of Book I as 'la republica Utopia', while in the register of Gondomar's collection the manuscript is entered as *República Eutopía*.⁸ The only evidence that gives us any clue as to which Latin original has been used is to be found in the text itself: like the two editions of 1518, the translation has the error of twenty miles instead of twelve miles.⁹

The Gondomar manuscript contains no prefatory materials of its own, and it has unfortunately not been possible to uncover further evidence of its origin or destiny in the sixteenth century, but the major expansion of humanist – especially Erasmian – scholarship in the period must have created an ideal context for such a translation. One of the merits of the Gondomar manuscript is indeed that it places Spain, traditionally omitted, within the humanist sphere of Europe.

Medinilla's 1637 translation

The copy of Medinilla's translation we have consulted is from the Biblioteca Nacional in Madrid.¹⁰ Only Book II of *Utopia* is translated, but there is no mention of Book I being excluded. All the chapters and headings of the original Book II are translated, numbered from I to IX. It is not known which Latin edition Medinilla translated from, although it must have been no earlier than the 1518 editions, as the same error we noted for the Gondomar manuscript translation is repeated.¹¹ There is no evidence that he had access to the manuscript translation. Apparently the most widely disseminated texts by More at the time in Spain were the Latin complete works (Basel 1563, Louvain 1565 and 1566); there are various copies of these editions in Spanish libraries. None of the paratexts from the early Latin editions are included in Medinilla's translation.

The translation comprises a total of twenty-five paratextual elements, including a Latin quotation from Martial which replaces the brief epilogue placed after the 'FINIS' of the original text.¹² The preliminaries proper, title-

---

8   Carmen Manso Porto, *Don Diego Sarmiento de Acuña, Conde de Gondomar (1567–1626). Erudito, mecenas y bibliófilo* (n.p.: Xunta de Galicia, 1996), p. 621.
9   Gondomar MS, fol. 17 r ; cf. Cambridge 1995, p. 112, n. 4. The MS also has the variants indicated by the editors of Cambridge 1995 for the two 1518 editions on pp. 72, n. 9; 78, n. 10; 130, n. 13; and 136, n. 16.
10 For a description of the book, see López Estrada, 'La primera versión española de la *Utopía* de Moro, por Jerónimo Antonio de Medinilla (Córdoba, 1637)', in M. P. Hornik (ed.), *Collected Studies in Honour of Américo Castro's Eightieth Year* (Oxford: Lincombe Lodge Research Library, 1965), p. 291, n. 2.
11 See Córdoba 1637, fol. 2 r.
12 We suggest that this quotation of the second line of Martial's two-line epigram 91, placed after Medinilla's translation of chapter IX and thus closing the whole volume, serves as a defence of his translation against criticism: 'Either don't carp at ours, or publish your own.' For a different interpretation, see López Estrada, 'La primera versión española de la *Utopía*', p. 300.

page included, make up the first twenty-four folios with roman numbering. Apart from the title-page, index and colophon, we have four groups of paratexts: 1) preliminaries by the translator: dedication, preface and translator's commentary on chapter nine; 2) four letters of recommendation; 3) nine laudatory poems, two of which are in Latin; and 4) official civil and ecclesiastical approvals.[13]

The title-page is purely typographical, apart from the discreet ornament framing a quotation from Tacitus. Of the original Latin title, Medinilla has retained only the last word: UTOPIA. The title is placed first, in capital letters, followed by the name of the author in capitals in an even larger type. More's work was already commonly referred to by an abbreviated title from the time of the earliest editions, as is shown by the prefatory letters of Erasmus, Budé and More himself, and the authors of the various preliminaries to Medinilla's translation all call the work *Utopia*.[14]

The printer Salvador de Cea Tesa seems to have been a rather provincial figure in seventeenth-century Spanish printing. The vast majority of the books and pamphlets he is known to have printed in the period 1620–65 are on religious matters, which is in line with the general picture of printing at the time. He does, however, also print a few books on governing, such as Alonso Carrillo Lasso's *Virtudes reales* and *Soberanía del Reyno de España*, both printed in 1626, as well as works on the city of Córdoba in particular.

At the end of the sixteenth and beginning of the seventeenth century, Córdoba, and the Andalusian region in general, enjoyed a humanist flowering in which the Jesuit colleges played a significant role. The College of Santa Catalina, founded in Córdoba in 1553, was especially important, having one of the most substantial libraries in Spain at the time. Although Córdoba had reached its humanist peak some years earlier, it was still a centre of learning at the time of Medinilla's translation. However, it was probably not a major centre of printing, and according to López Estrada no other work issued by its printing-houses during this period was comparable to the translation of *Utopia*.[15] It was not reprinted in Medinilla's lifetime, and there are few seventeenth-century references to it, which suggests that it was not widely read in its own day. Editions were published in Madrid in 1790 and 1805. No new Spanish translation appeared until 1937, three hundred years after Medinilla's version.

13 Literary preliminaries were often abundant during the Spanish Baroque, but the paratexts to Medinilla's translation are numerous even by contemporary standards, as was the ancillary material of the first Latin editions of *Utopia*. Cervantes parodied this custom in the preliminaries to *Don Quixote* (1605).
14 The title is, however, not reduced to the name of the island in any printed edition before the early seventeenth century; see above, pp. 5, 20, 82, 87.
15 López Estrada, 'La primera versión española de la *Utopía*', pp. 291, 302.

The official civil approvals and privileges of Medinilla's translation are dated in Madrid between October and December 1635, two years before the work was actually printed. They are all summaries of the legal documents: only the essential information is reproduced. The privilege authorises Medinilla to print the work for a period of ten years, and he probably spent the first two years of this privilege circulating his translation in manuscript among his friends, colleagues and 'important connections'.[16] Since the preliminaries were not included in the calculation of the price, they represented an extra cost for the printer. Although such summaries of legal documents were not unusual in texts of this period, could it be that Medinilla kept these preliminaries to a minimum to give space to (and spend the extra cost on) the impressive array of recommendations and panegyrics of his translation?

The translator's preliminaries: *Utopia* as a manual of good governance

Jerónimo Antonio de Medinilla y Porres was born around 1590 and died in 1650. He belonged to a family of noble, rural origins, and like his father he became a Knight of the Order of Santiago (1614), the patron saint of Spain. As the front page and privilege indicate, and the headings to the other paratexts insistently repeat, Medinilla was Equerry of his Majesty and Lord of the towns of Bocos, Rozas and Remolino, and recently appointed Royal Representative and Chief Magistrate of the city of Córdoba and its territory. According to Bartolomé Jiménez Patón's 'Testimony'[17] he was also former governor of the town of Villanueva de los Infantes and its district. Medinilla is thus primarily a practical man of government. No other works by him are known to have been printed, but Jiménez Patón suggests that Medinilla had 'drafts' of other translations that he urges him to print.[18] The *Methodus ad faciliorem historiarum cognitionem* (1566) by the French political philosopher Jean Bodin is said to have been among these drafts. Bodin's major work is of course his work on 'perfect governing', *Les Six Livres de la République* (1576), which was influential well into the seventeenth century. However, it seems highly significant in our context that Medinilla showed an interest in Bodin's critical analysis of history.[19] Even though Bodin was anti-Machiavellian, he was still

---

16 See for example the prologue, dated May 1637, by the Augustinian Father Francisco de Cabrera to a work by Bartolomé Jiménez Patón on the question of dress, *Discurso de los tufos, copetes y calvas* (1639), which is dedicated to Medinilla and mentions his translation of *Utopia* that he (Cabrera) 'would like to see printed'.
17 See Part II, pp. 268–9.
18 See Part II, pp. 244–5.
19 Information on Medinilla's draft translation is found in Nicolás Antonio, *Bibliotheca Hispana Nova*, ed. Mario Ruffini (Turin: Bottega d'Erasmo, 1963; Rome, 1672), vol. 1, p. 567. In fact, Bodin's *République* had been translated into Spanish in 1590 by Gaspar de Añastro and printed in Turin. This version with 'Catholic emendations' was supervised by

regarded by most Spaniards as a disciple of Machiavelli. The Spanish political theorists attacked him, but were at the same time seduced by his writings. They recognised that Machiavelli's theory had been successful in practice and they saw the need for a pragmatic reason of state, but they could not accept a theory of state that separated politics from (Christian) morality.[20]

Medinilla's particular interest in works on government is reflected in the quotation from Tacitus that appears on the title-page of his translation. As López Estrada has pointed out, the quotation is cut rather abruptly, making the paragraph difficult to understand. The complete passage reads: 'For every nation or city is governed by the people, or by the nobility, or by individuals.[21] After the form of the state has been selected from these and constituted, it can more easily be praised than it can come into existence, or if it does come into existence, it can hardly be long-lasting.'[22] The quotation may not only imply that *Utopia* was impossible to realise, as López Estrada seems to argue;[23] it may also reflect Medinilla's political attitude. From Medinilla's perspective of practical politics, it was self-evidently relevant to search for solutions in the works of Tacitus, Bodin and More.

The vernacular reception of Tacitus in Spain is late, partly owing to the fear of his pernicious influence if read in translation. An anonymous seventeenth-century document[24] comments on the dangers of translating Tacitus into

---

the Inquisition in Murcia, and although it was found worthy of several expurgations, it was totally prohibited in Sandoval's *Index librorum prohibitorum et expurgatorum* (1612). This may explain why Medinilla opted for a translation of the *Methodus*, which had been prohibited in Quiroga's 1583 *Index et catalogus librorum prohibitorum*, but only had a few expurgations in the 1612 *Index*. See Ángel Alcalá, 'El humanista y cronista real Pedro de Valencia (1555–1620) y la crisis española de los siglos XVI-XVII' in Pierre Civil (ed.), *Siglos dorados: Homenaje a Agustín Redondo*, vol. I (Madrid: Castalia, 2004), p. 5.

20 See Elena Cantarino, 'Tratadistas político-morales de los siglos XVI y XVII (Apuntes sobre el estado actual de la investigación)', *El Basilisco*, 21 (1996), 4–7. For an updated contextualisation of this period in Spanish intellectual history in English, see Jeremy Robbins, 'The arts of perception: the epistemological mentality of the Spanish Baroque 1580–1720', *Bulletin of Spanish Studies*, 82 (2005), 1–289, especiallly chapters 3 and 4.

21 This first sentence is omitted by Medinilla. In the original, it reads as follows: 'Nam cunctas nationes et urbes populus aut primores aut singuli regunt' (Tacitus, *Annals* IV. 33, trans. John Jackson (London: William Heinemann and Cambridge, MA: Harvard University Press, Loeb Classical Library, 1937), pp. 56–7). Presumably Medinilla was not happy with the idea that the people might govern a city or nation.

22 Part II, pp. 234–5.

23 López Estrada, *Tomás Moro y España*, p. 83.

24 'Censura sobre los Annales e Historias de Caio Cornelio Tácito, para consultar si será bien imprimir su traducción en español' (MS 13086, Biblioteca Nacional, Madrid). See the doctoral thesis by María Teresa Cid Vázquez, 'Tacitismo y razón de estado en los "Comentarios Políticos" de Juan Alfonso de Lancina' (Madrid: Universidad Complutense de Madrid, 2001). Cid Vázquez argues that the document is written by the author and ambassador Diego Saavedra Fajardo (1584–1648), who embodies a typical Spanish attitude in both admiring Tacitus and expressing scepticism towards him in his emblem-book on political theory *Idea de un principe político-cristiano representado en cien empresas* (Munich

a language accessible to all sorts of people: Tacitus enumerates the vices of Tiberius in order to reprehend them, but his style is such that this can easily be misunderstood by the unlearned reader, according to the author. Nevertheless, Tacitus was translated into Spanish in the early seventeenth century. That his translators were more interested in the political than the philological aspects of the work is easily explained by the fact that they were all functionaries of the court: soldiers, jurists, historians, diplomats, rather than humanists. The story of the translation and reception of Tacitus thus furnishes at least two interesting parallels to Medinilla's translation of the 'modern' text *Utopia*: it was carried out by men of practical skills related to governance (like Medinilla)[25] rather than by humanists, and there was a fear of the work being 'misunderstood' by the common public.

In general, Spanish theorists tried to make the Machiavellian idea of the reason of state compatible with the traditional doctrine of the subordination of politics to morality and religion, giving rise to Spanish Tacitism as an original movement. References to Tacitus in seventeenth-century Spanish texts are legion, but the condemnation of the Roman historian also becomes a commonplace, since many authors regard the references to him as a covert way of passing on the Machiavellian message, considering both Tacitus and Machiavelli as belonging to the impious sect of *políticos*.[26] The most important means of access to the thoughts of Tacitus in Spain was through the (expurgated) Spanish translation of the Flemish humanist Justus Lipsius' work on politics *Politicorum libri sex*.[27] It is quite possible that Medinilla is not quoting Tacitus directly, but rather via the writings of Lipsius or other works on Tacitus.

Medinilla also highlights *Utopia* as a political manual in his dedication to Juan de Chaves y Mendoza, president of the Council of the military and religious orders as well as of His Majesty's Council and Chamber, offering him his translation in gratitude for favours related to the public offices granted him after his father's death. He recommends *Utopia* to a recipient who like himself is a man of practical politics, speaking of it not as a brilliant or witty humanist invention, but as a conception that can be put into practice: 'I chose

---

1640, Milan 1642), better known as *Empresas políticas*, which was widely read across Europe in vernacular as well as Latin translations.

25 One of these was Baltasar Álamos de Barrientos (1555–1643), whose translation with commentaries was completed in 1594 while he was in prison for his friendship with Antonio Pérez, Philip II's once highly trusted secretary who fell from favour. His translation was only printed twenty years later as *Tácito español ilustrado con Aforismos por don Baltasar Álamos de Barrientos. Dirigido a don Francisco Gómez de Sandoval y Rojas, Duque de Lerma* (Madrid: Luis Sánchez, 1614). The translation was based on Lipsius' edition of Tacitus.

26 'Politician' and 'politics' often had a pejorative meaning until well into the seventeenth century in Spain, sometimes used synonymously with the equally pejorative 'Machiavellian', or even 'atheist'; for an example from Medinilla himself, see Part II, pp. 240–1.

27 Translated by Bernardino de Mendoza and printed in Madrid in 1604. The fact that Lipsius reconverted to Catholicism in 1591 understandably boosted his influence in Spain.

the occasion of the translation of Thomas More's *Utopia*, an idea that until now was only wished for in this age, and not realised because thought to be impossible.'[28]

In his preface to the reader, Medinilla continues his elaboration of the political aspects of *Utopia*, comparing the laws and rules of More's ideal republic favourably to those of the Ancients, and he argues that even the most adept political thinker will find this text as rewarding as the most perfect works on government, such as those of Livy or Tacitus. More's *Utopia* represents a 'treasure' that Medinilla wants to make available to all varieties of people, thus serving his country.

The question of censorship: the 'Testimony' and the translator's note on chapter IX

Medinilla obviously felt the need to explain to his readers certain aspects of the chapter on the religions of the Utopians. He remarks on the way in which the words of the Catholic theologians and martyrs are often abused by people who are opposed to the orthodox faith and who propagate their own distorted doctrines. In the later part of his career, More himself would no doubt have shared the view Medinilla expresses here in the light of the Lutheran heresy which began to emerge in the year after the publication of *Utopia*.[29] This also sounds like an echo of the prologue by the Inquisitor General Cardinal Gaspar de Quiroga[30] to the Spanish *Index et Catalogus librorum prohibitorum* of 1583 where *Utopia* figures, although Thomas More is recognised as a man of true Christian faith.[31] In fact, the reception of More as a martyr in Spain is better documented than the reception of Medinilla's translation of *Utopia*. The news of More's martyrdom reached Spain through various channels: one of the first was a 'newsletter' by a Spanish merchant sent from London in 1535 and probably printed shortly thereafter.[32] Another work that is important

---

28 Part II, pp. 236–7.
29 See the well-known passage from Book II of the *Confutation of Tyndale's Answer* (1532): 'I saye therfore in these dayes in whyche men by theyr owne defaute mysseconstre and take harme of the very scrypture of god, untyll menne better amende, yf any man wolde now translate Moria [i.e. *The Praise of Folly*] in to Englyshe, or some works eyther that I have my selfe wryten ere this, all be yt there be none harme therin / folke yet beynge (as they be) geven to take harme of that that is good / I wolde not onely my derlynges bookes but myne owne also, helpe to burne them both wyth myne owne handes' (Thomas More, *Collected Works*, vol. 8, Part I, ed. L. A. Schuster *et al.* (New Haven and London: Yale University Press, 1973), p. 179).
30 Curiously, this Quiroga, born in 1512, is the nephew of Vasco de Quiroga, who some fifty years earlier attempted to put the Utopian ideals into practice in Mexico.
31 See *Index de L'Inquisition Espagnole. 1583, 1584*, ed. J. M. De Bujanda (Sherbrooke: Centre d'Études de la Renaissance, Université de Sherbrooke, and Geneva: Droz, 1993), p. 879; see also above, pp. 26–7.
32 *Carta enviada de Inglaterra por un mercader español: de la muerte gloriosa del maestro Tomás Moro, chanceller mayor de dicho reino* (see López Estrada, *Tomás Moro y España*, p. 25).

for the cultural transfer of this story is the *De origine ac progressu schismatis Anglicani* by the English Catholic Nicholas Sanders, which the Jesuit Pedro de Ribadeneira used as the main source for his history of the English schism, one of the period's most widely-read works in Spain.[33] Ribadeneira also wrote a brief 'life' of Thomas More. Another account of the martyr's glorious life and death was the Sevillan poet Fernando de Herrera's *Tomás Moro* (1592, printed in Madrid in 1617). References to More as a martyr are frequent in the paratexts of Medinilla's translation, which thus comes to occupy a place already prepared for it, in some sense, by More's exemplary status.

The 'Testimony', dated September 1637, forms one of the ecclesiastical permissions and is the last official approval included before the work was printed. As Quiroga's 1583 *Index* shows, *Utopia* was prohibited until expurgated; the few passages in need of expurgation are indicated in his 1584 *Index*.[34] Although *Utopia* did not appear in the Indexes of 1612 (with an appendix in 1614) and 1632, the translation into Spanish did of course attract the attention of the Inquisition.[35] Jiménez Patón, in his capacity as censor appointed by the Grand Inquisitors of Murcia, affirms that he has considered the present translation of *Utopia* according to the 'most recent Catalogue and Expurgatory Index' and that although other printings of *Utopia* needed some expurgations, this present edition does not. He even underlines that the translation's newly expurgated passages make it suitable for immediate publication, alluding to modifications that Medinilla made in his translation of Book II, especially chapter IX.[36]

Medinilla himself claims in his note on this chapter that he has 'not cut any of the text, and has kept the laws of translation', but he did actually make some modifications.[37] He has tried, he says, to 'convey more of the spirit of the author than of his words' and preferred brevity, 'to say much in a short space, to expand not pages, but thoughts'.[38] The principal deviation from the original is of course that the whole of Book I is silently omitted. As we have seen, the preliminaries underline the importance of *Utopia* as a political work,

33 *Historia eclesiástica del scisma de Inglaterra* (Madrid, 1588). For his work on the Anglican schism, Sanders drew on the lost biography of More by William Rastell; see Hugh Trevor-Roper, 'The image of Thomas More in England', in *La fortuna dell'Utopia*, p. 8.
34 Bujanda, *Index*, p. 1035. The *Index* refers to Basel 1563.
35 Of the works on the 1583 *Index* 74 per cent were in Latin, 8.5 per cent in Spanish and 17 per cent in other languages; see Henry Kamen, *The Spanish Inquisition: An Historical Revision* (London: Weidenfeld & Nicolson, 1997), p. 113.
36 See Part II, pp. 268–9.
37 We shall not make detailed comparisons between the Latin original and Medinilla's translation, but only comment on a few aspects. For further examples, see the section 'El criterio de la versión', in López Estrada, 'La primera versión española de la *Utopía*', pp. 304–8.
38 Part II, pp. 238–41. According to López Estrada, this strategy of concision sometimes obscures the text in Medinilla's translation, although the essential is preserved ('La primera versión española de la *Utopía*', p. 305).

an ideal of good governance. Thus, what interests Medinilla and his fellow authors of prefatory materials is More's construction of the Utopian republic that is displayed in Book II, while the sophisticated courtly dialogue in Book I where Hythloday, Giles and More debate specific political and social issues, typical of early sixteenth-century humanism, is considered of less relevance to the seventeenth-century Spanish reader.

The title of chapter IX, 'De religionibus utopiensium', is the only one which has not been translated accurately by Medinilla: he renders the plural 'religions' of the original by 'De la religión'. There are at least two other significant deviations from the original in this chapter: when the erroneous belief that animals have immortal souls is cited as a view that is not forbidden, this last part of the paragraph is omitted.[39] Likewise, at the end of the text after Hythloday has finished his story, the narrator in Medinilla's translation does not mention that he finds many of the things Raphael has recounted 'absurd'.[40] Medinilla probably wanted to rid the text of any doubts about the perfection of the Utopian model.

Perhaps he also believed that he had removed the absurdities. In fact, in his note on the chapter, Medinilla converts the various religions of the Utopians into practices within the 'Evangelical Roman Catholic' religion, mentioning the diversity of monastic and mendicant, as well as military, orders of his own times. Thus he has effectively 'normalised' – that is, censored – More's bold account of Utopian religions. However, as we have seen in relation to Spanish Tacitism, the question of religion is inseparable from the political debate in Medinilla's context: Spanish authors like Pedro de Ribadeneira[41] fiercely attacked what they considered the 'false reasons of state' of for example Machiavelli (using religion for a political purpose) or Bodin (permitting liberty of conscience and a plurality of cults), which did not give Christian morality priority in politics.[42]

Such problems may explain the absence of earlier translations;[43] indeed,

---

39 Córdoba 1637, fol. 43 r; cf. Cambridge 1995, pp. 224–5.
40 Córdoba 1637, fol. 51 r; cf. Cambridge 1995, pp. 246–7.
41 Ribadeneira's treatise on governing, *Tratado de la religión y virtudes que debe tener el príncipe cristiano para gobernar y conservar sus estados, contra lo que Nicolas Maquiavelo y los políticos deste tiempo enseñan* (Madrid, 1595; included in *Obras escogidas de Pedro de Ribadeneira*, ed. Vicente de la Fuente, Madrid; Atlas, 1952), was dedicated to the 'Christian Prince' and directed against the teachings of Machiavelli and the 'politicians of this age'.
42 See Alfonso Moraleja Juárez, 'Baltasar Gracián y el impío Bodino', in *Baltasar Gracián: ética, política y filosofía* (Oviedo: Fundación Gustavo Bueno, Pentalfa Ediciones, 2002), pp. 105–22.
43 Interestingly, the first Spanish translation of Montaigne's *Essais,* which was made at about the same time as Medinilla's translation of *Utopia*, was never printed. The reasons for this are somewhat unclear, as the translation had already received the necessary approvals by September 1637, but one hypothesis is that the preface of the translator himself (Diego de Cisneros, theologian and collaborator of the Holy Office), which drew attention to the

Quevedo bears witness to this in his letter of recommendation: 'There has been no lack of readers of good sense who have read some propositions of this book with indignation, judging that the liberties the author takes do not always tread securely within the boundaries of the Religion.'[44] However, the work of censors in removing suspect passages and the now widely recognised status of More as perhaps the first Counter-Reformation martyr, cancelling out More's earlier Erasmian associations, had finally made it possible to publish *Utopia* in Spain.

Humanists and politicians: the letters of recommendation

The names of the most famous contributors to Medinilla's carefully packaged volume reflect both the Spanish preoccupation with politics and Spanish humanism in this period. While the renowned humanist and professor of eloquence at Villanueva de los Infantes, Bartolomé Jiménez Patón, primarily emphasises Medinilla's merits as a translator in his letter, the celebrity contribution to the preliminaries, Francisco de Quevedo's 'Description, Judgement and Recommendation', is above all about Thomas More and the political relevance of *Utopia* rather than about Medinilla's translation.

Jiménez Patón praises Medinilla for obeying the rules of his namesake St Jerome, not translating word for word, but according to the sense. His praise of Medinilla's style of translation also includes a none-too-subtle highlighting of his own teachings and theory of translation, implying that Medinilla had been his student.[45] Quevedo claims to be the one who encouraged Medinilla to translate the book;[46] nevertheless, Medinilla's closest ally in his Utopian enterprise is most likely to have been Jiménez Patón, who flaunts his function as censor of this translation as well as panegyrist, and he is also one of very few contemporary sources who mention Medinilla's translation elsewhere in his own writings. As a final touch to his praise, Jiménez Patón emphasises that it is good that 'our homeland' can enjoy this excellent translation, since its 'first author Raphael Hythloday was Spanish'. Hythloday's nationality (in

---

supposedly unorthodox and 'dangerous' parts of Montaigne's work, made the Inquisition change its mind. The *Essais* were finally put on the Spanish Index of prohibited books in 1640. See Otilia López Fanego, 'Actualidad de Montaigne: Los *Essais*, una traducción por hacer', *1616: Anuario de la Sociedad Española de Literatura General y Comparada*, 4 (1981), 32.

44 Part II, pp. 246–7.
45 See López Estrada, 'La primera versión española de la *Utopía*', p. 294. Anton Martí comments that Jiménez Patón was 'childishly vain'; he had, for example, accumulated a great number of laudatory poems for the publication of his work on rhetoric, *Mercurius Trimegistus* (1621), just like his 'student' Medinilla (Martí, *La preceptiva retórica española en el siglo de oro* (Madrid: Gredos, 1972), p. 265, n. 74).
46 See Part II, pp. 246–7.

fact Portuguese, but Portugal was under Spanish dominion until 1640) is only mentioned in Book I, to which neither Jiménez Patón nor Medinilla makes any reference. Jiménez Patón states it as a matter of fact, apparently without taking account of Hythloday's fictional status; this apparent example of a willingness on the part of the authors of the Córdoba 1637 paratexts to enter into More's fictional game is so brief and residual that it demonstrates how far this perspective was from their minds.

Quevedo was Lord of the towns of Cetina and Torre de Juan Abad, situated about twenty kilometres from Villanueva de los Infantes. Torre de Juan Abad caused him long-drawn-out legal disputes and Medinilla was probably involved in part of this bureaucratic process due to his various offices as governor.[47] Both Medinilla and Quevedo belonged to the lower nobility and had been admitted to the Order of Santiago some twenty years earlier. However, whereas Quevedo was one of the outstanding authors of his time and had spent his life attached to the court in Madrid, Medinilla was serving the King as an administrator in the provinces. Quevedo's involvement in the politics of the time was of a different order: he undertook diplomatic missions to Italy in 1613–18 as counsellor to his friend the Duke of Osuna, Viceroy of Sicily and later of Naples, and he was granted the honorary title of Secretary to the King in 1632.

When Quevedo praises Medinilla's translation, he does not express an opinion visible in any of his other writings. In fact, in certain of his letters from the period 1635–37, he portrays Medinilla quite unfavourably as a harsh governor, accusing him of being a 'Nicolaíta', that is to say a Machiavellian,[48] and referring to an episode from the *Ragguagli di Parnasso* (1612–13) by the anti-Spanish Italian author Traiano Boccalini.[49] In mentioning the same work by Boccalini in his letter of recommendation, it is not unlikely that Quevedo is covertly giving his true opinion of Medinilla as a governor. However, now that Medinilla holds the important office of *corregidor* of Córdoba, Quevedo probably found it best to be on good terms with him. There is no mention of Medinilla's translation or of his own preface to the Spanish *Utopia* in Quevedo's letters.

In speaking of the prefatory letters of Erasmus and Budé as 'printed in the text of this book', Quevedo is clearly referring to his own Latin copy of

---

47 On Quevedo and Torre de Juan Abad, see Pablo Jauralde Pou, *Francisco de Quevedo (1580–1645)* (Madrid: Castalia, 1998), p. 223.
48 See the letter to Sancho de Sandoval (14 March 1637) in Francisco de Quevedo, *Obras completas. Obras en verso*, vol 2, ed. Felicidad Buendía (Madrid: Aguilar, 1986 (1943)), p. 957. According to López Estrada ('La primera versión española de la *Utopia*', p. 296), a marginal note by Sandoval in this letter explains that Quevedo is referring to Medinilla.
49 The first part of the *Ragguagli* was translated into Spanish by Fernando Peres de Sousa in 1634 in *Discursos politicos, y avisos del Parnasso*.

Utopia, Louvain 1548, and not to Medinilla's translation.[50] This copy carries only one marginal note in his hand in Book II, about how rich men conspire to exploit the poor, while Book I and some of the prefatory letters are heavily marked.[51] Quevedo himself provides an interesting example of the partial textual transfer of More's *Utopia* to Spain. Barely two years before Medinilla's translation was printed, Quevedo translated a passage from Book I in his political pamphlet *Carta al serenísimo, muy alto y muy poderoso Luis XIII* (12 July 1635), occasioned by France's declaration of war on Spain on 6 June that year.[52] Quevedo sees many parallels between the political-historical situation of More's day and his own. However, although he himself wrote satirical 'fictions' inspired by many of the same classical authors as More, including Lucian, and although he recognised that *Utopia* belonged to the same genre,[53] Quevedo too stresses the book's character as a political manual: 'If those who govern were to follow its precepts, and those who obey were to govern themselves by it, rulers would have no burdens and their subjects would have no cares.'[54] Quevedo himself is the author of several political works advising the sovereign, directly in some, more allegorically in others, but always rooted in Catholic orthodoxy. This is true for example of his bestseller within the genre, *Política de Dios, gobierno de Cristo y tiranía de Satanás* (Madrid, 1626), where Christ is the model for the ideal governor.

However, perhaps the most interesting paratext of Medinilla's translation takes us back to Spanish humanism. This is the third letter of recommendation, by the Jesuit Cipriano Gutiérrez, of whom we know virtually nothing, apart

50 See Part II, pp. 244–5. Quevedo's copy of Louvain 1548 is preserved in the Biblioteca Nacional de Madrid (shelfmark R 20494).
51 Several passages in Book I are marked as 'Erasmian'; see Royston O. Jones, 'Some notes on More's "Utopia" in Spain', *Modern Language Review*, 45 (1950), 480. The marginal notes in Quevedo's copy of *Utopia* have been studied by López Estrada, 'Quevedo y la *Utopía* de Tomás Moro', in *Homenaje al profesor Giménez Fernández* (Sevilla: Universidad de Sevilla, 1967), 155–96; and Carmen Peraita Huerta, 'Mapas de lectura, diálogos con los textos: la Carta al rey Luis XIII y las anotaciones en el ejemplar de la *Utopía* de Quevedo', *La Perinola*, 8 (2004), 321–41.
52 The passage translated is the one where Hythloday speaks of the necessity for kings to be philosophers and philosophers kings (Cambridge 1995, pp. 82–3). Quevedo comments on this, reminding how Thomas More 'foretold present events' and gave 'prudent counsel' (*Obras completas. Prosa*, ed. Felicidad Buendía (Madrid: Aguilar, 1992 (1932)), vol. 1, pp. 1007–8).
53 See Part II, pp. 244–7. In the paragraph where Quevedo explains the term 'Utopia' (there is no such place, that is, it is a 'fiction') several key words reveal the text's kinship with the satirical genre: 'reprehender' (criticise), 'fingir' (feign), 'fabricó' (constructed), 'reprehendió los desórdenes' (rebuked the misrule), 'a todos los reprehende' (rebukes everyone), and last but not least he mentions this in connection with the Menippean satire *Ragguagli di Parnaso* by Boccalini, whom he accuses of plagiarising More's *Utopia*. On Quevedo's relations with Boccalini, see Mercedes Blanco, 'Del Infierno al Parnaso: escepticismo y sátira política en Quevedo y Trajano Boccalini', *La Perinola*, 2 (1998), 173–93.
54 Part II, pp. 246–7.

from what the heading tells us: he was Master of the Holy Scripture at the Jesuit College of Santa Catalina in Córdoba. Gutiérrez's text may be characterised as a perfect synthesis of the Jesuit academic rhetoric of the time, with its classical learning, its quotations of *auctoritates* and its varied 'conceptist' word-play.[55]

For Gutiérrez, *Utopia* is 'a glorious idea', and as such a model for imitation, above all moral imitation. 'Idea' is here to be understood in the sense given by Covarrubias in his 'dictionary',[56] where he relates it to its etymological root meaning, 'to see', because to make something in imitation of an original or a model, one has to have the model in front of oneself, like a painter. Thus it is a model in a more concrete sense than the Platonic idea, a model to imitate rather than a model of perfection. Gutiérrez therefore situates More's text within two coordinates: as a work of moral reprehension, and as a work within the tradition of 'imaginary republics'. The prevalence of vice in all ages ('O ages, you are all alike!') calls for its repression by means of satire, or, as Gutiérrez puts it, 'bitter, barbed tracts' which 'hide the pill under a silver surface' or 'mask it with foreign words'.[57]

This leads him to explain why satire is necessary. He recalls how it was prohibited in classical times because it had been reduced to mere personal attacks; however, owing to the persistency of vice, satire returned with renewed forces. Even though his argument and examples are taken from classical texts, Gutiérrez is obviously alluding to the currency of satire in seventeenth-century Spain. Satire was less a precise genre than an attitude demonstrated in various kinds of texts, and this allows us to connect the view he expresses here with his manner of understanding *Utopia*; more particularly, it suggests that the constant reference he makes to 'foreign words' alludes to More's intention when employing the Greek construct 'Utopia' in his Latin text. By showing us the 'no place/good place', he reprehends the 'real place/bad place' – that is, the real world, full of vice. Gutiérrez proves this to be

---

55 Most of these paratexts, but Gutiérrez's in particular, display *conceptismo*, the main literary style of the Spanish seventeenth century, which emphasises the role of wit, as expressed in Baltasar Gracián's *Agudeza y arte de ingenio, en que se explican todos los modos y diferencias de conceptos* (1648). The word *ingenio* ('wit') denotes the mental faculty that produces and deciphers conceits (*conceptos*); these are expressed and codified in *agudezas* (subtleties of thought and language). The more difficult the conceit, the greater the pleasure in deciphering the meaning; this 'doctrine of difficulty' is essential to *conceptismo*, which requires an active and 'ingenious' reader. *Conceptismo* may also be seen as a style of thinking that reflects the struggle to keep together a cultural world on the verge of disintegrating. For a thorough examination of the phenomenon, see Mercedes Blanco, *Les Rhétoriques de la pointe: Baltasar Gracián et le conceptisme en Europe* (Paris: Editions Champion, 1992).
56 Sebastián de Covarrubias Horozco, *Tesoro de la lengua castellana o española*, ed. Martín de Riquer (Barcelona: Alta Fulla, 1993 (1611)), p. 726.
57 Part II, pp. 250–1.

More's intention by referring to Varro's Menippean satires, which bore Greek titles designed to veil their satirical subject.

Gutiérrez compares this satirical use of foreign names to the resources used by other authors of 'ideal republics' to reprehend the evil ways of the world: Cicero called his books on republics 'dreams', while Plato used the dialogue form, 'which served as a disguise for his indignant Philosophy'.[58] One notes also that Gutiérrez emphasises the masking, the concealment of these ideal republics in the form of dreams or dialogues, which brings out their fictitious, and thus moral, character.[59] The unattainable model – like More's *Utopia* –is a perfect example of reprehension, as Gutiérrez goes on to explain: 'a land and province that does not exist, so that the realm which should be will become that which is'.[60]

Even though both Medinilla and Gutiérrez regard *Utopia* as a model to imitate, an 'idea', their conception of this imitation is different. Gutiérrez sees the moral function of the book as operating through the fiction, while Medinilla perceives a need to put into practice the laws and rules given in the text, and thus proposes it as a political manual.[61] Likewise, as we have seen, Quevedo does not seem to pay attention to the satire or wit of *Utopia*, being more intent on actualising *Utopia* in the context of his own didactic-political works. This gives us an insight into the way *Utopia* was interpreted in the period, relegating its satirical character to a secondary level that only a humanist like Gutiérrez, less attentive to political questions, will bring to the fore. These parallel conceptions of *Utopia* lead to two different uses of the work: a practical realisation of Utopia in America, for example in the Jesuit communities of Paraguay; or the redeployment of the Utopian fiction in various texts, from the anonymous Counter-Reformation *Omnibona*, via *Don Quixote* and its 'Ínsula Barataria', to the eighteenth-century Utopian work *Sinapia*.[62]

However, Medinilla, Quevedo and Gutiérrez all share the reading of More's text as an attack on England. In much the same way as Quevedo's reading of *Utopia* is coloured by the post-schismatic English and European scene, so Gutiérrez directs his interpretation of the text towards a reprehension of England: by resorting to the non-existing, to fiction, to the unattainable ideal model, he suggests, *Utopia* censures the 'stubborn waywardness

---

58 Part II, pp. 252–3.
59 Cf. Aneau's preface to his French translation, discussed above, p. 76 (for the text, see Part II, pp. 188–93).
60 Part II, p. 252–3.
61 Juan Solórzano y Pereyra interprets the work in the same manner in his *Política indiana* of 1648, emphasising above all the laws that apply in *Utopia* and their functionality.
62 See Stelio Cro's comprehensive study, 'La utopía de las dos orillas (1453–1793)', *Cuadernos para investigación de la literatura hispánica*, 30 (2005), 15–268.

of the British regions' (Part II, pp. 252–3). That there 'is no such place' may thus be interpreted as a key to what lies behind this text: a direct attack on England, and by extension, on all badly governed 'republics'.

Installing the new Royal Representative

As already indicated, there is little evidence of the reception of Medinilla's translation of *Utopia* in the first half of the seventeenth century. What we do have is Medinilla's own framing of this translation through the abundant preliminaries. Our interpretation of this material suggests that Medinilla had two closely related concerns: the question of the reason of state, and his own 'self-fashioning'[63] as new Royal Representative and Chief Magistrate of Córdoba.

Medinilla searches for a model of good government with Christian authority and finds it in the 120-year-old *Utopia* of the martyr Thomas More. He may perhaps be placed among the 'realist Tacitists' (like Saavedra Fajardo) who searched for a 'true' as well as 'pragmatic' reason of state, without neglecting Christian principles.[64] Medinilla chooses to translate only Book II of *Utopia*, which he reads as a handbook (reinterpreting the Latin subtitle *libellus*) for the governor and the governed. Medinilla has no interest in the fictional frame and its elaboration in the letters of the sixteenth-century humanists, nor does it occur to him to read *Utopia* as 'a work of fantasy', as R. O. Jones puts it.[65] We thus return to the question of what happened to the fictional aspect of the work in the Spanish context.

Jones claims that by the early seventeenth century *Utopia* was no longer of the practical importance it had been to earlier Spanish humanists like Vasco de Quiroga. However, as we have seen, Medinilla and his contemporaries *do* read More's work as dealing with issues of pressing relevance to their times, as Jones argued that the first readers of *Utopia* did. We consider that Medinilla's primary purpose in communicating Utopia to his fellow countrymen is to make the praise of the ideal governance of Utopia reflect his own governance of Córdoba and its districts.[66] Thus in seventeenth-century Spain the func-

---

63 Although not in the more sophisticated sense elaborated by Stephen Greenblatt in *Renaissance Self-Fashioning: From More to Shakespeare* (Chicago: University of Chicago Press, 1980).
64 See J. A. Fernández-Santamaría, *Reason of State and Statecraft in Spanish Political Thought (1595–1640)* (Lanham, MD, New York and London: University Press of America, 1983), pp. 189 ff. and (on Saavedra Fajardo) 246–65.
65 Jones, 'Some Notes', p. 479.
66 Medinilla here seems to be entirely in line with what the anonymous 1553 Dutch translation underlines on the title page, namely that *Utopia* is a practical handbook 'for those who in the present day have to rule a town and district, a purpose which it is above all suited to serve' (see above, p. 105).

tion of *Utopia* as a political treatise is emphasised, marginalising the narrative element.[67] This is what governs the interpretative horizon of the reception of *Utopia* among Medinilla's contemporaries. We have seen that this model has various nuances. It may be used as a means of denigrating England,[68] or as a political model to be imitated. And, in Medinilla's case, the translation may also serve to praise his own polis or *civitas*.

The pivotal point of Medinilla's use of *Utopia* as a means of self-fashioning is of course his installation as the new *corregidor*. The author of the last letter of recommendation, Andrés de Morales y Padilla, and the authors of the laudatory poems, are 'occasional poets' holding administrative or ecclesiastical offices. They all follow the same line of eulogy: primarily celebrating the newly appointed Royal Representative and Chief Magistrate. When praising Medinilla as a translator and man of letters they equally praise him as a governor who has not only translated More's text but also put his precepts into practice in the administration of Córdoba and its districts. In the poems, the parallels drawn between More-England and Medinilla-Spain are constant, as are the parallels between Medinilla's administrative functions and his education in letters.

Following this line of interpretation, we suggest that the Spanish translation of More's *Utopia* served a personal and local interest, although it must be recognised that Medinilla's office as *corregidor* was a high-ranking position in Spain. Medinilla took special care with the edition, making sure that his official titles were repeated in the headings to the various preliminaries, together with praise of the translation *and* the translator. Perhaps Medinilla also alludes to his own position when he advertises the ideas of More's *Utopia* in his preface: 'It is one thing to portray republics as they are, and quite another to depict them as they should be. And it is not enough for those who govern to be good if they do not see to it that their subjects are good as well.'[69]

Conclusion: *Utopia* in seventeenth-century Spain

The cultural transfer of *Utopia* to Spain is not due to Medinilla's translation. The Latin editions were read and acknowledged by Spanish humanists and men of letters, and the book was perhaps also read in the anonymous translation that might have circulated in manuscript among the cultured elite of the

---

67 On the question of the relationship between the 'ironical-fictional' framework of Book I and the systematic exposition of the republic of the Utopians, see Werner von Koppenfels, 'Mundus alter et idem: Utopiefiktion und menippeische Satire', *Beihefte zu Poetica*, 13 (1981), 35.
68 Jones has pointed out how 'the various eulogists ... seem to consider the work to be primarily an attack on England, thus missing the chief point of the book' ('Some Notes', p. 480).
69 Part II, pp. 236–7.

sixteenth century. The most striking indication of this is the way Utopian ideas were transferred across the Atlantic with the Spanish colonialists and attempts made to put them into practice in the New World.

Even though the necessity of an ideal model is recurrent in the tradition of 'republics', the historical context of Spain in the seventeenth century made it a matter of urgency to actualise models of good governance and put them into practice in order to solve the problems of a kingdom that was going to pieces as a result of successive wars, poverty, depopulation, corruption and bureaucracy. There was a general sense that this was a time of crisis, and Medinilla's translation may be seen to form part of a considerable outpouring of political treatises offered to Spanish readers. The enormous number of such works written in Spanish was swollen still further by a major transfer of texts from the classical tradition, as we have seen with Tacitus, and of contemporary writings by Italian and French authors such as Virgilio Malvezzi[70] and Bodin. In choosing to translate More's *Utopia*, Medinilla also responds to a fashion that spurred many translations.

Medinilla thus belongs to this legion of practical men who – like the first Spanish translators of Tacitus, who were functionaries of the court, not humanists – contributed their solutions to the question of the 'republic' by presenting models of governance. *Utopia* is for Medinilla a manual of government that should be followed and imitated, a manual that had the great advantage over the works of Tacitus and Bodin that it had acquired quasi-divine status through More's martyrdom.

Randi Lise Davenport and Carlos F. Cabanillas Cárdenas

---

70 His *Il Romulo* (Bologna, 1629) was translated by Quevedo and printed in Pamplona in 1632.

AFTERWORD: TRANSFERRING *UTOPIA*

With the help of the documents published in this volume, visualise a library desk with a precious cargo of materials for studying *Utopia*. There are copies of recent paperback and hardback editions for convenience and reference. But the bulk of the surface is taken up with copies of the forty-five known Latin and vernacular editions printed before 1650, in pre-1900 bindings.[1] Such a desk would itself be a kind of Utopia, for there is literally no place in the world where all the rare books in question could routinely be accessed together. At the British Library in London, however, one can get quite close. For it lacks only eight of the necessary copies.[2] To proceed with the real-life experiment all we need is a trolley and permission to look at them all at once!

You turn first to the modern books. You notice that facsimiles and texts of ancillary material from the early sixteenth-century editions appear not only in the fusty Yale 1965 hardback but in the glossy Oxford 1999 paperback. Prefatory letters and poems catch the eye, as well as a woodcut of Hythloday, More, and Peter Giles conversing on a grass-covered bench, an attendant nearby (from the first page of the main dialogue in the Basel 1518 editions). There is clearly an acknowledgement, dating back to at least 1965, that these ancillary materials 'set the stage' – as the Yale editor Hexter puts it – for what follows in *Utopia*.[3] How, though, is this meant to affect your reading of the text?

You then open the other, digitally printed paperback of the edition of reference for our volume, and you discover that it also recognises the value of printing and translating the paratexts to the four early editions in which More had or might have had some hand.[4] But when you read the critical notes you find that the editors still firmly identify the work, 'Thomas More's *Utopia*', with a text written by More, with his 'intentions and aspirations' for that text, and that they do not consider the paratexts they have gone to the trouble of publishing to be primary 'interpretive contexts' – except insofar as they contain

---

1 The figure is based on the editions to which reference is made in parts 1 and 2 of the Bibliography to this volume. It includes collected works that offer a text of *Utopia*. It is not the result of an independent bibliographical analysis, and counts what bibliographers usually describe as separate issues of the same edition as separate editions.
2 The British Library contains no copies of Florence 1519, Venice 1566, Paris 1585, Paris 1611 (these last two are French translations of Sansovino's version of Lando's Italian translation), Milan 1620, Hoorn 1629–30, Hoorn 1634, Córdoba 1637.
3 Yale 1965, p. 575.
4 The paperback issue of Cambridge 1995 first became available in 2006.

clues concerning its genesis.[5] Of other early editions in Latin and vernacular languages, and their new paratexts, there is no mention; they simply have no place in a volume that aims above all to deliver the 'original' work.

But what is the original work? Sprawled across the rest of the desk lies a bewildering variety of printed and bound objects of different shapes, sizes and colours, many of which, when opened, expose the inky marks of their users. How do these relate to the 'text' delivered up for historical interpretation by the modern editions? You gravitate towards the two largest folios on the table, one with a hardboard cover (Hanau 1619) and one with a soft vellum cover (Paris 1598). But you find that it is difficult to locate *Utopia* in either, and that each offers a very different setting for the work. The copy of Hanau 1619 comprises a 1,000-page 'amphitheatre of serio-ludic Socratic wisdom' which in 1707 sat – according to a manuscript inscription on the title-page – in a private Parisian library. Among myriad sections collecting ancient and modern Latin writings on small animals and natural objects, you need to search quite hard to find one devoted to a Latin text of the 'Utopia' (with Latin paratexts). The copy of Paris 1598, again, does not even mention *Utopia* on the title-page, and only briefly in the preface. You finally find a French translation of Book II included as chapter 24 – the last – of a larger work on the state and forms of government. And the first paragraph proves to be completely unfamiliar. It amounts to a paratext within the text, a highly charged set of instructions about how to read the description of the island. You are to learn from a Catholic martyr, a martyr horribly and unjustly persecuted by the King of a corrupt country, that in the 'reformation or constitution of a new Republic' ('la reformation ou constitution d'une nouvelle Republique'), new and profitable measures can always be found.[6] You would need an expert to tell you that what follows is a French translation not of a Latin text, as claimed in the preface, but of an Italian one. 'More's *Utopia*' is here reduced to the description of the island in Book II and completely re-situated.

We have already gone a long way from the modern volumes with which we started. The closest equivalent to the Yale edition among the rare books on the table appears to be an editorial enterprise of the 1560s not mentioned by the modern editors and available in no fewer than four folio copies (Louvain 1565–1566). It collects Latin works in double columns, and starts with the *Utopia*. But sandwiching the standard Latin paratexts from the first four editions are two unusual paratexts: More's epitaph and his letter from prison before his condemnation. This book, it seems, is telling a story about More the virtuous martyr to a Catholic audience in the Low Countries.

---

5 Cambridge 1995, pp. 275, xvii–xxxiii.
6 I refer to the 1598 text of Chappuys's work because there is no copy of Paris 1585 in the British Library. For the 1585 text of the same paratext, see Part II, pp. 196–7.

You move across to the grandest-looking and fattest volume on the table, a quarto with an ornate early modern binding that – a note tells you – joined the private collection of Thomas Grenville (1755–1846) in 1828. This book situates the *Utopia*, in its March 1518 Basel incarnation, at the head of a whole variety of works by Erasmus and More, including their translations of Lucian and their epigrams. By looking at a slimmer quarto of the November 1518 Basel edition, which contains just the *Utopia* and the epigrams, you work out that Grenville's copy runs together the March 1518 edition with a late-1517 volume of More's and Erasmus' Lucianic works, a volume that pre-announces the March 1518 edition in a paratextual note added by the printer at the end.

You are already a little confused. But when you open the first of a related series of five large Italian quartos (Venice 1561, 1567, 1578, 1583, 1607), things get worse. There is again no mention of *Utopia* on the title-page. (This remains the case throughout the series until the 1583 and 1607 editions.) It advertises eighteen books on government by Francesco Sansovino, whose name does not catch the eye as prominently as the inked signature of a proud owner 'Gio. Maurizio'. The other Italian copy is just as puzzling (Venice 1548). It comes in a volume with 'Tracts 1548–55' gold-tooled on the binding. When you flick it open you find the Latin text of a Cologne edition of 1555, and have to go back to the first leaves to start reading, in Italian, a work called 'Eutopia' on the fourth line of the title-page.

Where is 'More's *Utopia*'? You look across your desk for the very earliest editions of the Latin original but you find they do not stick out and that they come in two very different forms. One (Paris 1517), a little octavo, has a cramped and wordy title-page and a series of paratextual poems and letters, but nothing that is visually very arresting. Its first leaf bears the dated signature of an English owner of 1652, while your eye is drawn throughout the text to inked underlinings and marginal notes. The other (Louvain 1516), a larger octavo, likewise tells us in ink on the more spacious title-page that it was 'bequeathed' in 1706. The following two pages attract you with a detailed map of an island and the key to a strange alphabet.

Have you not seen these before? Yes, there was a very similar – but not identical – double-page in the copy you have already picked up of Basel 1524, in German, only there someone has rather inaccurately copied out the first line of the sample Utopian verses at the bottom of the page. The other German volume (Leipzig 1612), you note, has *coloured* maps throughout. You soon realise, however, that most of the maps relate to a 'Utopia Part II' (1613) that is not by More, and that uses a Utopian letter on its title-page not to be found in any key to the Utopian alphabet available on your table.[7] Then

---

7 The British Library copy of Leipzig 1612 is bound together with a copy of Joseph Hall, *Utopiae pars II. Mundus alter et idem. Die heutige newe alte Welt*, trans. G. Wintermonat

you glance at the smallest books on the table. There is the tiny 1629 Cologne edition (32mo), whose pages measure no more than 9cm by 4.5cm, and whose title-page proudly declares it to have been expurgated by the authority of the Cardinal-Archbishop of Toledo. Not much bigger is the Lyon 1559 edition (16mo). These two could easily occupy a purse or a trouser pocket. *Utopia* is indeed in these cases a *libellus*: a small book, a handbook.

To handle this variety of rebound and restored volumes on a British library desk is not somehow to encounter *Utopia* exactly as early modern consumers would have done. But it does begin to suggest what makes paratexts, including the vernacular paratexts, worth publishing, and what it is that turns these traditionally peripheral texts into *primary* documents for study of *Utopia*, or Utopia (the fictive place of Hythloday's discourse, the no-place). The clues they offer are a crucial part of the trail we have to follow to make sense of each of the objects on the library desk before us. At the same time, to follow this trail – as the contributors to part I of this volume do – is to change the whole encounter with the object of interpretation, the 'work'. It becomes an inherently mobile object, a package of transportable goods. The meaning and use of these goods depends on the vehicles and the situations in which they are transferred and transacted not just by the author and his direct agents, but by all the producers and users in the early modern marketplace.[8]

Normally, editors and critics bring or transfer contexts *to* the static early modern text, which sits there in splendid isolation waiting obediently to be historicised. The contexts might be brought in traditional fashion from the author's intellectual life, or in new historicist fashion from anecdotes or intertexts that have caught the critic's eye. This of course remains a valuable and unavoidable enterprise – one in which all contributions to the present volume, including the current one, participate. I shall end by taking contexts back to the work as a 'text' that we read in a modern edition.

But to exhibit the text for modern readers in search of historical contexts is all too often to obscure the ways in which early modern agents constructively transfer the intellectual goods they have invented or found. To borrow an anthropological idiom, the settings brought in by modern analysts tend to displace the situations proactively defined by 'native' actors.[9] So critical

---

(Leipzig: Henning Grosse, 1613), which is ascribed erroneously on the title-page and in the British Library catalogue to Albericus Gentilus. The situation of Leipzig 1612 is of course different when consulted elsewhere as a separately bound volume; there is then no indication we should understand it to be 'Utopiae pars I'.

8 The Latin etymology of trans-ferral or trans-lation (from *trans-ferre*, p. part. *trans-latus*) denotes a bearing across of things or goods from one place to another; trans-action (from *trans* + *agere*) denotes a carrying through of an action, a negotiation.

9 See Peter Burke, 'Context in Context', *Common Knowledge*, 8:1 (2002), 152–77 (163, 174–5), where he is citing the work of the anthropologist James Clyde Mitchell.

introductions largely ignore the historical paratexts that their authors go to the trouble of reproducing. The obverse can be equally true. None of the native actors whose traces are to be found on our library desk even notes the existence of the hermeneutic puzzle given such prominence in modern introductions: how the reader is to solve the 'problem' of the relationship of Book II to Book I.

Through close study of copy-specific and edition-specific features such as paratexts, we can recover the situations the native actors *did* define. We catch them in the process of transferring and transacting their goods by means of literary artefacts (artefacts made of 'letters' in any medium, oral, written, or printed), or self-consciously telling stories – including witty, invented stories – about their own and others' translations and transactions of such goods. To start with an obvious example, the most common form of early modern book-transaction is the gift. As a little, festive book associated with Lucian, the *Utopia* produced in Louvain around Christmas 1516 was probably situated as a '*strena*, a present related to a holiday that in antiquity had subversive (albeit largely symbolic) associations'.[10]

But wherever we follow the documentary traces, goods are on the move or being transacted in carefully managed ways. Within the work, of course, an invented actor transfers knowledge of a fictive place to an audience of historical figures (including Giles) in a real place (Antwerp), an audience whose own reactions are part of the invention. On 3 September 1516, More writes from London to Erasmus in Antwerp, sending him a manuscript of a work he calls 'Nusquam nostram' ('our Nowhere'), with just the prefatory epistle to Peter Giles attached. Given its own woodcut border in the Basel 1518 editions, the epistle in question begins by sending Giles an overdue work now called 'libellum ... de Utopiana republica' ('a little book about the Republic of Utopia'). It goes on wittily to offer to purchase information about the exact location of the island in the New World on behalf of a bishop who desires to go there to further the Christian religion.[11] Erasmus sends Hutten a story about *Utopia* in a letter of 1519: the second book was written at leisure but the first book was composed in the heat of the moment, when an opportunity presented itself.[12] The remark gives Hutten – and J. H. Hexter, centuries later – a different *Utopia*, but it should be seen as an actively constructed epitext, a back-story for a work published the previous year by Froben in Basel. For the letter to Hutten appeared in a 1519 folio volume of correspondence, also

---

10 Carlo Ginzburg, *No Island is an Island: Four Glances at English literature in a World Perspective* (New York: Columbia University Press, c.2000), pp. 14–15; Yale 1965, p. clxxxiv.
11 Cambridge 1995, pp. 34–5.
12 Cambridge 1995, p. xxi; J. H. Hexter, *More's 'Utopia': the Biography of an Idea* (New York: Harper and Row, 1965), p. 29.

AFTERWORD: TRANSFERRING *UTOPIA*

published by Froben in Basel, a volume with agendas specific to a particular cultural and political moment. Erasmus was consolidating his influence and connections in England. Did he want to play down the degree of More's investment in the excoriating critiques of Book I?[13]

The current volume establishes that this whole process did not stop with Basel 1518 and with the More and Erasmus circle. *Utopia* wittily exploits and captures an early modern moment when the possibilities for transporting knowledge of distant places – distant in time, space and custom – into new contexts were dramatically multiplied by new technologies such as the compass and the printing-press; a moment, also, when it was increasingly difficult to tell how genuine the transported goods were. The paratexts collected and commented upon here show us that from Louvain 1516 to Amsterdam 1643, the producers and users understood themselves to be actors in the process of transferring the fictional but 'truthful' Utopia between times, spaces, languages, and peoples.

The theatrical metaphor suggested by 'actors' is worth extending. For the best way of re-conceptualising what is happening on the British Library desk, of comprehending the various situations prescribed in the paratexts, is in terms of distinct performances of different productions of the same work. On the one hand, each book can be described not only as a 'text' of the author's work but as a distinct, collaborative *event* in which choices have been made about the mise en scène, the cast, the tone. On the other hand, there is a given – if adaptable – scenario common to all performances. The work must bring the invented 'matter' (Hythloday's no-place) before our eyes (Book II), even if it does not use the scene-setting and political debate contained in Book I. (Several of the vernacular editions discard it in full or in part.)[14] From this perspective, each production is staging the 'original' performance of Hythloday, and transferring knowledge of an invented no-place on a given occasion to a new place, a new audience by means of a new invention, print. At the same time, each may be conscious of and draw upon prior productions and their trappings.

We can then begin to build a sense of the ways in which the mise en scène and the action vary from performance to performance. The work may be put

---

13 D. Erasmus, *Farrago nova epistolarum D. Erasmi Roterodami ad alios et aliorum ad hunc* (Basel: Froben, 1519). On this volume and its moment see Lisa Jardine, 'Before Clarissa: Erasmus, "Letters of Obscure Men", and epistolary fictions', in T. Van Houdt, J. Papy, G. Tournoy and C. Matheeussen (eds), *Self-Presentation and Social Identification: The Rhetoric and Pragmatics of Letter Writing in Early Modern Times* (Leuven: Brill, 2002), pp. 385–403.
14 This is the case in Basel 1524; Venice 1561, 1567, 1578, 1583, 1607; Paris 1585, 1598, 1611; Leipzig 1612; Córdoba 1637.

on a bare or a cluttered stage. The action may range from a gift of a worthy work to a general public audience, made with no particular timing, to a specific act of donation marking an occasion, or an intervention in specific circumstances. The Dutch or 'low German' edition (Antwerp 1553) has no paratext to speak of beyond a printer's privilege and colophon. Other editions are not much more elaborate. A number are equipped like London 1551 with a single, new dedicatory letter and one paratextual item from the Latin edition – though this already gives us much more to go on. Leipzig 1612 has no dedicatee; its place of publication appears to have no special significance, at least not a political or religious one.

This should not be taken to mean that editions with fewer paratexts necessarily point to simpler situations of transmission. Venice 1548 would be a case in point. It is just that these editions and their situations are less visibly elaborate – less easy to elaborate upon, for the modern scholar – than others such as Basel 1524 and Córdoba 1637. The paratextual clues suggest that Chansonnette used the work in 1524 as the means for a highly specific undertaking. He was mobilising the prestige of the Basel humanists to support a particular group on the Basel council. Córdoba 1637 was a major publishing event of its time and marked Medinilla's installation as the new *corregidor* of the city. No copy of this edition made it into the British Library collections and onto our desk. Was it less likely to travel for some reason? The edition is staged with a highly complex new mise en scène that barely draws at all on the Latin paratexts – by contrast with the first two French editions that co-opt Budé, for obvious reasons, as a significant protagonist in their productions.

Likewise, when *Utopia* was transferred to Italy it lost most of its Latin paratextual baggage and became the production of a whole network of polygraphers centered on Venice. The situation of the work comprehended entire books by Lando and Doni, if not – in Lando's case – the man himself, his whole life-and-works. The Italian situation proves to be elaborate, even though – by contrast with the Spanish case – the paratexts *printed with* the Italian editions are not. In the Italian case it is the modern scholar who has to reconstruct a complex paratext by following clues in a variety of places. In so doing, is she still recovering a situation defined by early modern actors, or constructing a setting by means of her own analysis? The distinction starts to blur.

Let us break down the components of these productions a little more systematically. Instead of something stably labelled 'More's *Utopia*' we are confronted with a whole array of titles and subtitles on title-pages and elsewhere to choose from, while chapter divisions and headings also vary. The title even varies between the first two editions of the 'original' Latin work

on our British Library desk (Louvain 1516 and Paris 1517). The two different wordings already point the reader in slightly different directions; in one case towards a work that is 'no less beneficial than playful' ('nec minus salutaris quam festivus'), in the other to a work that is no less useful than elegant ('nec minus utile quam elegans'), a formulation also used by Budé at the end of his prefatory letter. In some cases, significant classical tags are hung up to catch our eye – the Tacitean tag included on the title-page of the Spanish edition indicates an intersection between the Spanish *Utopia* and the transmission of Tacitus in Spain.

As we have already seen, visual and graphic elements are assembled in different combinations to different effect. In Doni's edition the prologue is a frontispiece device distinctive to his published works – a woman with a mask. Some editions attempt graphically to reproduce the Utopian alphabet – a more straightforward enterprise if you were in Basel and able to borrow the plates and forms from the Latin edition, but very tricky elsewhere. Maps and portraits of More are relatively rare. Paris 1550 begins the main text with an illustration not dissimilar to the Basel one reproduced in modern editions (see above, pp. 69–70), but it makes the participants in the dialogues look more classical, more Roman.

Another fundamental variable in the situations of the work is the suggested or actual presence of other works. We have already seen this in the case of Wintermonat's two-part *Utopia* – as it became in 1613. The paratexts to the first Latin editions of course associate the work with Erasmus' *Praise of Folly* and other serio-ludic works, as well as famous classical discussions of the best state of a commonwealth. In other editions, or in individual paratexts, the work is situated more definitely as either a playful fiction that hides deeper truths, truths to which the actors more or less explicitly point, even as they join in the play; or as a useful handbook that directly facilitates the practice of the political and pedagogical arts, whether or not we are at the same time directed to notice the work's fictional and satirical aspects. So Florence 1519 situates *Utopia* within a series of Lucianic texts, Venice 1561 within a series of descriptions of actual states (see above, pp. 16, 59–63).

The principle extends to collections of texts specially bound for one consumer, such as the fat quarto of Lucianic Moreana-and-Erasmiana that reached Grenville. Yale University's Rare Books collection includes a copy of Louvain 1516 that has been bound in with a brief history of England and a collection of texts for teaching Greek (or in one case, Greek and Hebrew). All are inscribed on their separate title-pages by Cuthbert Tunstall, who features in *Utopia* as a protagonist. The suggestion is that this is a teaching volume designed to draw together a circle between England and the Low Countries committed to the propagation of the new Greek studies – and the print

technology that went with it – so enthusiastically welcomed by the Utopians themselves.[15]

This brings us to geography. The geographical position of the island itself is cleverly left uncertain in More's work. But to which other locations, or network of locations, do the printed objects point us, and in which ways? Do they move in local, intra- or inter-cultural orbits? We have already had a hint that Córdoba 1637 might have been intended as a local, not an international event, and 'Leipzig' only seemed significant as the site of a book fair. One set of clues linking Florence 1519 (with its paratextual letter to Richard Foxe) and London 1551 leads us to the highly significant location of Corpus Christi College, Oxford. But the contents of Venice 1561 link Utopia to a whole chain of countries and cities of the contemporary Eurasian and classical worlds, from England and Germany to Tunisia and Fez, from Rome and Athens to Sparta and Persia. And detective work on its paratexts and those of the French editions leads us out into an inter-cultural, Franco-Italian network comparable with the England-Low Countries axis constructed by the Latin editions. Indeed, a hierarchy of cultural transmission does begin to suggest itself. The Latin, French and Italian *Utopia*-events are more international in scope, whereas the German-Dutch, Spanish and English look more local in reach and impact.

A whole further set of questions about protagonists can be opened up. How many actors, playing which types of roles, with what degree of authorial agency, participate in the various printed productions? What on-stage presence do the original writer and his persona have? The original scenario of course hides 'More' behind Hythloday, but to what extent is he brought out from his cover in performance, and in what guise – Catholic martyr, or citizen of London? The second Latin edition already reveals more of 'More' than the first, by appending a second letter to Peter Giles that gives away the game – at least to those 'in the know', with some Greek up their sleeves. We then begin to notice the printed traces of a whole group of editors and translators, ranging from the figure of Erasmus pulling the threads in early Latin editions, to Medinilla-as-Jerome in the Spanish edition. Certain printers and publishers such as Froben, Beatus Rhenanus and Bidelli have authoritative parts to play.

There is another, related category of textual intermediary: the critic, recommender or censor-judge wheeled on stage to approve the work before its prospective audience, and to join and/or deconstruct the fictional game. Budé is the most significant of these members of the on-stage audience, while the Spanish editions bring on a number, including Quevedo and Gutiérrez.

---

15 Lisa Jardine, *Erasmus, Man of Letters: The Construction of Charisma in Print* (Princeton, NJ: Princeton University Press, 1993), pp. 175–80.

Then there are the imposing personae of the patrons and dedicatees. The printer Bidelli gives Milan 1620 to Giulio Arese, the president of the senate of Milan, in open expectation of a return gift of protection. He compares Arese in learning and authority directly to More himself. In the case of England 1551, circumstances suggest that the patron, William Cecil, may have encouraged an old schoolfriend to translate the work, and that he may even have played a role in getting it printed. Busleyden and Juan de Chaves do not quite assume this role but they are nevertheless weighty protagonists in their respective *Utopia*-events. Other protagonists are less easy to pigeon-hole. Peter Giles is so important to the whole scenario across both text and paratext that his role is difficult to categorise.

There is one final but crucial variable to mention: the outcome of the production, both as envisaged by the performance itself and as realised by the actual audience. Budé becomes an almost authorial figure in Le Blond's edition of 1550, which follows Paris 1517 in making reference to his prefatory epistle in the title. Indeed, Le Blond bases his paratexts on Budé's letter, suggesting that he prefers the French scholar's description of *Utopia* to Thomas More's. The translated epistle itself stages what is intended to be the Parisian audience's reaction to reading the work: quasi-religious contemplation of what Le Blond – who was in holy orders – calls (in his paratextual poem) the holy morals ('sainctes meurs') of the Utopian paradise.[16]

In the translated letter itself, Budé writes from Paris to Thomas Lupset to thank him for the gift of a copy of *Utopia*. The situation he describes is the transfer of Greek learning into Latin. For Budé situates the gift in relation to a previous favour – Lupset's loan of Linacre's translations into Latin of a Greek work by Galen, which he has been hastily perusing. Budé carries the supplementary gift with him to his country house, where he is habitually absorbed in his rustic affairs. He is so affected by the book, however, that he 'almost' drops everything to contemplate the whole art of economy and its goals. Here, it seems that the envisaged outcome of Hythloday's 'sermon' is critical discussion of tacitly accepted social and economic injustices (of the kind staged within the work in Book I), rather than pragmatic action, though Budé-Le Blond ends by describing the work as a seedbed ('pepiniere') from which his own and other ages will pull up customs ('meurs', from the Latin 'translaticios mores'), adapting them for their own citizenries.[17]

Let us move from this to the real, off-stage case of Vasco de Quiroga, a judge and bishop in the Spanish New World. The Spanish were transporting books across the Atlantic from the early 1500s and a copy of Basel 1518N, now in Texas, made it into the library of the first bishop of Mexico, Fray Juan

---

16 See Part II, pp. 182–3.
17 See Paris 1550, fols *3 r, *8 r; cf. Cambridge 1995, p. 18.

de Zumárraga, who signed and annotated it.[18] The gist of the annotations is closely related to Quiroga's response to the work, which has naturally led scholars to conjecture that he read the text in Zumárraga's copy. The response in question is highly pragmatic; it takes the form of a judicial opinion about actions to be taken.

Quiroga did not travel in person to deliver his report on the New World, like his fictional counterpart Hythloday. His written opinion was placed in a wooden box with other administrative documents, and set sail from San Juan de Ulúa in July 1532, though storms delayed its arrival in the royal council in Spain until early 1533. The box carried a description of the land and personnel of New Mexico and the opinions of each judge regarding the organisation thought to be most suitable for the new kingdom. Quiroga's is lost, but we know from a legal brief he sent across in 1535 (together with a translation – not extant – of part of the *Utopia* into Spanish) that his opinion on the best form of government for the new province was drawn up as a pattern from More's work. Though the council appear to have shown no interest, Quiroga did eventually use Hythloday's discourse as a blueprint for the reforms he introduced – including communal ownership – in two hospital-villages near Santa Fe.[19]

Here, then, we have two concluding glimpses of *Utopia* on the move. In the first case, Le Blond co-opts the letter, solicited by Lupset, in which Budé self-consciously assists in transporting *Utopia* within Europe from Louvain to Paris, and stages an appropriate reaction for the Parisian reader who has acquired a copy for their country estate. In the second case, we see a copy of *Utopia* 1518 transported back to the New World of which – in More's fiction – it had brought knowledge to the Old World, and encounter a real-life report on the New World travelling in the opposite direction in a wooden box, followed a little later by a Spanish translation.

Let us now return to the library desk to see if the 'text' we actually read in our modern paperback looks any different. We glance again at the woodcut of the scene in More's garden, handily reproduced for us in the Oxford World's Classics edition ... .

Perched on a garden bench after a good lunch, Raphael Hythloday is telling Thomas More and Peter Giles about the training and studies of the Utopians. Before the Portuguese party arrived from across the equator the islanders

---

18 The copy is located in the Benson Collection (LAC-ZZ Rare Books) at the University of Texas, call number GZZ 321.07 M813D 1518.
19 Silvio Arturo Zavala, *Sir Thomas More in New Spain: A Utopian Adventure of the Renaissance* (Hispanic & Luso-Brazilian Councils: London, 1955), pp. 12–14 and *passim*; 'Nouvelles études sur Vasco de Quiroga', *Moreana*, 15–16 (1967), 380–4; 'Vasco de Quiroga, traducteur de l'Utopia', *Moreana*, 69 (1981), 115–17.

knew nothing of classical philosophy. Yet without its help they had found out just about the same things as the ancients had. When they did hear from their visitors about the literature and learning of the Greeks ('de literis et disciplina Graecorum') they were keen to study Greek letters with Hythloday and the others. They showed great aptitude, perhaps because both they and their language were descended in some way from Greek forebears. So, Hythloday reports, '[b]efore leaving on the fourth voyage I placed on board, instead of merchandise, a good-sized packet of books ...'. He goes on to list the Greek authors transferred in this way to the new world, including a Theophrastus mutilated on the journey, and 'a Sophocles in the small typeface of the Aldine edition'. Having seen these books, the Utopians undertake to make paper and print with type, where previously they had written only on vellum, bark and papyrus.[20]

On one level the passage is a witty refraction of grand narratives of More's day. These narratives brought the act of transfer centre stage by making the Roman discovery of Greek 'letters' the foundational moment of a cultural history that culminated in a third great revival of learning – the early sixteenth-century present, the present which had gone beyond antiquity by inventing the printing-press and the compass. This is why, in the story Hythloday tells in the passage under consideration, we encounter 'letters' not as static texts waiting to be interpreted but as transferrable goods ready to be transacted.

On the ship, philosophical knowledge of humanity and nature takes the place and the form of commodities, desirable inventions transported from one place to another, then exchanged and repackaged for use in new settings. On the one hand, they take intangible forms such as Greek 'letters', intellectual gifts, knowledge of many lands ('multarum cognitio terrarum'). These goods are stored in the memories of travellers like Hythloday ready to be accessed and transferred in exchanges with the Utopians. On the other hand, they take the tangible form of printed books such as the Aldine Sophocles with its small typeface, books that are stored alongside other merchandise on a ship for transportation to foreign climes. These books carry knowledge of letters in both philosophical and mechanical senses.

Hythloday goes on to describe how the Utopians' trading activity is designed to maximise their importation of knowledge goods. They do their own exportation so as to avoid letting strangers come there to fetch away their goods. The implicit exception, of course, is Hythloday himself, who is welcome as one who brings special intellectual gifts and knowledge of many countries, and who in turn carries knowledge of Utopia's people and customs back to Europe. He – and the book which carries his discourse – claim to be

20 Cambridge 1995, pp. 180–5.

transporting not empty words, but experiential, visual knowledge of what it is to live in Utopia. But what use is he to make of this knowledge? How can he translate or transact it in European contexts? A debate on just these questions is of course staged in Book I, which now begins to look more like part of the paratextual threshold to Hythloday's discourse, and less like what it is in modern editions, an integral part of the 'main text' completely distinct in status from the ancillary materials.

For what is often described as the debate on councillorship might more accurately be labelled as the debate on knowledge transfer. 'More' insists that the kind of knowledge Hythloday has is very much in demand from princes; Hythloday responds by imagining various scenes in which he can envisage no way of getting his knowledge effectively across to a receptive audience – the etymology of his name, after all, brands him 'an expert in nonsense'. But this 'getting across' is precisely what the paratextual materials aim to both dramatise and facilitate, in the vernacular editions as well as the Latin ones.

So the narratives and interactions staged in the vernacular paratexts ultimately confront the question raised in the original scenario: how to transfer and transact the knowledge Hythloday brings from Utopia, how effectively to transport it to new locations and people. End-users such as Quiroga face the same issue in their own situations. Our conclusion must therefore be that the text does look different once we have studied the books on the British Library desk. The 'original' *Utopia* appears to have a broader paratextual threshold once we see what varies most in the translations. Many of them replace Book I altogether with paratextual materials that transact Hythloday's knowledge in new situations.

In Francis Bacon's 1605 *Advancement of learning* we read that, by contrast with pictures and statues,

> the Images of mens wits and knowledges remaine in Bookes, ... provoking and causing infinit actions and opinions, in succeeding ages. So that if the invention of the Shippe was thought so noble, which carryeth riches, and commodities from place to place, and consociateth the most remote regions in participation of their fruits: how much more are letters to bee magnified, which as Shippes, passe through the vast Seas of time, and make ages so distant, to participate of the wisedome, illuminations, and inventions the one of the other?[21]

The function of 'letters', once again, is to facilitate the displacing and sharing of intellectual goods between different places, times and peoples. The printing press, like the compass, merely extends the efficiency and range of the transportation. Bacon's words might be used as a kind of archetypal epitext for the

---

21 Francis Bacon, *The Advancement of Learning: The Oxford Francis Bacon*, vol. 4, ed. Michael Kiernan (Oxford: Clarendon Press, 2000), p. 53.

early modern learned book. For the book tells a story of knowledge transfer; it self-consciously carries the artefacts and effects of human invention from one place and situation to another, aiming to provoke and cause actions and opinions in the process. Each act of carriage is different, with its own dedicated vehicle, its own travel documents or paratexts –whether Latin or vernacular, whether fact or fiction, whether manuscript or print. In one situation, secondhand goods prepared by other agents are quickly repackaged, moved and sold on (e.g. Paris 1611); in another, a whole new trade route is negotiated, and the goods are carefully administered so that a new market can participate (e.g. Córdoba 1637). Each and every book on the library desk tells a different story about the transferring and transacting of Utopia's riches and commodities.

Warren Boutcher

PART II
THE PARATEXTS

Amsterdam 1643: Title-page. By permission of the British Library

PRINCIPLES AND EDITORIAL CONVENTIONS

The vernacular paratexts are grouped here by language in the order of the corresponding chapters of Part I. As explained above in the preface, we have not included the original Latin paratexts that reappear here and there in translation in the vernacular versions of *Utopia*, since they are available, as far as their substance is concerned, in Cambridge 1995; their importance to particular translations is indicated in Part I.[1] With this exception, each group comprises a complete set of the substantive paratexts, that is to say titlepages, prefatory materials of all kinds, and other items which are relevant to the reading of the text in its particular context. Standard privileges, tables of contents and running heads are omitted.[2] Marginal annotations are also not reproduced in Part II, but they are discussed where relevant in Part I. After the vernacular paratexts, a single prefatory letter in Latin has been included because it appears to be the only 'new' prefatory text published in a Latin edition of *Utopia* between 1519 and 1650.

For each edition, omitted items are indicated in square brackets at the place where they occur so that the overall contents and sequence of each edition can be reconstructed by the reader. The descriptions of omitted items are brief and are not intended to provide a full bibliographical description. Where more details (e.g. of printer's marks and mottoes) are included, it is because those details seem particularly striking or because they are important to the argument of the corresponding introductory chapter. Absolute consistency in this respect was not thought necessary.

In keeping with the aims of the volume as a whole, the texts themselves have been transcribed (some would prefer to say 'edited') with only a minimum of editorial intervention in order to retain as much as possible of the sense of reading a text that belongs to a specific moment of the past. (See also below, 'Editorial conventions'.) Since there are virtually no variant versions (Venice 1583 being a marginal exception), we have not needed to provide a textual apparatus, except to indicate cases where we have corrected self-evident errors; no silent corrections are made. The punctuation has similarly been

---

1 A marginal exception has been made for the German verse translations of the Utopian quatrain, since they contain features of special interest and are not to be found in easily accessible modern editions.
2 In borderline cases, the contributors to this volume have made their own decisions with regard to what to include or exclude and whether items should be reproduced in Part II or cited in the relevant chapter of Part I.

adjusted as little as possible in order to avoid foreclosing interpretation and to preserve the rhythm of the original text. Occasionally, textual problems are indicated in a note, but in general, we felt that the availability of a translation for every text made it unnecessary to enter into interpretative subtleties.

The translations provided on facing pages aim to provide a literal version which is as idiomatic as fidelity to the original will allow, without false antiquarianism or archaism of style. In some instances, especially perhaps the Spanish paratexts, the rhetoric of the texts strained modern English idiom to the limit. Needless to say, we have not striven for aesthetic effect; the verse paratexts, for example, are rendered in continuous prose, since it was impossible to achieve a line-by-line translation which corresponded helpfully and at all points with the original. Allusions and special difficulties are explained in the footnotes that accompany the translations, but always sparingly; mythological and historical references which can be looked up in standard works of reference are not included. Names and other items explained in the corresponding introductory chapter in Part I are not annotated here, nor are cross-references provided: it is expected that readers seeking a commentary will read the chapter concerned, which supplies references to Part II for all passages quoted and discussed. No translation is provided for the paratexts of the English translation, but local difficulties are explained in notes.

Transcriptions, translations and annotations have been provided by the authors of the corresponding chapters in Part I unless otherwise indicated.

Editorial conventions

The transcription of early modern texts both in the introductory chapters as quotations and in Part II presented certain difficulties. A reasonably consistent set of principles had to be found that was applicable to seven different languages, each with its own orthographic and historical peculiarities; in addition, the editorial practices currently favoured for these languages vary a good deal according to national culture. We agreed we should respect early modern orthography as far as possible, but with certain concessions to modern habits of printing and reading. We also bore in mind that this volume is addressed in the first place to Anglophone readers. The conventions we agreed to adopt, which apply to the volume as a whole, not only Part II, are as follows:

1. All signs of abbreviation, such as ampersands (excepting '&c') and superscript signs indicating an omitted letter or syllable, are resolved.

2. In the early modern vernaculars, i/j and u/v are disambiguated (in practical terms, consonantal 'i' is written as 'j', consonantal 'u' as 'v' and vice versa). Thus French 'iouuence' becomes 'jouvence'; Spanish 'Ivan' becomes 'Juan'.

3. In Latin, conventional practice is followed in distinguishing between 'u' and 'v': 'uolo' is written 'volo', 'Vtopia' becomes 'Utopia', 'qva' becomes 'qua'. However, since consonantal 'i' (as in 'ius') is familiar to modern readers of Latin, we have preserved early modern orthography in the use of i/j (i.e. we print 'ius' or 'jus' according to the text being transcribed), with one exception: we render 'ij' ('filij') as 'ii' ('filii'); this applies also to numerals ('iii' for 'iij'). The accents sometimes used in early modern Latin have been omitted here. Latin 'æ', 'œ' are printed throughout as 'ae', 'oe'.

4. Black-letter type is replaced by roman. 'Long s' is rendered by 'round s'.

5. The punctuation of the original is respected in all but the most extreme cases, such as full points in the middle of sentences and missing full points at the end of sentences. These are corrected, but the correction is indicated in a footnote. No silent corrections are made. Use of the slash (/) as punctuation in certain texts is also preserved.

6. Since the title-page is the primary vehicle by means of which the book offers itself to the reader, the title of each translation is transcribed as far as possible in the way that it appears in the original (layout, use of roman or italics, capitals or lower case), but without attempting to imitate font size, use of colour, etc.[3] Other titles and headings in the texts of Part II are, however, transcribed without such features. Elsewhere in the volume, early modern titles are printed continuously and without special typographical features. No distinction is made between small and large capitals.

7. The use of capitals for initial letters and for whole words within early modern texts is respected throughout the volume except where capitalisation is a feature associated with layout and appears to have a solely typographical function (as in section titles and headings).

8. Page- and folio-numbers within the texts are indicated in square brackets, at the exact place where they occur, in the most economical form, i.e. '3' (not 'p. 3'), 'A ii r' (not 'fol. A ii r'). The distinction between pages and folios may easily be inferred from the sequence. Hyphens at page-turns have been suppressed.

9. Principles of transcription peculiar to individual texts are indicated in a footnote to the text (or group of texts) in question.

---

[3] We have justified all titles on the centre, a principle widely adopted in the early modern period, in order to avoid problems of spacing in the few cases (e.g. Paris 1550) where the original has left and right justification.

THE GERMAN PARATEXTS

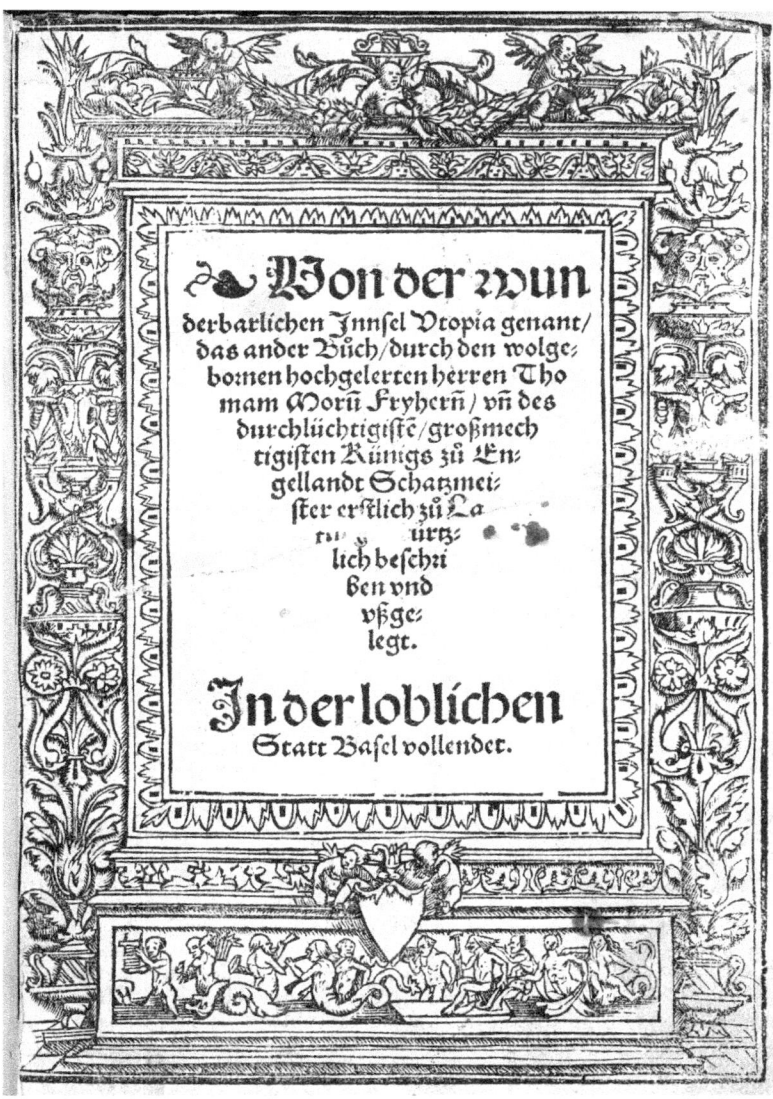

Basel 1524: Title-page. By permission of the British Library

Basel 1524

Von der wun
derbarlichen Innsel Utopia genant /[1]
das ander Bůch / durch den wolgebornen hochgelerten herren Tho
mam Morum Fryherren / und des
durchlüchtigisten / großmech
tigisten Künigs zů En-
gellandt Schatzmei-
ster erstlich zů La
tin gar kürtz-
lich beschri
ben und
ußge-
legt.

In der loblichen
Statt Basel vollendet.[2]

[map of Utopia]

[Aii r] [Utopian alphabet with Latin key; quatrain in Utopian script with roman transliteration]

Und ist die meynung diser obgeschribnen
versen in Teütscher sprach sovyl.

Utopus Hertzog hat mir gethon das /
Ein Insel gemacht / die ich nit was /

---

1 It should be noted that the slash (/) is not a symbol used by us to indicate the beginning of a new line. It is a punctuation mark used in the original text.
2 When transcribing the German paratexts, I have followed the following principles: 1. 'fz' and the (much rarer) 'ſſ' are rendered by the modern ligature *ß* provided the two letters belong to the same morph (this is always the case). 2. Like the normal form 'dafz', the abbreviation 'dz' is rendered by *daß*. 3. But 'ſſ' is always rendered *ss*. 4. 'uñ' is rendered *und* (not *unn*). 5. 'a', 'o' and 'u' modified by a small 'e' written above the letter are rendered *ä, ö, ü*. 6. But 'ů' (the diphthong written as a *u* with a small *o* above it) is retained. 6. The formula-like abbreviations in the 1524 preface that constitute an elaborate form of polite address are retained as they are. 7. A typographical symbol (like ", but placed lower) is used at the end of lines to indicate that the last letters of that line belong to the same word as the first letters of the following line. However, in the 1524 preface this symbol is often lacking. The words concerned are printed as one word, without comment, except in the title, where a modern hyphen is used.

THE GERMAN PARATEXTS 151

Basel 1524

About the wonderful island called Utopia, the second book, by the well-born highly learned Sir Thomas More, knight and treasurer of the most glorious and most mighty king of England, first rendered and explained quite briefly in Latin, made in the good city of Basel.

[map of Utopia]

[Aii r] [Utopian alphabet with Latin key; quatrain in Utopian script with roman transliteration]

And the meaning of the above verses in the German language is as follows: [German translation of the poem][1]

---

1 For an English translation of the quatrain, see Cambridge 1995, p. 23.

Und ich eyntzig uff erden fry
Hab on die kunst Philosophy
Alln tötlichen menschen zkennen geben
Zů füren ein burgerlich leben /
Und was ich hab mitteyl ich gern
Will on beschwärd gern bessers lern.

[Aii v] Denn Edlen / Strengen / Frommen / Vesten / Fürsichtigen / Ersamen / Wysen herrn / Adelberg Meyer Burgermeister und dem Rat der loblichen Statt Basel minen gnedigen und günstigen herren.

Alles heyl zuvor mit erbietung miner gar willigen dienst / Gnedigen unnd günstigen herrn / es ist ein alt harkommen und ein lobliche durch natürliche ingebung in die gemüter der menschen ingepflantzte art / das / so ettliche by und mit einander ein Burgerliche früntliche bywonung ein zytlang gehebt / und sich darnach begibt / daß eintweder teyl sich von dem andern sündern / und an ein ander ort (nach dem und menschliche sachen offt geendert werden) fügen soll / pfligt alsdann der selbig dem / von dem er scheidet / ettwas zů einer letze / unnd als ein pfand syns unnderdienstlichen gneigten willens zůzestellen / damit er als empfangner gůtwilligkeiten unnd früntschafft wenig ingedenck / oder ja als undanckbar nitt geachtet werde / In sonderheit dwyl und die undanckbarkeit an ir selbs ein sollichs heßlichs laster ist / das es nyemand gnůgsamlichen entwerffen mag / und vyl weger ist nüt weder nit gnůg darvon zůschriben. Uß semlichen ursachen / Gnedigen lieben herrn / nach dem ich etliche jar by üwer St.[Aiii r] E.W.[3] in iren diensten und bestellungen / in diser wyt berümpten hochloblichen Stat Basel / wol und eerlichen (des ich üwer St.W. hochflyssigen danck sag) gehalten worden / bin ich billich bewegt worden / so ich uff diß zyt allein von wegen gehorsamer pflicht / so ich meinem lieben vatter / der sollichs von mir sins krancken alters halb gehebt will haben / uß götlichem natürlichem recht zethůn bin / von V.W. wiewol gar ungern / für diß mal scheyden sol und můß / bemelten V.St.E.W. ein underdienstliche bezügknuß / dises in V.St.W. diensten gantz bereyten gemüts zůverlassen / uff das ich das obangezeygt schandtlichs laster der unndanckbarkeit / so ich all min leben lang mit höchstem flyß geflohen unnd gehasset / nit uff mich laden thů. Da ich aber ettliche tag in mir selbs beratschlagt / was sich am allergeschicklichsten gebüren würd / das V.St.W. ich zů einem sollichen pfand künfftiger gedechtnuß leystete / dwyl es minder sträflich ist / gar nüt überantwurten / weder das jhen / so man achtet nitt mögen angenommen werden. Nun hab ich offt und dick gelesen und

---

3 The letters in this and other similar abbreviated forms of address correspond to the initials of a selection of the adjectives of praise spelt out in the heading of the dedication.

To the noble, powerful, pious, steadfast, prudent, honourable, wise Lord Mayor Adelberg Meyer and to the Council of the good city of Basel, my gracious and benevolent lords.

First, all hail, with the offer of my most willing service, my gracious and benevolent lords! It is an ancient and praiseworthy custom, implanted in the minds of men by natural suggestion, that, whenever people have lived together in friendly society for some time and it afterwards comes to be that one of them must part from the others and go elsewhere (since human affairs are often subject to change), the one who leaves then usually gives something to comfort the one he parts from as a pledge of his humble good will, in order that he may not seem to disregard the services and friendship he has received, or even to be ungrateful; particularly since ingratitude in itself is such an ugly vice that none can condemn it sufficiently, and it would be much better to write nothing about it than not to write enough. For this same reason, gracious, dear lords, after having been kept some years well and honourably in the employ and service of your Lordships in this famous and excellent city of Basel (for which I give eager thanks to your Lordships), I have with good reason been moved – since I now (but only in obedience to the duty I by divine and natural law owe to my dear father, who asks this of me because he is old and sick), must (but only very unwillingly) for this time part with your Lordships – to give to your same Lordships a humble pledge of my eager willingness to serve your Lordships, so that I may not fall into the above-mentioned shameful vice of ingratitude that I have hated and done my utmost to avoid all my life.

So I spent some days considering within myself what it would be most fitting that I should offer to your Lordships as a pledge of my continuing regard – for it is less blameworthy to give nothing at all than to give that which one suspects will not be well received. I have often and many times read

vermerckt / wie der hochgelerten vyl (deren ich ein liebhaber / nitt als inen zůzerechnen[4] bin) so sy inen fürnement ire underdienstliche neygung / gegen ettwa einem Fürsten oder einer Statt zůerzeigen / dise nachvolgende gewonheit habent / Namlich / das sy sich beflyssent gemelts Fürsten oder sollicher Statt herkommen / wesen / Regimment und dapffere herliche geschichten / mit einem zierlichen hoch geblümpten brechtlichen gedicht uffs lobwirdigest zůbeschriben. Deren meynung wiewol ichs nitt verwirff / kan ouch mit glimpff nit verworffen werden / [Aiii v] yedoch hatt die mir in disem val nitt anmütig syn wöllen / nit allein darumb / das es für ein kleinfügige sach gerechnet wirt / da man nüt anders schribt weder allwegen nach vorbildung der vorgeender / sonders ouch (und das am fürnemlichsten) ursach halb / das das lob einer Statt Basel / so manigfeltig und fürtreffend ist / das es nit eins eintzigen monats / nit eins kleinen büchlins bedarff / soll das selb echter recht nach würdigkeit ußgelegt werden / und vor langest so wyt berümpt / und in das gantz Tütschland / ja in die gantze Christenheit der massen ußgespreyt ist / daß semlich ir lob weder min noch anderer lüten gezügknuß erfordert. Zů letst nach erwegung aller umbständ / hatt mich ein andere meinung für gůt angesehen / nemlich das glycherwyse und yederman pfligt von denen eerlichen händeln / die im gemein und bekant synd mit lust zůreden und zůhören / als der recht Adel von lobsamen ritterlichen sachen / von beschirmung der wytwen und weysen / ein recht geystlicher priester / von waren gottes diensten / ein rechter Theologus allein von der lutern heiligen geschrifft / ein rechter kouffman von syner getrüwen kouffmanschafft / ein kriegsman von eerlichen kriegsübungen unnd sunst in allen andern sachen / ein yedes ding fröwet sich syns glychen. Also ouch ist der warheit glych und gemäß / das ein yede wolgeordnete Stat und policy höre gern und mit höchsten fröwden von ir glychen / das ist / von andern wol und recht gehandthabten gemeinen wesen reden. Harumb byn ich zwyfel on / gnedigen unnd günstigen herren V.St.E.W. (als die einer sondern gůten policy mit höchster vernunfft und gerechtigkeit ye wölten [Aiiii r] nit unbillich / wie ich dann selbs erfaren hab / gelobt synd gsyn und noch) werdent kein mißfallens empfahen ab der anzeigung eins glückseligen Regiments / so inen ander lüt fürgenommen habent. Nun aber in der zal aller hochberümptester policy / find ich keine die der Utopianern langhargebruchtem gemeinen wesen verglychen mög / dann wiewol man in den Historien vylerley policy und ordnung burgerlichs wesens verlesen thůt / als under anndern / die erste policy Socratis / die er angesehen aber nyemand angenommen[5] hatt / die andere policy desselbigen / so by den Magnesiern ein zyt gewert / die policy Phalee in der Statt Carthago / Hippodami by den Milesiern / Minois by den

---

4 1524: zůzerechen
5 1524: angonommen

and noticed that many of the highly learned (I am an admirer of these, but am not of their number), when they set out to show their humble respect, for example for a prince or for a city, have the following habit: namely that they do their best to praise as highly as possible the origin, nature, constitution and glorious feats of valour of the prince or the city in question in an elegant, flowery and magnificent poem.

The opinion of these people – though I do not condemn it and though it cannot reasonably be condemned – would not suit me in this case. Not only because it is considered a thing of little account to write nothing other than what has been said by one's predecessors, but also (and that is more important) because the story of the city of Basel is so manifold and so excellent that one single month and one little book would not suffice to describe and explain it according to its true worth – and it has already for a long time been so widely known and so widely famed in the whole of Germany, indeed, in the whole of Christendom, that this same glory has no need of my testimony nor of that of others.

Finally, after considering all the circumstances, I found another opinion preferable, namely, that just as everybody with pleasure speaks and hears about those good actions that are of a kind familiar to him (a good nobleman about praiseworthy knightly deeds, the protection of widows and orphans; a good spiritual priest about the true service of God; a good theologian only about the pure holy scripture; a good merchant about his honest line of trade; a good soldier about honourable warfare – and so on in every other domain: everything takes joy in what is like unto itself), in the same way it is true and proper that every well organised state and polity should take the greatest delight in hearing about those that resemble it, that is to say other societies that are organised well and justly. I therefore have no doubt, gracious and benevolent Lords, that you (who, as I know by experience, never want unjustly to be praised for governing a particularly good polity with the highest degree of reason and justice) will not be displeased if I draw attention to a happy social order established by others.[2]

Among all the most famous polities, however, I find none that are worthy to be compared with the long-established society of the Utopians; for even if one can read about a great number of different polities and social systems in the histories (such as, among others, Socrates' first polity, which he devised, but which nobody adopted; the second polity of the same, which the Magnesians adopted for a time; Phaleas' polity in the city of Carthage; Hippodamus' among the Milesians; Minos' among the Cretans, that are now

---

2 This sentence is particularly difficult. The translation is conjectural.

Cretensern / so man yetzund Candianer nennet / Lycurgi by den Lacedemoniern / und Solonis by den Atheniensern / von welchen zwyen zůletst ernempten policyen / die alten Römer den anfang und ursprung irer gesätz und geschribner weltlichen rechten / sodann irs gmeinen burgerlichen Regiments erlangt haben / Wiewol (sprich ich) dise und der glychen vyl ordnungen eins gmeinen wesens / hoch und wyt berümpt gewesen / und uß den selbigen syent vyl herrliche manliche tathen beschehen / habent ouch semliche policy vyl hundert jaren einen grünenden bestand gehebt / yedoch synd die dermassen in abnemen gefallen / das sy irem alten wesen in keinen weg zůverglychen sind. Das da (als mich ansicht) des merern theils uß dem entsprungen / daß in semlichen policyen / die ouch dem Regiment diser loblichen Innsel Utopie wyt müssent wychen / dry tugent in sonderheit gemangelt haben / so in Utopia gar frömcklich und unzerbrochenlich [Aiiii v] mit höchstem flyß gehandthabt werdent / Und sind namlich dise des ersten ordenliche gemeinschafft aller dingen / so der natur nach mitgeteylt mögen werden / Zům andern ein glychheit in allen ußteylungen der belonungen / der straffen und noturfftigen sachen / Zum dritten ein fridsamme einhelligkeit burgerlicher bywonung / Dann die Utopianer haltent dise dry Artickel (wie dann sollichs uß erwegung der hystory verstanden wirt) für die fürnemsten irs gantzen regiments / und lůgent in allweg mitt höchster fürsichtigkeit / das der selbigen Artickel keiner werde von dem andern gesündert / besonder uß diser ursach / daß ein schlechte unverscheydne gemeinschafft aller dingen / gar nüt ußgenommen / dadurch eim yeden was im gelieben ouch erloubt würde (wie dann die erste policy Socratis semlichs uffsetzen thät) were der mennschlichen burgerlichen bywonung gantz und gar widerig / Dann do die glychheit nit gehalten / sonders werdent die gůten unnd bösen / die wol herkommen und schnöden / die vernünfftigen und thoren glych empfangen / da wirt ein solliche glichheit der unglychen in ein höchste unglychheit bewendt / nit anders dann so man dem bůchstaben des weltlichen geschribnen rechtens oder der Burgerlichen Statuten und gesätz in allweg hertigklich nachgon will / so die umbständ ettwa eins handels ein billiche milterung erheischent / da wirt in dem val semlichs Recht / ein allerhöchste ungerechtigkeit unnd schmachheit genempt. Harumb versorgent die Utopianer / das alle ding so von art und natur gmein syn mögent / der massen gmein sygent / das dennocht glychheit und einigkeit vor augen schwebe. Sy flie-[Av r]hent ouch dargegen uffs flyssigest dry widerwertige laster / namlich zwytracht / gytz des gelts / und eergytigkeit / dann wa deren eins inryssen / möchtent die vorbestimpte dry tugent nit verblyben / und müßte also ir Regiment zerstört und umbkert werden / glych wie es sich by den Römern erzeigt hatt / dann diewyl sy dise drü laster uß irem Regiment vertryben und die vorbestimpte dry tugend handthaben thätend / herschtent sy über das

called Candians; Lycurgus' among the Lacedaemonians; and Solon's among the Athenians – from which two last-mentioned polities the old Romans took the beginning and origin of their written laws and legal system, and then the whole organisation of their civic government – , even if (I say) these and many other ways of organising a society have been highly and widely famed, and even if they gave rise to many wonderful and manly deeds, and although the same polities lasted and thrived for many hundreds of years – even so, they have now fallen into such a decay that they can in no way be compared to what they were. That, it seems to me, is mainly due to the fact that in these polities – which are also far inferior to the government of this praiseworthy island of Utopia – in particular lacked three virtues that in Utopia are piously and adamantly cultivated with the greatest of care. These are, first, the common ownership of all things that are of such a nature that they may be shared; secondly, equality in the giving out of all rewards, punishments and necessities; thirdly, a peaceful unity among the citizens living together. For the Utopians regard these three articles (as one will see by a consideration of the story) as the principal ones of their whole government, and always see to it with great care that none of these articles be separated from the others; particularly for this reason, that the simple undifferentiated common ownership of all things, with no exceptions, so that everyone would be allowed to do what he liked (more or less as was postulated by the first polity of Socrates), would be totally contrary to the humane living together of the citizens. For when equality is not regulated, when the good and the bad, the well-born and the base, the wise and the foolish are received in the same way, then such an equality of the unequal is transformed into the highest form of inequality – much as, if one rigorously follows the letter of secular written law or of civil statutes and ordinances (so that, for example, the mitigating circumstances of a fight are not taken into consideration), then in that case the same justice is called the highest form of injustice and infamy. The Utopians therefore see to it that all things that according to their nature can be held in common, are held in common in such a way that one does not lose sight of equality and unity. They therefore also with all their might avoid three abominable vices, namely strife, greed for money and ambitiousness – for where one of these moves in, the above-mentioned three virtues cannot remain, so that their government must be destroyed and overturned, just as it happened among the Romans, for as long as they banned these three vices from their government and maintained the above-mentioned three virtues, they ruled over the

meerteyl der gantzen welt / so bald aber sy bemelte laster in ire policy und gemüter inwurtzlen liessent / da wurdent unverzogenlich all ir anschleg / ir burgerlich wesen und gewalt in abfal bracht / und wie dann sollichs ougenschynlich ernidert unnd zertrent. Diewyl nun dise policy der Innsel Utopia / wie ob angezeygt die baßgeordnete ältiste unnd bestendtlicheste yewelten gewesen und noch syn soll / so von den mennschen ye angesehen worden / hab ich darumb die histori sollicher Innsel E.St.E.W. als waren liebhabern aller recht uffgesetzten policyen und burgerlichen Regiments / zů einem pfand wie obanzeygt / uß der latinischen in die Tütsche sprach / so ich in diser loblichen Statt Basel gelernet / transferieren wöllen / Wiewol ich des vertütschens halb wol bekenn / das man an ettlichen orten die verborgne art und zierliche manyer des latins nit gantz eygentlich erfolgen mag / besonder in der wol gezierten und geblümpten latinischen red des wol gebornen und hochgelerten herrn Thome Mori Fryherrn / und des durchlüchtigisten großmechtigisten Künigs zů Engelland Schatzmeisters / der da (wie er selbs anzeigt) dise History eigentlich und nit anderst beschriben hatt / weder wie die unge[Av v]varlichen vor syben oder acht jaren in bysin / syn Thome Mori und des fürnemen wolgelerten herren Peters Egydii Grichtschribers zů Antdorff / durch einen hocherfarnen Portugaleser / mit namen Raphaelem Hythlodeum / der in der Insel Utopia ob fünff jar wonhafft gewesen / und dise policy erfaren habe / erlüteret und erzelt worden ist / wie dann der anfang irer der obgemelten dryen gesselligen früntschafft / und wie sy von disen sachen zůred worden / zůsampt ettlichen annderen sachen / so die Engellender gar nach allein betreffend / und zům verstand des Utopianischen wesens von unnöten / in dem ersten bůch der Utopia (welchs ich darumb nit hab vertütschen wöllen / ouch die zyt semlichs zůthůn nit gehebt) mit meren worten vergryffen unnd ußgelegt synd. Nun möcht yemand befremdden wie es doch keme / das dise Innsel Utopia als ein wytberümpte herlichiste Innsel in der zal anderer Inseln / so die alten ußmesser der welt und des erdtrichs / als Pomponius Mela / Strabo / Plinius / Solinus /Claudius Ptolemeus und andere / denen alle Region und landschafft der gantzen welt bekant gewesen synd / nit gefunden wirt / diewyl wol zůvermůten / wa sy so lange zyt in einem sollichen wesen verblyben / hettent die obgemelten Geography nit nüt darvon geschryben / Uff semliche inred schrybt herr Thomas Morus daß Raphael Hythlodeus / mitt diser antwurt im syge begegnet / namlich das / wenn schon die Cosmographi wenig meldung von diser Innsel gethon hetten / were das dennocht kein wunder / diewyl und nit lychtigklich mag zůgon / daß ein

greater part of the whole world, but as soon as they allowed the three said vices to take root in their polity and minds, at once all their enterprises, their society and power fell into a decline, and were thus undeniably brought down and broken up.

Because the polity of the island of Utopia, as I have said before, was and reputedly still is the best organised, the oldest and the most enduring that has ever been devised by men, I decided – as a pledge, as has been said above – to translate for your Lordships (as true lovers of well-organised polities and civic governments) the description of this island from the Latin into the German language, which I had learned in this good city of Basel.

As far as the translation is concerned, however, I must admit that one cannot, in some places, completely follow the hidden art and elegant manner of the Latin, particularly in the very elegant and flowery style of the well-born and highly learned Sir Thomas More, Knight and Treasurer[3] of the most glorious and most mighty King of England, who (as he says himself) gave this comprehensive description just as it was explained and recounted about seven or eight years ago, in his (Thomas More's) presence and in that of the noble, highly learned Mr Peter Giles, city clerk[4] of Antwerp, by a highly experienced Portuguese, by the name of Raphael Hythloday, who had lived in the island of Utopia for more than five years and had experienced this polity – just as the beginning of the companionable friendship of the three above-mentioned and how they came to speak of these matters, together with some others, that only concern the English, and that are of no use for the understanding of the conditions of Utopia, are dealt with and explained with many words in the first book of *Utopia* (which I therefore decided not to translate – nor would I have had time to do this).

Now, one may find it strange that this island of Utopia, being a widely famed, wonderful island is not – according to those who in ancient times described the world and the earth, such as Pomponius Mela, Strabo, Pliny, Solinus, Ptolemy and others, to whom all the regions and districts of the whole world were known – found among the other islands; for it must be supposed that, if it has remained in such a condition for such a long time, then the above-mentioned geographers would not have failed to write about it. Thomas More writes that Raphael Hythloday gave him the following answer concerning this objection, namely that, if it were the case that the cosmographers had said little about this island, that would be no wonder, since it

---

3 More was knighted and made Under-Treasurer in 1521; he was not made Chancellor until 1529.
4 The German word is *Grichtschriber*, i.e. *Gerichtsschreiber*, literally 'writer of a court of law'. Cambridge 1995 (p. xx) says that Giles was 'city clerk of Antwerp and as such deeply involved in the business of that cosmopolitan shipping and commercial centre'.

ußlendig frembd Schiff in das selb land kommen und das gestad erreichen [Avi r] möge / wie dann das im anfang der history der lenge nach erklert wirt / Zů dem mag sich wol begeben haben / das dise Innsel nit allein einest sonders zůmer malen iren namen verendert habe / glych wie mitt andern Innseln meer beschehen ist / als mit der Insel Nygropont / die vor zyten Euboea genant ist gsin / Die man yetz Candiam nennet / hat vor zyten Creta geheissen / Die Innsel Corfun / hand die alten Corcyram genempt / Peloponesus heisset yetzund Morea / Die zwey künigrych Maiorica und Minorica sind by den alten Baleares Innsule gewesen / Die Insel oder Künigrych Engelland und Schotland hand den namen Albion lange zytt getragen / und der glychen Innsel und landschafften meer / so mit der zyt einen nüwen namen überkommen haben / Dem allem nach volgt klärlichen / das ein solliche inred kein irrung bringen mag / dadurch dem Hythlodeo minder zůglouben gewesen syge weder sunst. Harumb gnedigen und günstigen herrn / wellen üwere St.E.W. diß vertütscht büchly als ein gewiß pfand mins underdienstlichen gegen inen und einer loblichen Statt Basel gantz geneigten gemüts gůtwilligklichen von mir empfahen und uffnemen / dann so ich vernimm sollichs üwern wyßheiten gesellig gewesen syn / will ich mich hernach desterflyssiger in grössern und merern sachen keiner arbeit beduren lassen / zů willfar und gefallen gemelter V.St.E.W. die mir als irem gantz bereyten diener allzyt zů gebieten habent.

V. St. E. W. Gantz williger diener Claudius Cantiuncula von Metz.

[woodcut: More, Giles and Hythloday in conversation on bench]
[Book II]
[woodcut as above]
[colophon]

may not easily happen that a foreign strange ship may come to that country and reach the shore, as is amply explained at the beginning of the description. Besides, it may have happened that this island has changed its name, not only once, but several times, as has happened to several other islands, such as Negropont, that used to be called Euboea. The one people now call Candia used to be called Crete. The island of Corfu the Ancients called Corcyra. The Peleponnese is now called the Morea. For the Ancients, the two kingdoms of Majorca and Minorca were the Balearic Islands. The island and the kingdoms of England and Scotland long bore the name of Albion – and so on with several islands and districts that with time have received a new name. Out of this it clearly follows that the objection should not confuse us and make us believe Hythloday any less than we would without it. Therefore, graceful and benevolent lords, I hope your Lordships will willingly receive and accept this little book that I have translated into German as a certain pledge of a mind that is all set humbly to serve you and the good city of Basel, for if I shall learn that this has proved pleasing to your Lordships, I shall henceforth with all the more industry (and in greater and more numerous matters) not shun any work that may be pleasing to your Lordships, who may always command, as your most obedient servant,

your esteemed Lordships' wholly devoted servant Claudius Cantiuncula of Metz

[woodcut: More, Giles and Hythloday in conversation on bench]
[Book II]
[woodcut as above]
[colophon]

Leipzig 1612

De optimo Reipublicae Statu,
Libellus vere aureus.
Ordentliche und Außführliche
Beschreibung
Der uberaus herrlichen und gantz
wunderbarlichen / doch wenigen
bißhero bekandten Insul
UTOPIA:
Sampt umbständlicher Erzeh-
lung aller derselben Gelegenheiten / Städten /
und der Einwohner des Lands Sitten / Gewohnhei-
ten und Gebräuchen: Darinnen gleichsam in einem Mu-
ster oder Model eigentlich fürgestellt und angezeigt wird /
die beste weis und art einer löblichen und wolbestellten Policey
und Regiments: Zumahl fast kurtzweilig und auch
nützlich zu lesen und zu betrachten:
Erstlich durch den hochgelährten und
Weitberümpten Herrn *Thomam Morum,*
des Königreichs Engelland Obristen Cantzler / in Lateinischer Sprach an tag gegeben: Nun aber mit sonderm
fleiß in unser Deutsche Sprach ubergesetzt:
Durch
Smdygmxirnhdrh
Mxisofm[6]
Gedruckt zu Leipzig / in verlegung Henning
Grossen des Jüngern / Anno 1612.

[ii r] Vorred des *Interpretis*, An den günstigen Leser.[7]

Es seynd numehr beynahend in die hundert jahr verschienen / seither der fürtreffliche und herrliche Mann Thomas Morus / weyland Königlicher Rath und oberster Cantzler in Engelland / gegenwertiges Werck von der newen Insul *Utopia*, mit grossem fleis gestellet und beschrieben hat: welches dann / fast allen gelehrten und redlichen Leuten / so zu seiner zeit gelebt / und denen es fürkommen / sehr angenem gewesen / auch von dem mehrerntheil derselben

---

6 This name is written in Utopian letters; see above, p. 40.
7 The Latin quotations, words and names in the text are set in roman, the rest in Fraktur. I render the original roman by italics and the Fraktur by modern roman characters. I do not render the sign „ which is printed in the margin before the start of each line of the two Latin quotations. When copying the Latin names and quotations in this text I write out in full, in brackets, those names and other words that are abbreviated with a point.

Leipzig 1612

On the best State of a Commonwealth, A truly golden handbook.[5] Proper and comprehensive description of the most wonderful and most marvellous, but hitherto little known island of UTOPIA, with a thorough presentation of the conditions of the said island, of its towns, and of the traditions, habits and customs of the inhabitants of the land, in which a kind of example or model of the best manner and form of a praiseworthy and well-organised polity and government is properly presented and pointed out; at the same time most entertaining and also useful to read and to consider; first published in the Latin language by the highly learned and widely famous Sir *Thomas More*, High Chancellor of the Kingdom of England, but now translated with particular care into our German language by Smdygmxirnhdrh Mxisofm. Printed at Leipzig for the publishing house of Henning Grosse the Younger in the year 1612.

Preface by the *Translator* to the Good Reader

Almost a hundred years have now passed since that excellent and glorious man *Thomas More*, once royal councillor and High Chancellor of England, with great diligence put together and wrote the present work about the new island of *Utopia*, which almost all learned and honest people who were alive in his day and who came into contact with it then found so pleasing and

---

5 Translation from Cambridge 1995, p. 3.

mit solchem *applausu* und frolocken ist angenommen worden / daß unlangs hernach der gewaltige Mann *Erasmus Roterodamus*, nicht umbgehen können / gedachtes Werck in offentlichen Druck zu geben: Inmassen dann solches auff sein Com[ii v]mendation / zu Basel / im Jahr 1517 von *Ioh[anne] Frobenio* ist publicirt worden. Was aber ermelter Erasmus von diesem Tractätlin gehalten / ist leichtlich zu erkennen aus dem Titul / den er demselben fürgesetzt: welcher also lautet: *De optimo Reip[ublicae] statu, deque; nova Insula Utopia, libellus vere aureus, nec minus salutaris, quam festivus, &c.* Gleicher massen hat auch der fürneme Mann *Guilielmus Budaeus*, so ein sonderliche zierd des gantzen Franckreichs gewesen / dieses werck in einem Sendschreiben / so demselben im Druck beygefügt / sehr hoch gerühmt: Da er unter andern diese *verba formalia* setzet: *MORUM de Utopia novi Orbis Insula, summe et amo et veneror. Ejus [e]n[im] historiam aetas nostra, posteraeque; aetates, habebunt velut elegantium utiliumque; institutorum seminarium, unde translatitios mores in suam quisque civitatem importent et accommodent, &c.* [iii r] Nicht weniger haben auch sonst mehr ansehlige und treffliche Leut diesem Werck grosses lob verliehen: Als / *Gerhardus Noviomagus, Petrus Aegidius, Hieron[imus] Buslidius, Cornelius Graphaeus, Ioh[annes] Bodinus*, und viel andere / deren wort allhie anzuziehen unnot / und an diesem ort viel zu lang seyn würde. Wie angenem aber auch den frembden Nationen diß Büchlin gewesen / ist daraus leichtlich abzunemen / weil dasselbig nach und nach in etliche unterschiedliche Sprachen ist transferirt worden: Inmassen dann auch der fürneme Jurist *Claudius Cantiuncula* solches wirdig geachtet / das es in Deutsche Sprach möchte ubersetzet werden. Aus welchen ursachen dann ich jüngst bin beweget worden / dem günstigen Leser zu gefallen / mich solcher version zu unterfangen / und die ubrige stunden / so andere mit spaciren / spie[iii v]len oder schlaffen hinbringen / hierauff zu wenden.

Demnach aber innerhalb der nechst verschienen hundert jahren / seither nemlich diese Insul *Utopia*, von *Th[oma] Moro* beschrieben worden / die Portugeser / Spanier / Engelländer / See- und Holländer / viel newe den Europeern zuvor unbekante Insulen und Landschafften erfunden (Inmassen wir dann erst vor wenig wochen zeitung aus Engelland gehabt / das daselbs die kurtze Reiß und Schiffarth nach der *China*, durch die Nordsee gegen Mitternacht / nach welcher so viel Jahr und so lange zeit / auch mit unseglichen grossen kosten und gefahr / man bißher vergebens getrachtet / und dieselbe gesucht hat / endlich sol erfunden seyn worden) Also möchte sich / und zwar nicht unbillich der guthertzige Leser darüber nicht we[iiii r]nig verwundern / wie es doch immer zugehe / daß bisher nie keiner aus allen

which was received by the greater number of these with such applause and rejoicing that, a short time afterwards, that great man *Erasmus of Rotterdam* could not refrain from having the said work printed and presented to the public, so that it was, on his recommendation, published by *Johann Froben* in Basel in the year 1517.[6] What the above-mentioned Erasmus thought about this little tract can easily be seen from the title under which he presented it: *On the Best State of a Commonwealth and on the New Island of Utopia. A Truly Golden Handbook, No Less Beneficial than Entertaining*[7] etc. In the same way that outstanding man *Guillaume Budé*, who was a particular ornament to the whole of France, praised this work very highly in a dedication that was printed along with it, using *these very words*, among others: *I particularly love and revere MORE for what he has written about this island of the New World, Utopia. Our own age and ages to come will discover in his narrative a seedbed, so to speak, of elegant and useful concepts from which they will be able to borrow practices to be introduced into their own several nations and adapted for use there*[8] *etc.* No less have many other considerable and excellent people also given great praise to this work, such as *Gerard Geldenhouwer, Peter Giles, Jerome De Busleyden, Cornelis De Schrijver, Jean Bodin* and many others, all of whose words it would be unnecessary to quote here: that would take much too long. How pleasing this book has been to foreign nations also can easily be seen by the fact that it has in the course of time been translated into several different languages; thus also the outstanding jurist *Claude Chansonnette* found that it was worthy to be translated into the German tongue. For these reasons I have recently been moved, to please the kind reader, to undertake such a translation and to spend on this the free hours that others spend on walks, on play or on sleep.[9]

Since, however, during the hundred years that have passed since this island of *Utopia* was described by *Thomas More*, the Portuguese, Spanish, English, Zealanders and Hollanders have discovered many islands and countries that were before unknown to the Europeans (thus we just a few weeks ago got news from England that the short passage to *China* northwards through the North Sea – which had until now been sought and looked for in vain for so many years and during such a long time and at unutterably great expense and danger – is said to have been found at last), so the kind reader might – and not unreasonably – wonder not a little how it may still be that not one of

---

6 This could be a misprint or a confusion with Paris 1517. But a book printed in March 1518 'new style' would of course most likely be printed in 1517 'old style' (according to which the year began on the 25th of March).
7 As above, p. 163, n. 5.
8 This is the end of Budé's letter to Lupset. Translation from Cambridge 1995, p. 19.
9 This curious sentence may have been inspired, directly or indirectly, by Cicero, *Oratio pro Archia poeta* VI.13.

Weltreisern / Kriegs- Schiff- und Kauffleuten in diese Insul *Utopiam* kommen sey / der da hette können relation thun / wie es noch heutiges tages darinnen stehe.

Hierauff ist zwar nicht leichtlich zu antworten / ich gib aber diesen bescheid: daß nemlich diese lange zeit her / wie jedermänniglich bewust / so viel allerley sorten Schiff / die nach den Ost- und WestIndien / auch anderswohin gegen Sud und Nord / aus den Meergräntzenden Landen der Christenheit weggesegelt / seynd ausgeblieben / da man nicht weis wo sie hin kommen / das wol ein grosse Armada mit denselben / so sie verhanden weren / könte ausgerüstet werden. Wer weis nu / ob nicht dieselbigen in der Insul *Utopia* vielleicht seynd ankommen. Zu dem so [iiii v] ist glaublich / da jemand in einem so glückseligen Land ankömpt / da jederman gnug hat / und niemand arm ist / das er ihm nicht mehr heraus begere. Endlich / so tregts vermutlich der Nam *Utopia* auff sich / das diese Insul werde schwerlich mögen gefunden werden. Doch wirds die zeit geben / welche alle verborgne ding pflegt an tag zu bringen. Hiezwischen wölle der günstige Leser mit gegenwertiger version für lieb nemen / und thu ich uns letzetlich[8] hiemit dem gnedigen Schutz Gottes mit fleis befehlen. *Datum* den 1. Januar. *Anno* 1612.

[table of contents]

[vi r] Vier Verß in Utopianischer Sprach.
[Utopian poem in roman transliteration]

Diese Verß lauten von wort zu wort in Lateinischer Sprach also:
[Latin translation of poem]
Und ist diß die meynung in Deutscher Sprach:

> Mich hat Herr Utop wol bedacht /
>   Aus festem Land zur Insul gemacht.
> Ich bin allein auff Erden frey /
>   So ohn die Kunst Philosophey /
> Den Menschen hab zu erkennen gebn /
>   Zu führen ein Politisch lebn.
> Was ich nu hab / mittheil ich gern:
>   Wer bessers kan von dem ich lern.

[typographical ornament]

---

8 1612: tzetlich

all the world-travellers, military, maritime and commercial men, has come to this island of *Utopia*, so that he could have given an account of how things may still stand there now at the present day.

It may not be easy to answer this, but I give this reply: namely, that during this long time, as everyone knows, so many ships of all kinds – sailing from those countries in Christendom that have a seabord towards the East and West Indies, and also elsewhere, towards the South and North – have been lost that one could make of them, if they were to be had, a great armada. Now who knows whether these may not perhaps have arrived in the island of *Utopia*. It is probable, besides, that if someone should come to such a happy country, where everyone has enough, and no one is poor, then he would not wish to leave it. And finally, the very name *Utopia* seems to imply that this island may hardly be found. But time will tell, that usually brings all hidden things to light. May the good reader, in the meantime, content himself with this present translation; and I end[10] by diligently recommending us both to God's merciful care. Dated on the 1st day of January in the year 1612.

[table of contents]

[vi v] Four lines in the Utopian language.
[Utopian poem in roman transliteration]

These lines signify word for word in the Latin language the following:
[Latin translation of the poem]
And this is the meaning in the German language:
[German translation of the poem][11]

[typographical ornament]

10 This translation depends on the conjectural emendation of the text referred to in my note on the original.
11 See above, p. 151, n. 1.

[portrait of More]
[map of Utopia]
[Book I (beginning and end only)]
[Book II]
Ende der Beschreibung der wunderbarlichen/noch bißher wenig bekanten Insul *Utopia*.

Soli DE[O] gloria.
[typographical ornament]
[colophon: place, printer, date]

[portrait of More]
[map of Utopia]
[Book 1 (beginning and end)]
[Book II]
The end of the description of the marvellous, until now little-known island of *Utopia*.

Glory to GOD alone.
[typographical ornament]
[colophon: place, printer, date]

THE ITALIAN PARATEXTS

LA REPVBLICA NVOVAMENTE RITROVATA, DEL GOVERNO DELL'ISO, LA EVTOPIA, NELLA QVAL SI VE, de nuoui modi di gouernare Stati, reggier Popoli, dar Leggi à i senatori, con mol, ta profondità di sapienza, storia nõ meno vtile che necessaria.
Opera di Thomaso Moro Cittadino di Londra.

IN VINEGIA, M D XLVIII

Venice 1548: Title-page. By permission of the British Library

Venice 1548

LA REPUBLICA
NUOVAMENTE RITROVATA,
DEL GOVERNO DELL'ISO-
LA EUTOPIA, NELLA QUAL SI VE-
de nuovi modi di governare Stati, reggier
Popoli, dar Leggi à i senatori, con mol-
ta profondità di sapienza, storia non
meno utile che necessaria.
Opera di Thomaso Moro Cittadino di Londra.

[Frontispiece image: the 'masked woman']

In Vinegia, M D XLVIII.

[2 r] Al gentilissimo M. Gieronimo Fava

Messere Jacopo vostro padre m'è paruto un'huomo tanto ben composto, e ordinato, cosi nelle facende del mondo, come ne governi della famiglia: che io giudico la casa vostra un'ottima republica. Poi s'io volessi entrare nel lodare quanto egl'habbia ben allevati tanti figliuoli e figliuole, havrei preso troppo carico sopra le mie spalle, perchè bisognerebbe ch'io mi facessi dai buon costume, dalla realtà, dalla religione, dalla fede, dall'amore dalla carità, e cosi venissi virtù per virtù lodando quella, e honorando quell'altra, talmente che io non farei mai fine: poi s'io havessi à far noto al mondo la pace, non saprei dipingere mi[2 v]glior esempio, ne maggior specchio, che mostrar cinque fratelli che voi siate, cosa rara veramente. Però essendo tanto la virtù del padre, la bontà della madre, e la realtà di voi altri figliuoli cosi nota come chiara: tacerò per non ne saper dir quel bene, che meritate che sia detto, e verrò al particular mio. Perche havendomi dato a questi di passati, un' libretto nelle mani d'una ottima Republica feci subito disegno d'inviarlo a voi accio facesse paragone con la Republica della casa vostra, e cosí essendo stampata ve ne fo un' dono, e ve la dedico, ben è vero che maggiore è l'animo del Doni, che non son le forze per donare: pure questo sara un principio e un saggio, non tanto da conservar l'amicitia, quanto a ringratiar vi in parte de benificii ricevuti: voi [3 r] troverete in questa Republica ch'io vi mando, ottimi costumi, ordini

Venice 1548

The recently rediscovered Republic. On the government of the island Eutopia, in which may be seen new ways to govern states, to rule peoples, to provide laws for the senators, with most profound wisdom, a history no less useful than necessary. A work by Thomas More, citizen of London.

[The 'masked woman']

In Venice, 1548

To the most noble Master Geronimo Fava

Master Jacob, your father, always appeared to me to be a man so balanced and well-ordered, both in the affairs of the world and in the governing of his family, that I judge your home to be an excellent republic. But if I were to embark on the praise of how well he has raised so many sons and daughters, I would have taken too heavy a burden on my shoulders, because necessarily I should have to take into account their good manners, their nobility, their religion, their faith, their love and their charity, and thus I should proceed virtue by virtue, praising this one and honouring the other, to such a degree that I should never come to an end; or if I had to make known to the world what peace is, I could not offer a better example or a more ample mirror than by depicting you five brothers and sisters, a rare thing indeed. But as your father's virtue, your mother's goodness and the nobility of you brothers and sisters are as well-known as they are illustrious, I shall keep silent, not being able to express all the good that deserves to be said about you, and instead I shall come to my point. A little book about an excellent Republic having come into my hands in the last few days, I immediately decided to send it to you, so that you could compare it with the Republic of your home, and now, as it has been printed, I offer it as a gift to you, and dedicate it to you, even if the mind of Doni is larger than his power to give.[1] Yet this will be a beginning and a sample, not so much to preserve our friendship as in part to thank you for the favours I have received. In this Republic which I send you, you will

---

1 The original has a play on words here between Doni's name, the noun *dono* (plural *doni*), 'gift', and the verb *donare*, 'to give'.

buoni, reggimenti savi, amaestramenti santi, governo sincero, e huomini reali, poi ben composte le città, gl'officii, la giustitia, e la misericordia, che ne havrete sommo diletto, e non picciol contento: che piú, leggendo il libretto intenderete cose bellissime, e considerando questa lettera, ci troverete sculpito il cuor mio tutto devoto alla gentilezza vostra, e alla gentil creanza di tutti, à i quali parimente mi raccomando.

Vostro affettionatissimo il Doni.

[La tavola d'alcune cose principali, che nell'Opera si contengono]
[Tavola del libro secondo]

[More to Giles I]
[Book I]
[Book II, omitting last paragraph: 'Interea... quam sperarim.']

find excellent manners, good laws, wise regulations, holy education, sincere government and men of noble spirit, as you will find that the cities, the public offices, the dispensation of justice and charity are well devised. All this will give you the highest pleasure and no little satisfaction: because furthermore when you read this little book you will learn of very beautiful things, and when you meditate on this letter, you will find carved in it my heart, which is wholly indebted to your noble spirit and to the good will of all, to whom I equally recommend myself.

Your most affectionate Doni

[Table of some important topics contained in the work]
[Table of contents of Book II]

[More to Giles I]
[Book I]
[Book II, omitting last paragraph: 'Meantime ... expect to see.']

Venice 1561

        Del governo
        de i regni
        et delle republiche
        cosi antiche come moderne
        libri XVIII

*Ne quali si contengono
i magistrati, gli offici, e gli ordini proprii che s'osservano ne predetti principati*

        Dove si ha cognitione
        di molte historie particolari, utili e necessarie al viver civile

        Di Francesco Sansovino.
        Con privilegio.

        In Venetia.[1]

[fol. 184 r]   Del governo della Rep. d'Utopia.
                        Libro decim'ottavo.

Tomaso Moro cittadino di Londra, e huomo santissimo di vita, e pieno di vera giustitia, e di divina religione fu Secretario di Arrigo Ottavo Re d'Inghilterra. Costui venuto grande col suo proprio valore, non volendo consentire alle scelerate voglie del Re che volendo scacciar la propria e leggitima moglie desiderava di farsi sposa una dishonestissima femina, e con suo gran biasimo privar la figliuola, fu sforzato a dire in publico alla presenza del popolo la sua ragione, di ch'egli riportò da quell'irato Principe l'esser come un ladrone vergognosamente fatto morire, et non volle che fosse lecito a pietosi parenti del morto dar sepoltura alle sue lacere membra. Ora questo huomo dottissimo havendo a noia i corrotti costumi del nostro secolo scrisse molto ornatamente in quella Regione della gente beata questa Repub. governata da ottimi leggi, e ridotta in somma pace, et in felicità, accioche gli huomini imparassero

---

1 The title-page also features the printer's mark used by Sansovino and his son. The work was reissued in 1556, 1567, 1578, 1583 and 1607 by different printers. The number of chapters increases progressively (1566, 1567 and 1578 have twenty-one, 1583 has twenty-two). The title also becomes more detailed in later editions. The account of Utopia is placed at the end in all editions. It has not been thought necessary to reproduce all the title-pages here, but the full titles will be found in the Bibliography.

Venice 1561

On the government of kingdoms and republics both ancient and modern, eighteen books, in which are contained the particular magistrates, offices and orders observed in the above-mentioned principalities, and where one can acquire knowledge of many individual histories which are useful and necessary to civil life.

By Francesco Sansovino
With privilege

In Venice

On the government of the Republic of Utopia
The eighteenth book

Thomas More, citizen of London, and a man of most saintly life, full of true justice and divine religion, was the Secretary of Henry VIII, King of England. Having achieved greatness through his own merit, and unwilling to consent to the criminal desires of the King, who wanted to repudiate his true legitimate spouse and take to wife a most immoral woman, and to his great discredit disinherit his daughter, More was forced to give his reasons in public before the people, for which the angry King repaid him by having him shamefully put to death like a thief and forbidding the dead man's pitiable relatives to give burial to his dismembered body. Now, since this very learned man was sick of the corrupt customs of our time, he composed in a most elegant style this Republic situated in that region of fortunate people,[2] a republic governed by excellent laws and brought to a state of absolute peace and happiness, so

---

2 This phrasing is a conjectural interpretation of the rather obscure syntax and word-order of the original.

dalla sua piacevolissima fittione di trovar il vero modo di viver bene, e felicemente, la quale noi habbiamo voluto por nell'ordine di queste altre, e ultima, percioche ne pare ch'ella sia molto piu risoluta, di quella di Platone.

[In the 1583 edition, the final sentence is extended as follows:]
[...quella di Platone]; e accioche da questa lettura cosi imaginata considerando il lettore, le cose vere che si contengono nelle antecedenti Rep. possa vedere, che si può sempre in riformare, o constituire una nuova Rep. ritrovar qualche cosa di nuovo, che sia utile e buona.

[Book II]

that men might learn from his most pleasing fiction how to find the true way of living well and happily, which we wished to include in the series of other republics, placing it last, because it appears to be much more thoroughly worked out than Plato's.

[...]; and so that from this imaginary reading the reader might see, when considering the true matters contained in the preceding Republics, that in reforming or constituting a new Republic, one can always find something new that is useful and valuable.

[Book II]

Translations by Kristin Gjerpe and Lone Klem

THE FRENCH PARATEXTS

LA DESCRI-
PTION DE L'ISLE D'VTOPIE
OV EST COMPRINS LE MIROER

des republicques du monde, & l'exemplaire de vie heureuse: redigé par escript en stille Treselegant de grand' haultesse & maiesté par illustre bon & scauant personnage Thomas Morus citoyé de Londre & chãcelier d'Angleterre Auec l'Espistre liminaire composée par Monsieur Bude maistre des requestes du feu Roy Francoys premier de ce nom.

Auec priuilege.

Les semblables sont a vendre au Palais à Paris au premier pillier de la grand'Salle en la Bouticque de Charles l'Angelier deuant la Chappelle de Messieurs les Presidens.

1550.

Paris 1550: Title-page. By permission of the British Library

Paris 1550

LA DESCRI-
PTION DE L'ISLE D'UTOPIE
OU EST COMPRINS LE MIROER
des republicques du monde, et l'exemplaire de vie
heureuse: redigé par escript en stille Treselegant de
grand' haultesse et majesté par illustre bon et scavant
personnage Thomas Morus citoyen de Londre et chan
celier d'Angleterre Avec l'Espistre liminaire composée par Monsieur Bude maistre des requestes du feu
Roy Francoys premier de ce nom.

Avec privilege.

Les semblables sont a vendre au Palais à Paris
au premier pillier de la grand' Salle en la Bouticque de Charles l'Angelier devant la Chappel
le de Messieurs les Presidens.

1550.

[Extraict des registres de Parlement]

[Guillaume Budé à Thomas Lupset Angloys]

[viii v]   Dixain du translateur
à la louenge de la saincte vie des Utopiens.

Si on veoit le poëte renaistre
Qui escripvit les champs Elisiens,
Je pense moy qu'il vouldroit descognoistre
Ce terme la, et diroit qu'es vers siens
Il avoit mis les champs Utopiens,
Je dy cecy car quand bien on lyra,
Les sainctes meurs d'Utopie, on dira
C'est paradis au prix du lieu ou sommes,
Touchant les gens on les estimera
Estre espritz sainctz plus tost que mortelz hommes.

Paris 1550

The description of the isle of Utopia, comprising the mirror of the republics of the world and the model of a happy life, set down in writing in a most elegant and elevated style of great majesty by the illustrious, good and learned person Thomas Morus citizen of London and Chancellor of England, with the prefatory epistle composed by Monsieur Budé, Master of Requests of the late King Francis, the first of that name.

With privilege.

Copies are for sale at the Palace[1] in Paris at the first pillar of the great Hall, in the shop of Charles l'Angelier facing the Chapel of their Lordships the Judges.

1550

[Extract of the Registers of Parlement (privilege)]
[Budé's letter to Lupset]

> Ten-line stanza by the translator
> in praise of the saintly life of the Utopians

If the poet who wrote of the Elysian Fields[2] were to be reborn, I for my part think that he would wish to disavow that phrase and say that he had put into his verses the Utopian Fields. I say this because if one studies carefully the saintly customs of Utopia, one will say that it is paradise compared to the place where we are. As for the people, they will be considered to be saintly spirits rather than mortal men.

---

1 The Palais de Justice (Law Courts).
2 Probably Ovid, *Metamorphoses* XIV.111.

[1 r] Le premier livre.

[Woodcut depicting More, Hythloday, Giles and Clement in conversation]

Les excellentz propos que teint en Flandres un singulier homme nommé RAPHAEL HYTLODEUS, Portugalloys, touchant le bon regime, de la republicque: Ensemble le recit qu'il fit des meurs, Loix, Coustumes et Pollice, Bien ordonnée des habitans d'Utopie, nouvelle Isle, n'a pas long temps trouvée, et descouverte: Aussi de la description d'icelle: de laquelle n'avoit faict jamais mention aulcun Geographe au paravant. Le tout redigé [1 v] par escript en stille treselegant de grand haultesse et majesté. Par illustre, bon, et scavant personnaige Thomas Morus Citoyen de Londres et Chancelier d'Angleterre. Traduict en langue Françoyse par Maistre Jehan le Blond d'Evreux.

[Book I]
[Book II][1]

[Oii r] Cy fine le devis et propos dapres[2] disner, de Raphael Hythlodeus, touchant les loix et meurs de l'Isle d'Utopie, qui n'est encore à gueres de gens congneue, mis en elegance latine par illustre, tresdocte, bien renommé personnaige le seigneur Thomas Morus Chancelier d'Angleterre, et tourné en langue Françoyse par maistre Jehan Le Blond.

[Motto in cartouche:]
Espoir en mieulx

[Oii v] l'Autheur au lecteur.
[Woodcut of More writing in his study]
Ne sois offence amy lecteur, si en ceste mesme petite tradition, tu trouves oultre les loix et reigles de tourner quelque œuvre, que jaye aulcunefois usé de Paraphrases. Je lay faict pour rendre les sentences de lautheur plus intelligibles.

---

1 Each chapter of Book II begins with a woodcut depicting the following, in the order of the chapters: Thomas writing in his study; the city of Amaurot in the background with three armour-clad riders in the foreground; the governor of a town inspecting an open book (presumably of laws) that is being presented to him; a repeat of the woodcut prefacing Book I; a seated governor with accusing finger pointing at a guilty-looking man; a man arriving at steps leading to a temple-like structure and presenting an offering (?) to an old man, perhaps a priest, with another standing behind; a bound man on a horse being brought to a seated governor; a repeat of the woodcut with the guilty-looking man; a repeat of the woodcut with the man arriving at the steps of a temple-like structure.

2 We have not felt it necessary to add the apostrophe which is omitted in this and a number of other contracted forms in the French paratexts.

The first book.

[Woodcut depicting More, Hythloday, Giles and Clement in conversation]

The excellent discourse given in Flanders by an extraordinary man named RAPHAEL HYTHLODEUS, a Portuguese, on the right way to run a republic, together with his narration of the customs, laws and well-ordered governance of the inhabitants of Utopia, a new island that has only recently been found and discovered. Also his description of the island, of which no geographer had previously made mention. All this set down in writing in a most elegant style of great elevation and majesty by the illustrious, good and learned person Thomas Morus citizen of London and Chancellor of England. Translated into French by Master Jehan Le Blond of Evreux.

[Book I]
[Book II]

Here ends the after-lunch conversation and remarks of Raphael Hythlodeus concerning the laws and customs of the Isle of Utopia, which is still unknown to most people, put into elegant Latin by the illustrious, most learned and widely-renowned person Sir Thomas Morus, Chancellor of England, and translated into the French language by Master Jehan Le Blond.

[Motto in cartouche:]
Hope for better things.

The author to the reader
[Woodcut of More writing in his study]
Don't be offended, dear reader, if in this little translation of mine you find that, in addition to the laws and rules of translating a work, I have sometimes used paraphrases: I have done so in order to render the author's intentions more

Et consequemment si en traduisant j'ay ramené en nostre usaige françois certains termes infrequentz.[3] On ne se doibt mal contenter si un personnaige faict renaistre et reduit en cours quelques vacables [*sic*] trouvez en autheurs Idoines, et sil sefforce donner nouveaulte aux parolles anciennes, et ne souffre totalement perir les motz qui par la coulpe des temps sont tournez en desacoustumance. En sorte que si nous n'usions que de termes vulgaires et communz à chascun, nostre langue nen enrichiroit d'un flocquet, et fauldroit tousjours faire comme les tabellions et notaires, qui en leurs actes ne changent ne ne muent de stille.

[Oiii r] [title in cartouche:]
Au lecteur.
Afin que tu ne penses Ami que de mon privé, et seul jugement je t'ay mis en lumiere en nostre langue ceste description de l'isle d'Utopie considerant comme il est escript que l'homme ne se doibt appuier sur son privé sens et prudence et aussi que au tesmoignage de deux ou de trois toute chose doibt estre arrestée non content du seul tesmoignage de Thomas Morus qui premier a redigé en latin ladicte description je me suis grandement fondé sur ce que defunct de bonne et immortelle memoyre monsieur Bude en a dict en une epistre cy apres inserée, traduicte de latin en nostre langue par laquelle on peult congnoistre combien iceluy tant pur et excellent jugement d'homme a estimé ce petit livre digne d'estre leu chose qui me sera, comme j'espere envers tout bon esprit argument suffisant de n'avoir temerairement et sans conseil par privilege de la court de Parlement mis en lumiere ce livre en quoy[4] j'ay pretendu, comme de tout aultre mien labeur, faire chose qui soit a l'utilité et proffit de la republicque.
A dieu.

[S'ensuit la table des chapitres du premier et second livre de la description de l'Isle d'Utopie et premierement.]
[Fautes survenues a l'impression.]
[colophon: printer's device and name]

---

3 1550: [lacks full stop]
4 1550: en quoy duquel

intelligible; nor should you be offended, furthermore, if in translating I have reintroduced into our French usage certain unfamiliar terms. One should not be displeased if someone revives and brings back into use a number of words found in suitable authors, and if he attempts to give novelty to ancient words and does not allow words altogether to perish which through the ravages of time have fallen out of custom. So that if we only used standard terms common to everybody, our language would not be enriched by one jot, and one would always have to behave like secretaries and notaries, who in their documents neither change nor vary their style.

To the reader.
I would not wish you to believe, my friend, that it is only on the basis of my own personal judgement that I have published in our language this description of the Isle of Utopia, considering that, as it is written, man should not depend upon his private understanding and prudence and therefore that all matters should be settled on the testimony of two or three persons.[3] Not contenting myself, therefore, solely with the testimony of Thomas Morus, who first composed this description in Latin, I have based my judgement largely upon what the late Master Budé, of blessed and immortal memory, said of it in an epistle inserted hereafter, translated from Latin into our language, by which one may know to what extent this man's judgement, so pure and excellent, considered this little book to be worth reading. This will, I hope, be counted by any well-disposed mind as sufficient proof that it is not rashly and ill-advisedly that I have, with the privilege of the court of Parlement, published this book, in which I have aimed, as in all my other work, to do something that is useful and profitable to the republic.
Farewell.

[Table of contents]

[List of printing errors]
[colophon]

---

3 1 Cor.14, 29.

Lyon 1559

LA
REPUBLIQUE
D'UTOPIE, PAR THO-
MAS MAURE, CHAN-
CELIER D'ANGLE-
TERRE,
Œuvre grandement utile et profi-
table, demonstrant le parfait
estat d'une bien ordon-
nee politique:
Traduite nouvellement de Latin
en Françoys.

[printer's mark (bird with a serpent's tail) and motto in surrounding frame:
ULTRO SUCCEDERE VOTIS]

A LYON,
Par Jean Saugrain.
M.D.LIX.

[2]   Dizain.
Si on voyoit le Poëte renaistre
Qui ha décrit les Champs Elysiens:
Je pense et croy, qu'il voudroit décognoistre
Ce terme là: et diroit qu'es vers siens
Il avoit mis les champs Utopiens:
Je dy cecy: Car quand bien on lira
Les saintes mœurs d'Utopie, on dira
C'est paradis au pris du lieu ou sommes.
Touchant les gens, on les estimera
Estre espritz saintz, plustost que mortelz hommes.

[3] Advertissement declaratif de l'œuvre.
Par M.B.A.

Comme les Anciens Poëtes souz la fabuleuse mythologie ont couvert, et adombré la vraye Philosophie: Ainsi le prudent Chancelier d'Angleterre S.

Lyon 1559

The Republic of Utopia, by Thomas More, Chancellor of England,
A highly useful and profitable work demonstrating the perfect state of a well-organised form of government.

Newly translated from Latin into French.

[printer's mark and motto: 'To have one's prayers answered unasked']

At Lyon, printed by Jean Saugrain
MDLIX

Ten-line stanza

If the poet who described the Elysian Fields were to be reborn,[4] I think and believe that he would wish to disavow that word and say that he had put into his verses the Utopian Fields. I say this because if one studies carefully the saintly customs of Utopia, one will say that it is paradise compared to the place where we are. As for the people, one will regard them as saintly spirits rather than mortal men.

Note explaining the work
by M.B.A.

Just as the ancient poets, under the veil of mythological fable, concealed true philosophy, so too the wise Chancellor of England, Sir Thomas Maure, under

---

4 See above, p. 183, n. 2.

THOMAS MAURE souz une feinte narration de la nouvelle isle D'UTOPIE, ha voulu figurer une morale Republique, et tresparfaite politique: voire si tresparfaite que jamais telle ne fut, ne est, ne paraventure sera. Car à la maniere que les graves Stoïques, ont figuré leur parfait Sage, et le treseloquent Ciceron ha formé son parfait Orateur: desquelz la description est tant souveraine, que telz Sages, et telz Orateurs ne furent onques veuz; ne se voyent à present: ne sont esperez à l'advenir: mais telz les ont depeintz, qu'il les conviendroit estre en leur absoluë perfection, si l'imbecilité humaine y pouvoit atteindre. A L'image desquels ceux qui plus pres adviendront plus excellens en Sapience, et en art Oratoire estimez ils seront: Ainsi le magnifique Thomas Maure tres-subtil [4] ouvrier de ingenieusement inventer, et de bien dire: souz fiction Chorographique d'une isle nouvellement trouvee, et trescivilement regie, ha coloré l'Image d'une tresexcellente police de Republique, non certes telle, qu'elle ait jamais ainsi esté, ou soit en nul lieu: mais telle qu'en tous lieux elle devroit estre: Et pource il l'ha nomme, LA REPUBLIQUE D'UTOPIE, c'est à dire de nul lieu: et Monsieur Bude en sa magnifique epistre liminaire de lœuvre, lha nomme UDEPOTIE, c'est à dire, qui ne fut jamais. Tous deux donnans à entendre que en nul lieu, et en nul temps ne fut; et n'est et ne sera une telle et si bien formee Republique: et encores souz telle couleur reprenans les defaux des Politiques, qui sont à present toutes perverties et corrompues, en leur representant au vif le patron de ceste Utopique, auquel pour les amender et ameliorer, il les faudroit conformer, et les imiter le plus pres qu'il seroit possible. Mais considerant ce prudent Chancelier Anglois, que telle reprehension, et exemplaire reformation des gouvernemens, ne seroit agreablement receuë en plate forme de nue et découverte demonstration: Affin de la rendre plus plaisante, plus agreable, et plus acceptable, [5] il l'ha voulu figurer souz nouvelle et étrange histoire, qu'il feint avoir entendu d'un étrangier peregrinateur, et lointain voyageur, qu'il nomme RAPHAEL HYTHLODAEUS: Et cela fait-il si subtilement, y donnant couleur de versimilitude historiale: que lon diroit proprement estre un vray recit, entendu par autruy, des lieux, personnes, et choses, qui sont en nature, combien que ce n'est qu'un contemplatif argument, tresbon et tresraisonnable, inventé par ce grand personnage Londrois THOMAS MAURE: comme manifestement en donnent indice les noms Grecz convenablement imposez aux personnes

the cover of a fictional narration of the new Isle of Utopia, sought to represent a moral republic and a most perfect form of government: so utterly perfect, indeed, that such a thing never existed, nor does it exist today, and perhaps never will. For as the austere Stoics imagined their perfect sage, and the most eloquent Cicero formed his perfect orator, who are described in such absolute terms that such sages and such orators have never been seen, nor are they seen in our day, nor can one hope they will appear in the future: but they are depicted in the form that would be appropriate to them in their absolute perfection, if human weakness could attain it; and those who come closest to that ideal will be judged to be the most excellent in wisdom and the art of oratory. Likewise, the lofty Thomas More, that most cunning craftsman of ingenious invention[5] and eloquence has painted in bright colours, in the form of a chorographical fiction of an island recently discovered and ruled in a very orderly fashion, the image of a most excellent form of government for a republic – not, it is true, such as anything of the kind ever existed or is actually to be found in some place, but such as it ought to be everywhere. And for this reason he named it the Republic of Utopia, which means of no place; and Master Budé in his magnificent prefatory epistle to the work named it 'Udepotia', that is, something that never existed. Both gave us to understand that it was never to be found in any place or at any time, and that there is not and never will be so well-formed a Republic. Both also by means of this image reprehended the defects of present-day forms of government, which are all perverted and corrupt, by vividly staging for them the model of this Utopian system, which they should be made to conform to and imitate as closely as possible in order to amend and improve them. But because this wise English Chancellor thought that such a rebuke, such an exemplary reformation of governments, would not be received with pleasure in the plain form of a naked and unconcealed demonstration, he sought to represent it, in order to make it more pleasant, more agreeable and more acceptable, by means of a new and strange story, which he pretends that he heard from a widely-travelled foreigner, come from far away, whom he calls Raphael Hythlodaeus. And this he does in such a subtle way, giving it the colour of historical probability, that one would say it really is a true story, heard by others,[6] about places, persons and things that exist in nature, although it is nothing but an imaginary account, an excellent and most reasonable invention of this great person Thomas Maure of London, as the Greek names fittingly assigned to persons

---

5 This word should be understood in its rhetorical sense, i.e. the discovery by the writer of suitable materials.
6 Aneau is apparently referring here to the fictional setting in which Hythloday tells the story of Utopia to More and Giles. However, the phrase could also be taken to mean 'heard via someone else'.

et aux choses, car UTOPIE est à dire nul lieu, nom de Isle phantastique qui en nul lieu ne se trouve, ny en la Geographie, ny au monde: ne la situation d'icelle Isle, comme l'Auteur mesme, et M. Bude; et Pierre Gilles en leurs epistres Latines le donnent à entendre, disans par maniere de couverture, avoir oblié de demander à HYTHLODAEUS, en quelle mer et region, et souz quel Climat est celle Isle situee. Joint qu'il apert celuy HYTHLODAEUS estre un personnage feint et introduit expressement souz un nom imposé à plaisir, HYTHLODAEUS, si[6]gnifiant en Grec: facteur de non veritables et plaisans propos: lequel en propre nom il appelle RAPHAEL, nom d'un Ange spirituel, signifiant que de son propre et bon esprit, ha esté inventee ladite Republique de nul lieu. Les autres vrays personnages introduitz assistans au discours de Raphaël, qui sont Clement, et Pierre Gilles d'Anvers, celuy pour qui Erasme ha écrit l'Epithalame: sont adjointz comme témoins, pour mieux déguiser et rendre plus vray semblable la controuvee bonne invention, en forme de historiale narration: tendant à delectable et utile fin de remonstrer par un plaisant discours, les fautes des Republiques presentes, et figurer un Archetype parfait de vraye Politique, auquel les autres se devront conformer, ou pour le moins le plus pres que possible sera en approcher.

[Book I]
[Book II]

[352] Cy fine le devis et propos d'apres disner, de Raphaël Hythlodeus, touchant les Loix et mœurs de l'Isle d'Utopie, qui n'est encores à gueres de gens congneuë, mis en elegance Latine par illustre, tresdocte, et bien renommé personnage le seigneur Thomas Morus Chancelier d'Angleterre, et nouvellement tourné en langue Françoyse.

Espoir en mieux.

and things clearly indicate, for Utopia means no place, the name of a fantasy island which is to be found nowhere, neither in geographical writings nor in the world itself; nor can its location be determined, as the author himself, and M. Budé and Peter Giles give us to understand in their Latin epistles, saying by way of pretext that they forgot to ask Hythlodaeus in what ocean and region and in which clime this island is located. It is moreover apparent that Hythlodaeus is a fictional figure, introduced explicitly by means of a name coined at the author's pleasure, HYTHLODAEUS, which signifies in Greek 'creator of untrue and playful discourse', his given name being Raphael, the name of a spiritual angel, meaning that the author has invented this republic of no place out of his own excellent wit. The other real persons introduced as being present at Raphaël's discourse, namely Clement and Peter Giles of Antwerp, the man for whom Erasmus wrote his *Epithalamium*, are included as witnesses, in order better to disguise and to make more plausible the excellently forged invention in the form of a historical narration. All this has the delightful and useful aim of reprehending, by means of a playful discourse, the defects of present-day republics and of representing the perfect archetype of a true form of government, which all others ought to conform themselves to, or at least approach as closely as possible.

[Book I]
[Book II]

Here ends the after-lunch conversation and remarks of Raphael Hythlodeus concerning the laws and customs of the Isle of Utopia, which is still unknown to most people, put into elegant Latin by the illustrious, most learned and widely-renowned person Sir Thomas Morus, Chancellor of England, and recently translated into the French language.

Hope for better things.

Paris 1585

L'ESTAT, DESCRIPTION ET GOUVERNEMENT DES ROYAUMES ET REPUBLIQUES DU MONDE, TANT ANCIENNES QUE MODERNES.
Comprins en XXIIII Livres.
Contenans divers reiglemens, ordonnances, loix, coustumes, offices, Magistrats et autres choses notables appartenantes à l'histoire, et utiles à toutes manieres et conditions d'hommes, tant en affaires d'Estat que de la Police, et propres en temps de paix et de guerre.[5]

Par Gabriel Chappuys, Tourangeau.
Au Roy Tres-Chrestien Henry III.

[Printer's device]
A PARIS,

Chez Pierre Cavellat, ruë Sainct Jacques à l'Enseigne de l'Escu de Florence.
M.D.LXXXV.

AVEC PRIVILEGE DU ROY

[298] DE LA REPUBLIQUE D'UTOPIE
Estat et Gouvernement d'icelle.
LIVRE VINGT-QUATRIESME.
Description de l'Isle d'Utopie: Cinquante quatre villes d'Utopie: Amaurot principale ville: Anidre fleuve: Agriculture, exercice principal entre les Utopiens.

Chapitre I
Le Chancelier d'Angleterre, Thomas Morus, personnage de tres-saincte vie, remply d'une vraye justice, et d'une grande religion; au demourant tres-docte, estant fasché des mœurs corrompues de nostre siecle, a escrit, avec ornement, ceste Republique gouvernee par bonnes loix, et reduite en grande paix et felicité, à fin que les hommes aprinssent, par sa tres aggreable fiction, à trouver le vray moyen de bien et heureusement vivre. Or avons nous bien voulu la mettre au rang de ces autres, pource qu'elle semble estre beaucoup plus resoluë et parfaicte, que celle de Platon, et à fin que de ceste lecture ainsi imaginee,

---

5 This is the first of the French versions of Venice 1561 (see above, p. 178, note 1). We have not reproduced here the title-page of Paris 1598, essentially a reprint of Paris 1585, or of Paris 1611, which contains much the same materials (but see above, p. 82).

Paris 1585

The state, description and government of the kingdoms and republics of the world, both ancient and modern. Comprised in XXIIII books. Containing different regulations, decrees, laws, customs, offices, Magistrates, and other notable things pertaining to history, and useful to all kinds and conditions of men, in affairs of state as well as of administration, appropriate for times of both peace and war.

By Gabriel Chappuys of Tours.

To the Most Christian King Henri III.

At the printing-house of Pierre Cavellat, in the rue Saint-Jacques at the sign of the coat of arms of Florence.
MDLXXXV

With royal privilege

On the Republic of Utopia, its state and government.
Twenty-fourth book.

Description of the Isle of Utopia: fifty-four Utopian towns; the capital Amaurot; the river Anidre; agriculture, the principal occupation among the Utopians.

Chapter I
Being indignant at the corrupt customs of our age, the Chancellor of England, Thomas More, a man of a most saintly life, replete with true justice and great religious faith, and also most learned, wrote this elegant account of a republic governed by good laws and brought to a state of peace and happiness, so that men may learn, by his most pleasing fiction, to find the true means to live well and happily. Now, we thought it right to place it alongside the others because it seems much more complete and perfect than Plato's, and in order that the reader, when considering the true matter contained in the preceding republics, may see by means of this imaginary

le lecteur considerant les choses vrayes, qui sont contenuës aux precedentes Rebubliques, puisse voir, que l'on peut tousjours, en la reformation ou constitution d'une nouvelle Republique, trouver quelque chose de nouveau qui soit bonne et profitable. Ce Thomas Morus citoyen de Londres, et parvenu à ce hault degré par sa propre valeur, sous le regne du Roy Henry huictiesme, ne voulant consentir aux mauvaises volontez du Roy, lequel vouloit repudier sa propre et legitime femme, et en espouser une autre, en privant par un sien grand blasme, sa fille, fut contrainct de dire en public, devant le peuple, sa raison pour empescher un tel acte: et pour ceste cause ce Prince irrité le fit honteusement mourir, comme un larron: et ne voulut pas qu'il fust licite aux pitioyables parens du mort de donner sepulture à ses pauvres membres deschirez. Or pour prendre desormais le fil de ce que nous avons proposé de reciter.

[Book II]

reading that one may always, in the reformation of a republic or the constitution of a new one, devise something fresh that is good and beneficial. Since Thomas Morus, citizen of London, who reached this high rank by his own merit, did not wish during the reign of King Henry VIII to consent to the evil desires of the King, who sought to repudiate his true legitimate wife and marry another, thereby, to his great discredit, disinheriting his daughter, he was forced to declare in public, before the people, his reason for resisting such an act. And because of this the angry Prince put him to a shameful death, like a thief, and would not allow the pitiable relatives of the deceased to give his poor torn limbs a proper burial. Let us now take up the thread of what we have set out to tell.

[Book II]

Amsterdam 1643

> L'UTOPIE
> DE
> THOMAS MORUS
> Chancelier d'Angleterre,
> *Traduicte par*
> SAMUEL SORBIERE
>
> [printer's device: a small globe]
>
> A Amsterdam
> *Chez* Jean Blaeu
> MDCXLIII.[6]

[The title appears on a kind of curtain attached to a frame at the top and reaching halfway down the page. Below, as in a scene from a play, three figures sit at a table in a garden; on the table, there is a map, half unrolled, and a pair of compasses. The figure facing out of the picture is not difficult to identify as Hythloday, telling his story to More and Giles.][7]

[2 r] A Monseigneur, Monseigneur Frederic Magnus, Comte Sauvage du Rhin, Comte de Salms et Seigneur de Venestranges, quatriesme personne de la Cavallerie, Gouverneur de l'Escluse, et Colonel.

Monseigneur,
Voicy une Republique dont le plan fust tracé il y a six vingts ans passés par l'un des plus grands hommes de son siecle; qui ayant consideré profondement le train des affaires du monde voulut en [2 v] remarquer les defauts dans cest escrit. Apres l'estime qu'Erasme, Budée, et tous les doctes en ont faite, je ne puis rien adjouster en sa recommandation. Mais pour ne pas taire mon sentiment de ce que j'ose vous presenter, je diray que ceste piece me semble avoir en son genre toute la perfection dont elle estoit capable, qu'elle est comme ces tableaux ausquels il n'y a pas un seul coup de pinceau à desirer, et que Platon tout divin qu'on le nomme n'a point travaillé sur ceste matiere avecque tant de netteté et d'heureux succez. L'utile et l'agreable se rencontrent icy meslés en sorte qu'on ne sçait le[3 r]quel y entre en plus grande mesure. Car on lit une fable aussi ingenieusement inventée qu'on en puisse trouver dans ces livres

---

6 Old-style roman numerals have here been transcribed according to modern norms.
7 This title-page is reproduced above, p. 143.

Amsterdam 1643

The Utopia of Thomas Morus Chancellor of England, translated by Samuel Sorbière

[printer's device]

In Amsterdam at the printhouse of Jean Blaeu 1643

[see description of title-page on p. 198, reproduced above, p. 143]

To My Lord, Lord Frederik Magnus, Wald- and Rhinegrave, Count of Salm and Lord of Fénétrange, Brigadier-General of the Cavalry,[7] Governor of Sluis, and Colonel.

My Lord,
Here is a Republic the plan of which was sketched out a hundred and twenty years ago by one of the greatest men of his age, who, having given profound consideration to the course of the world's affairs, wished to note its defects in this written account. After the homage paid to it by Erasmus, Budé and all men of learning, there is nothing I can add to recommend it. But in order not to conceal my own opinion of what I take the liberty of presenting to you, I may say that this piece seems to me of its kind to possess all the perfection of which it was capable, that it is like those paintings in which not one single stroke of the brush is left wanting, and that Plato, although they call him divine, did not treat this subject with such clarity and with such a happy outcome. The useful and the agreeable come together here blended in such a way that one cannot say which plays the greater part. For one reads here a fable as ingeniously invented as one can find in books written solely to

---

7 The French phrase translated here is a rendering of the Dutch 'vierde grootofficier der cavalrie'; the rank held is the fourth highest in the cavalry.

qui ne sont faits que pour le divertissement de ceux qui les lisent; et parmi les plaisirs que l'imagination reçoit de la beauté des fictions, et de la naifveté des choses representées, la partie intellectuelle de l'ame s'instruit, et le jugement du lecteur se purifie et se forme au bon sens, lors mesme qu'il ne pense pas d'en tirer tous ces advantages. Cela m'a fait souhaiter souvent que quelcune de ces plumes, que nous voyons aujourdhuy si bien taillées en nostre lan[3 v]gue, entreprit la traduction de cest ouvrage; et peut estre je seray cause l'ayant entreprise qu'un autre rendra à mon autheur toute son eloquence, de laquelle j'advoue que je luy fais perdre une bonne partie. Je m'assure neantmoins qu'il me pardonneroit aisement ceste injure sur ma confession, et considerant que mon principal dessein a esté celuy de vous desennuyer aux heures de vostre loisir; c'est à dire, lors que vous relascherés un peu du soin continuel que vous apportés à l'agrandissement de ces Illustres Estats. Tous les gens de bien, Monseigneur, se rejouissent de voir ceste [4 r] genereuse emulation avec laquelle lors que vous vous picqués de les servir, ils se picquent d'honorer vostre vertu, et chacun en tire un prognostique infaillible de l'eternelle prosperité des affaires publiques. Ce qu'on apprehende est, que vostre courage ne prejudicie à nostre bon-heur, et que vous n'alliés trop souvent au milieu de ces dangers, où en ceste derniere campagne vous n'eustes que fort peu de personnes qui osassent vous suivre, de deux mille qui vous accompagnoient. Mais on voit bien qu'il seroit difficile de vous persuader l'usage d'une valeur moins heroïque, et de rom[4 v]pre une habitude que la coustume de vaincre a trop puissamment confirmée; c'est pourquoy on n'employe que des vœux pour vostre conservation. J'en fais, outre ceux la, qui regardent Messieurs vos fils, et qui leur promettent des triomphes, lors qu'ils iront où leur naissance les appelle, et que ces excellentes semences qu'on remarque en eux seront en leur saison de produire. Je ne desadvoueray jamais, Monseigneur, les grandes obligations que je vous ay du favorable accueil que j'ay eü chez vous, de l'employ que vous m'avés donné et que j'estime tres-honorable, et du repos que [5 r] vous m'avés fait esperer: mais toutes ces pensées, et tous ces mouvements que je viens de vous descouvrir, ne naissent en mon cœur que de l'interest qu'un bon citoyen doit prendre au bien public, et de la cognoissance particuliere que j'ay des choses sur lesquelles je raisonne. S'il vous plaist de les reçevoir aussi comme des preuves de mon zele et de ma fidelité à vostre service, vous ne vous esloignerés pas de la verité; quoy que je ne pretende point de la faire paroistre en ceste occasion, ny autrement que par de solides effects; qui n'estant point des payemens d'une debte, ne [5 v] recognoissent aucun autre

entertain those who read them; and among the pleasures that the imagination receives from the beauty of fictions and the natural quality of the things represented, the intellectual part of the mind is instructed, and the reader's judgement is purified and imbued with good sense, even when he is not aware of drawing all these advantages from it. This has often made me wish that one of those pens that we see nowadays so well-sharpened in the use of our language would undertake the translation of this work; and maybe I shall be responsible, having undertaken it, for encouraging somebody else to restore to my author all his eloquence, a significant part of which, I admit, I have made him lose. I nevertheless reassure myself that he would easily have forgiven me this offence on hearing my confession, and considering that my main purpose has been to distract you in your leisure time, that is to say, when you allow some slackening of the continuous care you devote to increasing the glory of these illustrious States. All people of quality, my Lord, rejoice in seeing this worthy emulation by which, when you spur yourself on to serve them, they spur themselves on to honour your virtue, and everyone draws from it an infallible prognostication of the eternal prosperity of public affairs. What we all fear is that your courage might prejudice our good fortune, and that you might venture too often into the midst of those dangers where, in this last campaign, there were but few, among the two thousand persons who accompanied you, who dared follow you. But it is evident that it would be difficult to persuade you to display a less heroic valour and break a habit powerfully reinforced by constant victory; all we can do, therefore, is offer prayers for your conservation. In addition to these, I am offering others in favour of your noble sons, promising triumphs for them one day when they go where they are called by their birth, and when those excellent seeds we discern in them have reached the season where they bear fruit. I shall never disavow, my Lord, the great obligations I owe you for the favourable welcome I have had in your home, for the employment that you have given me and that I consider to be most honourable, and for the security you have allowed me to hope for; but all the thoughts and all the feelings I have revealed to you here arise in my heart solely from the interest a good citizen should take in the public good and from the particular knowledge that I have of the things I am speaking of. If it pleases you to receive them also as proofs of my devotion and faithfulness in your service, you will not stray far from the truth, even though I do not pretend to make it manifest on this occasion, nor otherwise than by solid effects, which, since they are not payments for a debt, recognise no other

principe que la passion avec laquelle je veux estre toute ma vie,

Monseigneur,

Vostre tres-humble, tres-obeissant et
tres-affectionné serviteur

A La Haye ce 1 de Novembre 1642.

Samuel Sorbiere

[More to Giles I]
[Book I]
[Book II]

principle than the passion with which I shall remain my whole life,

>My Lord,
>Your most humble, obedient and devoted servant

At The Hague, 1st November 1642.

>Samuel Sorbière

[More to Giles I]
[Book I]
[Book II]

>*Texts edited and translated by*
>*Gro Bjørnerud Mo and Kirsti Sellevold*

THE ENGLISH PARATEXTS

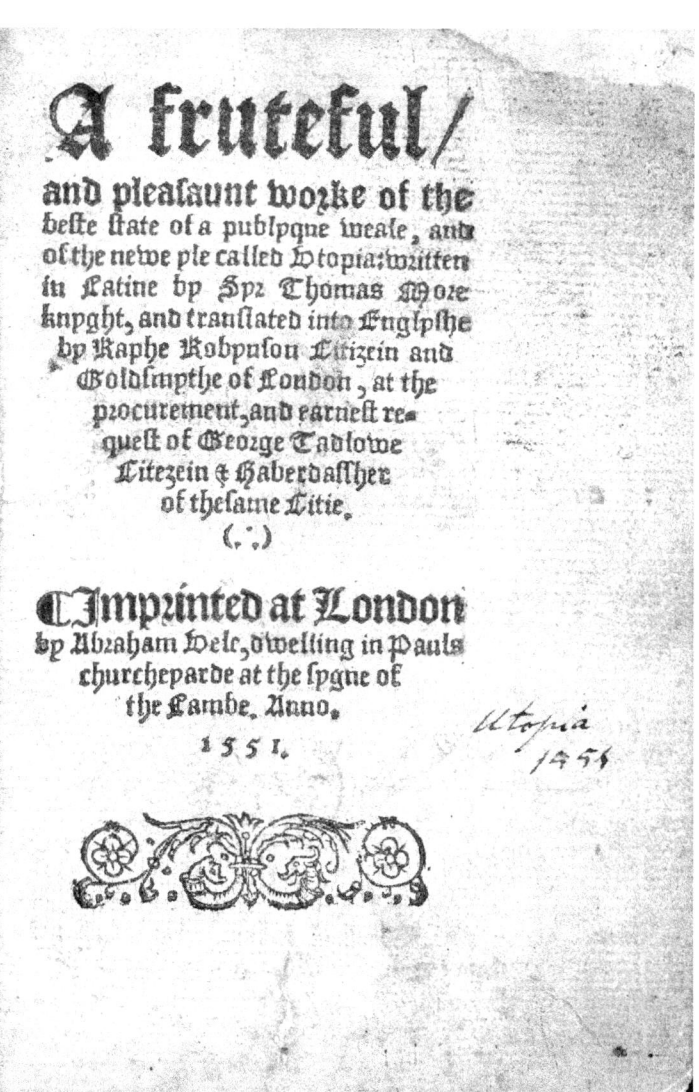

London 1551: Title-page. By permission of the British Library

London 1551

A fruteful /
and pleasaunt worke of the
beste state of a publyque weale, and
of the newe yle called Utopia: written
in Latine by Syr Thomas More
knyght, and translated into Englyshe
by Raphe Robynson Citizein and
Goldsmythe of London, at the
procurement, and earnest request of George Tadlowe
Citezein and Haberdassher
of the same Citie.

Imprinted at London
by Abraham Vele, dwelling in Pauls
churcheyarde at the sygne of
the Lambe. Anno,
1551.

[ii r] To the right honourable, and his verie singuler good maister, maister William Cecylle esquiere, one of the twoo principal secretaries to the kyng his moste excellent majestie, Raphe Robynson wissheth continuaunce of health, with dayly increase of vertue, and honoure.

Upon a tyme, when tidynges came too the citie of Corinthe that kyng Philippe father to Alexander surnamed the Great, was comming thetherwarde with an armie royall to lay siege to the citie: The Corinthians being forth with stryken with greate feare, beganne busilie, and earnestly to looke aboute them, and to falle to worke of all handes. Some to skowre and trymme up harneis, some to carry stones, some to amende and buylde hygher the walles, some to rampiere[1] and fortyfie the [ii v] bulwarkes, and fortresses, some one thynge, and some an other for the defendinge, and strengthenynge of the citie. The whiche busie labour, and toyle of theires when Diogenes the phylosopher sawe, having no profitable busines wherupon to sette himself on worke (neither any man required his labour, and helpe as expedient for the commenwealth in that necessitie) immediatly girded about him his phylosophicall cloke, and began to rolle, and tumble up and downe hether and thether upon the hille syde, that lieth adjoyninge to the citie, his great barrel or tunne, wherein he dwelled:

---

1 rampiere: strengthen

for other dwellynge place wold he have none. This seing one of his frendes, and not alitell musynge therat, came to hym: And I praye the Diogenes (quod he) whie doest thou thus, or what meanest thou hereby? Forsothe I am tumblyng my tubbe to (quod he) bycause it were no reason that I only should be ydell, where so many be working. In semblable maner, right honorable sir, though I be, as I am indede, of muche lesse habilitie then Dio[iii r]genes was to do any thinge, that shall or may be for the avauncement and commoditie of the publique wealth of my native countrey: yet I seing every sort, and kynde of people in theire vocation, and degree busilie occupied about the common wealthes affaires: and especially learned men dayly putting forth in writing newe inventions, and devises to the furtheraunce of the same: thought it my bounden duetie to God, and to my countrey so to tumble my tubbe, I meane so to occupie, and exercise meself in bestowing such spare houres, as I beinge at the becke, and commaundement of others, cold conveniently winne to me self: that though no commoditie of that my labour, and travaile to the publique weale should arise, yet it myght by this appeare, that myne endevoire, and good wille hereunto was not lacking. To the accomplishement therfore, and fulfyllyng of this my mynde, and purpose: I toke upon me to tourne, and translate out of Latine into oure Englishe tonge the frutefull, and profitable boke, which sir Thomas more knight compiled, and made of the new yle Uto[iii v]pia, conteining and setting forth the best state, and fourme of a publique weale: A worke (as it appeareth) written almost fourtie yeres ago by the said sir Thomas More the authour therof. The whiche man, forasmuche as he was a man of late tyme, yea almost of thies our dayes: and for the excellent qualities, wherewith the great goodnes of God had plentyfully endowed him, and for the high place, and rowme, wherunto his prince had moste graciously called him, notably wel knowen, not only among us his contremen, but also in forrein countreis and nations: therfore I have not much to speake of him. This only I saye: that it is much to be lamented of al, and not only of us English men, that a man of so incomparable witte, of so profounde knowledge, of so absolute learning, and of so fine eloquence was yet neverthelesse so much blinded, rather with obstinacie, then with ignoraunce that he could not or rather would not see the shining light of godes holy truthe in certein principal pointes of Christian religion: but did rather cheuse to persever, and continue in his wilfull and stub[iv r]bourne obstinacie even to the very death, this I say is a thing much to be lamented. But letting this matter passe, I retourne again to utopia. Which (as I said befor) is a work not only for the matter that it conteineth fruteful and profitable, but also for the writers eloquent latine stiele pleasaunt and delectable. Which he that readeth in latine, as the authour himself wrote it, perfectly understanding the same: doubtles he shal take great pleasure, and delite both

in the swete eloquence of the writer, and also in the wittie invencion, and fine conveiaunce, or disposition of the matter: but most of all in the good, and holsome lessons, which be there in great plenty, and aboundaunce. But nowe I feare greatly that in this my simple translation through my rudenes and ignoraunce in our english tonge all the grace and pleasure of the eloquence, wherwith the matter in latine is finely set forth may seme to be utterly excluded, and lost: and therfore the frutefulnes of the matter it selfe muche peradventure diminished, and appayred[2]. For who knoweth not whiche knoweth any thyng, that an eloquent styele setteth [iv v] forth and highly commendeth a meane matter? Where as on the other side rude, and unlearned speche defaceth and disgraceth a very good matter. According as I harde ones a wise man say: A good tale evel tolde were better untold, and an evell tale well tolde nedeth none other sollicitour. This thing I well pondering and wayinge with me self, and also knowing, and knowledging the barbarous rudenes of my translation was fully determined never to have put it forth in printe, had it not bene for certein frendes of myne, and especially one, whom above al other I regarded, a man of sage, and discret witte, and in worldly[3] matters by long use well experienced, whoes name is George Tadlowe: an honest citizein of London, and in the same citie well accepted, and of good reputation: at whoes request, and instaunce I first toke upon my weake, and feble shoulders the heavie, and weightie bourdein of this great enterprice. This man with divers other, but this man chiefely (for he was able to do more with me, then many other) after that I had ones rudely brought the worke to [v r] an ende, ceassed not by al meanes possible continualy to assault me, until he had at the laste, what by the force of his pitthie argumentes and strong reasons, and what by hys authority so persuaded me, that he caused me to agree and consente to the impryntynge herof. He therfore, as the chiefe persuadour, must take upon him the daunger, whyche upon this bolde, and rashe enterpryse shall ensue. I, as I suppose, am herin clerely acquytte, and discharged of all blame. Yet, honorable Syr for the better avoydyng of envyous and malycyous tonges, I (knowynge you to be a man, not onlye profoundely learned, and well affected towardes all suche, as eyther canne, or wyll take paynes in the well bestowing of that poore talente, whyche GOD hath endued them wyth: but also for youre godlye dysposytyon, and vertuous qualytyes not unworthelye nowe placed in aucthorytye, and called to honoure) am the bolder humblye to offer and dedycate unto youre good maystershyppe thys my symple woorke. Partly that under the sauffe conducte [v v] of your protection it may the better be defended from the obloquie of them, which can say well by nothing, that pleaseth not their fond, and corrupt judgementes,

2 appayred: impaired
3 1551: wordly

though it be els both frutefull and godly: and partlye that by the meanes of this homely present I may the better renewe, and revive (which of late, as you know, I have already begonne to do) the old acquayntaunce, that was betwene you and me in the time of our childhode, being then scolefellowes togethers. Not doubting that you for your native goodnes, and gentelnes will accept in good parte this poore gift, as an argument, or token, that mine old good wil, and hartye affection towardes you is not by reason of long tract of time, and separation[4] of our bodies any thinge at all quayled and diminished, but rather (I assuer you) much augmented, and increased. This verely is the chieffe cause, that hath incouraged me to be so bolde with youre maistershippe. Els truelye this my poore present is of such simple and meane sort, that it is neyther able to recompense the least portion of your [vi r] great gentelnes to me, of my part undeserved, both in the time of our olde acquayntance, and also now lately again bountifully shewed: neither yet fitte, and mete for the very basenes of it to be offered to one so worthy, as you be. But almighty god (who therfore ever be thanked) hath avaunced you to such fortune, and dignity, that you be of hability to accept thankefully as well a mans good will as his gift. The same god graunte you and all yours long, and joyfully to contynue in all godlynes and prosperytye.

[More to Giles I]
[Book I]
[Book II]

4 1551: separrtion

London 1556

A frutefull
pleasaunt, and wittie worke,
of the beste state of a publique
weale, and of the new yle, called Utopia: written in Latine, by the right worthie and famous Syr Thomas More
knyght, and translated into Englishe by
Raphe Robynson, sometime fellowe
of Corpus Christi College in Oxford, and nowe by him at this seconde edition newlie perused and corrected, and
also with divers no-
tes in the margent
augmented.

Imprinted at London, by
Abraham Vele, dwellinge in
Pauls churchyarde, at the signe
of the Lambe.

[Aii r] The translator to the gentle reader.
Thou shalte understande gentle reader that thoughe this worke of Utopia in English, come now the seconde tyme furth in Print, yet was it never my minde nor intente, that it shoulde ever have bene Imprinted at all, as who for no such purpose toke upon me at the firste the translation thereof: but did it onelye at the request of a frende, for his owne private use, upon hope that he wolde have kept it secrete to hym self alone. Whom though I knew to be a man in dede, both very wittie, and also skilful, yet was I certen, that in the knowledge of the Latin tonge, he was not so well sene, as to be hable to judge of the finenes or coursenes of my translation. Wherfore I wente the more sleightlye through with it, propoundynge to my selfe therein, rather to please my sayde frendes judgemente, then myne owne. To the meanesse of whose learninge I [Aii v] thoughte it my part to submit, and attemper my stile. Lightlie therefore I overran the whole woorke, and in shorte tyme, with more hast, then good spede, I brought it to an ende. But as the latin proverbe sayeth: The hastye bitche bringeth furth blind whelpes. For when this my worke was finished, the rudenes therof shewed it to be done in poste haste. How be it, rude and base though it were, yet fortune so ruled the matter

that to Imprintinge it came, and that partly against my wyll. Howebeit not beinge hable in this behalfe to resist the pitthie persuasions of my frendes, and perceaving therfore none other remedy, but that furth it shoulde: I comforted myselfe for the tyme, only with this notable saying of Terence.

> *Ita vita est hominum, quasi quum ludas tesseris.*
> *Si illud, quod est maxume opus, iactu non cadit:*
> *Illud, quod cecidit forte, id arte ut corrigas.*[5]

In which verses the Poete likeneth or compareth the life of man to a dice-plaiyng or a game at the tables[6]: Meanynge therin, if that chaunce rise not, whiche is most for the plaiers advauntage, that [Aiii r] then the chaunce, whiche fortune hathe sent, ought so connyngly to be played, as may be to the plaier least dammage. By the which worthy similitude surely the wittie Poete geveth us to understande, that though in any of our actes and doynges, (as it ofte chaunceth) we happen to faile and misse of our good pretensed[7] purpose, so that the successe[8] and our intent prove thinges farre odde[9]: yet so we ought with wittie circumspection to handle the matter, that no evyll or incommoditie, as farre furth as may be, and as in us lieth, do therof ensue. According to the whiche counsell, though I am in dede in comparison of an experte gamester and a conning player, but a verye bungler, yet have I in this by chaunce, that on my side unwares hath fallen, so (I suppose) behaved myself, that, as doubtles it might have bene of me much more conningly handled, had I forethought so much, or doubted any such sequele at the beginninge of my plaie: so I am suer it had bene much worse then it is, if I had not in the ende loked somwhat earnestlye to my game. For though this worke [Aiii v] came not from me so fine, so perfecte, and so exact yet at first, as surely for my smale lerning, it should have done, yf I had then ment the publishing therof in print: yet I trust I have now in this seconde edition taken about it such paines, that verye fewe great faultes and notable errours are in it to be founde. Now therfore, most gentle reader, the meanesse of this simple translation, and the faultes that be therin (as I feare muche there be some) I doubt not, but thou wilt, in just consideration of the premisses, gentlye and favourablye winke at them. So doynge thou shalt minister unto me good cause to thinke my labour and paynes herein not altogethers bestowed in vaine.
Vale.

---

5 Terence, *Adelphoe* II. 739-41. Robinson paraphrases the quotation in the sentence that follows ('In which verses... least dammage').
6 the tables: a board game akin to backgammon.
7 pretensed: intended
8 successe: outcome
9 farre odde: very different

[More to Giles I]
[Book I]
[Book II]
[Giles to Busleyden]

[S vi v] A meter of .iiii. verses in the Utopian tongue, briefely touchinge aswell the straunge beginning, as also the happie and wealthie continuance of the same common wealth.
[Utopian quatrain, transliterated only]

Which verses the translator, accordinge to his simple knowledge, and meane understanding in the Utopian tongue, hath thus rudely englished.
[English translation of the Utopian quatrain]

A shorte meter of Utopia, written by Anemolius poete laureate, and nephewe to Hythlodaye by his sister.
[S vii r] [Anemolius' poem]

Gerard Noviomage of Utopia.
[Noviomagus' poem]

[S vii v] Cornelius Graphey to the Reader.
[Grapheus' poem][10]

[S viii r] The Printer to the Reader.
The Utopian Alphabete, good Reader, whiche in the above written Epistle[11] is promised, herunto I have not now adjoyned, because I have not as yet the true characters or fourmes of the Utopiane letters. And no marveill: seyng it is a tongue to us muche straunger then the Indian, the Persian, the Syrian, the Arabicke, the Egyptian, the Macedonian, the Sclavonian, the ciprian, the Scythian etc. Which tongues though they be nothing so straunge among us, as the Utopian is, yet their characters we have not. But I trust, God willing, at the next impression hereof, to perfourme that, whiche nowe I can not: that is to saye: to exhibite perfectly unto thee, the Utopian Alphabete. In the meane time accept my god wyl. And so fare well.

---

10 Robinson's translations of all these Latin paratexts are available in Oxford 1999.
11 i.e. the letter from Giles to Busleyden, which mentions the Utopian alphabet and the addition of marginal notes; the marginalia are also included in this edition.

London 1597

A
Most pleasant, fruit-
full, and wittie worke, of
the best state of a publique weale, and of
the new Yle called *Utopia*:
Written in Latine, by the right worthie and famous Syr
Thomas Moore Knight: and translated into English by *Raphe Robinson*, sometime fellow
of *Corpus Christi* Colledge
in *Oxford*.
*And now this third Edition, newly corrected
and amended.*

[Printer's device: naked woman wearing crown, scourged by rods held in hand descending from clouds; motto in surround: 'virescit[12] vulnere veritas'[13]]

London
Printed by Thomas Creede.
1597.

[More to Giles I]
[Book I]
[Book II]
[Giles to Busleyden]
[Utopian quatrain transliterated and translated]
[Anemolius' poem]
[Noviomagus' poem]
[Grapheus' poem][14]

---

12 1597: viressit
13 'Truth flourishes when wounded.'
14 The poems carry the same headings as in London 1556; the same applies to London 1624.

London 1624

SIR THOMAS MOORE'S
UTOPIA:
CONTAINING,
AN EXCELLENT, LEARNED,
WITTIE, AND PLEASANT
Discourse of the best state of a Publike Weale,
as it is found in the Government of the new
Ile called *Utopia*.
FIRST WRITTEN IN LATINE,
by the Right Honourable and worthy of all Fame,
Sir THOMAS MOORE, Knight, *Lord Chauncellour* of *England*; And translated into English
by RAPHE ROBINSON, sometime
Fellow of *Corpus Christi* Colledge
in *Oxford*.
And now after many Impressions, newly Corrected and
purged of all Errors hapned in the
former Editions.
LONDON,
Printed by *Bernard Alsop*, dwelling in *Distaffe* lane
at the Signe of the *Dolphin*.
1624.

[A 2 r] To the Honourable descended Gentleman Cresacre More, of Moreplace in North-Mimes, in the Countie of Hertford, Esquire; next in Bloud to Sir Thomas More, Lord Chauncellour of England, and Heire to the aunciant Familie of the Cresacres, sometime Lords of the Mannor of Bamborough,[15] in the Countie of Yorke, in the time of Edward the first.

Howsoever (in these wretched daies) the Dedication of Bookes is growne into a wretched respect; Because the Inducements looke a wrie, sometimes from vertue, pointing at ostentation (which is grosse,) or at flatterie (which is more base,) or else at gaine, which is the most sordid of all other: yet (worthy Sir) I beseech you be pleased better to conceive of this present; for the Inducements which have drawne me to this boldnesse, cary (I might say a Noble, but I dare be bold to say) an honest countenance: to omit the excellencie of the Worke (yet unparaleld in that nature) or the noble parts of the more excellent Authour (whose remembrance is a myrror to all succeeding

---

15 1624: Bamorough

Nobilitie) both which might challenge Caesar for a Patron: yet when I looke into your Honourable Pedegree, and finde you the undoubted heire of his Bloud, me thought it was a [A2 v] theft of the worst nature, to give to another the inheritance of his vertue, and I might as well take from you the Lands of the Honourable and auncient Family of *Cresacre* (with which God and your right hath endowed you) as bestow upon a stranger this glorious Commonwealth, to which your owne Bloud, your Auncestours vertue, and my dutie must necessarily intaile you: This consideration, when you please to take to your memory, I doubt not but it will much lessen my presumption, and you will out of the goodnesse of your owne vertue thinke, since it is my fortune to bestow upon him the new Edition, I could not with good manners[16] but bring him to kisse the hand of his true owner, wishing that as this Booke is eternall for the vertue, and shall live whilest any Booke hath being: so your name and goodnesse may continue amongst us, ever flourishing and unwithered, so long as the Sunne and Moone endureth:
Your Worships ever to be commanded,
BERNARD ALSOP.

[More to Giles I]
[Book I]
[Book II]
[Giles to Busleyden]
[Utopian quatrain transliterated and translated]
[Anemolius' poem]
[Noviomagus' poem]
[Grapheus' poem][17]

---

16 1624: good manners)
17 This is the order in two of the copies of London 1624 that I have examined. However, in another copy (Bodleian Library: Crynes 935), the sequence is as follows: More to Giles I; Giles to Busleyden; Utopian quatrain transliterated and translated; Anemolius's poem; Noviomagus's poem; Grapheus's poem; Book I; Book II. The pages are numbered as in the other copies; since Book I begins with a new page-number, and the paratexts have only signature numbers, this causes no problems.

London 1639

[Frontispiece: a slightly shorter version of the title, in a decorative surround, beneath a portrait of More flanked by 'Prudentia' and 'Eloquentia'; details of bookseller below, with date; 'W. Marshall sculpsit' in the surround; title-page on next recto:]

THE COMMON-
WEALTH
OF
UTOPIA:
Containing a Learned and
pleasant Discourse of the best
state of a Publike Weale, as it
is found in the Government of the new Ile called
Utopia.
WRITTEN
By the right Honourable,
Sir THOMAS MOORE,
Lord *Chauncellour* of
England.
LONDON,
Printed by *B. Alsop* and *T. Fawcet*, and
are to be sold by *Wil. Sheares*, at his
shop in *Bedford-street* in *Coven-garden*
neere the *New Exchange.*
1639.

[A r] To the Hon[ourable] descended Gentleman, Cresacre Moore, of More place in North-Mimes, in the County of Hertford, Esquire: Next in Bloud to Sir Thomas Moore, L[ord] Chancellor of England, and Heire to the ancient Family of the Cresacres, sometime Lord of the Mannor of Bamborough, in the County of Yorke, in the time of Edward the first.

Sir,
I have found you so Noble in the first Dedication, that I should much derogate from your true Worth, and wrong my selfe to make choise of a new Pa[A v]tron for the second (exactly done with applause) wherein though I presume, yet persume, t'will bee no sinne to multiply my obligation. Your name, and nature, claimes, and deserves it, 'tis your due and my duty, and were I able to express more MOORE should have it, for I must alwayes acknowledge your

goodnesse in whatsoever quality fortune shall bestow me. SIR, I know you are wise. In a word I am, really what I am.
Your worships ever to be commanded.
Ber. Alsop.

[Book I]
[Book II]

Texts edited by Christina Sandhaug
with the collaboration of Terence Cave

THE DUTCH PARATEXTS

De Utopie van Thomas Morus, in zijnen tijden Cancellier van Enghelant: Een boeck seer profijtelijck ende vermakelijck om lesen, bysondere den ghenen die heensdaechs een Stadt ende ghemeynte hebben te regeren, daer hy meestendeel toe dienende is. Nu eerst ourghe= sedt in neder Duytssche.

Gheprint Thantwerpen in de Camerstrate in den Salm, by Hans de Laet. Anno. 1553.
Met Gratie ende Preuilegie.

Antwerp 1553: Title-page. By permission of the British Library

Antwerp 1553

        De Utopie van
Thomas Morus / in zijnen
tijden Cancellier van Enghelant: Een boeck
seer profijtelijck ende vermakelijck om lesen /
bysondere den ghenen die heensdaechs
een Stadt ende ghemeynte hebben te
regeren / daer hy meestendeel toe
dienende is. Nu eerst overghe-
sedt in neder Duytssche.

[emblem]
Spes alit agricolas

Gheprint Thantwerpen
in de Camerstrate in den Salm / by
Hans de Laet. Anno. 1553.
Met Gratie ende Previlegie.

[privilege]
[Book I]
[Book II]

[L viii v] Ghevisiteert ende gheabprobeert by eenen gheleerden Heere / Licenciaet inder Godheyt / vander K[eiserlijcke] M[ajesteit] daer toe gheadmitteert.

[Details of printer as on title-page, with slight differences of presentation]

Antwerp 1553

The Utopia of Thomas Morus, in his time Chancellor of England: a book most profitable and pleasing to read, especially for those who in the present day have to rule a town and district, a purpose which it is above all suited to serve. Now translated for the first time into Dutch.

[emblem]
Farmers are nourished by hope.

Printed in Antwerp in the Camerstrate in the Salm by Hans de Laet. In the year 1553.

With grace and privilege.

[privilege]
[Book I]
[Book II]

[L viii v] Inspected and approved by a learned gentleman, Bachelor of Divinity, appointed for that purpose by his Imperial Majesty.

[Details of printer as on title-page]

Antwerp 1562

[title and emblem as in 1553]

<blockquote>Gheprint Thantwerpen
in die[1] Camerstrate in die Rape / by
Hans die Laet. Anno 1562.
Met Gratie ende Previlegie.</blockquote>

[the contents of this edition are in other respects identical to those of the 1553 edition]

---

1 The three instances of 'die' in this and the following line are as printed on the original title page.

Antwerp 1562

[title and emblem as in the 1553 edition]

Printed in Antwerp in the Camerstrate in the Rape by Hans de Laet. In the year 1562.

With grace and privilege.

[the contents of this edition are identical to those of the 1553 edition]

Hoorn 1629

De Utopia van
Thomas Morus / in sijn
leven Cancellier van Enghelandt: Een Boeck seer profitelijck ende vermakelijck om lesen / bysonder den
genen / die hedens daeghs een Stadt
ende Gemeynte hebben te regeren / daer't meesten-
deel toe dient.

Over-geset in 't Nederduytsch:
En in vele plaetsen van onghebruyckelijcke woorden ende druck-
fauten ghebetert.

[typographical ornament]

TOT HOORN,
By Marten Gerbrantsz. Boeckverkooper / Anno 1629.[2]

[3] Aen den Christelijcken weet-gerighen Leser.

Christeliicke Leser: daer en is voor Landen ende Steden geen sake gheluckigher ende meerder te wenschen dan goede Politie ende de ware Religie. Want door goede Politie worden de Landen ende Steden wijsselijck voorsien tegen hare uyt-heemsche vyanden; ende van binnen (soo veel mogelick is) van alle quaet-doenders ende oproerige geesten gesuyvert. Ende door de ware Religie, wel gemaintineert sijnde, wordt de suyvere Godts-dienst opgherecht ende voort-gheplant onder de Onderdanen, ende de oprechte vreese Godts gestabilieert, ende wordt also de Almachtige God tot een onverwinlijcke Patroon ende beschermer der selver Landen ghemaeckt, diese dan oock also met een vierighe muer gestadelijck ront[4]om beschut ende bewaert. Tot desen eynde streckt den heylsamen raedt van Jethro den Vader van Mosis huysvrouwe, Exod. 18.21.22. De trouwe vermaninge des Godsaligen Coninghs Davids, Psalm 2.10.11. ende Josaphats, 2. Paral. 19. De voorsegginge des Propheten Esaie 49. 't Ghebedt dat voor de Overheden bevolen werdt te doen. 1. Timot. 2. Eyndelijck

---

2 The sign '=' used in the original at the end of lines to indicate word-breaks has been rendered here by the modern hyphen.

Hoorn 1629

The Utopia of Thomas Morus, in his lifetime Chancellor of England: a book most profitable and pleasing to read, especially for those who in the present day have to rule a town and district, a purpose which it is above all suited to serve. Translated into Dutch. And in many places purged of words no longer in use and printing errors.

[typographical ornament]

At Hoorn, by Marten Gerbrantsz. Bookseller. In the year 1629.

To the Christian reader who is eager for knowledge.

Christian reader: there is nothing more fortunate and desirable for countries and towns than good Government and true Religion. For through good Government countries and towns have a sure protection against their enemies from outside, and from within they are purged (as far as possible) of all wrongdoers and rebellious spirits. And through true Religion, when it is properly maintained, a pure faith is established and promoted among the subjects and an upright fear of God implanted, and thus Almighty God becomes the invincible Lord and defender of these same countries, so that they are in this way protected and preserved, encircled in a wall of fire.[1] This was the aim of the salutary advice of Jethro, the father of Moses' wife, Exodus 18.21.22; the faithful exhortations of the Blessed King David, Psalms 2.10–11, and of Josaphat, 2 Chronicles 19; the prophecies of Isaiah 49; the prayer that we are commanded to offer for those in authority, 1 Timothy 2; and finally,

---

1 See Zacharias II.9.

het treffelijck exempel Davids, psalm. 101. Het ware van herten te wenschen dat alle Christen Potentaten ende Overheden hare gantsche Regeringe daer nae aenstelden, soo souden de Landen ende Steden op 't Heerlijckste floreren ende bloeyen in goeden vrede ende voorspoet. Maer om dat in beyde stucken groote nalatigheyt wert befonden (God betert) so ist dat de Landen ende Steden uytwendigh met langhduerighen bloedigen Oorloge, midtsgaders met andere plagen inwendigh swaerlijck worden te huys besocht, ende soo daer gheen beteringh in geschiet, eyndelijck wel mochten, door Gods rechtveerdigh Oordeel, t'eenmael verdorven ende ver[5]destrueert werden, ghelijck wy verscheyden exempelen, over ghelijcke sonden connen lesen geschiet te zijn den volcke Gods in 't Oude Testament ende in verscheyden plaetsen ter werelt nae de Hemmelvaert des Heeren Christi, jae oock in onse nabueren de verheerde Nederlanden. Om nu tot verbeteringhe der Politie een goede ooghe te slaen, dient voor al den heylsamen raedt Jethrons ghevolght ende de voorschreven vermaninghen in 't werck gestelt. Daer by dan niet ondienstelijck, maer met geneuchte sal konnen ghelesen worden, dese cierlijcke afbeeldinghe der Politie, die den gheleerden Thomas Morus Cancellier des Coninghs van Enghelandt hier ontworpen heeft in zijn Utopiâ ofte Achoriâ. Want alhoewel daer verscheyden dingen in zijn die hy selve oordeelt berispelijck te wesen, (ende ooc sodanigh zijn,) in hare zeden, krijghs-handel, Religie ende Godts-dienst: so ist nochtans dat hy (die overslaende) niet alleenlijck wenscht, maer genoeghsam aenradet, die selve Utopiensen in een groot [6] deel der Politie ende generale stucken der Religie nae te volghen ende ghelijck te zijn: ghelijck insonderheydt voor de Politie dientstigh soude zijn den dwangh voor de quaedt-doenders om haer vande ledigheyt ende bedelirije af te houden, de goede opvoedinghe der Kinderen, de verachtinge van de Rijckdommen tegen de gierigheyt, &c. Item, die generale puncten der Religie in 't 9. Cappitel beschreven. Ick wensche u.l. mede, Christelijcke Leser, wie ghy zijt dit boeck alsoo te moghen lesen, dat yegelijck in sijne beroepinghe desen voorslagh soecke in 't werck te stellen, (daer sy niet teghen Godts woordt en strijdt) ende alsoo de Politie ende Religie de helpende handt te bieden met ernstighe gebeden, woorden ende wercken. Daer toe verleen ons sijnen rijcken zegen, die daer is een eenigh Godt in wesen, ende drie eenigh in personen over al te prijsen inder eeuwigheyt. Amen.

the excellent example of David, Psalm 101. It is sincerely to be desired that all Christian potentates and authorities should establish their entire mode of government according to this principle; thus countries and towns would wonderfully flourish and bloom in perfect peace and prosperity. But where both[2] suffer from neglect (may God send improvement), countries and towns will be grievously afflicted by long-lasting bloody wars from without, and from within by other troubles, and if there be no improvement in them, they will at last be ruined and destroyed by God's righteous judgement, as we may read happened to God's people for similar sins in various examples in the Old Testament and in various places of the world after the Ascension of Christ the Lord, and indeed also to our neighbours, the occupied Netherlands.[3] Let us now cast a glance at political improvement. Here above all Jethro's salutary advice must be followed and the above-mentioned admonitions put into practice. In addition, this elegant image of a Polity, which the learned Thomas Morus, Chancellor of the King of England, has sketched out in his Utopia or Achoria, may be read, not unprofitably, but with enjoyment. For even if it contains various things that he himself judges to be worthy of reproof (as indeed they are), in the Utopians' customs, manner of waging war, religion and worship of God, there are nevertheless others where, when he gives consideration to the matter, he not only desires but as good as recommends us to follow and imitate the Utopians themselves with regard to a great deal of their politics and the general aspects of their religion.[4] Thus, in the political domain, the compulsion for wrongdoers to be kept from unemployment and beggary would be particularly valuable, together with the proper upbringing of children, the contempt for riches and the rejection of avarice, etc. Similarly, the main points of religion described in chapter 9. I desire you also, Christian Reader, whoever you are who may read this book, that each of you in his calling shall seek to put into practice what More proposes (insofar as it is not in conflict with God's word), and also to give Politics and Religion a helping hand with your earnest prayers, words and works. May He give us for this purpose his rich blessings, He who is one in essence and three in one in persons, worthy of praise above all else, world without end. Amen.

---

2 This may refer to the 'countries and towns' of this and the previous sentence (both types of community had their own form of government), but it seems more likely that the antecedent is 'political and religious government'.
3 The Spanish-ruled southern Netherlands. At the time this preface was written, the eighty-year-long war with Spain was not yet over, and many Netherlanders from the north of the country, especially Calvinist supporters of the House of Orange, dreamed of setting the southern provinces free.
4 This sentence refers to the comments attributed to More at the end of Book II, after Hythloday has withdrawn from the scene.

[Book I]
[Book II]

[201] 't Boeck des doorluchtigen Thomas Morus, eertijdts Cancellier des Coninghs van groot Britanien, *van den besten staet eener Republijcke, ende van het nieuwe Eylandt Utopia.* Een recht gouden Schrift, ende niet min heylsaem als geneughlijck, twelck voor den genen die daer aen moghten twijffelen klaer sal blijcken uyt de lofbrieven Erasmi van Rotterdam, Gulielmi Budaei, ende andere treffelijcke mannen, de welcke wy dierhalven hier achter aen ghevoeght hebben.

[More to Giles I]
[Erasmus to Froben]
[Budé to Lupset]
[Busleyden to More]
[Giles to Busleyden]
[Noviomagus' poem[
[Grapheus' poem]
[Anemolius' poem]

[colophon:]
Tot Hoorn.
Ghedruckt by Isaäc Willemsz. Boeckverkooper / op 't noordt in 't Schrijfboeck.
Anno 1630.

[Book I]
[Book II]

The book of the illustrious Thomas Morus, sometime Chancellor of the King of Great Britain, on the best state of a Republic and on the new Island Utopia. A truly golden text, no less salutary than enjoyable, which, for those who might doubt it, is clearly seen from the letters of praise of Erasmus of Rotterdam, Guillaume Budé, and other excellent men, which we have therefore added here.

[More to Giles I]
[Erasmus to Froben]
[Budé to Lupset]
[Busleyden to More]
[Giles to Busleyden]
[Noviomagus' poem[
[Grapheus' poem]
[Anemolius' poem]

[colophon:]
In Hoorn.
Printed by Isaäc Willemsz. Bookseller in the north at the sign of the Writing-Book.
In the year 1630.

Hoorn 1634

De *Utopia* van
Thomas Morus, in
sijn leven Cancellier van
Enghelandt:
Seer profitelijck ende vermakelijck
om lesen / bysonder den genen / die hedens-
daeghs een Stadt ende Ghemeynte hebben
te regeren / daer 't meestendeel
toe dient.
Hier achter sijn by-gevoeght de Lof-
Brieven van Erasmus van Rotterdam, Guilh.
Bud. ende andere treffelijcke Mannen.
Over-gheset in 't Nederduytsche; en in vele
plaetsen van onghebruyckelijcke woorden ende
druck-fauten ghebetert.

[typographical ornament, different from 1629]

Tot HOORN,
By Marten Gerbrantsz. Boeckverkooper
in de kerck-straet / in 't ABC.
Anno 1634.[3]

---

[3] Except for the title-page, the contents of this edition are identical to those of Hoorn 1629-30.

Hoorn 1634

The *Utopia* of Thomas Morus, in his lifetime Chancellor of England: most profitable and pleasing to read, especially for those who in the present day have to rule a town and district, a purpose which it is above all suited to serve. After it have been added the letters of praise of Erasmus of Rotterdam, Guillaume Budé and other excellent men. Translated into Dutch; and in many places purged of words no longer in use and printing errors.

[typographical ornament, different from 1629]

In Hoorn, by Marten Gerbrantsz. Bookseller in the Kerck-Straet at the sign of the ABC.

In the year 1634.

THE SPANISH PARATEXTS

VTOPIA DE THOMAS MORO,

TRADVCIDA DE LATIN en Castellano por Don Geronimo Antonio de Medinilla i Porres, Cauallero de la Orden de Santiago, Cavallerizo de su Magestad, Señor de las Villas de Bocos, Rozas, i Remolino, Corregidor, i Iusticia mayor de la Ciudad de Cordova, i su tierra.

A D. IVAN DE CHAVES I MENDOZA Cavallero de la Orden de Santiago, Presidente del Real Consejo de las Ordenes, del Consejo, i Camara de su Magestad, Conde de S. Cruz, i Señor de la Calçada, &c.

Dilecta ex his, & constituta Reipublicę forma, laudari faciiius, quàm evenire, vel si evenit, haut diuturna esse potest. *C. Corn. T. Ann. lib. 4.*

CON PRIVILEGIO.
En Cordova. Por SALVADOR DE CEA. A. 1637.

Córdoba 1637: Title–page. By permission of the Biblioteca Nacional, Madrid

Córdoba 1637

UTOPÍA
De
THOMÁS MORO,
*TRADUCIDA DE LATIN
en Castellano por Don Gerónimo*[1] *Antonio de
Medinilla i Porres, Cavallero de la Orden de
Santiago, Cavallerizo de su Magestad, Señor
de las Villas de Bocos, Rozas, i Remolino,
Corregidor, i Justicia mayor de la Ciudad
de Córdova, i su tierra.*

A D[ON] JUAN DE CHAVES I MENDOZA
Cavallero de la Orden de Santiago, Presidente
del Real Consejo de las Órdenes, del Consejo, y
Cámara de su Magestad, Conde de S[anta] Cruz, i
Señor de la Calçada, &c.

Dilecta ex his, et constituta Reipublicae forma, laudari facilius,
quam evenire, vel si evenit, haut
diuturna esse potest. *C.*[2] *Corn. T.
Ann. lib. 4.*

CON PRIVILEGIO
En Córdova. Por SALVADOR DE CEA. A. 1637.

[ii r] A D[on] Juan de Chaves i Mendoça, Cavallero de la Orden de Sanctiago, Presidente del Consejo de las Órdenes, del Consejo i Cámara de su Magestad, Conde de Sancta Cruz, i Señor de la Calçada, &c.

Aviendo V[uestra] S[eñoría] sido el primero, después del fallecimiento de mi padre (que esté en el cielo) que con su favor, i autoridad me ha honrado, i ayudado mi soledad, no cumpliera yo con las leyes de mi obligación, si debiendo tanto de amparo a V.S. [ii v] (como el mundo sabe) no confesara

---

1 Accents have been made consistent according to modern norms throughout. Abbreviations of titles and terms of address (e.g. 'D.' for 'Don', 'v. md.' for 'vuestra merced') have been expanded in square brackets when they first occur but otherwise left as in Córdoba 1637.

2 'C.' is an error for 'P[ublius]'. The text of this and other classical quotations in the paratexts of Córdoba 1637 varies in certain details from that of standard modern editions.

Córdoba 1637

Thomas More's *Utopia*, translated from Latin into Castilian by Don Jerónimo Antonio de Medinilla y Porres, Knight of the Order of Santiago, Equerry of his Majesty, Lord of the towns of Bocos, Rozas, and Remolino, Royal Representative and Chief Magistrate of the City of Córdoba and its territory.

To Don Juan de Chaves y Mendoza, Knight of the Order of Santiago, President of the Royal Council of the Orders,[1] of the Council and Chamber of His Majesty, Count of Santa Cruz, and Lord of la Calzada etc.

After the form of the state has been selected[2] from these[3] and constituted, it can more easily be praised than it can come into existence, or if it does come into existence, it can hardly be long-lasting. (Tacitus, *Annals*, Book IV)

With Royal Privilege
In Córdoba. By Salvador de Cea. In the year 1637.

To Don Juan de Chaves y Mendoza, Knight of the Order of Santiago, President of the Council of the Orders, of the Council and Chamber of His Majesty, Count of Santa Cruz, and Lord of la Calzada, etc.

Your Lordship having been the first to honour me with your favour and authority and to help me in my loneliness after the passing of my father (may he rest in peace), I would not discharge my obligation if, owing so much to your Lordship's protection (as everyone knows), I were not to confess the debt

---

[1] The military orders, like the Order of Santiago, which was founded in the twelfth century and played a crucial role in the Reconquest of Spain
[2] We have translated according to the text of modern editions, which read 'delecta' for 'dilecta'; 'dilecta' makes no sense here.
[3] i.e. democracy, aristocracy, and monarchy, which Tacitus states in the passage that precedes the one that is quoted.

públicamente la deuda, i mostrara a V.S. el reconocimiento que puedo en toda ocasión. Elegí la de la versión de la Utopía de Thomás Moro, idea hasta aora desseada en el siglo, i por impossible no conseguida. Autor de perpetua memoria, insigne por virtud, sabiduría, i fortuna. Consideraciones, i discursos contiene el assunto, dignos de alabança, en nuestro tiempo de admiración, imitación en todos. V.S. obra lo que éste escrive, hallándose en su gran sujeto, erudición, esperiencia, i prendas naturales aventajadas, en cuya ponderación no tiene parte el afe[iii r]cto, ni la lisonja. Los loores de V.S. han llegado ya a no tener necessidad della, que es la mayor alabança. Espero que en el ánimo de V.S. (que tanto se lleva de la razón) hallará la acogida que aguarda mi intento. Este será perpetuamente manifestar a V.S. i al mundo mi reconocimiento, en la merced que recibo de su mano, que beso muchas vezes. Guarde Dios a V.S. como yo he menester. Córdova 20. de Octubre de 1637.

Don Hierónimo Antonio
de Medinilla i Porres.

[iii v] Al Lector.
Entre los que forman Ideas, i Repúblicas desseadas, fue el más acertado Thomás Moro (gran Canciller de Inglaterra)[3] cuya constancia en la Fe, junto con la prudencia del siglo, hizo bienaventurada su memoria. Es diverso el poner las Repúblicas como ellas son, o como debrían ser. I no basta sea bueno el que govierna,[4] si no haze que sus súbditos lo sean. Por huir de la envidia que causa la reprehensión, escrivió más cómo avían de ser los hombres, que cómo eran los de su edad, dando institutos, i le[iiii r]yes, que no alcançaron Lacedemonios, Atenienses, ni Romanos. Fundó la felicidad de un estado perfectamente dichoso, estableciendo la virtud, destruyendo el vicio, cortó la raíz de competencias entre los hombres, reduciéndolas a vivir en común, sin posseer alguna cosa en particular; de tal suerte, que qualquiera acción pública, o privada, no se encamine a la codicia de muchos, ni al antojo, i mal desseo de pocos. Antes toda esta su imagen mira a la Justicia, i constante igualdad común, mejorando nuestra flaqueza, i descubriendo los riesgos de la ambición. Es su estilo tan grave, i tan [iiii v] cubierto el artificio, que haze competir una materia estrecha, i estéril en la apariencia, con las más finas de Estado, i con quantos misterios suele querer colegir el más Político de Tito Libio, i Cornelio Tácito: porque haze historia de afectos humanos, i no panegyrico de

---

3 1637: (gran Canciller de Inglaterra(
4 1637: govierno

publicly and show your Lordship all the gratitude that I can at every opportunity. I chose the occasion of the translation of Thomas More's *Utopia*, an idea[4] that until now was only wished for in this age, and not realised because thought to be impossible. He is an author whose memory will be everlasting, renowned for virtue, wisdom, and fortune. His subject encompasses considerations and discussions worthy of applause in our time, and of admiration and imitation in all ages. Your Lordship puts into effect what he writes, since your noble character encompasses erudition, experience, and exceptional natural talents, which may be discerned without recourse to personal feeling or flattery. The eulogies of your Lordship have now reached a point where they have no need of such flattery, and this is itself the highest praise. I hope that in your Lordship's mind (which is so much in tune with reason) this work will find the reception that corresponds to my intention, this being to demonstrate unceasingly to your Lordship and to the whole world my gratitude for the favours I receive from your hand, which I kiss many times. May God protect your Lordship, as it is also my duty to do. Córdoba, 20 October 1637.

Don Jerónimo Antonio de
Medinilla y Porres.

To the reader.
Among those who construct ideal models and imaginary republics, the most discerning was Thomas More (the great Chancellor of England) whose constancy in the faith, together with worldly prudence, made his memory blessed. It is one thing to portray republics as they are, and quite another to depict them as they should be. And it is not enough for those who govern to be good if they do not see to it that their subjects are good as well. In order to escape the envy aroused by censure, he wrote more about how men should be than about how they were in his day, prescribing rules and laws that neither the Lacedaemonians, the Athenians, nor the Romans achieved. He founded the happiness of a perfectly prosperous state, establishing virtue, destroying vice; he cut the root of competitiveness among men, requiring them to live in common, without owning anything individually, in such a way that no public or private action fosters the avarice of the many, nor the whims and base desires of the few. Rather, this whole imaginary conception of his aims at justice and constant common equality, remedying our frailty and exposing the risks of ambition. His style is so weighty, and his artistry so subtle that he brings together a material that is apparently quite simple and sterile with the most recondite matters of state and with all the mysteries the most adept political thinker could wish to compile from Livy and Tacitus. For he is constructing

---

4 i.e. an ideal model.

alabanças. Esta admiración [me] produxo humor curioso, i desseos de servir a la Patria, haziendo común este tesoro. Comuniqué el intento con personas sabias, i vistos algunos pedaços, ultimadamente me alentaron a poner esta versión, en la opinión del mundo. E procurado en el traducir, dar más el espíritu del Autor, [v r] que sus palabras. Ame la brevedad, dezir mucho en poco: enchir no planas, sino sentencias: mas es tan delicado el fastidio de los hombres, que aun de no cansarse se cansan. Desseé hazer común a toda[5] suerte de gentes, lo que en mayor volumen pudiera ser de pocos. El que lo cotejare con el original Latino, reconocerá el travajo, que ha costado. Éste tendré por logrado, si fuere recibida con agrado mi intención, ofreciendo en recompensa desta aceptación algunas obras no menos útiles, que han servido de onesta diversión a diferentes ocupaciones. No propongo estos exemplares [v v] como quien los sabe, sino como quien los dessea aprender.

[vi r] Nota al capítulo nono, i último desta Obra, hecha por el Tradutor.

Como los Santos Doctores i felices Mártyres tenían assentadas en su coraçón las verdades comunes de nuestra Religión Católica, seguros de su Fe, i de la de aquellos a quienes[6] escribían, hablaron a las vezes tan concisa, i brevemente, que de sus palabras, i precissión, se valen los mal intencionados i contrarios a nuestra Religión, para ampliar, i estender sus proposiciones, i doctrinas torcidas: i para esto traen la autoridad de los Santos, citándolos no como ellos hablaron, mas como quieren que hablen. En esta atención los Prelados de la Iglesia Cató[vi v]lica, i las Inquisiciones della, a la malicia de los unos se vieron en obligación de prevenilles con cauciones, i limitaciones, i declaraciones en los libros de los Padres Santos de la Iglesia, como se reconoce en las que han puesto en los Expurgatorios de España, i Portugal, en los Tratados, i obras de muchos Mártyres, i Doctores, como son; San Ignacio, San Victorino, San Zenón, San Prudencio, i otros en gran número. Esto mismo ha acontecido al Mártyr Santo Thomás Moro, que según su fervorosa Fe, i de la de aquellos a quien escrivía introdujo algunas cláusulas, que en el sentido dellas, eran, i son Católicas: pero según el estado que oi tiene el siglo pueden dañar: por lo qual los Expurgatorios de España, [vii r] santamente ordenaron, no anduviese

5 1637: todo
6 1637: quien

a story of human feelings, and not a panegyric or encomium. My admiration for his work generated a strong motivation and desire to serve my country by making this treasure common property. I communicated my attempt to certain wise persons, and having seen some pieces of it, they finally urged me to put this translation to the test of public opinion. In it, I have tried to convey more of the spirit of the author than of his words. I preferred brevity, to say much in a short space, to expand not pages, but thoughts; but people are so hard to please that they get bored even with not being bored. I wished to make available to all varieties of people a text which in a larger volume would have been available to only a few. He who compares it with the original Latin will recognise the work it has cost. I will consider my work successful if my intention is received with approval, and I offer in recompense for this acceptance some no less useful works that have served as honest diversion from other occupations.[5] I present these works not as one who already possesses the knowledge they contain, but as one who wishes to learn from them.

Translator's Note on Chapter Nine, the Final Chapter of this Book.

Since the Holy Doctors of the Church and blessed Martyrs confidently held the fundamental truths of our Catholic religion in their hearts, and were sure of their faith and of the faith of those for whom they wrote, they sometimes spoke so concisely and briefly that the precision of their words was used to advantage by the ill-intentioned and contrary to our religion in order to expand and extend their own twisted propositions and doctrines; and for this purpose they draw upon the authority of the Saints, quoting their words not as they spoke them, but as they want them to speak. In view of the artful guile of such individuals, the Prelates of the Catholic Church and her Inquisitions were obliged to thwart them by including cautions and limitations and declarations in the books of the Holy Fathers of the Church, as one sees in those they have inserted, in the Spanish and Portuguese indexes[6] of prohibited books, into the treatises and works of many Martyrs and Doctors, such as Saint Ignatius, Saint Victorinus, Saint Zeno, Saint Prudentius and others in great number. This has likewise happened to the holy martyr Thomas More who, according to his fervent faith and the faith of those for whom he wrote, introduced certain clauses which were and are Catholic in sense, but which could prove damaging due to the state of the world today. For this reason the indexes of prohibited books in Spain piously ordered that this book not be

---

5 Perhaps a reference to Medinilla's putative translation of Jean Bodin's *Methodus ad faciliorem historiarum cognitionem*.
6 Both the Spanish and the Portuguese Inquisitions operated independently of the Roman Index, but the Portuguese Inquisition accepted and promoted the Roman catalogues, and even surpassed them in rigour.

este libro sin reformarle. Al principio engañaron los enemigos invisibles al mundo, i a sus mayores sabios, introduciendo la pluridad de dioses para la Idolatría. Este[7] error lo derribó el Salvador del mundo Christo nuestro Señor con su advenimiento, en tal manera, que no ai rastro dél en gente de razón, i ya no permanece sino entre unos pocos bárbaros, que avitan el fin de la tierra. A procurado el engaño en lo último de la edad pervertir al mundo, quitándole el verdadero conocimiento de Dios, por medio del Ateísmo, estableciendo en los ánimos estraños, que el ánima del hombre es mortal, i se acava con la muerte, como la de los brutos irracionales, i juntamente travaja en persuadir, [vii v] que a cada qual es permitido honrar a Dios con la Religión que quisiere, aunque sea contra la unión del Evangelio. El piadoso mártir Thomás Moro, discurre en el capítulo de la Religión de los Utopianos, acerca[8] de la variedad que permitían en la República: i aunque los Expurgatorios no limitan algo deste capítulo, como lo advierte el testimonio del Maestro Bartolomé Ximénez Patón, a quien justamente el S[anto] Tribunal ha cometido limpiar obras, que necesitan de corrección, todavía ha parecido prevenir la ocasión, que puede tomar el Ateísta, i Político, contra lo que el glorioso Mártir procuró: i atendiendo a esto, dispuse esta nota, por no quitarle al testo, i guardar las leyes de tradutor, con que se encamina el sentido Ca[viii r]tólico del Mártir. I es cierto, que conviene que aya mucha variedad de Religiones, cultos, leyes, ceremonias dentro de la Religión Evangélica, Católica Romana, i assí veemos que la ha avido, i ai para siempre. Porque como dize el Apóstol S[an] Pablo, *Multiformis sapientia Dei*. O como lee el texto Siriaco, *Sapientia Dei differentiis plena*. I en los Cantares se lee: *Mille Clypei pendent ex ea*. Un modo de govierno, leyes, i ceremonias uvo en la Primitiva Iglesia, guardando lo sustancial, que aora no esta en plática, como se vee en muchos Cánones de los Apóstoles, i a cada Era le ha tocado varios usos. En el presente ai tanta diferencia de ceremonias en la Missa, i Breviarios de Griegos, con reliquias del Ritual Romano, tanta variedad, i di[viii v]versidad de Religiones Monásticas, Mendicantes, i Militares, con diversos ábitos, e institutos, tanta variedad de leyes, i diversidad de decretos Canónicos, unos admitidos en unos pueblos, i no en otros.

7 1637: este
8 1637: a cerca

published without first being revised. In the beginning the invisible enemies deceived the world and its wisest men, introducing the plurality of gods in the service of Idolatry. Christ our Lord, the Saviour of the World, overthrew this error with his advent, in such a way that there is now no vestige of it in people of reason, and it no longer persists except among a few barbarians who live at the ends of the earth. This spirit of deception has endeavoured to pervert the world in the latter age, depriving it of the true knowledge of God by means of Atheism, establishing in estranged souls the notion that the soul of man is mortal and ends with death,[7] like that of irrational brutes. At the same time, the deception works to persuade people that every man is permitted to honour God with the religion that he chooses, though it be contrary to the integrity of the Gospel. In his chapter on the religion of the Utopians, the pious martyr Thomas More discusses the variety of religions they permitted in the Republic; and although the Indexes have not censored this chapter in any way, as advised by the testimony of Master Bartolomé Jiménez Patón, whom the Holy Tribunal has justly charged with the purging of works that need correction; however, it has seemed necessary to prevent the atheist or political thinker from taking the opportunity of perverting the glorious Martyr's intentions. With this in mind, I have prepared this note in order not to have to cut any of the text and to keep the laws of translation, by which the Martyr's Catholic sense is conveyed. And certainly, it is desirable that there should be a wide variety of religions, sects, laws and ceremonies within the Evangelical, Catholic and Roman religion, and accordingly we see that there have been, and always will be many varieties. Because as the Apostle Paul says: *God's wisdom has many forms.*[8] Or as the Syriac text reads, *God's wisdom is full of differences.*[9] And in the Song of Songs one reads, *A thousand shields hang from it.*[10] There was only one form of government, laws, and ceremonies in the Primitive Church, preserving the essentials, but this is now no longer in practice, as is seen in many canons of the Apostles, and every age has had diverse customs. At present there are the very different ceremonies of the Greek Mass and Breviaries, with relics of the Roman ritual, and great variety and diversity of monastic religions, of mendicant and militant orders, each with its own habits and rules; there is such a multiplicity of laws and different canonical decrees, some being adopted by some nations and not by others. No less is

---

7 The fifth Lateran Council (1512-17) affirmed the dogma of the immortality of the soul, but did not succeed in ending the philosophical debate on this controversial question. It continued for example with Pietro Pomponazzi's *The Treatise on the Immortality of the Soul* (1516), which denied the separate existence of the soul.
8 Ephesians III.10.
9 The same verse in a Latin translation of the Syriac version of the Bible.
10 Song of Songs IV.4, where the beloved's neck is likened to the tower of David; the 'thousand shields' defend it against its innumerable foes.

No es menos la disonancia de espíritus, unos de vida Activa, otros de Contemplativa, unos solitarios, i otros que viven en comunidad. Los que no se contentan con seguir a los Santos, sólo se contentan con perseguirlos: i por no dezir lo que dixeron, dizen lo que ellos mandaron, que no se dixesse: por esto nuestro Religioso Autor, ceñido en sus doctrinas, i assegurado en el fundamento de la Fe, enseña con seguridad de conciencia, la certeza de la sabiduría del mundo.

[ix r] El maestro Bartolomé Ximénez Patón, Cathedrático de eloquencia de Villanueva de los Infantes, i sus partidos, i Notario del S[anto] Oficio. A Don Gerónimo Antonio de Medinilla i Porres, Cavallero del Ábito de Santiago, Cavallerizo de su Magestad, Señor de las Villas de Bocos, Roças, i Remolino, Corregidor, i Justicia mayor de la Ciudad de Córdova, i su tierra.

Lo perfecto del arte, es evidente cosa que consiste, en que a la execución se disimule. No de otra suerte la excelencia, i elegancia de las traduciones de una en otra lengua, en que no lo parezcan: antes todos las juzguen invención libre del Autor, en que declara los pensamientos agenos, como propios, con dialectos, idioma, i frases tales. Esta eminencia esperimentamos en la que v[uestra] m[erce]d ha hecho de la Utopía del insigne, i piadoso Thomás Moro de lengua Latina en Castellana, siguiendo la doctrina del Máximo Doctor Gerónimo (agradecido a su nombre) ponderando las sentencias, sin faltar a lo sustancial dellas, sin atender al número de las palabras. Ela[9] visto, i considerado con atención [ix v] mui de espacio, i siempre me parece más bien. I no quiero negar el contento que recibo de ver en ella el lucimiento de mi doctrina, que v.md. con tanta afición se ha dignado de honrar, siguiéndola con tal afecto, i propensión; como las demás facultades que ha professado, preciándose no de la medianía, con que otros se contentan; antes llegando a competir con sus maestros, aviéndolos sido los más eminentes de la Europa, en el manejo de los Cavallos, en el uso de armas, i en la contemplación de la Astronomía. Entre los quales (aunque sea el ansar con los cisnes) no por elección, sino por buena suerte mía (i destos partidos) no merecido, alcancé este nombre en las buenas letras, que llaman de humanidad, (por la nobilísima de v.md.) dando lugar a

---

9 1637: E la

the dissent among minds: some prefer the active life, others the contemplative; some are solitary, while others live in community. Those who are not content to follow the Saints are only satisfied by persecuting them; and in order not to say what the Saints said, they say what the Saints commanded us not to say. For this reason, our Religious Author, armed with his doctrines and firmly grounded in the Faith, is able with a secure conscience to teach us about human affairs as they really are.

Master Bartolomé Jiménez Patón, Professor of Eloquence in Villanueva de los Infantes[11] and its districts and Notary of the Holy Office,[12] to Don Jerónimo Antonio de Medinilla y Porres, Knight of the Order of Santiago, Equerry of His Majesty, Lord of the towns of Bocos, Rozas, and Remolino, Royal Representative and Chief Magistrate of the City of Córdoba and its territory.

Clearly, the perfection of art lies in concealing the artistic execution. Such, too, is the perfection of those translations from one language to another which in their excellence and elegance do not seem like translations; rather, all would judge them to be the free inventions of the author, in which the translator sets forth the author's thoughts as his own, in his own dialect, language, and phrasing. We experience this excellence in the translation you have made of the *Utopia* of the distinguished and pious Thomas More from the Latin tongue into Castilian, in accordance with the teaching of the eminent Doctor Jerome (thanks be to his name),[13] giving weight to the ideas without betraying their substance and without paying attention to the mere number of words. I have seen the translation, and after considering it several times at length and with close attention, it seems better to me each time I read it. And I would not deny the contentment I receive from seeing in your translation the illustration of my own teaching, which you have deigned to honour with such devotion, following it with the same passion and aptitude as the other arts you have cultivated, not priding yourself on mediocrity, as others are content to do, but attaining a position of parity with those who instructed you, who were the most eminent in Europe in horsemanship, the use of weapons, and astronomical contemplation. Among these men, I (though a mere goose among swans), not by choice, but by my own undeserved good fortune (and that of these districts), have achieved this title of mine[14] in the literary arts which they call the humanities (by your most noble humanity), securing a

---

11 Villanueva de los Infantes was the political and ecclesiastical capital of the Montiel district from the sixteenth century, the seat of the Government of the Order of Santiago and a spiritual and cultural centre of La Mancha during the Spanish Golden Age.
12 The Inquisition of Murcia.
13 St Jerome, the model *par excellence* for his Latin translation of the Bible.
14 i.e. 'Maestro'.

las pocas mías, i haziéndolas más, i mayores, con el grande aprovechamiento de su eminente ingenio, como de aquellas primeras ocupaciones, tiene dados testimonios en la patria común (i propia de v.md. Madrid) mui notorios a todos, con assistencia, i aprobación de nuestro Monarca, i de muchos Príncipes désta: bien es le dé a toda España con la tradución presente, tan fiel, tan elegante, i con lenguaje tan casto, natural, i propio, como si en ella se uviera engendrado, i nacido. I es bien, que déste goze nuestra patria; pues el primer autor Rafael Hilthodeo [*sic*] fue Español. No dilate v.md. la publicación, desseoso de darla mejo[x r]rada (pues lo está) ni se le opongan temores del acierto (pues lo ha conseguido) antes intrepidamente la comunique a todos, porque todos la esperan con la gran satisfación, que tienen de su perspicidad, i talento; i está v.md. ya tan empeñado, que a vozes la piden como de justicia (de cuya buena administración tanto v.md. se precia) i no sólo ésta, pero las demás obras, que tiene en borrador, es justo que se pongan en limpio, i salgan a luz, obligándole lo de Marcial a Faustino.

Post te victurae, per te quoque vivere chartae
Incipiant: cineri gloria sera venit.

Assí Dios guarde a v.md. con los premios, i felicidad, que le desseo muchos años. Deste su estudio todo el de v.md.

El Maestro Bartolomé Ximénez Patón.

[x v] Noticia, juicio i recomendación de la Utopía, i de Thomás Moro.
Don Francisco de Quevedo Villegas, Cavallero del Ábito de S. Jacobo, Señor de las Villas de Cetina, i la Torre de Juan Abad.

La vida mortal de Thomás Moro escrivió en nuestra habla Fernando de Herrera varón docto, i de juicio severo; su segunda vida escrivió con su sangre su muerte, coronada de victorioso martirio, fue su ingenio admirable, su erudición rara, su constancia santa, su vida exemplar, su muerte gloriosa, docto en la lengua Latina, i Griega. Celebráronle en su tiempo Erasmo de Roteradamo, i Guillelmo Budeo, como se lee en dos cartas suyas, impressas en el texto desta obra, llamola Utopía, voz Griega, cuyo significado es, no ai tal lugar. Vivió en tiempo, i en Reino, que le fue forçoso, para reprehender

place for my own meagre writings, increasing their number and merit with the great benefit of your outstanding wit, just as those first achievements of yours are acknowledged and well-known to all throughout our common homeland (and specifically yours, namely Madrid),[15] in the presence and with the approval of our Monarch and of our country's many Princes. It is well that all of Spain is given in this present work a translation so faithful, so elegant, and in a language so pure, natural, and correct, as if the original had been conceived and born in it. And it is well that our homeland will enjoy it, for the first author Raphael Hythloday was Spanish. Do not delay publication in the desire to improve it (for it is already improved), nor should you let fears about its accuracy trouble you (for you have achieved accuracy), but rather spread it boldly abroad to all, because all are waiting for it, already fully cognisant of your lucidity and skill; and you find yourself compelled to do so, for they cry out for it and with justice (on the administration of which you so justly pride yourself), and not only for this, but also for the other works you are composing. It is only right that you should give them the finishing touch and bring them into the light of day; I urge you, as Martial urged Faustinus: *Let your writings, which will live after you, also live through you; glory comes too late when it comes to the ashes.*[16]

And so may God preserve you, with the rewards and happiness that I desire for you, for many years. From his study, your obedient servant Master Bartolomé Jiménez Patón.

Description, Judgement and Recommendation of the *Utopia*, and of Thomas More. Don Francisco de Quevedo Villegas, Knight of the Order of Saint James,[17] Lord of the towns of Cetina and Torre de Juan Abad.

Fernando de Herrera, a distinguished scholar of rigorous judgement, wrote in our language of the earthly life of Thomas More, whose second life was written with his blood, his death crowned with victorious martyrdom. His intellect was remarkable, his erudition rare, his constancy saintly, his life exemplary, and his death glorious. He was a scholar of Latin and Greek. He was celebrated in his day by Erasmus of Rotterdam and Guillaume Budé, as one can read in their two letters printed in the text of this book. He called it *Utopia*, a Greek word meaning 'there is no such place'. He lived in an age and a kingdom that obliged him to feign conformity in order to criticise the government under which

---

15 Medinilla was not from Madrid as Jiménez Patón here seems to suggest but from the rural town of Bocos in Castilla La Vieja.
16 Martial, *Epigrammata* I.xxv.7-8. This is one of the epigrams that Jiménez Patón comments on in his *Declaración magistral de los epigramas de Marcial* (1628).
17 The Military Order of Santiago (= St James).

el govierno, que padecía, fingir el conveniente. Yo me persuado que fabricó aquella política contra la tyranía de Inglaterra, i [xi r] por esso hizo Isla su Idea, i juntamente reprehendió los desórdenes de los más Príncipes de su edad, fuérame fácil verificar esta opinión; empero no es difícil, que quien leyere este libro la verifique con esta advertencia mía: quien dize que se ha de hazer lo que nadie haze, a todos los reprehende: esto hizo por satisfazer su celo nuestro autor. Hurtos son de cláusulas de la Utopía los más Repúblicos Raguallos del Bocalino, preciso caudal es, el que obligó, a que fuesse ladrón a tan grande autor. No han faltado lectores de buen seso, que han leído con ceño algunas proposiciones deste libro, juzgando, que su libertad, no pisava segura los umbrales de la Religión, siendo assí, que ningunas son más vasallas de la Iglesia Católica, que aquellas entendida su mente, que piadosa se encaminó a la contradición de las novedades, que en su patria nacieron robustas, para tan llorosos fines. Escrivió aquella alma esclarecida, con espíritu de tan larga vista, que como yo mostré en mi carta al Rei Christianísimo antevió los sucessos presentes, assistiendo con saludable consejo a las cabeças de los tumultos.

El libro es corto, mas para atenderle como merece, ninguna vida será larga, escrivió poco, i dijo mucho: si los que goviernan le obedecen, i los que obedecen se goviernan por él, ni [a] aquellos será carga, ni a éstos cuidado. Por esto viendo yo a Don Gerónimo Antonio de Medinilla i Porres [xi v] que le llevava por compañía en los caminos, i le tenía por tarea en las pocas oras, que le dejava descansar la obligación de su govierno de Montiel le importuné, a que hiziesse esta tradución: assegurándome el acierto della, lo cuidadoso de su estilo, i sin afectación; i las noticias políticas, que con larga lección ha adquirido, executándolas en quanto del servicio de su Magestad se le ha ordenado, i con gran providencia, i desinterés, en el govierno que tuvo destos partidos. Quien fuere tan liberal, que en parte quiera pagar algo de lo que se deve a la santa memoria de Thomás Moro, lea en la Celta Dilettere de Bartolomé Zucchi de Monja, la carta que escrivió el Cardenal de Capua a Monseñor Marino Cardenal i Governador de Milán, i verá quantos méritos tuvo su muerte para canonizar las alabanças de su vida, i de su doctrina. En la Torre de Juan Abad, 28. de Septiembre de 1637.

Don Francisco de Quevedo Villegas

he suffered. I am persuaded that he constructed his system of government in opposition to the tyranny of England, and for this reason he presented his idea as an island, and simultaneously rebuked the misrule of so many Princes of his age. It would be easy for me to verify this opinion, or at the very least it is not difficult, for whoever reads this book will verify it with this remark of mine: he who says that one must do that which no one does, rebukes everyone. Our author did this in order to satisfy his zeal. Most of the republican *Ragguagli* of Boccalini are made up of phrases stolen from the *Utopia*, and its priceless wealth compelled him to become a thief of so great an author. There has been no lack of readers of good sense who have read some propositions of this book with indignation, judging that the liberties the author takes do not always tread securely within the boundaries of the Religion; but in fact, no propositions are more subject to the Catholic Church than these, if one correctly understands the author's mind, which piously applied itself to combating the new ideas that sprang up vigorously in his country to such lamentable effect. That illuminated soul wrote with such a visionary spirit that, as I showed in my letter to the Most Christian King,[18] he foresaw present events, providing leaders of disturbances with salutary advice.

The book is short, but no life could be too long to give it the attention it deserves; he wrote little, and said much. If those who govern were to follow its precepts, and those who obey were to govern themselves by it, rulers would have no burdens and their subjects would have no cares. Therefore, seeing that Don Jerónimo Antonio de Medinilla y Porres carried it with him for company along the way and made it his task in the few hours which his obligations as governor of Montiel left him for rest, I put him to the trouble of doing this translation. I have no doubts as to its accuracy, its meticulous style and lack of affectation, and the political knowledge, which with long reading he has acquired, employing it whenever the service of his Majesty so demanded, and with great foresight and impartiality in his government of these districts. He who would be so generous as to want to pay back in part something of that which is owed to the blessed memory of Thomas More, should read in the *Scelta di lettere* by Bartolomé Zucchi de Monza[19] the letter that the Cardinal of Capua wrote to Monsignor Marino, Cardinal and Governor of Milan: he will see there how much merit More's death carried with it to canonise the many glories of his life and his teaching. From Torre de Juan Abad, 28 September 1637.

Don Francisco de Quevedo Villegas.

18 The French King Louis XIII.
19 Bartolomeo Zucchi di Monza's *Scelta di lettere di diversi eccellentiss. scrittori* (Venice, 1595) includes the letter that Nicholas Schönberg, Cardinal of Capua, wrote on 12 August 1535 to the Cardinal of Milan, Marino Caracciolo, on the news of More's death.

[xii r] Juicio, i sentir de la Utopía, i su Tradutor, por el P[adre] Cypriano Gutiérrez de la Compañía de JESUS, i Maestro de Sagrada Escritura en su Collegio de Córdova.

Aquesta gloriosa Idea, si vivo exemplar de bien ordenadas Repúblicas, tan airosamente copió viveza, i valentía de su peregrino original, eternizando a mucho siglo dilatadas Políticas en compendiosas dogmas de la ya desde oi famosa Utopía. Noble argumento del mayor Canciller de Monarquías, tres i quatro vezes de la Romana Iglesia en la gran Bretaña esclarecido Mártyr Thomás Moro, por Fe, letras, virtudes, i santo celo a immortales aras consagrado: que pudiera mui bien el Apolo de aquellas Islas admirado de sí, invidiarse a sí[10], por sí mesmo a nuestro vulgar felizmente traducido; i aun inclinar su pluma de oro a pluma tan ennoblecida, propria, veloz, constante, breve, grave, i sentenciosa: Elogios todos de nuestro conciudadano, Epíst[ola] 46. al ingenioso libro de su Lucillo. *Librum tuum quem mihi promiseras accepi, quid ingenii iste habuit? quid impetus?*[11] *tenor, compositio virilis, et sancta; nihilo*[xii v]*minus interveniebat dulce illud et loco lene; grandis, et rectus est.*[12] I en duplicados aprecios respetar también pudiera, erudición no común, concisa Magestad, vivas, i eficaces razones con primores no pocos de eloquencia. Aplauso singular deste mi sentir, la varia de Casiodoro 49. lib[ro] I. a las traduciones de Euclydes, Nicomastro, Aristóteles, i Pytágoras por el generoso Héroe, e ínclyto Patricio Boecio. *Quos tanta* (dize el Senador) *verborum luculentia:* (poco antes *Translationibus tuis) reddidisti claros, tanta linguae proprietate conspicuos, ut potuissent et illi opus tuum praeferre*[13] *si utrumque didicissent.*

Gloria, que no assí fácil se alcança por serlo difícil, i mucho, la corriente de un estilo, i más de una Tradución, cuyo tenor para ser intelligible, debe ser en sus cláusulas constante, i si se falta a su orden, i quiebra el hilo de oro, presto se da en obscura proligidad; interpretando unas palabras por otras con supersticioso enfado, i cansancio a pocos renglones; la unión de los periodos

---

10 1637: assí
11 These two phrases should no doubt be read as exclamations rather than questions.
12 1637: et sancta nihilominus interveniebat, dulce illud et loco lene, grandis, et rectus est.
13 1637: proferre

Judgement and opinion on the *Utopia* and its Translator, by Father Cipriano Gutiérrez of the Society of Jesus, and Master of Sacred Scripture at their College in Córdoba.

This glorious idea, the very exemplar of well-ordered republics, imitated with great elegance the penetration and power of its extraordinary original, perpetuating for ages to come the copious political ideas, expressed in succinct formulas, of the now famous *Utopia*. A noble theme[20] by the greatest Chancellor of any Monarchy, the three- and fourfold illustrious martyr of the Roman Church in Britain, Thomas More, consecrated by his faith, learning, virtues, and saintly zeal on the altar of immortality; such that the Apollo of those Islands could very well first admire himself, and then be envious of himself, seeing himself so felicitously translated into our common language; his golden pen might even make obeisance to that other pen, so elevated, correct, fluent, consistent, brief, serious and pithy – all terms of praise used by our fellow-citizen[21] in his forty-sixth letter,[22] on the brilliant book of his Lucilius: *I have received your book, which you had promised me. What talent it is full of! What power! There is a steady flow, and the composition is both virile and high-minded. Nevertheless, something sweet and mild, so to speak, is mixed in with it. It is sublime and it is virtuous.* And, adding still more expressions of appreciation, he could also respect his uncommon erudition, concise majesty, lively and efficacious arguments made with not a few exquisite examples of eloquence. Praise appropriate to this opinion of mine in Cassiodorus' *Varia*, Book I, Epistle 49,[23] on the translations of Euclid, Nicomachus, Aristotle, and Pythagoras by the generous hero and illustrious *patricius*[24] Boethius. *You*[25] *have (in your translations*, mentioned above) *rendered them illustrious by such splendour of verbal expression, and conspicuous by such a correct use of language, that even they* [i.e. the original authors] *might have preferred your work, had they been acquainted with both.*

Glory which is not easily won merely by overcoming difficulties, less easily in capturing the fluency of a style, and still less in a translation, whose tenor must be consistent in its phrasing in order to be intelligible; and if it be lacking in order and break the golden thread, it quickly gives way to obscure prolixity, taking one word for another with narrow-minded insistence and tediously working line by line; the sentences woven together in a polished

---

20 Gutiérrez's paratext is more in the mode of a humanist commentary than a letter of recommendation: hence the sentences without main verbs.
21 Lucius Annaeus Seneca, 'Seneca the Younger', born in Córdoba.
22 *Epistulae morales ad Lucilium* I.46.
23 In modern editions, this epistle is no. 45.
24 From the time of the Emperor Constantine, '*patricius*' was a title given to a person in high office at court.
25 i.e. Boethius.

tersos i rodados, *sermo rotatus*,[14] de quien Juvenal Sátyra 6. [dice] más dulce, i regalada al gusto, que todas las delicias de el Ambrosía, i Néctar. El Ticiniense Prelado, i culto, S. Ennodio lindamente lo ponderava a la erudición miliflua de su Olibrio. *Dum favos loqueris,* epíst[ola] 10. *et per domos cereas eloquentiae nectare liquentis elementi mella componis, peregrinum labiis meis saporem epuli divitis infudisti.*

[xiii r] Suave es el lenguaje, alto el assunto, la materia esclarecida, leyes, fueros, avisos de una República, que no fue, i ser debría. O tiempos todos sois unos! fiscalean vicios ásperos, i picantes documentos, ocultándose la píldora en superficies de plata, i enmascarándose en peregrinas vozes lo libre atrevido (mejor dixera) verdadero, de una sátyra a los vicios. Prohibiéronla antiguas leyes, es assí, porque ya la licenciosa demasía descaradamente tocava a personas, a quien no podía tocar por el salvo conducto de la sanctidad de sus vidas con no poca gracia lo tocava el Lyrico,

>   *Quin etiam lex*
>   *Poenaque dicta malo, quae nollet carmine quenquam*
>   *Describi. vertere modum formidine fustis,*
>   *Ad benedicendum, delectandumque redacti.*

Británico a las Sátyras de Juvenal *lege lata per Alcibiadem siluerunt.* I el Bado con más claridad a las Sátyras persianas, *Prooemio, cumque honestae*[15] *personae foedius notarentur, lata Romae lex, ut siquis malum carmen, in quemquam scripsisset, eius rei ius, iuditiumque esset, ita metu paenae scenici a male*[16] *dicendo destiterunt.* No duraron mucho las violencias de aqueste freno, i mordaza, antes artificiosamente[17] se recataron de la pena, i con traza presto se bolvieron a sus ingenios picantes, la culpa tenían las culpas, que a grandes vozes

---

14 1637: sermo rotatus [roman]
15 1637: *bonestae*
16 1637: *mele*
17 1637: artificisamente

and fluent manner, in accordance with the *concise style,* which Juvenal in his Satire 6 says is more sweet and pleasurable to the taste than all the delights of ambrosia and nectar. The learned Prelate of Ticinum, Saint Ennodius,[26] suavely praised the mellifluous erudition of his Olybrius: *As you speak honeycombs,* Epistle 10,[27] *and, by means of the liquid element of nectar, produce honey from the waxen mansions of eloquence, you have been pouring into my lips the foreign taste of a rich meal.*

The language is smooth, the subject elevated, the content made clear: laws and statutes, tidings of a republic that never existed, but should exist. O ages, you are all alike! Vices are castigated in bitter, barbed tracts, hiding the pill under a silver surface and masking with foreign words the outspoken opinions (or to put it better) the true import of a satire on vices. The ancient laws prohibited satire, and they did so because licentious excess was now brazenly attacking certain persons whom it had not previously been able to touch because they were under the safe-conduct of the sanctity of their lives. The Lyric Poet[28] touched upon it with no little wit and charm: *When a law had been laid down, and a penalty, forbidding anyone to be portrayed in a malevolent poem, they changed their habits out of fear for the stick, and were led back to praise and entertainment.*[29] Britannicus on the *Satires* of Juvenal:[30] *When a law had been proposed by Alcibiades, they kept silent.*[31] And Badius with more clarity on the *Satires* of Persius: *When respectable people were cruelly branded with infamy, a law was proposed in Rome, saying that if anyone wrote a malevolent play against someone, the case should be brought to trial and judgement; and so, out of fear of punishment, the actors desisted from malevolent speech.*[32]

The violence of this bit and bridle[33] did not last for long; instead, the satirists cleverly evaded punishment, and with agile sleight-of-hand returned to their barbed devices; the blame lay with human vices, which were stridently calling

---

26 Ennodius was Bishop of Pavia, formerly Ticinum.
27 Book I, epistle 9 in modern editions.
28 Horace.
29 Horace, *Epistulae* II.i.152-5.
30 This remark is to be found in the introduction to Johannes Britannicus' early sixteenth-century commentaries on Juvenal's satires.
31 In fifth-century BCE Athens, it was common to ridicule individuals by name on the stage. In an anecdote recounted by Aelius Aristides, who also refers to laws forbidding this practice, Alcibiades was said to have thrown into the sea someone who had ridiculed him in the manner of an actor. The story is apocryphal, and there is no contemporary evidence that a law against the practice ever existed. See Stephen Halliwell, 'Comic satire and freedom of speech in classical Athens', *Journal of Hellenic Studies,* 111 (1991), 48-70.
32 The quotation has not been identified; it is presumably derived from one of the many editions of the commentaries on Persius's satires by Josse Bade (Badius) and Johannes Britannicus (first published in 1499). In invoking the names of these two celebrated humanist philologists, Gutiérrez is aligning himself with a long tradition of Renaissance commentary. The quotations refer to the practice in Athens and Rome respectively.
33 i.e. the satires.

pedían atrozes reprehensiones, echaron velo de estrangeras vozes al vituperio de sus exorbitancias. [xiii v] Del más erudito Romano Marco Varrón me dio noticia en su Adversarios, lib. 18. cap[ítulo] 28. Alexandro[18] Turnebo: ἑὼς ποτεπνϱιῶμ,[19] idest *liber de temporibus*, de los tiempos de ahora;[20] ταϱέ μέΰίπου,[21] idest *de sepultura*, títulos Griegos,[22] retiravan de la vista los avisos libres, que encerravan en sus libros. Tulio con nombre de sueños promulgó seis libros de su República, uno gozó nuestra era, el del Africano Scipión, después de aquellos incendios: el divino Platón diez libros de República, i Justo régimen entre nombres varios de Diálogos, disfrazes de su indignada Filosofía, a costumbres, dedicó al cedro: i con más valiente espíritu nuestro invencible Mártir castigó la contumaz rebeldía de sus Británicas Regiones en voz de UTOPÍA, retirándose al nombre Griego de Provincia que no fue Τῖ μέ οντα,[23] Plato de legibus, *res quae nullae sunt*, tierra, i Provincia, que no es, para que sea la que deve la que es, introduce la que sería a merced, i beneficio de sus heroicas enseñanças.

Ilustres Diálogos, grandiosas políticas, divinos goviernos, si confederados con la práctica, uso, i esperiencia de la agudeza de sus documentos: Sócrates, i Platón juzgaron por impossible exercitarse acá en la tierra la soberana idea de Repúblicas, que formavan verse sólo su exemplar allá en el cielo. *Intelligo equidem, quod ea in Civitate dicis, quam nos condidimus in praesentia,* [xiiii r] *quae et verbis solum, in terris vero nunquam,*[24] *ut arbitror extat; at forte in*[25] *caelo, illius extat exemplar, conspicuum ei, qui ut intueri voluerit, et se ipsum ad illud, cum intuitus est, instituere. Nihil autem refert, sive uspiam sit, sive erit, quae enim illius officia sunt agere solum, quae alterius sunt nequaquam consentaneum est.* Esta es la UTOPÍA, i su sagrada Filosofía, sutileza, i enseñança de costumbres,

---

18 Error for 'Adriano'.
19 This and the following Greek phrase appear to have been transcribed from the manuscript text by a printer ignorant of Greek and not subsequently corrected. We read the phrase as ἕως ποτε, περὶ ὡρῶν.
20 1637: de aora [semi-colon lacking]
21 Rather: ταφὴ Μενίππου.
22 The two Greek phrases are titles of lost satires by Varro.
23 Rather: Τὰ μὴ ὄντα.
24 A comparison between the quotation and early modern Latin translations of Plato indicates that Gutiérrez is here quoting from Ficino's translation; see for example *Omnia Divini Platonis Opera, tralatione Marsilii Ficini, emendatione et ad Graecum codicum collatione Simonis Grynaei. Nunc recens summa diligentia repurgata* (Basel: Froben, 1532), p. 653. However, Gutiérrez's quotation contains the following deviations from this text: 'nunquam' for 'nusquam', 'agere' for 'aget' and 'nequaquam consentaneum' for 'nequaquam. Consentaneum'.
25 1637: *iu*

out for terrible punishments. They threw a veil of foreign words over their exorbitant vituperations. A[drianus] Turnebus, in Book 18, Chapter 28 of his *Adversaria*,[34] drew my attention to that most scholarly Roman, Marcus Varro: *Until Some Time, About the Times*, that is, *A Book about the Times*, on the present period; 'Menippus' burial', that is, *On Burying* (Greek titles)[35] – they removed from sight those frank admonitions which they included in their books. Cicero announced six books of his *De republica*, calling them dreams; one of them, the dream of Scipio the African,[36] has survived the fires to be enjoyed in our era. The divine Plato wrote ten books on the idea of a Republic and on just government and customs in the form of variously-titled dialogues which served as disguises for his indignant Philosophy. These he consigned to cedar.[37] With more valiant spirit, our invincible Martyr rebuked the stubborn waywardness of the British regions under the term UTOPIA, taking refuge in the Greek name for a province which did not exist: *Things having no existence*, Plato on Laws, *things which are nothing*:[38] a land and province that does not exist, so that the realm which should be will become that which is; it introduces that which should be, by grace and favour of his heroic teachings.

Famous dialogues, grand political conceptions, divine governments, indeed, if they are combined with the practice, use, and experience of these profound writings. Socrates and Plato judged the implementation of the supreme idea of all republics to be impossible here on earth, since for them its exemplar could only be formed up there in the heavens: *I understand: you are talking about the state that we have founded here and now, which exists only in words, but never on earth, in my opinion. But perhaps there is an exemplar of it in heaven, visible to him who wants, as it were, to examine it, and when he has done so, to model himself on it. It does not matter whether it exists somewhere, or is going to; for it is reasonable to perform only the duties of that state, and not at all the duties of another.*[39] This is the *Utopia* and its sacred Philosophy, its subtlety and its teaching of morals, put into practice with happy

---

34 *Adriani Turnebi philosophiae, et graecarum literarum regii professoris, Adversariorum libri triginta, in tres tomos divisi, tomus secundus* (Paris: Martin Le Jeune, 1580), p. 170. The *Adversaria* is a huge compilation of noteworthy items from the author's readings.
35 See facing page, note 22.
36 Book VI, the *Somnium Scipionis*.
37 This is probably a reference to cedar as a symbol of cultural preservation and enduring memory.
38 Plato uses this expression not only in the *Laws* (*passim*) but frequently in other works also, where ontology is at issue.
39 Plato, *Republic* 592 A-B. On Gutiérrez's source text, see facing page, note 24. We have translated according to Gutiérrez's reading; his source gives 'nowhere' for 'never', and, for the last sentence, 'one will perform only the duties of that state, and not at all the duties of another. This was agreed upon.'

practicada con felices aciertos, créditos, i fianças de multiplicados goviernos en los partidos de Murcia, Villanueva de los Infantes, i oi en nuestra Colonia Patricia, Cabeza, i Principado de toda la España Anadaluz. Sydonio Apolinar, Lib. I. Epíst. 7. *Privilegiis geminae praefecturae per quinquennium repetitis fascibus rexerat.*
Conducense pues glorias de acertados empleos a la subtileza del genio, fortuna de la pluma, dándose las manos práctica, i theórica, govierno, i su vida, i agregándose obras a órdenes de tan experto Magistrado, a quien assistiendo la prudente Astrea, alternando con destreza de Marte, i de Mercurio, de la pluma el uso, exercicio de la espada, ora del azero los azeros, ora del caduceo la eloquencia: estos nuevos augmentos, i aún mayores haze, que le assistan al noble escudo de esclarecidos progenitores, mucho fuera la generosa emulación, victoria de honor quien la presumiera? [26] *Veteris decora prosa*[xiv v]*piae novelli*[27] *vincis nitore colloquii, sat fuerat parentum tuorum desideriis seniora te familiae ornamenta aemulari, vincere posse, sicut nemo credidit ita nullus optauit.* Epíst. I. S. Ennodio. Soliciten repetidos méritos, repetidos lauros, e inmortales trofeos de aquesta UTOPÍA. Este es mi sentir, en nuestro Colegio de Santa Catalina de la Compañía de Jesús de Córdova, Otubre 17. de 1637.

Cypriano Gutiérrez.

[xv r] Carta de D. Andrés de Morales i Padilla, Cavallero[28] Veintiquatro de la Ciudad de Córdova.
A la Utopía, i a su Tradutor.

Siempre honra Dios sus amigos, i les dispone lo mejor en sus obras, tanto que si para las suyas mismas que se contienen en las divinas letras, proveyó de un Gerónimo, que las tradujesse en nuestra lengua Latina. Assí en la obra de su amigo el insigne varón, i Mártir Thomás Moro le proveyó de otro Gerónymo, que con tanta eminencia nos ha dado su *Utopía* en nuestro vulgar Castellano. I como él escrivió aquella República en la forma, que desseava, que las demás se governassen: assí también le dio Dios a v.md. para que le tradujesse en la

---

26 This question is again to be read rather as an exclamation.
27 1637: nobelli
28 1637: Gavallero

assurances, credits and guarantees by many governments in the districts of Murcia, Villanueva de los Infantes, and today in our Patrician Colony,[40] Head and Principality of all of Andalucian Spain. Sidonius Apollinaris in Book 1, Epistle 7: *He had ruled for five years through the privileges of his double prefectship, after the position had been renewed.*[41]

The glories of exact application being thus conferred on the brilliance of genius, a triumph of the pen; practice joining hands with theory, governance with life, adding new works to the ordinances of such an expert Magistrate, attended by prudent Astraea, alternating the skills of Mars and Mercury, the use of the pen and the exercise of the sword, now blades of steel, now the eloquence of the caduceus. These new exploits, and even greater ones, ensure that he will be included in the noble coat of arms of illustrious ancestors. Emulating such ancestors would be a great act. O he who could pretend to such a victory of honour! *You surpass the splendour of your ancestors by the beauty of your novel speech. It would have been enough for you, according to the wishes of your parents, to emulate your forefathers, those ornaments of your family; as for outdoing them, no one thought it possible, so no one attempted it.* Ennodius, Epistle 1.[42] May those forefathers derive ever-renewed deserts, ever-renewed laurels and immortal trophies from this *Utopia*! This is my opinion, given in our College of Santa Catalina of the Society of Jesus in Córdoba, 17 October 1637.

Cipriano Gutiérrez.

Letter from Don Andrés de Morales y Padilla[43], Alderman[44] of the City of Córdoba. To the *Utopia* and its Translator.

God always honours His friends and ordains the best for them in their works. If for His own works, contained in the divine Scriptures, He provided a Jerome to translate them into our Latin language, so for the work of His beloved friend, the distinguished man and martyr Thomas More, He provided another Jerome, who with such eminence has given us his *Utopia* in our own Castilian vernacular. And just as More wrote that Republic in the form in which he desired that other republics should be governed, in the same manner God granted that you translate it in the most desirable form,

---

40 i.e. Córdoba, called 'Colonia Patricia' because it was the seat of prominent citizens during the Roman occupation.
41 Sidonius, *Epistulae* I.7.
42 Ennodius, *Epistulae* I.i.4.
43 There exists a manuscript by Morales y Padilla on the history of Córdoba, *Historia general de Córdoba*, written in the period 1625-49. The original is kept in the City Hall of Córdoba.
44 Twenty-four noblemen made up the city council in many of the Andalucian cities and towns, hence their title 'Veintiquatro'.

forma mejor, que pudo dessear, i con tanto acierto en todo, que le tuvo hasta en sacar a luz en esta Ciudad su libro: porque su Autor en la descripción de la Ciudad de Amauroto cabeça de aquella Isla, parece, que sacó a luz un retrato de algunas de las aventajas partes, con[xv v] que dotó a la de Córdova el Autor de la naturaleza, que guarde a v.md. mui felizes años, como lo desseo. En 21. de Otubre de 1637.

Don Andrés de Morales y Padilla.

[xvi r] De D. Francisco Roco Campofrío i Córdova, Cavallero Veintiquatro della, a la tradución de la Utopía.

Soneto.

La que el Moro político Britano
   Utopía fabricó, segundo Numa,
   Por no hurtar a el govierno alguna suma,
   Oi la traduce vuestra culta mano;
Por ella a un tiempo el Betis mira Hispano,
   Vidriera clara su rizada espuma,
   Regir la vara, leyes dar la pluma,
   Inspiradas de vuestro Genio cano.
Si esta i aquella, a Córdova govierna,
   Caduca de Marcelo su memoria,
   Por vos Señor de Bocos será eterna:
Que si la instruye la Utopiana historia,
   la reedifica vuestra vara alterna,
   Fábrica vivirá de inmortal gloria.

[xvi v]   Del mismo don Francisco de Córdova.

Décimas.

En el Anglia Thomás Moro
en rojas cenizas yaze,
y de ellas Fenix renace
a España vivo tessoro.
Con pluma si fiel de oro
en su Utopía traducido
oi por vos Señor ha sido;
i en culto buelo segundo,
él será inmortal a el mundo,
i vos por el aplaudido.

and give such meticulous care to everything until your book saw the light of day in this city; for in the description of Amaurot, the capital of that Island, the author seems to offer a representation of some of the outstanding features with which nature's Author endowed our city of Córdoba. May He reserve many prosperous years for you, as I desire. On 21 October 1637.

Don Andrés de Morales y Padilla.

From Don Francisco Roco Campofrío y Córdoba, Alderman of that city, to the translation of the Utopia.

Sonnet

The Utopia, which More the British man of politics – that second Numa[45] – constructed, in order that the art of government be robbed of no advantage, is today translated by your scholarly hand.

Thanks to that hand, Spaniard, the Betis,[46] its curling foam like shining glass, sees both the rod of justice wielded and the laws penned that are inspired by your venerable mind.

If pen and rod rule Córdoba, the memory of Marcellus[47] will fade; for you, Lord of Bocos, memory will be eternal.

If the Utopian story instructs it, your rod, alternating with the pen, will reconstruct it and it will live as an edifice of immortal fame.

By the same Don Francisco de Córdoba.

A poem in ten-line stanzas

In Anglia, Thomas More lies in russet ashes, and like a Phoenix is reborn from them as a living treasure for Spain. With a pen of gold, he has been faithfully translated today by you, Sir, in his Utopia; in a learned second flight he will live for ever in the world, and you will earn the world's applause.

---

45 Numa Pompilius was the legendary second king of Rome, successor to Romulus. According to tradition, as recorded by Plutarch, he received laws from the gods, established peace and justice in early Rome, organised religious institutions and promoted a free-market economy.

46 The river Betis or Guadalquivir flows through Córdoba.

47 Claudius Marcellus, according to tradition, founded Córdoba as the Roman city of Corduba, c. 152 BCE, and proved to be a humane governor.

Si bien su volumen breve,
i de Moro disciplina
grande, perfecta doctrina,
en sus preceptos se bebe.
A su novedad se deve
el deleitar enseñando,
i a vos, Córdova, que obrando
lo que erudito imprimís,
govierne lo que escrevís,
i escribáis bien governando.

[xvii r] De Don Melchor Guajardo Fajardo, Cavallero Veintiquatro de Córdova, a la *Utopía* traducida, i a su Autor.

Soneto.

La antiguedad de Apeles celebrava,
   Quando obrando su mano, conocía
   De su pincel la mucha valentía,
   Que el cuerpo, i aun el alma, retratava,
Desprecie ya lo mesmo que admirava:
   Pues a su copia no se le devía,
   Del espíritu ver la gallardía,
   Quando lo humano sólo trasladava.
En el govierno, que prudente tratas,
   I en el que docto copias, i dispones
   Del Moro Inglés, cuya opinión dilatas;
A devidos aplausos oi te expones:
   Pues con la vara el alma le retratas,
   I con la pluma el cuerpo le compones.

[xvii v] De Agustín de Galarza Contador de Resultas de su Magestad, a la tradución de la Utopía.

Soneto.

No con buril, en bronce, la memoria
De tu nombre eternize Medinilla,
La Fama, pues por rara maravilla,
Le deve a tu discurso mayor gloria.

Though it be small in size and More's teachings great, perfect doctrine may be absorbed from its precepts. That it gives delight as it teaches is due to its novelty; and to you, Córdoba is in debt for putting into practice what you have published as a scholar, for you govern as you write, and write as you so excellently govern.

From Don Melchor Guajardo Fajardo,[48] Alderman of Córdoba, to the *Utopia* in translation and to its Author.

Sonnet

Antiquity extolled the nimble exploits of Apelles' brush, which, as his hand laboured, portrayed the body and even the soul.

Now scorn the very thing they once admired, for his copy did not allow the lively grace of the spirit to be seen: he translated only the human aspect.

Both in that governance you practice with such high prudence and in your learned imitation and setting forth of the English More, whose fame you spread abroad, you present yourself today for well-earned applause: for with the regent's rod you paint his soul, and with the pen you compose his body.

From Agustín de Galarza,[49] Auditor of Internal Revenue to his Majesty, to the translation of the *Utopia*.

Sonnet

Let not Fame render the memory of your name eternal, Medinilla, with burin blade on bronze, for, by some rare marvel, greater glory is due to your words.

---

48 Melchor Guajardo Fajardo y Molina became a member of the Order of Santiago in 1671.
49 Agustín Galarza was an enthusiast for occasional poetry and had his own Academy in which authors like Gabriel Bocángel, Luis Quiñones de Benavente, Juan Vélez de Guevara and others participated.

En pedaços de cielo haga notoria
　　La dicha, que por ti gana Castilla;
　　Pues si tu pluma en paz sabe regilla,
Flecha en la guerra, ofrece la victoria.
Siempre luce la ciencia en la nobleza,
　　Como (más que en su Autor) se mira eterno
　　(Deste libro) en tu pluma esclarecida.
Débante pues los Reinos su firmeza,
　　Que traducir preceptos de govierno
　　Es descrebir exemplos de tu vida.

[xviii r] Del mismo Contador Agustín Galarza.

　　　　　Décimas.

Preceptos de governar
un Inglés al mundo dio,
(i aunque doctos) los dejó
rústicos, i por labrar.
Oi Medinilla acendrar
has querido este tessoro,
con que más que a Thomás Moro
te deve el mundo Español
pues quedó con tu crisol
puro, i acendrado el oro.

Bien claros exemplos das,
de que lo que dizes obras;
pues se adelanta en tus obras
tu crédito mucho más.
Al mundo glorias darás,
si en él con tal dicha vives,
que dize, quando recibes
aclamaciones eternas,
que escribes, como goviernas
i goviernas como escribes.

Publish to the world in celestial constellations the great fortune that Castile earns through you; for if your pen knows how to rule in times of peace, in war it becomes an arrow and offers victory.

The light of knowledge forever shines in noble men, just as it shines in your luminous pen, conferring on this book an eternal fame which surpasses that of its author. The Realms owe their constancy to the fact that to translate the precepts of government is to cite models from your life.

By the same Royal Auditor Agustín Galarza.

A poem in ten-line stanzas

An Englishman endowed the world with precepts for good government, and though they were learned, he left them rough-hewn, in need of polishing. Today you have sought to purify this treasure, Medinilla, for which the Spanish world owes more to you than to Thomas More, since, passing through your crucible, the gold is left refined of dross and pure.

You offer clear examples of the fact that what you say, you do; for in your works your good repute is greatly increased. You will bestow glory on the world if you live there with such good fortune; for they say, when you receive eternal applause, that you write as you govern and govern as you write.

[xviii v] Del Licendiado Joseph de Rivas i Tafur, Capellán maior del Cabildo de la Ciudad de Córdova, a la Utopía, i a su Tradutor.

Soneto.

De aquel Moro, de aquel Moral prudente,
    Que la Consular pú[r]pura ceñido;
    Donde la Fe, si la miró vestido;
    Aun más gloriosa, la admiró corriente.
Deste pues el espíritu excelente,
    Medinilla, Político advertido,
    El govierno del mundo has reducido,
    A preceptos, a estilo doctamente.
Legislador, moderador famoso,
    El Thámesis, ya Bético, tu gloria,
    I el Betis, ya Británico, la aclama.
Sea ya Porres a el Orbe su Coloso,
    Sea ya Bocos el templo a la memoria,
    I el mundo sea la trompa de tu fama.

[xix r] Del P. M[aestro] Fr[ay] Hierónimo de Pancorvo, Rector del Colegio de S. Roque de Córdova. A la tradución de la *Utopía*, i a su Tradutor.

Octava.

Tiene en la diestra la eloquente pluma,
I en la otra mano la temida vara,
El que Córdova admira, nuevo Numa,
El de alto ingenio, si de estirpe clara;
De Oliva coronado, i blanca espuma
Le canta el Betis, i su curso para
Al son armonioso, que retumba
De la cuna del Sol, hasta la tumba.

From the Licentiate Joseph de Rivas y Tafur, Chief Chaplain of the Municipal Council of the City of Córdoba, to the *Utopia* and its Translator.

Sonnet

That wise Moral mulberry[50] was enrobed in consular purple: thus dressed, he beheld Faith and marvelled how, unrobed, she was yet more glorious.

Then, from this superior spirit, Medinilla, as a seasoned politician, you reduced the government of nations to precepts in a learned style.

Famous legislator and judge, the Thames, now Baetican, and the Betis, now British, applaud your glory. May Porres be colossus to the world, Bocos the temple of memory, and the world the trumpet of your fame.

From Padre Maestro Friar Hierónimo de Pancorvo,[51] Rector of the College of San Roque of Córdoba, to the translation of the *Utopia* and its Translator.

Octave

He holds in his right hand the eloquent pen, and in the other the rigorous rod of government, this latter-day Numa, whom Córdoba marvels at, a man of lofty mind and illustrious stock.

Crowned with olive trees and with white foam, the Betis sings his praises and stops in its course at the harmonious sound that resounds from the cradle of the sun to its grave.

---

50 The mulberry (Sp. *moral*) is the tree that blossoms last and was characterised as 'prudent' and 'wise' by the Ancients. This was one of the many puns on More's name that were popular from Erasmus' *Encomium Moriae* onwards.
51 Pancorvo was a Carmelite friar who published a handful of religious works. The Sevillan humanist Rodrigo Caro who wrote poems in both Spanish and Latin dedicated a brief bilingual composition to Pancorvo.

[xix v] Ad D[octum] D[ominum]²⁹ Hieronymum de Medinilla et Porres Equestris Ordinis Iacobei, Dominum Oppidorum de Bocos, Rozas, et Remolino, Cordubae eiusque Provinciae Praetorem.
Consalvi Navarri Castellani I[uris] U[triusque] studiosi.

> Elegiacum Carmen:

Personet Aonio Parnassia carmina Phoebus
    Cantu, Calliope personet Aonio.
Terpsichore dulci citharam modulamine pulset,
    Euterpe calamos inflet arundineos.
Carmine gesta canens, resonet vivacia, Clio,
    Pindaricos hymnos proferat, atque Erato,
Gestibus harmonicis cantet Polymneia, plectro
    Barbita Melpomene tendat Apollineo.
Psallat lascivos numeros modulata Thalia,
    Uranieque poli pervigil astra notans.
Et tibi puniceis felicia tempora circum
[xx r]   Floribus innectant laurea serta comas.
Denique pro meritis donent tibi numina Pindi
    Sacra Medusaei flumina fontis equi.
Sed te, quae poterunt, Hieronyme digna manere
    Praemia? quae poterunt nomine dona tuo?
Non si Mnemosidum dulcissima turba sororum
    Laudibus usque tuum tollat in astra decus.
Non tibi si impediat crines Pataraea corona,
    Non tibi si viridans nectat oliva caput.
Nam tecum ingenio contendere? nobilitate
    Quis poterit? tecum nullus utroque valet.
Quid veterum memorem tantorum gesta virorum
    Famosae stirpi stemmata clara tuae?³⁰
Scilicet armipotens potis est equitare Minerva,
    Scilicet, et Mavors reddere iura potest.
O me felicem! tantas si promere laudes
    Possem, sed tantas quis celebrare queat?
Quis celebrare queat mortali corpore cretus
    Heroem tantum! quis celebrare queat?

---

29 It is possible that the initials should be expanded as 'dominum doctorem', but there is no evidence that Medinilla had a doctorate, whereas he was certainly learned.
30 1637: tuae.

To the learned Don Gerónimo de Medinilla y Porres, Knight of the Order of Santiago, Lord of the towns of Bocos, Rozas and Remolino, and Chief Magistrate of the City of Córdoba and its territory, by Gonzalo Navarro Castellanos,[52] a student of both laws,[53]

A poem in elegiac metre

Let Phoebus chant the poems of Parnassus in Aonian song, let Calliope chant in Aonian song.

Let Terpsichore strike the lyre with sweet modulation, let Euterpe blow the reed-pipes.

Let Clio sing, celebrating enduring deeds in verse, and let Erato give voice to Pindaric hymns.

Let Polyhymnia sing with harmonious gestures, let Melpomene tune the lyre with Apollo's plectrum.

Let Thalia play on the cithara the wanton verses she has set to music, while all night long she observes the stars of Urania's heaven.

And let them fasten in your hair a laurel wreath, woven with crimson flowers, encircling your happy brow.

Finally, let the divine powers of Mount Pindus give you, for your merits, the sacred rivers flowing from the fountain of the Medusa-horse.[54]

But what prizes are there that can still be worthy of you, Jerónimo? What gifts can still be worthy of your name?

Not if the sweet circle of sisters, the Muses, were to lift your honour up to the very stars in praise.

Not if Apollo's garland were to embrace your hair. Not if green olive were to be fastened about your head.

For who would be able to compete with you in talents? Who in nobility? No one is able to rival you in either.

Why should I mention the deeds of all those great men of days gone by, the glorious pedigree of your famous family?

Of course the warlike Minerva is able to ride, and of course Mars is able to establish justice.

How happy would I be if I could express such great praises! But who could celebrate such glories?

What man who inhabits a mortal body could celebrate so great a hero? Who could celebrate him?

---

52 Gonzalo Navarro Castellanos is above all known for a work attacking the modern Spanish comedy.
53 i.e. of both Roman and canon law.
54 i.e. inspiration: the fount of the Muses sprang from the earth where it was struck by the hoof of Pegasus, the winged horse who was born from the blood of Medusa.

Quem propter terras habitat, quas fugerat olim
    Astraea et cunctis, iusque suumque datur.
Quondam iura dabas patriis Infantibus, eheu
    Heu patria infelix hoc caritura patre.
O felix (nec vana fides) nunc Corduba tanto
    Digna viro, summum quem penes imperium!
Munere pro tali grates persolve Philippo,
    Misit qui mores in tua regna suos.
Ut tandem ingenio par sit tua fama superstes,
    Iam canit ingenium Morus in Orbe tuum.
[xx v] Morus ab Ausoniis nuper revocatus ad oras
    Hesperias, cives instruit arte pios.
Non te More decus patriae flevisse decebit,
    Barbarus eripuit quod tua fata ferox.
Gaude (si quicquam gaudi[31] caelestia praeter)
    Quae dederas, populis dogmata cuncta patent.
Phoebus, Calliope, Euterpe, Polymneia, Clio,
    Terpsicore, Uranie, Melpomene, atque Erato,
Culta Thalia simul reddant discrimine mille
    Vocis, ut Aonio concelebrare choro.
Baetis Cecropia crines redimitus oliva,
    Naiades inter fundito dulce melos.
Pierides tandem, iuste si munera[32] posco,
    Carmina dum famae, serta parate comis.

[xxi r] Lic[entiati] Didaci de Cea et Zayas Theologi presbyteri, in Hispanicam Utopiam[33] D. D. Hieronimi Antonii de Medinilla et Porres Equitis Iacobaei, Cordub[ae] meritiss[imi] Praetoris, Domini Oppidorum de Bocos, Roças, et Remolino, &c.

    Epigramma.

Quisquis eris, Lector, parvum ne sperne libellum,[34]
Maior nam parvis gratia inesse solet.
Anglia dat Morum latio sermone loquentem,
Morumque Hispano dat Medinilla loqui.

---

31 1637: gaudI
32 1637: mnnera
33 1637: Utopiam. [with full stop]
34 1637: parvum, ne sperne libellum

Because of him Astraea,[55] who had fled long ago, now lives on earth, and just laws and rights are given to all.

Once upon a time you bestowed justice on the children of your fatherland: alas, alas, unhappy land, that is now deprived of its father.

Oh, happy (no empty word) Córdoba now, worthy of such a great man, in whom the supreme power lies.

Show your gratitude for such a gift to Philip, who sent his good government to your territories.[56]

In order that your fame may at last be for ever equal to your talents, More now celebrates them throughout the world.

More, who was recently called back from the Ausonian coasts to the Hesperian, taught the art [of government] to pious citizens.

It does not become you, More – the glory of your country – to weep because that cruel barbarian[57] snatched away your life.

Rejoice (if there are joys elsewhere than in Heaven)! All the doctrines that you once gave are now made manifest to the peoples.

Let Phoebus, Calliope, Euterpe, Polyhymnia, Clio, Terpsichore, Urania, Melpomene and Erato,

Joining with elegant Thalia, sing out in thousandfold polyphony,[58] giving voice to your praises together in an Aonian choir.

O Baetis, crowned with Cecropian olive in your hair, pour forth a sweet song amid the Naiads.

Finally, Muses, if I may justly claim these gifts, prepare wreaths for his hair, together with the songs of fame.

By Licenciate Diego de Cea y Zayas,[59] theologian and priest, on the Spanish Utopia of the learned Don Jerónimo Antonio of Medinilla y Porres, Knight of the Order of Santiago, well-deserved Chief Magistrate of Córdoba, Lord of the towns of Bocos, Rozas and Remolino, etc.,

Epigram

Whoever you are, reader, do not despise this little book: small things are often more appealing.

England gives us More speaking in the language of Latium, and Medinilla gives him to us speaking in the Spanish tongue.

---

55 Justice.
56 i.e. Philip IV has sent his good government in the form of Medinilla himself.
57 Henry VIII.
58 Literally 'in the thousand levels of the voice'; probably a reference to the elaborate polyphonic music that was in vogue in the early seventeenth century in Spain, as for example in the works of the composer Tomás Luis de Victoria.
59 Franciscan friar who published several sermons in Seville in the first half of the seventeenth century.

Cernis inauditae gentis moderamina, mores
Otia cum studiis, cumque toga arma vides.
Certe opus excultum, sapienti, ac Pallade dignum,
Lusus, ac ingenii, quod Medinilla tui est.

[xxi v] Testimonio del M. Bartolomé Ximénez[35] Patón, Cathedrático de eloquencia de Villanueva de los Infantes, i sus partidos, i Notario del S. Oficio, por orden, i comissión del Tribunal de la Inquisición de Murcia.

El Maestro Bartolomé Ximénez Patón, Notario del Santo Oficio, i con especial comissión de los Señores Inquisidores, que residen en el Tribunal Apostólico de Murcia, para la expurgación de los libros, certifico, i hago fee, a los que el presente vieren, que el texto de la Utopía, que compuso Thomás Moro Inglés, i tradujo Don Gerónimo Antonio de Medinilla i Porres en Castellano: (Cavallero del Ábito de Santiago, Governador que fue en esta Villa, i sus partidos, Cavallerizo del Rei Señor nuestro, i su Corregidor en la Ciudad, i Provincia de Córdova, Señor de las villas de Bocos, Rozas, i Remolino) no sólo no está prohibido, pero si en algún tiempo tuvo alguna margen, que expurgar en otras impressiones, en la presente no la tiene; porque la he visto, i con[xxii r]siderado una, i muchas vezes, no sólo por la expurgación del más moderno Catálogo, i Expurgatorio, mas aun por la censura de los Antiguos. I por esto, i por las nuevas censuras, que dicha tradución tiene, puede i debe imprimirse, sin escrúpulo, ni sospecha de mala doctrina: antes su lección es de curiosidad Cristiana, i piadosa: i por ser assí en testimonio desta verdad lo firmé, i signé en Villanueva de los Infantes, en veinte i siete de Setiembre de mil i seiscientos i treinta siete años.

En testimonio [+] de verdad
vera fides
El Maestro Bartolomé Ximénez Patón.

[xxii v] Suma de la Aprobación por el Ordinario de Madrid.

Dio su Aprobación por orden del Licenciado Lorenço de Iturrizara Vicario

---

35 1637: Ximínez

You see the government and the way of life of a people that has never been heard of before; you see its recreations and its studies, its warfare and its civil pursuits.

It is certainly a refined work, worthy of a wise man and of Pallas, for it comes, Medinilla, from your poetic skills and your mental powers.

Testimony of Master Bartolomé Jiménez Patón, Professor of Eloquence of Villanueva de los Infantes and its districts, and Notary of the Holy Office, by order and commission of the Tribunal of the Inquisition in Murcia.[60]

Master Bartolomé Jiménez Patón, Notary of the Holy Office, and by special commission of the Grand Inquisitors residing in the Apostolic Tribunal of Murcia, for the expurgation of books: I certify and bear witness to anyone who sees the present work that the text of the *Utopia*, composed by the Englishman Thomas More, and translated into Castilian by Don Jerónimo Antonio de Medinilla y Porres (Knight of the Order of Santiago, former Governor of this town and its districts, Equerry of our Lord the King, and his Chief Magistrate in the City and Province of Córdoba, Lord of the Towns of Bocos, Rozas, and Remolino) not only is not prohibited, but if at some time it had some marginal need for expurgation in other printings, the present edition has none; for I have inspected and considered it over and over again, not only for the expurgation of the most recent Catalogue and Expurgatory Index,[61] but also for the censure of the Ancients. And for this reason, and because of the new expurgated passages that the said translation contains, it can and should be printed, without scruple or suspicion of false doctrine: rather, its lesson is one of pious Christian zeal, and in order thus to bear witness of this truth, I signed and endorsed it in Villanueva de los Infantes, on 27 September 1637.

In testimony [+] to the truth.
vera fides. [the true faith]
Master Bartolomé Jiménez Patón

Summary of the Approbation given by the Vicar-General of Madrid.

Father Agustín de Castro[62] of the Company of Jesus gave his Approbation

---

60 The Inquisition in Murcia was established in 1488, during the visit of Queen Isabel and King Ferdinand, and was one of twelve peninsular Tribunals of the Spanish Inquisition, the most prestigious being those of Toledo and Seville.
61 The most recent index would have been the *Novus Index librorum prohibitorum et expurgatorum* (Madrid, 1632) of Antonio de Zapata, Cardinal and Archbishop of Burgos and General Inquisitor 1627-35, where *Utopia* was not included.
62 Agustín de Castro (1589-1671) was preacher to the King and censor of the Holy Office before becoming Vicar-General. He was censor of the Expurgatory Index of 1632. Gracián quotes

general de la Villa de Madrid el Padre Agustín de Castro de la Compañía de Jesús. Dada en su Collegio Imperial de Madrid en veinte i nueve de Otubre de 1635.

[xxiii r] Suma de la Licencia del Ordinario de Madrid

Tiene licencia su Autor del Licenc[iado] Lorenço de Iturrizara Vicario general de la Villa de Madrid, por lo que a él toca, como consta de la licencia firmada de su nombre, i refrendada de Gabriel de Rojas Notario. Dada en Madrid a veinte i nueve de Otubre de mil i seiscientos i treinta i cinco años.

[xxiii v] Suma de la Aprobación por mandado de los Señores del Consejo Real.

Aprobó este libro, por mandado de los Señores del Consejo Real Don Jusepe Antonio González de Salas. Su fecha en Madrid, a veinte i uno de Noviembre de mil i seiscientos i treinta i cinco años.

[xxiiii r] Suma del privilegio.

Tiene Privilegio de su Magestad Don Gerónimo Antonio de Medinilla i Porres Cavallero del Ábito de Santiago, Cavallerizo de su Magestad, Señor de las Villas de Bocos, Roças, i Remolino, Corregidor de la Ciudad de Córdova, por diez años para imprimir este Libro. Su fecha en Madrid, a tres de Diziembre de mil i seiscientos i treinta i cinco años. Firmado del Rei N[uestro] Señor, i refrendado de Francisco Gómez de Lasprilla su Secretario.

[index of chapters]
[Book II]

[51 v] *Carpere vel noli nostra, vel ede tua.*
Marcial. lib. I. Epig. 93.
FIN. [typographical ornament]

Spanish texts edited by Carlos F. Cabanillas Cárdenas;
Latin and Greek texts edited by Vibeke Roggen.

by order of the Licenciate Lorenzo de Iturrizara, Vicar-general of the City of Madrid. Granted in the Imperial College of the Company of Jesus in Madrid on 29 October 1635.

Summary of the Licence from the Vicar-General of Madrid.

The author is given licence by the Licenciate Lorenzo de Iturrizara, Vicar-general of the City of Madrid, for that which appertains to him, as is stated by the licence signed in his name, and countersigned by Gabriel de Rojas, Notary. Granted in Madrid on 29 October 1635.

Summary of the Approbation given by order of the Lords of the Royal Council.

Don Jusepe Antonio González de Salas[63] approved this book by command of the Lords of the Royal Council. Dated in Madrid on 21 November 1635.

Summary of the Privilege.

Don Jerónimo Antonio de Medinilla y Porres, Knight of the Order of Santiago, Equerry of his Majesty, Lord of the Towns of Bocos, Rozas, and Remolino, Chief Magistrate of the City of Córdoba, has his Majesty's Privilege to print this Book for the space of ten years. Dated in Madrid, 3 December 1635. Signed by the King Our Lord, and countersigned by Francisco Gómez de Lasprilla, his Secretary.

[index of chapters]
[Book II]

Either don't carp at ours, or publish your own.
Martial Book 1, Epigram 93.[64]
END. [typographical ornament]

Spanish texts translated by Tyler Fisher and Kathleen Mountjoy in collaboration with Randi L. Davenport and Carlos F. Cabanillas Cárdenas; Latin and Greek texts translated by Vibeke Roggen.

Castro for an example of a conceit of 'enigmatic deliberation' ('agudeza de ponderación misteriosa') in his *Agudeza y arte de ingenio* (1648).
63 Jusepe Antonio González de Salas (1588-1651), classical philologist, friend of Quevedo and editor of his poetry.
64 Martial, *Epigrams* I.xci.2 (modern editions are numbered differently from their early modern predecessors).

A LATIN PARATEXT: MILAN 1620

ILLVSTRIS VIRI THOMAE
Mori, Regni Britaniarum
Cancellarij.

DE OPTIMO
REIPVBLICÆ STA-
TV, DE QVE NOVA IN-
sula Vtopia,

LIBRI DVO:
HAC POSTREMA EDITIO-
ne Superiorum iussu emendati.

AD ILLVSTRISSIMVM
Senatus Mediol. Præsidem
D.D. Iulium Aresium.

Mediolani, Apud Io. Bapt. Bidellium 1620.

Milan 1620: Title-page. By permission of the Folger Shakespeare Library

Milan 1620

[Dedicatory epistle]

Illustrissimo D. Iulio Aresio Senatus Mediol[anensis] Praesidi ampliss[imo] Io[annes] Baptista Bidellius F[ecit].

[A2 r] Magno meo bono mihi venit in manus, Illustriss[ime] Praeses, libellus hic, parvus quidem corpore, sed sapientia grandis, a Thoma Moro ingenii amoenissimi viro, eleganti stylo ac leporis pleno conscriptus, qui Reip[ublicae] [A2 v] bene temperatae formam, ad Platonis imitationem, sub nomine Insulae Utopiae, politiae studiosis exhibuit[1]. Simul ut vidi, cogitatio subiit animum, tibi a me opus excusum, mihi a te patrocinium operis deberi. Quam similis tu Moro, tui Morus? Doctrinis eloquentia conditis ille floruit: Tu scientia iuris cum vi persuadendi splendescis. Ille probitate praestitit aequalibus suis: tu virtutibus illuminas aequales tuos. Thomas rerum gerendarum peritus: Iulius rebus praeclare gestis exercitatus. Morus denique supremi Cancellarii munus in Angliae regno cum laude sustinuit: Aresius Senatui Insubriae, quae regno propemodum aequatur, cum omnium commendatione praesidet. Quid quod in regio consilio arcanorum, quae ad rem publicam sive [A3 r] in pace, sive in bello pertinent, locum habes honestissimum? Tua plurimum intererit in consilio dando nosse, quae ludendo vera dixit; observasseque monita et praecepta, quae per iocum serio dedit rectoribus provinciarum, vir ille perinsignis in utraque fortuna, qui tandem pro tuenda Catholica Religione, fortiter occubuit. Tua vero tutela mihi, tantum thesaurum publica restituenti debetur; quod nemo sit in hoc Mediolanensi typographorum collegio, qui plus, aut tuam benevolentiam affectet, aut dignitatem revereatur, aut virtutes suspiciat ac praedicet. Vale diu Regi, Senatui, clientibus. E typographaeo kal. Juliis MDCXX.

1 1620: hxhibuit

Milan 1620

[Dedicatory epistle]

Giovan Battista Bidelli made [this edition] for the noble lord Giulio Arese, the highly esteemed President of the Senate of Milan.

This little book, truly small in size but great in wisdom, came into my hands, noble President, to my great advantage. It was written by Thomas More, a man of the most delightful mental powers, in an elegant style, full of wit, and it has demonstrated to those who are occupied with state administration the outline of a Republic that is well governed, in imitation of Plato, under the name of the island Utopia. The moment I saw it, the thought occurred to me that I owed you a book printed by me, whereas you owed me protection for the book. How similar you are to More, and More to you! He flourished in learning, founded on eloquence; you derive lustre from the science of law, coupled with the power of persuasion. He surpassed his contemporaries in probity; your virtues shine like a beacon for your peers. Thomas was expert in practical affairs; Giulio is past master in affairs excellently conducted. Finally, More held with renown the office of Chancellor in the Kingdom of England; Arese presides, with the praise of all, over the Senate of Insubria,[1] which is almost equal to a kingdom. And what about the fact that you hold the most distinguished position in the royal Privy Council,[2] which deals with secret matters of state in both peace and war? It will be of great advantage to you when you come to give advice to know the truths he expressed in a playful spirit, to observe the advice and precepts that he – seriously, through humour – gave to those who ruled provinces. He was a man who famously endured both kinds of fate[3] and who finally died bravely defending the Catholic religion. But you owe me your protection, such a great treasure for one who is restoring state affairs; for there is no one in this corporation of Milan printers who to a higher degree strives after your benevolence, respects your dignity, or admires and commends your virtues. Live well and long for the sake of the King,[4] the Senate, and those you serve. The printing house, 1 July 1620.

---

1 Insubria is the region that surrounds Milan, the duchy of Milan.
2 The *consiglio segreto*.
3 That is, good luck as well as bad.
4 During this period, Milan was under Spanish rule. The king in question was Philip III (1598-1621).

TABLES OF PREFATORY MATERIAL
IN LATIN EDITIONS

Table 1 Editions in More's lifetime

Prefatory material ↓	Editions →	Louvain: Martens, 1516	Paris: Gourmont, 1517	Basel: Froben, 1518 March	Basel: Froben, 1518 November	Florence: Giunta, 1519
I	Map	1 (1516 map)		4 (1518 map)	4 (1518 map)	
II	Utopian Alphabet	2		5	5	
III	Utopian poem	3		6	6	
	a) In Utopian b) In transcription					
	c) In Latin translation					
IV	Anemolius' hexastichon	4	1	3	3	
V	Giles to Busleyden	5	3	7	7	
VI	Paludanus to Giles	6	4			2
VII	Paludanus' poem	7	5			
VIII	Noviomagus' poem	8	10	11	11	5
IX	Grapheus' poem	9	11	12	12	6
X	Busleyden to More	10	9	10	10	4
XI	More to Giles I	11	6	8	8	3
	Book I	After 11	After 6	After 8	After 8	After 3
	Book II					
XII	Marginal notes	12	7	9 *Helvetii* note omitted	9 *Helvetii* note omitted. Three notes added.	
XIII	Colophon	13	13	13		7
XIV	Printer's device			14	13	8
XV	Budé to Lupset		2	2	13	
XVI	More to Giles II		8		2	
XVII	Errata		12	1	1	
XVIII	Erasmus to Froben			(After 2nd title page): 15 Rhenanus to Pirckheimer, introducing the epigrams	(After 2nd title page): 14 Rhenanus to Pirckheimer, introducing the epigrams	1 Erasmus to Foxe
XIX	Other material					After 2: trans. from Lucian by More and Erasmus

Table 2 Sixteenth-century editions published after More's death

Editions → Prefatory material ↓	Louvain: Sassen, 1548	Cologne: Birckmann, 1555	Basel: Episcopius, 1563	Louvain: Zangre, 1565 and 1566; Louvain: Bogard. 1565 and 1566	Wittenberg: Krafft, 1591
I Map			10 (1563 map)		
II Utopian Alphabet					
III Utopian poem a) In Utopian b) In transcription c) In Latin translation	5 (only c.)	2 (only c.)	6 (only c.)		
IV Anemolius' hexastichon	4	1	5	12	1
V Giles to Busleyden	6	7	3	8	2
VI Paludanus to Giles				4	3
VII Paludanus' poem				5	4
VIII Noviomagus' poem	10	3	7	6	5
IX Grapheus' poem	11	4	8	7	6
X Busleyden to More	9	10	11	9	7
XI More to Giles I	7	8	4	10	8
Book I	After 7	After 8	I: After 8	After 15	After 8
Book II			II: After 10		
XII Marginal notes	8	9 1518 N included	9 1518 N incl.	15 1518 N incl.	9
XV Budé to Lupset	3	6	2	3	10
XVI More to Giles II	2	5	1		
XVII Erasmus to Froben					
XVIII Other material	1 Privilege		12 Rhenanus to Pirckheimer X Errata (at the end of the volume)	1 Privilege 2 More's epitaphs 11 More's prison letter 13 Table of contents 14 Censorship attestation 16 Rhenanus to Pirckheimer	

Table 3 Editions from the early seventeenth century

	Editions → Prefatory material ↓	Frankfurt: Saur, 1601 and Hanau: Henne, 1613	Hanau: Wechel's heirs,[1] 1619	Milan: Bidelli, 1620	Amsterdam: Blaeuw, 1629; 'Cologne: Cornelius ab Egmond' 1629;[2] Amsterdam: Jansson 1631
III	Utopian poem a) In Utopian b) In transcription c) In Latin translation				
IV	Anemolius' hexastichon		1	1	10
V	Giles to Busleyden	6	6	7	5
VI	Paludanus to Giles				6
VII	Paludanus' poem				7
VIII	Noviomagus' poem	7	7	8	8
IX	Grapheus' poem	8	8	9	9
X	Busleyden to More	5	5	6	4
XI	More to Giles I	2	2	4	1
	Book I	After 8	After 8	After 9	After 10
	Book II				
XII	Marginal notes	9 1518 N incl.	9 In the latter part of Book II only.[3]	10 1518 N incl.	
XV	Budé to Lupset	4	4	5	3
XVI	More to Giles II				
XVII	Erasmus to Froben	3	3		2
XVIII	Other material		The edition is part of a compilation, the *Amphitheatrum* of Dornavius	2 Imprimatur 3 Bidelli to Arese[4]	

1 See above, pp. 18–9.   2 See above, p. 19.   3 It seems as if the notes have been forgotten until the chapter 'De servis' in Book 2.   4 Reproduced above, Part II, pp. 274–5.

BIBLIOGRAPHY

Early modern Latin editions of *Utopia*

Louvain 1516: *Libellus vere aureus nec minus salutaris quam festivus de optimo reip. statu, deque nova insula Utopia authore clarissimo viro Thoma Moro inclytae civitatis Londinensis cive et vicecomite cura M. Petri Aegidii Antverpiensis, et arte Theodorici Martini Alustensis, Typographi almae Lovaniensium Academiae nunc primum accuratissime editus. Cum gratia et privilegio.*

Paris 1517: *Ad lectorem. Habes candide lector opusculum vere aureum Thomae Mori non minus utile quam elegans de optimo reipublicae statu, deque nova Insula Utopia, iam iterum, sed multo correctius quam prius, hac Enchiridii forma ut vides multorum tum senatorum tum aliorum gravissimorum virorum suasu aeditum. Quod sane tibi aediscendum non modo in manibus quotidie habendum censeo. Cui quidem ab innumeris mendis undequaque purgatio praeter Erasmi annotationes ac Budaei epistulam:*[1] *virorum sane qui hoc saeculo nostro extra omnem ingenii aleam positi sunt: Addita est etiam ipsius Mori epistula eruditissima. Vale. Cum gratia et privilegio.*

Basel 1518 March: *De optimo reip. statu, deque nova insula Utopia libellus vere aureus, nec minus salutaris quam festivus, clarissimi dissertissimique viri Thomae Mori inclytae civitatis Londinensis civis et Vicecomititis. Epigrammata clarissimi disertissimique viri Thomae Mori, pleraque e Graecis versa. Epigrammata Des. Erasmi Roterodami. Apud inclytam Basileam.*

Basel 1518 November: *De optimo reip. statu, deque nova insula Utopia, libellus vere aureus, nec minus salutaris quam festivus, clarissimi dissertissimique viri Thomae Mori inclytae civitatis Londinensis civis et Vicecomititis. Epigrammata clarissimi disertissimique viri Thomae Mori, pleraque e Graecis versa. Epigrammata Des. Erasmi Roterodami. Apud inclytam Basileam.*

Florence 1519: *Luciani opuscula Erasmo Roterodamo interprete: Toxaris, sive de Amicitia. Alexander, qui et Pseudomantis. Gallus, sive somnium. Timon, seu Misanthropus. Tyrannicida, seu pro tyrranicida. Declamatio Erasmi contra tyrannicidam. De iis, qui mercede conducti degunt. Et quaedam eiusdem alia. Eiusdem Luciani Thoma Moro interprete. Cynicus. Menippus, seu Necromantia. Philopseudes, seu incredulus. Tyrannicida. Declamatio Mori de eodem. Eiusdem Thomae Mori De optimo Reip. statu deque nova insula Utopia libellus vere aureus.*

Louvain 1548: *De optimo reipu. statu, deque nova insula Utopia, libellus vere aureus, nec minus salutaris quam festivus, clarissimi disertissimi viri Thomae Mori, inclytae civitatis Londinensis civis et Vicecomitis. Lovanii, Excudebat Servatius Sassenus impensis viduae Arnoldi Birkmanni.*

Cologne 1555: *De optimo reipub. statu deque nova insula Utopia, libellus vere aureus,*

---

[1] For the proposed emendation of this last phrase to 'propter Erasmi annotationes ac Budaei epistula', see above, pp. 22–3.

nec minus salutaris quam festivus clarissimi disertissimique viri Thomae Mori, inclytae civitatis Londiniensis civis et Vicecomitis. Coloniae, Apud heredes Arnoldi Birckmanni.

Basel 1563: *Thomae Mori, Angliae ornamenti eximii, lucubrationes, ab innumeris mendis repurgatae. Utopiae Libri II. Progymnasmata. Epigrammata. Ex Luciano conversa quaedam. Declamatio Lucianicae respondens. Quibus additae sunt duae aliorum Epistolae, de vita, moribus et morte Mori, adiuncto rerum notabilium Indice. Basil. apud Episcopium F[ilium].*

Louvain (Zangre) 1565: *Thomae Mori Angli, viri eruditionis pariter ac virtutis nomine clarissimi, Angliaeque olim cancellarii, Omnia, quae hucusque ad manus nostras pervenerunt, Latina Opera: quorum aliqua nunc primum in lucem prodeunt, reliqua vero multo quam antea castigatiora. Horum omnium elenchum Pagina duodecima commonstrabit. Lovanii, Apud Petrum Zangrium Tiletanum, sub Fonte.*

Louvain (Bogard) 1565: *Thomae Mori Angli, viri eruditionis pariter ac virtutis nomine clarissimi, Angliaeque olim cancellarii, Omnia, quae hucusque ad manus nostras pervenerunt, Latina Opera: Quorum aliqua nunc primum in lucem prodeunt, reliqua vero multo quam antea castigatiora. Horum omnium elenchum Pagina duodecima commonstrabit. Lovanii, Apud Ioannem Bogardum, sub Bibliis Aureis.*

Louvain (Zangre) 1566: *Thomae Mori Angli, viri eruditionis pariter ac virtutis nomine clarissimi, Angliaeque olim cancellarii, Omnia, quae hucusque ad manus nostras pervenerunt, Latina Opera: Quorum aliqua nunc primum in lucem prodeunt, reliqua vero multo quam antea castigatiora. horum omnium elenchum Pagina duodecima commonstrabit. Lovanii, Apud Petrum Zangrium Tiletanum, sub Fonte.*

Louvain (Bogard) 1566: *Thomae Mori Angli, viri eruditionis pariter ac virtutis nomine clarissimi, Angliaeque olim cancellarii, Omnia, quae hucusque ad manus nostras pervenerunt, Latina Opera: Quorum aliqua nunc primum in lucem prodeunt, reliqua vero multo quam antea castigatiora. Horum omnium elenchum Pagina duodecima commonstrabit. Lovanii, Apud Ioannem Bogardum, sub Bibliis Aureis.*

Wittenberg 1591: *Libellus vere aureus nec minus salutaris quam festivus de optimo reip. statu, deque nova insula Utopia authore clarissimo viro Thoma Moro inclytae civitatis Londiniensis, cive et vicecomite cure M. Petri Aegidii Antverpiensis, et arte Theodorici Martini Alustensis, Typographi almae Lovaniensium Academiae nunc primum accuratissime editus: Witebergae, Ex officina Cratoniana.*

Frankfurt 1601: *Illustris viri Thomae Mori Regni Britanniarum Cancellarii, De optimo reipublicae statu, deque nova insula Utopia, libri duo: Scriptum vere aureum, nec minus salutare, quam festivum, quod ex Erasmi Roterodami, Guilielmi Budaei, aliorumque magnorum virorum commendationibus, quae Epistolis praefixis continentur, liquidum dubitantibus evadet. Nunc tandem bibliotaphis subreptum, et in gratiam Politicorum, consilio et cura Magnifici Domini Eberarti von Weihe illustriss. ac potentiss. Principi ac Domino, Dn. Mauritio, Hessiae Landgravio, etc. a consiliis, editum. Francofurti Ex Officina Chalcographica Ioannis Saurii, sumptibus Petri Kopffii.*

Hanau 1613: *Illustris viri Thomae Mori Regni Britanniarum Cancellarii, De optimo reipublicae statu, deque nova Insula Utopia, libri Duo: scriptum vere aureum, nec minus salutare, quam festivum, quod ex Erasmi Roterodami, Guilielmi Budaei, aliorumque magnorum virorum commendationibus, quae Epistolis praefixis continentur, liquidum dubitantibus evadet. Hanoviae Typis Joannis Jacobi Hennëi, sumptibus Petri Kopffii.*

Hanau 1619: *'Illustris viri Thomae Mori regni Britanniarum cancellarii, de optimo reipublicae statu, deque nova insula Utopia, libri duo: scriptum vere aureum, nec minus salutare, quam festivum, quod ex Erasmi Roterodami, Guilielmi Budaei, aliorumque magnorum virorum commendationibus, quae Epistolis praefixis continentur, liquidum dubitantibus evadet',* in *Amphitheatrum sapientiae Socraticae joco-seriae, hoc est, encomia et commentaria autorum, qua veterum, qua recentiorum prope omnium: quibus res, aut pro vilibus vulgo aut damnosis habitae, styli patrocinio vindicantur, exornantur: Opus ad mysteria naturae discenda, ad omnem amoenitatem, sapientiam, virtutem, publice privatimque utilissimum: in duos tomos, partim ex libris editis, partim manuscriptis congestum tributumque, a Caspare Dornavio philos. et medico. Cum gratia & privilegio S. Caesareae Maiestatis. Hanoviae, Typis Wechelianis, Impensis Danielis ac Davidis Aubriorum, & Clementis Schleichii.*

Milan 1620: *Illustris viri Thomae Mori Regni Britanniarum Cancellarii, De optimo reipublicae statu, deque* NOVA INSULA UTOPIA, *libri duo: hac postrema editione Superiorum iussu emendati. Ad illustrissimum Senatus Mediol[anensis] Praesidem D. D. Iulium Aresium. Mediolani, Apud Io[annem] Bapt[istam] Bidellium.*

Amsterdam 1629: *Thomae Mori Utopia, a mendis vindicata. Amsterodami, Apud Guili. Iansonium Blaeuw.*

Cologne 1629: *Thomae Mori Utopia, a mendis vindicata, et iuxta Indicem libror[um] Expurgat[orum] Card[inalis] et Archiep[iscopi] Toletani correcta. Coloniae, Apud Corn[elium] ab Egmond.*

Amsterdam 1631: *Thomae Mori Utopia, a mendis vindicata. Amsterodami, Apud Ioannem Ianssonium.*

Early modern vernacular editions of *Utopia*

Manuscript

'La Uto[p]ia de Tomas Moro en castellano', MS II/1087, Biblioteca Real de Palacio (Count of Gondomar Collection), Madrid.

Printed editions

The full titles of all these editions except the second and later editions of the Italian 'Sansovino' series (Venice 1561, 1566, 1567, 1578, 1583, 1607), and Paris 1611, are provided above in Part II; full titles are therefore provided here only for these exceptional cases.

Basel 1524: *Von der wunderbarlichen Innsel Utopia genant / das ander Bůch*, trans. Claudius Cantiuncula (Claude Chansonnette), Basel: Johann Bebel, 1524

Venice 1548: *La republica nuovamente ritrovata, del governo dell'Isola Eutopia*, trans. Ortensio Lando, Venice: Aurelio Pincio, 1548

Paris 1550: *La description de l'isle d'Utopie ou est comprins le miroer des republicques du monde, et l'exemplaire de vie heureuse*, trans. Jean Le Blond, Paris: Charles L'Angelier, 1550

London 1551: *A fruteful / and pleasaunt worke of the beste state of a publyque weale, and of the newe yle called Utopia*, trans. Ralph Robinson, London: Abraham Vele, 1551

Antwerp 1553: *De Utopie van Thomas Morus / in zijnen tijden Cancellier van Enghelant*, Antwerp: Hans de Laet, 1553

London 1556: *A frutefull pleasaunt, and wittie worke, of the beste state of a publique weale, and of the new yle, called Utopia*, trans. Ralph Robinson, London: Abraham Vele, 1556

Lyon 1559: *La Republique d'Utopie, par Thomas Maure, Chancelier d'Angleterre*, trans. [Jean Le Blond], ed. Barthélemy Aneau, Lyon: Jean Saugrain, 1559

Venice 1561:[2] *Del governo de i regni et delle republiche cosi antiche come moderne libri XVIII*, Venice: Francesco Sansovino, [1561]

Antwerp 1562: *De Utopie van Thomas Morus*, Antwerp: Hans de Laet, 1562 (reprint of Antwerp 1553)

Venice 1566: *Del governo de regni et delle repubbliche antiche et moderne di M. Francesco Sansovino libri XXI. Ne quali si contengono, i magistrati, gli offici, e gli ordini proprii che s'osseruano ne predetti principati. Dove si ha cognitione di molte historie particolari, utili e necessarie al viver civile. Con nuova aggiunta di piu Repubbliche e regni in diverse parti del mondo*, Venice: Giovan Battista & Marchiò Sessa and brothers, 1566

Venice 1567: *Del governo de regni et delle republiche antiche et moderne di m. Francesco Sansovino libri XXI, ne quali si contengono diversi ordini, magistrati, leggi, costumi, historie, e cose notabili, che sono utili e necessarie ad ogni huomo civile e di stato. Con nuova aggiunta di piu repubbliche e regni in diverse parti del mondo*, Venice: Giovan Battista & Marchiò Sessa and brothers, 1567

Venice 1578: *Del governo et amministratione di diversi regni et republiche, cosi antiche come moderne di m. Francesco Sansovino, libri XXI. Ne' quali si contengono diversi ordini magistrati, leggi, costumi, historie, et altre cose notabili, che sono utili et necessarie ad ogni huomo civile et di stato. Con nuova aggiunta di piu republiche e regni in diverse parti del mondo*, Venice: Giovanni Antonio Bertano 1578

Venice 1583: *Del governo et amministratione di diversi regni, et republiche, cosi antiche, come moderne, di M. Francesco Sansovino libri XXII. Cioè di Germania. Francia. Spagna. Inghilterra. Polonia. Portogallo. Napoli. Turco. Persia. Tunisi. Fessa. Roma antica. Roma moderna. Athene. Sparta. Venetia. Genova. Lucca. Svizzeri. Norimberga. Ragugi. Utopia. Ne' quali si contengono diversi ordini, leggi, magistrati, usanze, costumi, ed altre cose notabili, appartenenti alla historia, utili ad ogni huomo di stato e civile, e buone cosi à tempi di pace, come di guerra*, Venice: Altobello Salicato, 1583

Paris 1585: *L'Estat, description et gouvernement des royaumes et republiques du monde, tant anciennes que modernes*, trans. Gabriel Chappuys, Paris: Pierre Cavellat, 1585

London 1597: *A most pleasant, fruitfull, and wittie worke, of the best state of a publique weale, and of the new Yle called Utopia*, trans. Ralph Robinson, London: Thomas Creede, 1597

Paris 1598: *L'Estat, Description et gouvernement des royaumes et republiques du monde, tant anciennes que modernes*, trans. Gabriel Chappuys, Paris: Regnault Chaudière, 1598 (reprint of Paris 1585)

---

2 In all of the Italian 'Sansovino' editions, together with Paris 1585 and 1598, *Utopia* forms the last book of the volume, regardless of the number of books in a particular edition; the only exception is Paris 1611, where *Utopia* is the twenty-second of twenty-four books.

Venice 1607: *Del governo et amministratione di diversi regni, et repubbliche cosi antiche, come moderne ... libri XXII*, Venice: Altobello Salicato, 1607 (reprint of Venice 1583)

Paris 1611: *Du Gouvernement et Administration de divers estats, Royaumes et Republiques, tant anciennes que modernes. Contenant diverses ordonnances, loix, statuts, Magistrats, institutions, coustumes, usances, descriptions de païs. Avec plusieurs autres choses notables appartenantes à l'histoire, utile à tout homme d'Estat et Civil, tant en paix, qu'en guerre. Par François Sanssovin Jurisconsulte*, Paris: François Huby, 1611[3]

Leipzig 1612: *De optimo Reipublicae Statu, Libellus vere aureus. Ordentliche und Auβführliche Beschreibung Der uberaus herrlichen und gantz wunderbarlichen / doch wenigen biβhero bekandten Insul* Utopia, trans. Smdygmxirnhdrh Mxisofm[4] (Gregor[ius] Wintermonat), Leipzig: Henning Grosse, 1612

London 1624: *Sir Thomas Moore's Utopia: containing, an excellent, learned, witties, and pleasant Discourse of the best state of a Publike Weale, as it is found in the Government of the new Ile called* Utopia, London: Bernard Alsop, 1624

Hoorn 1629: *De Utopia van Thomas Morus / in sijn leven Cancellier van Enghelandt*, Hoorn: Marten Gerbrandtsz, 1629 [colophon: Isaäc Willemsz, 1630]

Hoorn 1634: *De Utopia van Thomas Morus, in sijn leven Cancellier van Enghelandt*, Hoorn: Marten Gerbrandtsz, 1634

Córdoba 1637: *Utopía de Thomas Moro, traducida de Latin en Castellano por Don Gerónimo Antonio de Medinilla i Porres*, Córdoba: Salvador de Cea, 1637

London 1639: *The Commonwealth of* Utopia: *Containing a Learned and pleasant Discourse of the best state of a Publike Weale, as it is found in the Government of the new Ile called* Utopia, London: Bernard Alsop, 1639

Amsterdam 1643: *L'Utopie de Thomas Morus Chancelier d'Angleterre*, trans. Samuel Sorbière, Amsterdam: Jean Blaeu, 1643

Modern editions of *Utopia*

Oxford 1895: J. H. Lupton, *The Utopia of Sir Thomas More in Latin from the Edition of March 1518, and in English from the First Edition of Ralph Robynson's translation in 1551 with Additional Translations, Introduction and Notes*, Oxford: Clarendon Press, 1895

Yale 1965: *The Complete Works of Thomas More*, vol. 4, ed. J. H. Hexter and Edward J. Surtz, New Haven and London: Yale University Press, 1965

Leeds 1966: *Libellus vere aureus nec minus salutaris quam festivus de optimo reip. statu*, Leeds: Scolar Press, 1966 (facsimile reprint of Louvain 1516)

Paris 1970: Thomas More, *La description de l'Isle d'Utopie, traduction française de 1550*, intro. Michel Jeanneret, Wakefield: S. R. Publishers Ltd; New York, Johnson Reprint Corporation; Paris, Mouton, 1970

Turin 1971: Thomas More, *Utopia*, ed. Luigi Firpo, Turin: Unione Tipografico-

---

3 The privilege of this edition states that the printer Jean Milot had legally transferred the privilege to François Huby so that both could enjoy it jointly.
4 This is a transcription of the Utopian letters in which the name is printed in the original; see above, p. 40.

Editrice Torinese, 1971 (Book I transl. Firpo, Book II transl. Lando)
Paris 1978: *L'Utopie de Thomas More: Présentation, texte original, apparat critique, exégèse, traduction et notes*, ed. André Prevost, Paris: Mame, 1978
Hildesheim 1980: Morus, Thomas, *Von der wunderbaren Insel Utopia*, Klassiker der utopischen Literatur, 1, Hildesheim: Gerstenberg Verlag, 1980 (facsimile reprint of Basel 1524)
London 1992: Thomas More, *Utopia*, ed. Jenny Mezciems, London: Everyman's Library, 1992 (based on London 1551, with modern orthography)
Cambridge 1995: Thomas More, *Utopia*, ed. George M. Logan, Robert M. Adams and Clarence H. Miller, Cambridge: Cambridge University Press, 1995 (paperback reprint 2006)
Goldbach 1995: Caspar Dornau (Dornavius), *Amphitheatrum Sapientiae Socraticae Joco-Seriae. Schauplatz scherz- und ernsthafter Weisheiten. Neudruck der Ausgabe Hanau 1619*, ed. Robert Seidel, Goldbach: Keip Verlag, 1995 (includes *Utopia*: see above, Hanau 1619)
Oxford 1999: Thomas More, *Utopia*, in *Three Early Modern Utopias*, ed. Susan Bruce, Oxford: Oxford University Press, 1999 (based on London 1556, with modern orthography)

Other primary sources

Alamos de Barrientos, Baltasar, *Tacito español ilustrado con Aforismos por don Baltasar Álamos de Barrientos: Dirigido a don Francisco Gómez de Sandoval y Rojas, Duque de Lerma*, Madrid: Luis Sanchez, 1614
Aneau, Barthélemy, *Alector ou le coq. Histoire fabuleuse*, ed. Marie Madeleine Fontaine, 2 vols, Geneva: Droz, 1996
—— *Trois premiers livres de la Metamorphose d'Ovide, Traduictz en vers François. Le premier et second, par Cl. Marot. Le tiers par B. Aneau ... Avec une preparation de voie à la lecture et intelligence des Poëtes fabuleux*, Lyon: Guillaume Rouille, 1556
Antonio, Nicolás, *Bibliotheca Hispana Nova*, ed. Mario Ruffini, Turin: Bottega d'Erasmo, 1963
Aristotle, *The Politics*, trans. Ernest Barker, Oxford: Clarendon Press, 1968 (1946)
Bacon, Francis, *The Advancement of Learning: The Oxford Francis Bacon*, vol. 4, ed. Michael Kiernan, Oxford: Clarendon Press, 2000
Baldwin, William, *Beware the Cat: The First English Novel*, ed. William A. Ringler, Jr. and Michael Flachmann, San Marino, CA: Huntingdon Library, 1988
Boccalini, Traiano, *Discursos politicos, y avisos del Parnasso / de Trajano Bocalini ... tradujolos de la lengua toscana en la española, Fernando Peres de Sousa*, Madrid: María de Quiñones, 1634
Bodin, Jean, *Methodus ad facilem historiarum cognitionem*, Paris: Martin Le Jeune, 1566
—— *Les Six Livres de la république*, ed. Christiane Frémont, Marie-Dominique Couzinet and Henri Rochais, Paris: Fayard, 1986
—— *Los seis libros de la Republica de Juan Bodino*, trans. Gaspar de Añastro, Turin: for the heirs of Bevilaqua, 1590
Campanella, Tommaso, *La Città del Sole*; Francesco Patrizi (of Cherso), *La Città felice*, Genoa: Marieti, 1996

BIBLIOGRAPHY

'Censura sobre los Annales e Historias de Caio Cornelio Tácito, para consultar si será bien imprimir su traducción en español', MS 13086, Biblioteca Nacional, Madrid

Cicero, *Paradoxa Stoicorum*, trans. H. Rackham, in *Cicero*, vol. 4, London: William Heinemann and Cambridge, MA: Harvard University Press (The Loeb Classical Library), 1942

Covarrubias Orozco, Sebastián de, *Tesoro de la lengua castellana o española*, ed. Martín de Riquer, Barcelona: Alta Fulla, 1993

De Brune, Johan (the Elder), *De Grondsteenen van een vaste Regieringe gheleyt end wthestelt tot bericht end nuttigheyt van elle goede Vader-landers*, Middelburgh: Hans vander Hellen for Ian Pietersen vande Venne, 1621

Doni, Anton Francesco, *I Mondi e gli Inferni*, ed. P. Pellizzari, intro. Marziano Guglielminetti, Turin: Einaudi, 1994

—— *Les Mondes, celestes, terrestres et infernaux. Le Monde petit, Grand, Imaginé, Meslé, Risible, des Sages et Fols, et le Tresgrand ... Tirez des œuvres de Doni Florentin*, trans. Gabriel Chappuys, Lyon: Barthelemy Honorati, 1578

Dürr, Emil and Paul Roth (eds), *Aktensammlung zur Geschichte der Baselr Reformation in den Jahren 1519 bis Anfang 1534*, Basel: Verlag der Historischen und antiquarischen Gesellschaft, Staatsarchiv, 1921–1950

Erasmus, Desiderius, *Dialogus Ciceronianus*, ed. Pierre Mesnard, *Opera omnia*, Amsterdam: North-Holland Publishing Company, 1969–, Part I, vol. 2; trans. Betty I. Knott, *Collected Works of Erasmus*, Toronto, Buffalo and London: University of Toronto Press, 1974–, vol. 28

—— *Opus epistolarum Des. Erasmi Roterodami, denuo recognitum et auctum*, 12 vols, ed. P. S. Allen, Oxford: Clarendon Press, 1906–58

—— *The Correspondence of Erasmus* (*Collected Works of Erasmus*, vol. 1), 5 vols, trans. R. A. B. Mynors and D. F. S. Thomson, annotated by Wallace K. Ferguson, James K. McConica and Peter G. Bietenholz, Toronto, Buffalo and London: University of Toronto Press, 1974–79

—— *Farrago nova epistolarum D. Erasmi Roterodami ad alios et aliorum ad hunc*, Basel: Froben, 1519

—— *The praise of Folie. Moriae Encomium a boke made in latine by that great clerke Erasmus Roterodame. Englisshed by Sir Thomas Chaloner knight*, London: Thomas Berthelet, 1549

Erasmus, Desiderius and More, Thomas, *Luciani opuscula ... ab Erasmo Roterodamo et Thoma Moro ... in Latinorum linguam traducta*, Paris: Josse Bade, 1506

Index de L'Inquisition Espagnole. 1583, 1584, ed. J. M. De Bujanda, Sherbrooke: Centre d'Études de la Renaissance, Université de Sherbrooke, and Geneva: Droz, 1993

Jiménez Patón, Bartolomé, *Discurso de los tufos, copetes y calvas*, Baeza: Juan de la Cuesta, 1639

Lando, Ortensio, *Commentario delle più notabili e mostruose cose d'Italia e altri luoghi. Catalogo de gli inventori delle cose che si mangiano e beveno*, eds Guido and Paola Salvatori, Bologna: Edizioni Pendragon, 1994

—— *Paradossi cioè sentenze fuori del comun parere*, ed. A. Corsaro, Rome: Edizioni di storia e letteratura, 2000

Lipsius, Justus, *Los seis libros de las políticas o doctrina civil de Justo Lipsio que sirven para el gobierno del Reino o Principado*, trans. Bernardino de Mendoza, Madrid: Estevan Bogia for Juan Flamenco, 1604

Lucian, *How to Write History*, trans. K. Kilburn, in *Lucian*, vol. 6, London: William Heinemann and Cambridge, MA: Harvard University Press (The Loeb Classical Library), 1959

Machiavelli, Niccolò, *Il Principe*, ed. Mario Martelli and Nicoletta Marcelli, Rome: Salerno Editrice, 2006

Montaigne, Michel de, *Les Essais*, ed. P. Villey and V.-L. Saulnier, Paris: PUF, 1965

More, Thomas, *The workes of Sir Thomas More Knyght, sometyme Lorde Chauncellor of England, wrytten by him in the Englysh tonge*, London: John Cawood, John Waly and Richard Tottell, 1557

—— *Collected Works*, vol. 8, Part I, *The Confutation of Tyndale's Answer*, ed. L. A. Schuster et al., New Haven and London: Yale University Press, 1973

—— *The Correspondence of Sir Thomas More*, ed. Elizabeth Frances Rogers, Princeton, NJ: Princeton University Press, 1947

—— *Sir Thomas More: A Play by Anthony Munday and Others*, ed. Vittorio Gabrieli and Giorgio Melchiori, Manchester and New York: Manchester University Press, 1990

—— see also above, Erasmus and More

Nashe, Thomas, *The Unfortunate Traveller and Other Works*, ed. J. B. Steane, London: Penguin, 1985 (1972)

Patrizi (of Siena), Francesco, *Le Livre de police humaine, contenant briefve description de plusieurs choses dignes de memoire ...*, Paris: Charles l'Angelier, 1549 (1544)

Patrizi (of Cherso), Francesco, *La città felice*, see Campanella, Tommaso

Plato, *Laws*, ed. and trans. R. G. Bury, London: William Heinemann and Cambridge, MA: Harvard University Press (Loeb Classical Library), 1994 (1926)

Quevedo, Francisco de, *Obras completas: Prosa*, vol. 1, ed. Felicidad Buendía, Madrid: Aguilar, 1992 (1932)

—— *Obras completas: Obras en verso*, vol. 2, ed. Felicidad Buendía, Madrid: Aguilar, 1986 (1943)

Quiroga, Gaspar de, *Index librorum expurgatorum*, Madrid: Alfonso Gomez, 1584

Quiroga, Vasco de, *La Utopía en América*, ed. Paz Serrano Gassent (Madrid: Dastin, 2002)

Rabelais, François, *Œuvres complètes*, ed. Mireille Huchon and François Moureau, [Paris]: Gallimard, 1994

Ribadeneira, Pedro de, *Obras escogidas de Pedro de Rivadeneira*, ed. Vicente de la Fuente, Madrid: Atlas, Biblioteca de Autores Españoles, 1952 (1868)

Saavedra Fajardo, Diego, *Obras completas*, ed. Ángel González Palencia, Madrid: Aguilar, 1946

Sansovino, Francesco, *Ortografia delle voci della lingua nostra, o vero dittionario volgare et latino: nel quale s'impara a scriver correttamente ogni parola cosi in prosa come in verso, per fuggir le rime false e gli altri errori che si possono commettere favellando e scrivendo*, Venice: F. Sansovino, 1568

Sidney, Philip, *Miscellaneous Prose*, ed. Katherine Duncan-Jones and Jan van Dorsten, Oxford: Clarendon Press, 1973

Sorbière, Samuel, *Discours sceptiques*, ed. Sophie Gouverneur, Paris: Champion, 2002

Tacitus, *The Annals*, trans. John Jackson, London: William Heinemann and Cambridge, MA.: Harvard University Press (Loeb Classical Library), 1937

Zuccolo, Ludovico, *La Repubblica d'Evandria e altri dialoghi italiani*, pref. R. De Mattei, Roma: Colombo Editore, 1944

Secondary works

Alcalá, Ángel, 'El humanista y cronista real Pedro de Valencia (1555–1620) y la crisis española de los siglos XVI–XVII' in Pierre Civil (ed.), *Siglos dorados: Homenaje a Agustín Redondo*, vol. 1, Madrid: Castalia, 2004, pp. 1–14

Allen, Peter R., '*Utopia* and European humanism: the function of the prefatory letters and verses', *Studies in the Renaissance*, 10 (1963), 91–107

Allgemeine deutsche Biographie, auf Veranlassung Seiner Majestät des Könings von Bayern herausgegeben durch die historische Commission bei der Königlichen Akademie der Wissenschaften, Leipzig: Duncker und Humblot, 1875–1912

Baker, David Weil, *Divulging Utopia: Radical Humanism in Sixteenth-Century England*, Amherst: University of Massachusetts Press, 1999

Bataillon, Marcel, *Erasmo y España*, trans. A. Alatorre, Mexico: Fondo de Cultura Económica, 1966 (original version 1937)

Bennell, John, 'Robinson, Ralph (1520–1577)', in *Oxford Dictionary of National Biography*, Oxford University Press, www.oxforddnb.com/view/article/23863 (accessed 27.08.05)

Berschin, Walter, 'Neulateinische Utopien im alten Reich (1555–1741)', in W. Berschin, *Mittellateinische Studien*, Heidelberg: Matte, 2005, pp. 377–87

Bethencourt, Francisco, *História das Inquisições: Portugal, Espanha e Italia*, n.p.: Temas e Debates, 1996

Bietenholz, Peter G. and Thomas B. Deutscher (eds), *Contemporaries of Erasmus*, 3 vols, Toronto, Buffalo and London: University of Toronto Press, 1985–87

Binder, James, 'More's *Utopia* in English: a note on translation', *Modern Language Notes*, 62 (1947), 370–6

Bing, Gertrude, 'Nugae circa Veritatem: notes on Anton Francesco Doni', *Journal of the Warburg Institute*, 1 (1937–38), 304–12

Biot, Brigitte, 'Barthélemy Aneau, lecteur de l'*Utopie*', *Moreana*, 121 (1995), 11–28

Bishop, Malcolm, 'Ambrosius Holbein's *memento mori* map for Sir Thomas More's *Utopia*. The meanings of a masterpiece of early sixteenth-century graphic art', *British Dental Journal*, 199 (2005), 107–12

Blanco, Mercedes, *Les Rhétoriques de la pointe: Baltasar Gracián et le conceptisme en Europe*, Paris: Editions Champion, 1992

—— 'Del Infierno al Parnaso: escepticismo y sátira política en Quevedo y Trajano Boccalini', *La Perinola*, 2 (1998), 173–93

Blühm, Elger and Rolf Engelsing (eds), *Die Zeitung: Deutsche Urteile und Dokumente von den Anfängen bis zur Gegenwart*, Bremen: Carl Schünemann Verlag, 1967

Boutcher, Warren, '"A French Dexteritie, & an Italian Confidence": new documents on John Florio, learned strangers and Protestant humanist study of modern languages in Renaissance England from c.1547 to c.1625', *Reformation*, 2 (1997), 39–109

Bremond, Claude, Jacques Le Goff and Jean-Claude Schmitt, *L'«exemplum»* (Typologie des sources du moyen âge occidental, fasc. 40), Turnhout: Brepols, 1996

Burckhardt, Paul, *Geschichte der Stadt Basel*, Basel: Helbing und Lichtenhahn, 1942

Burke, Peter, 'Early modern Venice as a center of information and communication', in J. Martin and D. Romano (eds), *Venice Reconsidered. The History and Civilization of an Italian City-State 1297–1797*, Baltimore and London: Johns Hopkins University Press, 2000, pp. 389–419

—— 'Context in context', *Common Knowledge*, 8:1 (2002), 152–77
Burnett, Amy Nelson, *Teaching the Reformation: Ministers and their Message in Basel 1529–1629*, Oxford: Oxford University Press, 2006
Buyens, Vincent, 'Over edele tegenvoeters en welvarende Hollanders: ideal en droom in de zeventiende-eeuwse literatuur', in A. Decelle and A. Faems (eds), *Aan de voet van de regenboog: De utopie in de Nederlandse literatuur*, Leuven: Peeters, forthcoming
Cantarino, Elena, 'Tratadistas político-morales de los siglos XVI y XVII (Apuntes sobre el estado actual de la investigación)', *El Basilisco*, 21 (1996), 4–7
Cappelli, Adriano, *Lexicon abbreviaturarum: Wörterbuch lateinischer und italienischer Abkürzungen*, Leipzig: J. J. Weber, 1928
Cave, Terence, 'Epilogue', in Neil Kenny (ed.), *Philosophical Fictions and the French Renaissance*, London: Warburg Institute, 1991, pp. 127–32
Céard, Jean, 'La Fortune de l'*Utopie* de Thomas More en France au XVIe siècle', in *La fortuna dell'Utopia di Thomas More*, pp. 43–75
Cecchi, Alessandro, 'In margine a una recente monografia sul Salviati', *Antichità viva*, 33 (1994), 12–22
Cid Vázquez, María Teresa, 'Tacitismo y razón de estado en los "Comentarios Políticos" de Juan Alfonso de Lancina', PhD dissertation, Universidad Complutense de Madrid, 2001
Collinson, Patrick, 'Sir Nicholas Bacon and the Elizabethan *via media*', in *Godly People: Essays on English Protestantism and Puritanism*, London: Hambledon Press, 1983
Cooper, Richard (ed.), *Maurice Sceve: The Entry of Henri II into Lyon, September 1548*, Tempe, AZ: Medieval & Renaissance Texts & Studies, 1997
Cro, Stelio, 'La utopía de las dos orillas (1453–1793)', *Cuadernos para la investigación de la literatura hispánica*, 30 (2005), 15–268
Davis, J. C., *Utopia and the Ideal Society: A Study of English Utopian Writing 1516–1700*, Cambridge: Cambridge University Press, 198
Dillon, Anne, *The Construction of Martyrdom in the English Catholic Community, 1535–1603*, Aldershot and Burlington, VT: Ashgate, 2002
Dizionario biografico degli Italiani, vol. 4, Rome: Istituto della enciclopedia italiana, 1962, p. 83 (Arese), and vol. 10, Rome: Istituto della enciclopedia italiana, 1968, p. 358 (Bidelli)
Enciclopedia Italiana di scienze, lettere ed arti, Rome: Istituto della enciclopedia italiana, 1949
Evans, R. J. W., *The Wechel Presses: Humanism and Calvinism in Central Europe 1527–1627*, Oxford: Past and Present Society, 1975
Fernández-Santamaría, J. A., *Reason of State and Statecraft in Spanish Political Thought (1595–1640)*, Lanham, MD, New York and London: University Press of America, 1983
Firpo, Luigi, 'Thomas More e la sua fortuna in Italia', in L. Firpo (ed.), *Studi sull'Utopia*, Florence: Olschki, 1977, pp. 31–58
Fontaine, Marie Madeleine, 'Quelques traits du cicéronianisme lyonnais: Claude Guilliaud, Florent Wilson, Barthélemy Aneau et Simon de Vallambert', in *Scritture dell'impegno dal rinascimento all'età barocca*, Fasano: Schena, 1994, pp. 35–72

La fortuna dell'Utopia di Thomas More nel dibattito politico europeo del '500, Florence: Olschki, 1996
Freeman, John, 'Discourse in More's *Utopia*: alibi / pretext / postscript', *English Literary History*, 59 (1992), 289-311
Franckenstein, Jacob August et al. (eds), *Großes vollständiges Universal-Lexicon aller Wissenschaften und Künste*, Halle and Leipzig: Johann Heinrich Zedler, 1732-54, vol. 57, col. 991
Füglister, Hans, *Handwerksregiment: Untersuchungen und Materialien zur sozialen und politischen Struktur der Stadt Basel in der ersten Hälfte des 16. Jahrhunderts*, Basel and Frankfurt am Main: Helbing und Lichtenhahn, 1981
Genette, Gérard, *Seuils*. Paris: Editions du Seuil, 1987
Ginzburg, Carlo, *No Island is an Island: Four Glances at English Literature in a World Perspective*, New York: Columbia University Press, [2000]
Gleason, Elisabeth G., *Gasparo Contarini: Venice, Rome, and Reform*, Berkeley: University of California Press, 1993
Gómez, Fernando, *Good Places and Non-Places in Colonial Mexico: The Figure of Vasco de Quiroga (1470-1565)*, Lanham, New York and Oxford: University Press of America, 2001
Graves, Michael A. R., *Burghley: William Cecil, Lord Burghley*, London and New York: Longman, 1998
Greenblatt, Stephen, *Renaissance Self-Fashioning: From More to Shakespeare*, Chicago: University of Chicago Press, 1980
Grendler, Paul F., *Critics of the Italian World 1530-1560: Anton Francesco Doni, Nicololò Franco and Ortensio Lando*, Madison: University of Wisconsin Press, 1969
Guggisberg, Hans R., *Basel in the Sixteenth Century: Aspects of the City Republic before, during and after the Reformation*, St. Louis, Missouri: Center for Reformation Research, 1982
Hallowell, Robert E., 'Jean Le Blond's defense of the French language (1549)', *Romanic Review*, 51 (1960), 86-92
Hester, Nathalie, 'Stolen texts? Gabriel Chappuys' *L'estat, description et gouvernement des royaumes et républiques du monde*', in P. Cherchi (ed.), *Sondaggi sulla riscrittura del cinquecento*, Ravenna: Longo, 1998, pp. 133-148
Hexter, J. H., *More's 'Utopia': The Biography of an Idea*, New York: Harper and Row, 1965
Historisch-biographisches Lexicon der Schweiz, Neuenburg: Viktor Altinger, 1921-34
Hosington, Brenda, 'Early French translations of Thomas More's *Utopia*: 1550-1730', *Journal of Neo-Latin Studies*, 33 (1984), 116-34
Hoyer, Siegfried, 'Utopia deutsch: Zu den Gleichheitsvorstellungen im Baselr Humanistenkreis', *Jahrbuch für Geschichte des Feudalismus*, 5 (1981), 237-54
Israel, Jonathan I., *The Dutch Republic: Its Rise, Greatness, and Fall. 1477-1806*, Oxford: Clarendon Press, 1995
Jardine, Lisa, *Erasmus, Man of Letters: The Construction of Charisma in Print*, Princeton, NJ: Princeton University Press, 1993
—— 'Before Clarissa: Erasmus, "Letters of Obscure Men", and epistolary fictions', in T. Van Houdt, J. Papy, G. Tournoy and C. Matheeussen (eds), *Self-Presentation and Social Identification: The Rhetoric and Pragmatics of Letter Writing in Early Modern Times*, Leuven: Brill, 2002, pp. 385-403
Jauralde Pou, Pablo, *Francisco de Quevedo (1580-1645)*, Madrid: Castalia, 1998

Jones, Royston O., 'Some notes on More's "Utopia" in Spain', *The Modern Language Review*, 45 (1950), 478–82

Kamen, Henry, *The Spanish Inquisition: An Historical Revision*, London: Weidenfeld & Nicolson, 1997

Kenney, E. J., *The Classical Text*, Berkeley, Los Angeles and London: University of California Press, 1974

Killy, Walther (ed.), *Deutsche biographische Enzyklopädie*, Munich, New Providence, London and Paris: K. G. Saur Verlag, 1995–2003

King, John N., *English Reformation Literature: The Tudor Origins of the Protestant Tradition*, Princeton, NJ: Princeton University Press, 1982

Kisch, Guido, *Gestalten und Probleme aus Humanismus und Jurisprudenz: Neue Studien und Texte*, Berlin: Walter de Gruyter & Co., 1969

—— *Claudius Cantiuncula: Ein Baselr Jurist und Humanist des 16. Jahrhunderts*, Basel: Helbing und Lichtenhahn, 1970

Koppenfels, Werner von, 'Mundus alter et idem: Utopiefiktion und menippeische Satire', *Beihefte zu Poetica*, 13 (1981), 16–66

La Garanderie, Marie-Madeleine de, 'Guillaume Budé lecteur de l'*Utopie*', in *Miscellanea Moreana: Essays for Germain Marc'hadour*, Binghamton: Medieval & Renaissance Texts & Studies, 1989, pp. 327–38

Lavocat, Françoise, 'Fictions et paradoxes: Les nouveaux mondes possibles à la Renaissance', in *Vox Poetica* 20.02.06, www.voxpoetica.org/t/lavocatart.html (page consulted 12.03.06)

López Estrada, Francisco, 'La primera versión española de la *Utopía* de Moro, por Jerónimo Antonio de Medinilla (Córdoba, 1637)', in M. P. Hornik (ed.), *Collected Studies in Honour of Américo Castro's Eightieth Year*, Oxford: Lincombe Lodge Research Library, 1965, pp. 291–309

—— 'Quevedo y la *Utopía* de Tomás Moro', in *Homenaje al profesor Giménez Fernández*, Sevilla: Universidad de Sevilla, 1967, pp. 155–96

—— *Tomás Moro y España: Sus relaciones hasta el siglo XVIII*, Madrid: Editorial de la Universidad Complutense, 1980

—— 'Une traduction précoce de *L'Utopie* de Thomas More', *Moreana*, 111–12 (1992), 15–18

—— 'La fortuna de Tomás Moro y su *Utopía* en la España del Siglo de Oro', in *La fortuna dell'Utopia di Thomas More*, pp. 75–91

López Fanego, Otilia, 'Actualidad de Montaigne. Los *Essais*, una traducción por hacer', *1616: Anuario de la Sociedad Española de Literatura General y Comparada*, 4 (1981), 25–34

MacCaffrey, Wallace T., 'Cecil, William, first Baron Burghley (1520/21–1598)', *Oxford Dictionary of National Biography*, Oxford University Press, www.oxforddnb.com/view/article/4983 (accessed 06.11.05)

McCutcheon, Elizabeth, 'More's *Utopia* and Cicero's *Paradoxa Stoicorum*', *Moreana*, 86 (1985), 3–22

Manso Porto, Carmen, *Don Diego Sarmiento de Acuña, Conde de Gondomar (1567–1626). Erudito, mecenas y bibliófilo*, n.p.: Xunta de Galicia, 1996

Martí, Antonio, *La preceptiva retórica española en el siglo de oro*, Madrid: Gredos, 1972

Martins, José V. de Pina, 'L'*Utopie* de Thomas More au Portugal: au XVIe et au début du XVIIe siècle', *Moreana*, 69 (1981), 137–56

Minerva, Nadia (ed.), *Per una definizione dell'utopia: Metodologie e discipline a confronto*, Ravenna: Longo Editore, 1992
—— 'D'une définition à l'autre: sur quelques préfaciers français d'*Utopia* de Thomas More', in Nadia Minerva (ed.), *Per una definizione dell'utopia*, pp. 51–61
Montague, Jennifer, *An Index of Emblems of the Italian Academies*, London: The Warburg Institute, 1988
Moraleja Juárez, Alfonso, 'Baltasar Gracián y el impío Bodino', in *Baltasar Gracián: ética, política y filosofía*, Oviedo: Fundación Gustavo Bueno, Pentalfa Ediciones, 2002, pp. 105–22
Moro, Elena, 'Dall'utopia all'eutopia: dal disegno ideale della città alla sua concretizzazione', in Nadia Minerva (ed.), *Per una definizione dell'utopia*, pp. 449–55
Nieuw nederlandsch biografisch woordenboek, Leiden: A. W. Sijthoff, 1911–27
Norbrook, David, *Poetry and Politics in the English Renaissance*, rev. edn, Oxford: Oxford University Press, 2002
Peggrum, Reed Edwin, 'The first French and English translations of Sir Thomas More's *Utopia*', *Modern Language Review*, 35 (1940), 330–40
Peraita Huerta, Carmen, 'Mapas de lectura, diálogos con los textos: la Carta al rey Luis XIII y las anotaciones en el ejemplar de la *Utopía* de Quevedo', *La Perinola*, 8 (2004), 321–41
Pintard, René, *Le Libertinage érudit dans la première moitié du XVIIe siècle*, Paris: Boivin, 1943
Plaisance, Michel, 'L'Académie Florentine de 1541 à 1583: permanence et changement', in D. S. Chambers and F. Quiviger (eds), *Italian Academies of the Sixteenth century*, London: The Warburg Institute, 1995, pp. 127–35
Postman, Neil, *Amusing Ourselves to Death: Public Discourse in the Age of Show Business*, New York: Viking, 1985
Rahir, Edouard (ed.), *Catalogue d'une collection unique de volumes imprimés par les Elzevier et divers typographes hollandais du XVII siècle*, Nieuwkoop: B. de Graaf, 1965 (1896)
Rivoletti, Christian, *Le metamorfosi dell'Utopia: Anton Francesco Doni e l'immaginario utopico di metà Cinquecento*, Lucca: M. Pacini Fazzi, 2003
Robbins, Jeremy, 'The arts of perception: the epistemological mentality of the Spanish Baroque 1580–1720', *Bulletin of Spanish Studies*, 82 (2005), 1–289
Saulnier, V. L., 'Mythologies pantagruéliques. L'*Utopie* en France: Morus et Rabelais', in R. Klein (ed.), *Les Utopies à la Renaissance*, Brussels: Presses Universitaires, 1963, pp. 137–63
Schama, Simon, *The Embarrassment of Riches: An Interpretation of Dutch Culture in the Golden Age*, London: Collins, 1987
Schenkeveld, Maria A., *Dutch Literature in the Age of Rembrandt*, Amsterdam and Philadelphia: John Benjamins Publishing Company, 1991
Schoeck, R. J., 'Bodin's opposition to the mixed state and to Thomas More', in Horst Denzer (ed.), *Jean Bodin*, Munich: C. H. Beck, 1973, pp. 399–412
Scrivano, Riccardo, 'Ortensio Lando traduttore di Thomas More', in *Studi sulla cultura lombarda: in memoria di Mario Appolonio*, vol. 1, Milan: Pubblicazioni della Università Cattolica del Sacro Cuore, 1972, pp. 99–108
Seidel, Robert, *Späthumanismus in Schlesien: Caspar Dornau (1577–1631). Leben und Werk*, Tübingen: Max Niemeyer Verlag, 1994

Seidel Menchi, Silvana, 'Ortensio Lando cittadino di Utopia: un esercizio di lettura', in *La fortuna dell'Utopia di Thomas More*, pp. 95–119

Sellevold, Kirsti, 'Some "hardis repreneurs" in sixteenth-century France: Du Bellay, Aneau, Chappuys', in Hall Bjørnstad (ed.), *Borrowed Feathers: Plagiarism and the Limits of Imitation in Early Modern Europe*, Oslo: Unipub, 2008, pp. 53–65

Serrano y Sanz, Manuel, 'Libros manuscritos o de mano', *Revista de Archivos, Bibliotecas y Museos*, 8 (1903), 65–8, 225–8, 295–300

Sharratt, Peter, 'The Imaginary City of Bernard Salomon', in Philip Ford and Gillian Jondorf (eds), *Intellectual life in Renaissance Lyon*, Cambridge: Cambridge French Colloquia, 1993, pp. 33–49

Sivefors, Per, '"Yet their characters we have not": The Utopian alphabet and the production of textual control' (unpublished paper)

Sørensen, Knud, 'Notes on the first English translation of More's *Utopia*', in Graham D. Caie and Holger Nørgaard (eds), *A Literary Miscellany Presented to Eric Jacobsen*, Copenhagen: University of Copenhagen, 1988, pp. 326–37

Steczowicz, Agnieszka, *The Defence of Contraries: Paradox and the Late Renaissance Disciplines*, Unpublished D.Phil thesis, University of Oxford, 2006

Storia di Milano, vol. 10 ('L'età della riforma cattolica'), Milan: Fondazione Treccani degli Alfieri, 1957

Storia di Milano, vol. 11 ('Il declino spagnolo'), Milan: Fondazione Treccani degli Alfieri, 1958

Teuteberg, René, *Baselr Geschichte*, Basel: Christoph Merian Verlag, 1986

Trevor-Roper, Hugh, 'The image of Thomas More in England 1535–1635', in *La fortuna dell'Utopia di Thomas More*, pp. 5–23

Tucker, George Hugo, *Homo Viator: Itineraries of Exile, Displacement and Writing in Renaissance Europe*, Geneva: Droz, 2003

Venard, Marc (ed.), *Il tempo delle confessioni (1530–1620/30)*, in *Storia del cristianesimo: Religione-Politica-Cultura*, vol. 8, Rome: Borla/Città Nuova, 1992

Wackernagel, Rudolf, *Geschichte der Stadt Basel*, Basel: Helbing und Lichtenhahn, 1907–24

Zavala, Silvio Arturo, *Sir Thomas More in New Spain: A Utopian Adventure of the Renaissance*, Hispanic & Luso-Brazilian Councils: London, 1955

—— 'Nouvelles études sur Vasco de Quiroga', *Moreana*, 15–16 (1967), 380–8

—— 'Vasco de Quiroga, traducteur de l'*Utopia*', *Moreana*, 69 (1981), 115–17

Zuber, R., *Les 'Belles Infidèles' et la formation du goût classique*, Paris: Armand Colin, 1968

INDEX

For the paratexts reproduced in Part II, page-numbers refer to the translated version only, with two exceptions: names cited in footnotes to the original version, and the editions of *Utopia* where the whole page-run is given for that edition. Phrases such as 'the translator' are taken as the equivalent of the translator's name; where an item of prefatory material can be ascribed to a particular person, whether explicitly named or not, the page-run for the whole translated version of that item is given. The letter 'n' after a page reference indicates that the item appears in a note on that page.

Academia degli Inquieti 29
Academia peregrina 53
Accademia degli Elevati 56
Aegidius, Petrus *see* Giles
Aelius Aristides 251n
Agostini, Ludovico 63n
Álamos de Barrientos, Baltasar 116n
Albergati, Fabio 63n
Alberti, Leon Battista 51, 77
Alciati, Andrea 18
Alcibiades 251
Alexander III the Great, King of Macedonia 206
Alsop, Bernard 88, 101, 214–17
Amaurot 66, 72, 77, 77n, 184n, 195, 257
Amsterdam 82–4, 106, 108, 109, 199
Amyot, Jacques 68, 68n
Añastro, Gaspar de 114n
Aneau, Barthélemy 4–6, 10, 67, 68, 73–8, 79n, 81, 84, 124n, 189–93
Anemolius 21, 24, 50, 95, 107, 212, 213, 215, 229
Antwerp 4, 5n.1, 7, 8, 15, 104, 106, 132, 134, 159, 193, 221, 223
Arese, Giulio 29, 29n, 137, 275
Aretino, Pietro 48
Aristotle 9, 33, 38, 51, 97, 249
Astraea 255, 267
Athens, Athenians 35n, 136, 157, 237, 251n
Aubri, Daniel 18

Aubri, David 18
d'Aurigny, Gilles 68

Bacon, Francis 5, 140
Bade, Josse (Badius) 251
Baldwin, William 103
Basel 3, 4, 7, 9, 15, 17, 23, 30, 32–9, 41, 45, 46, 84, 99, 134, 135, 151–61, 165
Batavians 108, 109n
Beatus Rhenanus 23, 136
Bebel, Johann 32–4
Bergamo 27
Berthelet, Thomas de 95n
Bible (and Biblical references) 26, 33, 37, 51, 70, 72, 95, 107–9, 111, 241n, 243n, 187n, 225, 227, 241
Bidelli, Giovan Battista 19, 29, 30, 136, 137
Birckmann family 16, 18, 30
Birckmann, Arnold 16, 30
Birckmann, Franz 16
Blaeu(w) family 19n, 82, 86
Blaeu, J(e)an 19n, 82, 84n, 199
Blaeuw, Willem 19, 30, 82
Bocángel, Gabriel 259n
Boccaccio, Giovanni 16, 60
Boccalini, Traiano 121, 122n, 247
Bodin, Jean 43, 114, 115, 119, 127, 165, 239n
Boethius 249

Bogard, Jean 17
Bologna 56
Borromeo, Cardinal Federico 28–9
Borromeo, Saint Carlo 28
Britannicus, Johannes 251
Bronzino, Agnolo 52n
Brucioli, Antonio 56
Bruges 63n, 104
Brussels 17, 106
Budé, Guillaume 5, 6, 7, 10, 12, 19, 22, 24–7, 39n, 43, 69–76, 83, 86, 90n, 99, 107, 111, 113, 121, 134–8, 165, 183, 187, 191, 193, 199, 229, 231, 245
Bullinger, Heinrich 95
Buonamici, Matteo 63n
Buonvisi family 56, 57
Buonvisi, Antonio 56
Buonvisi, Vicenzo 56, 57
Burghley, Lord *see* Cecil
Burnet, Gilbert 87
Busleyden, Hieronymus van 6, 7, 22, 24, 35n, 38, 39, 43, 96, 104, 107, 111, 137, 165, 212, 213, 215, 229

Cabrera, Francisco de 114n
Calvin, Jean 73
Calvinists, Calvinism 5, 18, 19, 28, 73, 85, 99, 106–9, 227n
Campanella, Tommaso 5, 63–5
Candia, Candians *see* Crete, Cretans
Cantiuncula, Claudius *see* Chansonnette
Capucin order 27
Caracciolo, Cardinal Marino 247n
Caro, Rodrigo 263n
Caron, Johann 68
Carrillo Lasso, Alonso 113
Carthage 38, 155
Cassiodorus 249
Castro, Agustín de 269
Catherine de Médicis 7, 77n
Catherine of Aragon 3
Catullus 18
Cea Tesa, Salvador de 113, 235
Cea y Zayas, Diego de 267

Cecil, William (Lord Burghley) 9, 84, 87, 91–9, 137
Cervantes, Miguel de 113n
Cetina 121, 245
Chaloner, Sir Thomas 92, 93n
Chansonnette, Claude (Claudius Cantiuncula) 3, 6, 10, 32–9, 42, 44, 45, 153–61, 165
Chappuys, Gabriel 7, 10, 54n, 68, 78–82, 129n, 195
Charles V, Emperor 3, 106, 110, 111
Chaves y Mendoza, Juan de 116, 235
Cicero 10, 11, 55, 74–6, 92, 124, 165n, 191, 253
Cisneros, Cardinal Francisco Jiménez de 111
Cisneros, Diego de 119n
Claudius Marcellus 257
Clement, John 69, 185, 193
College of San Roque 263
College of Santa Catalina 113, 123, 255
College of the Three Languages 4, 104
Cologne 7, 16, 19, 20, 25–8
Contarini, Cardinal Gasparo 62, 63n
Córdoba 11, 110, 113, 114, 121, 123, 125, 126, 235, 237, 243, 249, 255–9, 263–71
Cornelius ab Egmond 19
Corpus Christi College, Oxford 87, 88–90, 99, 136, 210, 213, 214
Council of Trent 26, 111
Counter-Reformation 26, 61, 80, 120, 124
Covarrubias Horozco, Sebastián de 123
Coverdale, Miles 95
Creede, Thomas 100, 101, 213
Crete, Cretans 155–7, 161
Cromwell, Oliver 101
Cromwell, Thomas 91

David (Old Testament king) 225, 227, 241n
De Brune, Johan (the Elder) 109n
De Laet, Hans 105, 221, 223
Della Casa, Giovanni 51

INDEX

De Schrijver, Cornelis *see* Grapheus
Desmarez, Jean *see* Paludanus
Diogenes 90, 206–7
Dolet, Etienne 57
Doni, Anton Francesco 5–11, 47–66, 134, 135, 173–5
Dornau, Caspar 18
Douai 100n
Du Bellay, Joachim 69, 79n

Edward VI, King of England 12, 87–92
Elizabeth I, Queen of England 12, 97–9
Elysian Fields 70–2, 183, 189
Empire, Holy Roman 5–6, 63n, 108
English Prayer Book 102
Ennodius, Saint 251, 255
Episcopius, Nicolaus the Elder 17
Episcopius, Nicolaus the Younger 16, 17
Erasmus, Desiderius 3, 4, 5, 7, 8, 9, 11, 12, 14n, 15, 23, 24, 25, 27, 30, 31, 34n, 37, 40, 43, 48, 51, 56n, 70, 72, 83, 88, 90, 93n, 97, 98, 99, 103, 104, 107, 111, 113, 121, 130, 132–3, 135, 136, 165, 193, 199, 229, 231, 245, 263n
Euclid 249
Evreux 185

Fava, Geronimo 48, 50, 51, 53, 173
Ferdinand, King of Spain 269n
Ferrara 51n, 56
Florence 7, 11, 15, 49, 51, 52, 53n, 55, 195
Florio, John 98n, 102
F.N.D. 79, 82
Foxe, Richard 16, 88, 90, 136
François I, King of France 68, 73
Frankfurt am Main 7, 16, 17, 28, 42, 64
Frederik Magnus, Wald- and Rhinegrave, Count of Salm 83–6, 199
Froben, Hieronymus 17
Froben, Johann(es) 3, 4, 8, 15–17, 19, 20, 22–4, 30, 34, 111, 132, 133, 136, 165, 229
Froben, Justina 17

Galarza, Agustín (de) 259, 261

Galen 33, 137
Gassendi, Pierre 83
Geldenhouwer, Gerard *see* Noviomagus
Gerbrantsz, Marten 106, 225, 231
Ghent 106
Giles, Peter 6–7, 8, 15, 21, 22, 23, 24, 32, 38, 39n, 40, 43, 48, 50, 69, 81n, 83, 87, 90, 96, 103, 104, 107, 111, 119, 128, 132, 136, 137, 138, 159, 161, 165, 175, 185, 191n, 193, 198, 203, 209, 212, 213, 215, 229
Giovio, Paolo 29
Giunta family, Giunta press 16, 51, 54, 55
Giunta, Filippo 16
Goldsmiths' Company 89
Gómez de Lasprilla, Francisco 271
Gondomar, Count of *see* Sarmiento de Acuña
González de Salas, Jusepe Antonio 271
Gourmont, Gilles de 15, 23
Gracián, Baltasar 119n.42, 123n, 269n
Grapheus, Cornelius (Cornelis de Schrijver) 16, 21, 24, 43, 96, 107, 213, 215, 229
Grapheus, Johannes (Jan de Schrijver) 16
Greeks, the 139
Grosse, Henning 32, 42, 43, 131n, 163
Grotius, Hugo 83
Gryphe, Sébastien 56
Guajardo Fajardo y Molina, Melchor 259
Guazzo, Stefano 18
Gutiérrez, Cipriano 9, 11, 122–4, 136, 249–55

Hague, the 83, 203
Hall, Joseph 4, 7, 10, 40n, 43, 130n
Hanau 7, 18
Harmenszoon van Rijn, Rembrandt *see* Rembrandt
Henne, Johann Jakob 18
Henri II, King of France 77n
Henri III, King of France 10, 68n, 78, 80, 84, 195

Henri III, King of Navarre (later Henri IV, King of France) 80
Henri IV, King of France 82
Henrietta Maria, Queen of England 100
Henry VIII, King of England 3, 4, 8, 25, 44, 61, 68n, 80, 91, 98n, 104, 197
Hentenius, Johannes 26, 28, 30
Herrera, Fernando de 118, 245
Hessen-Kassel, Count of 28
Hippodamus 38, 155
Histoire du Grand et Admirable Royaume d'Antangil 67–8
Hobbes, Thomas 5, 85, 86
Holbein, Ambrosius 21
Holbein, Hans the Younger 8, 16, 42
Homer 18
Hoorn 106, 225, 229, 230n, 231
Horace 9, 50, 105
Huguenots 19, 84n
Hutten, Ulrich von 132
Hythloday, Raphael (Hythlod[a]eus) 8, 21, 22, 26, 32, 33, 34, 39, 44, 45, 69, 72, 83, 96, 103, 104, 108, 119, 120–1, 122n, 128, 131, 133, 136, 137, 138–40, 159–61, 185, 191, 198, 212, 227n, 245

Ignatius, Saint 239
Index 19, 26, 27, 115n.19, 117, 118, 120n, 239–41, 269
Inquisition 5, 27n, 28, 59n, 106, 111, 114n, 117, 118, 119n, 239, 243n, 269
Isabel, Queen of Spain 269n
Iturrizara, Lorenzo de 271

James V, King of Scotland 68
Jansson, Jan 19
Jerome, Saint 120, 243, 255
Jesuits 4, 8, 9, 106, 113, 118, 123, 124, 249, 255, 269, 271
Jethro 107, 225, 227
Jiménez Patón, Bartolomé 241, 243–5, 269
Jupiter 54
Juvenal 251

Kopff, Peter 18, 19, 30

Lacedaemonians 157, 237
Lando, Ortensio 4, 6–8, 11, 47–66, 74, 80, 128n, 134
Lantzenberger, Michael 32, 42, 43
Lateran Council, fifth 241n
Latius, Johannes *see* De Laet
Le Blond, Jean 4, 6, 9, 10, 68–86, 137, 138, 183–7
Leipzig 8, 32, 41, 42, 136, 163
Lipsius, Justus 116
Livy 41–2, 117, 237
London 8, 16, 21, 33, 56, 77n, 89, 96, 103, 128, 132, 136, 173, 177, 183, 185, 191, 197, 206, 208, 210, 213, 214, 216
Lope de Vega 29
Louis XIII, King of France 82, 247n
Louvain 3, 4, 6, 7, 8, 16, 17, 26, 30, 69n, 104, 105, 138
Lucca 56
Lucian 11, 16, 24, 51, 53, 56n, 90, 91, 103, 122, 130, 132, 135
Lupset, Thomas 15, 27, 39n, 71, 111, 137, 138, 165n, 183, 229
Luther, Martin 25, 26n, 37, 73
Lutheranism 25, 28, 37n, 117
Lycurgus 38, 157
Lyon 4, 54, 56, 57, 73–5, 77, 189

Maastricht 83
Machiavelli, Niccolò 13, 62, 81n, 85, 114–16, 119, 121
Madeleine of France 68
Madrid 110, 112, 113, 114, 116n, 118, 121, 245, 269, 271
Magnesia, Magnesians 38, 155
Malvezzi, Virgilio 127
Marcolini, Francesco 52
Marcus Varro *see* Varro
Marguerite de Navarre 73
Martens, Dirk 15, 104
Martial 112, 245, 271
Mary, Queen of England 25, 94, 96, 97, 106

Mary, Queen of Scots 99
Medinilla y Porres, Jerónimo Antonio de 3, 5, 6, 9, 11, 12, 26n, 84, 110, 112–27, 134, 136, 235–45, 247, 249, 255–71
Melanchthon, Philip 18
Meltinger, Heinrich 36, 45n
Mendoza, Bernardino de 116n
Metz 161
Meyer, Adelberg 36, 37n, 45n, 153
Michoacán 111
Milan 49, 56, 60, 63, 137, 247, 247n, 275, 275n
Miletus, Milesians 38, 155
Minos 38, 155
Misocacus civis utopiensis Philaletis 67
Momus 54
Montaigne, Michel de 13, 81n, 99, 102, 103, 120n
Morales y Padilla, Andrés de 126, 255, 257
More, Cresacre 5, 88, 101, 214–16
More (Maure, Morus), Thomas
  execution of 3, 4, 8, 12, 25, 56, 56n, 64, 74n, 89, 93, 110, 111, 118, 177, 197, 207, 267, 275
  family of 5, 8, 51, 88, 100, 101
  royal marriage question, and 3, 4, 8, 25, 61, 98, 177, 197
  as saint and martyr 4, 5, 8, 25, 30, 43n, 61, 80, 94, 97, 98n, 100, 105, 111, 117, 118, 120, 125, 127, 129, 136, 195, 237, 239, 241, 245–9, 255, 267, 275
  as statesman 17, 33, 34, 40, 43, 104, 151, 159, 163, 177, 183, 185, 189, 193, 195, 199, 207, 214, 216, 221, 225–31, 237, 249, 257, 275
  works of (other than *Utopia*) 11, 15–17, 30, 51, 56n, 90, 97, 103, 105, 117n, 130, 135
  see also Utopia
Moritz der Gelehrte *see* Hessen-Kassel
Munday, Antony 98

Naples 56, 64, 121
Nashe, Thomas 98, 103
Navarro Castellanos, Gonzalo 265
New Testament *see* Bible
New World 5n, 39, 58, 59, 81, 104, 127, 132, 137–9, 165
Nicomachus 249
Noviomagus, Gerardus (Gerard Geldenhouwer) 21, 24, 43, 96, 107, 165, 212, 213, 215, 229
Numa Pompilius 257, 263

Old Testament *see* Bible
Omnibona 124
Orange, house of 83, 84, 86, 108, 227n
Order of Santiago (St James, St Jacob) 114, 121, 235, 243, 245n, 259n, 265, 267, 269, 271
Osuna, Duke of 121
Ovid 76n, 183n

Paludanus, Joannes (Jean Desmarez) 17, 19, 23, 69
Pamplona 127n
Pancorvo, Hiéronimo de 263
Paris 7, 15, 56, 74, 82, 83, 85, 129, 137, 138, 141, 183
Patrizi, Francesco (da Cherso) 5, 9n, 63n, 69n
Patrizi, Francesco (da Siena) 9, 10, 68, 69n
Pavia 29, 251n
Peasants' War 45n
Peres de Sousa, Fernando 121n
Pérez, Antonio 116n
Persius 251
Petit, Samuel 83
Petrarch (Petrarca, Francesco) 16, 60
Phaleas 38, 155
Philip II, King of Macedonia 90, 206
Philip II, King of Spain 17n, 106, 116n
Philip III, King of Spain 275n
Philip IV, King of Spain 267
Piacenza 57
Pincio, Aurelio 48, 52

Plantin, Christophe 105
Plato 9, 10, 22, 39, 44n, 45, 62, 74n, 75n, 76, 77, 85, 96, 123, 124, 179, 195, 199, 252n, 253, 275
Pléiade 70
Pliny (the Elder) 159
Pomponazzi, Pietro 241n
Pomponius Mela 159
Proclus 33
Protestants, Protestantism 28, 43n, 80, 83, 86, 95, 97, 99, 106, 107
  see also Calvinists, Huguenots, Puritans, Reformation
Prudentius, Saint 239
Ptolemy 159
Puritans, Puritanism 101
Pythagoras 249

Quevedo, Francisco de 6, 12, 120, 121, 122, 124, 127n, 136, 245–7, 271n
Quiñones de Benavente, Luis 259n
Quintilian 70n
Quiroga, Cardinal Gaspar de 26, 27, 115n, 117, 118
Quiroga, Vasco de 111, 117n, 125, 137, 138, 140

Rabelais, François 11, 67, 90, 99, 103
Rastell, William 97, 118n
Reformation 3, 5, 7, 12, 25, 26, 34, 36, 37, 45n, 51, 56, 61, 66, 73, 80, 97, 99, 106, 107, 120, 124
  see also Calvinsts, Huguenots, Protestants, Puritans
Rembrandt Harmenszoon van Rijn 109
Ribadeneira, Pedro de 118, 119
Richelieu, Cardinal 84
Rivas y Tafur, Joseph de 263
Robinson, Ralph 4, 5, 9, 11, 12, 87–103, 106, 205–12, 213, 214
Rojas, Gabriel de 271
Rome, Romans (ancient) 35, 42, 63n, 71, 103, 108, 109n, 116, 135, 136, 139, 157, 237, 251, 253, 255n, 257n, 265n

Rome, Roman (modern, ecclesiastical) 25, 43, 49, 119, 239n, 241, 249

Saavedra Fajardo, Diego 115n, 125
Sabbioneta 50n
Saint-André, Jacques de 77n
St Bartholomew's Day massacre 19
St John's College, Cambridge 92n, 99
Salm, Count of see Frederik Magnus
Salviati, Francesco 52n, 53n
Sanders, Nicholas 118
Sandoval, Sancho de 115n, 121n
San Marino 63n
Sansovino, Francesco 4, 7, 9, 10, 48, 49, 59–65, 79–82, 84–6, 176n, 177–9, 284n
Santiago see Order of Santiago
Sarmiento de Acuña, Diego, Count of Gondomar 110, 112
Sassen, Servaes van 16
Saugrain, Jean 73, 189
Saur, Johann 17
Scève, Maurice 77n
Schleich, Clemens 18
Schönberg, Cardinal Nicholas 247n
Seneca 52, 249n
Seville 267n, 269n
Seymour, Edward, Duke of Somerset 92, 93
Sforza, Isabella 56n
Sgualdi, Vincenzo 63n
Shakespeare, William 98, 100, 103
Sidney, Sir Philip 97, 98
Sidonius Apollinaris 255
Sir Thomas More see Munday
Skelton, John 103
Sluis 83, 199
Socrates 18, 38, 155, 157, 253
Solinus 159
Solon 38, 157
Solórzano y Pereyra, Juan de 124n
Sophocles 139
Sorbière, Samuel 5, 19n, 82–6, 199–203
Sparta 35n, 136
Speroni, Sperone 51

INDEX

Stapleton, Thomas 100n
Stiblin, Kaspar 5
Stoic, Stoics, Stoicism 10, 55, 74n, 74–6, 191
Strabo 159
Stuart, house of 100, 101

Tacitus 113, 115–17, 127, 135, 235, 237
Tadlowe, George 89, 91, 93, 94, 206, 208, 210
Tasso, Torquato 51
Terence 211
Tissart, Marguerite 84
Toledo, Archbishop of *see* Quiroga
Tomasi, Tomaso 63n
Torre de Juan Abad 121, 245, 247
Tory, Geoffroy 67
Tours 195
Tudor, house of 100
Tunstall, Cuthbert 44, 135
Turin 114n
Turnebus, Adrianus 253

Ulysses 44
Utopia, editions of, 1516–1643
  Spanish manuscript translation 3, 5, 110–12, 126
  Louvain 1516 14–15, 20, 21, 22, 24, 33n, 42, 89n, 130, 132, 133, 135
  Paris 1517 15, 22–4, 33n, 69–71, 73, 89, 107n, 130, 135, 137, 165n
  Basel 1518 March 3, 6, 15, 16, 18n, 21, 24, 33n, 34, 40, 42–3, 69, 112, 128, 130, 132, 133, 165n
  Basel 1518 November 3, 6, 15, 16n, 17, 18, 21, 24, 33n, 34, 40, 42–3, 69, 111, 112, 127, 130, 132, 133, 137
  Florence 1519 11, 15, 16, 19, 20, 23, 24, 51, 56n, 88, 90, 128n, 135
  Basel 1524 2, 3, 8, 9, 32–9, 41, 44–6, 84, 99, 130, 133n, 134, 149–61
  Louvain 1548 3, 4, 6, 16, 17, 20, 25, 26, 89n, 104, 122
  Venice 1548 3, 10, 11, 47, 49–66, 130, 134, 171–5
  Paris 1550 4, 8, 68–86, 135, 137, 181–7
  London 1551 8, 11, 84, 87–103, 134, 136, 137, 205–9
  Antwerp 1553 4, 5n, 104–9, 125n, 134, 219–23
  Cologne 1555 16, 20, 25–7, 130
  London 1556 4, 87, 88, 94–7, 100, 101, 210–12, 213n
  Lyon 1559 4, 73–8, 131, 188–93
  Venice 1561 4, 48, 49, 59–66, 79, 130, 133n, 135, 136, 176–9
  Antwerp 1562 4, 105, 106, 107n, 222–3
  Basel 1563 5n, 16, 17, 20, 24, 25, 27, 30, 31, 112, 118n
  Louvain (Zangre and Bogard) 1565 17, 24, 26n, 27–8, 112, 129
  Louvain (Zangre and Bogard) 1566 17, 24, 27–8, 112, 129
  Venice 1566 59, 128n, 176n
  Venice 1567 59, 130, 133n, 176n
  Venice 1578 59, 130, 133n, 176n
  Venice 1583 59, 61, 62, 82, 85n, 130, 133n, 145, 176n, 178
  Paris 1585 78–82, 84, 128n, 129n, 133n, 194–7, 284n
  Wittenberg 1591 17, 31
  London 1597 87, 88, 101, 213
  Paris 1598 8, 79, 129, 133n, 194n, 284n
  Frankfurt 1601 17, 18, 20, 28, 30
  Venice 1607 59, 79, 130, 133n.14, 176n.1
  Paris 1611 79, 82, 128n, 133n, 141, 194n, 284n
  Leipzig 1612 1, 8, 32, 39–45, 130, 131n, 133n, 134, 162–9
  Hanau 1613 18, 29, 30
  Milan 1620 14, 19, 20, 27, 28, 29, 31, 63, 128n, 137, 273–5
  London 1624 87, 88, 101, 109, 213n, 214–15
  Hoorn 1629 106, 108n, 128n, 224–9
  Amsterdam 1629 5, 7, 19, 82–4, 108, 109
  Cologne 1629 19, 27–8, 109, 131

Amsterdam 1631 19, 108
Hoorn 1634 106, 128n, 230–1
Córdoba 1637 5, 10, 11, 26, 84, 109, 110, 112–27, 128n, 133n, 134, 136, 141, 233–71
London 1639 87, 88, 101, 109, 216–17
Amsterdam 1643 5, 19n, 68, 82–6, 133, 143, 198–203

Valdés, Alfonso de 111
Valerius Maximus 68
Valois, house of 99
Varro 124, 252n, 253
Veen, Otto van 109
Vele, Abraham 94–5, 97, 206, 210
Vélez de Guevara, Juan 259n
Venice 3, 4, 10, 47–9, 52, 55, 56n, 57–9, 62–5, 104, 134, 173, 177
Vespucci, Amerigo 58
Victorinus, Saint 239
Villanueva de los Infantes 114, 120, 121, 243, 255, 269
Vitruvius 77

Wechel family 18
Wechel, Andreas 18
Weihe, Eberhart von 17, 18, 28
Willemsz, Isaäc 106, 229
Wintermonat, Gregor(ius) 4, 7, 10, 32, 39–45, 130n, 135, 163–7
Wittenberg 7, 28

Xenophon 51, 95

Zangre, Pierre 17
Zapata, Antonio de 269n
Zealanders 165
Zeno, Saint 239
Zucchi de Monza, Bartolomé 247
Zuccolo, Ludovico 63–5
Zumárraga, Fray Juan de 137, 138